Reading Clinic

School of Education

Language In Education Division
Graduate School of Education
University of Pennsylvania
3700 Walnut Street
Philadelphia, PA 19104-6216

TOWARD A PSYCHOLOGY OF READING
The Proceedings of the CUNY Conferences

TOWARD A PSYCHOLOGY OF READING

The Proceedings
of the CUNY Conferences

edited by

ARTHUR S. REBER
DON L. SCARBOROUGH

BROOKLYN COLLEGE OF CUNY

LAWRENCE ERLBAUM ASSOCIATES, PUBLISHERS
1977   Hillsdale, New Jersey

DISTRIBUTED BY THE HALSTED PRESS DIVISION OF

JOHN WILEY & SONS

New York   Toronto   London   Sydney

Lawrence Erlbaum Associates, Inc., Publishers
62 Maria Drive
Hillsdale, New Jersey 07642

Distributed solely by Halsted Press Division
John Wiley & Sons, Inc., New York

Library of Congress Cataloging in Publication Data

Main entry under title:

Toward a psychology of reading.

Based on 2 conferences held at CUNY, Spring 1974, and
sponsored by Eastern Verbal Investigators League and
the Center for Research in Cognition and Affect.
Includes bibliographies.
1. Reading—Congresses.   2. Reading, Psychology of—
Congresses.   I. Reber, Arthur S.   II. Scarborough,
Don L.   III. Eastern Verbal Investigators League.
IV.   New York (City). City University of New York.
Center for Research in Cognition andAffect.
LB1049.95.T68   428'.4   76-47695
ISBN 0-470-99010-4

Printed in the United States of America

Contents

Preface   ix

1. The Structure and Acquisition of Reading I: Relations between
   Orthographies and the Structure of Language
   Lila R. Gleitman and *Paul Rozin*   1
   1 Introduction   1
   2 The Evolution of Writing   7
   3 Modern English Orthography   22
   4 From Phone to Acoustic Stimulus: The Problem of
      Segmentation   39
   5 Summary   49
      References   51

2. The Structure and Acquisition of Reading II: The Reading
   Process and the Acquisition of the Alphabetic Principle
   Paul Rozin and *Lila R. Gleitman*   55
   1 Introduction   55
   2 The Average Adult Reader   58
   3 The Preliterate Child   86
   4 Problems in Achieving Literacy   101
   5 Summary and Conclusions   130
      References   136

3. Visual Pattern in Fluent Word Identification
   Lee Brooks   143
   1 Introduction   143
   2 Possible Variations in Visual Form   143
   3 Theories of Fluency   148
   4 The Research   150

5 Conclusions and Discussion   178
References   180

4. Perceptual Processes in Reading: The Perceptual Spans
Keith Rayner and *George W. McConkie* 183
1 Introduction   183
2 The Perceptual Spans in Reading   185
3 Concerning Theories of Reading   201
4 Summary   203
References   204

5. Phonetic Segmentation and Recoding in the Beginning Reader
*Isabelle Y. Liberman, Donald Shankweiler, Alvin M.
Liberman, Carol Fowler,* and *F. William Fischer* 207
1 Introduction   207
2 Using the Alphabet to Full Advantage   208
3 The Phonetic Representation, Short-Term Memory, and
Reading   215
4 Summary   223
References   223

6. Reading Comprehension as a Function of Text Structure
Walter Kintsch 227
Introduction   227
1 Propositional Text Bases   228
2 Reading Rate and Recall as a Function of the Number of
Propositions in a Text Base   235
3 Reading Rate and the Repetition of Arguments   239
4 Further Analyses   248
5 Text Bases and Reading   253
References   256

7. Building Perceptual and Cognitive Strategies into a Reading
Curriculum
Joanna Williams 257
1 Introduction   257
2 Learning Strategies and Instructional Strategies   257
3 The Learning-Disabled Reader   260
4 Instructional Programs   263
5 Matching Instructional Treatment to Diagnostic
Category   266
6 The Tactile-Kinesthetic Modality   269
7 Psycholinguistic Factors   276

8   Curriculum Design   277
    References   285

8. **Assessment of Independent Reading Skills: Basic Research and Practical Applications**
    Robert C. Calfee 289
    1   Introduction   289
    2   An Example of a Reading Test   291
    3   Independent Skills in Reading   293
    4   "Clean" Tests   297
    5   Modifiability of Test Performance   310
    6   All-or-None Distributions of Test Scores   314
    7   Summary   320
        References   321

Author Index   325
Subject Index   331

Preface

The gap between laboratory research and its application often seems enormous. This seems particularly true in the area of reading. While hundreds of erstwhile researchers try to tap human perceptual, cognitive, and motor abilities, the hard-pressed educator in the field is often at a loss to find any fruits of these efforts that are useful in the task of teaching reading. The contents of this volume represent one attempt to span some of the differences between research and practice.

Although this book will not supply the practitioner with quick and easy answers to many real everyday problems, we think that researchers, teachers, and students concerned with the relationship between reading and the cognitive abilities underlying this skill will find productive and useful the cross fertilization between theory and application. The existing lacuna derives from the two overwhelmingly salient characteristics of reading: It is an exceedingly important social skill, and it is an extremely complex process. Many of the chapters in this book remind us that it is important to keep the complexity issue in mind when facing the social problems raised by reading.

The importance of reading has captured the attention of psychologists, pedagogues, social reformers, and parents. Pursuit of the goal of universal literacy has resulted in a field that has become the most fad ridden of the social sciences, a crazy-quilt array of pedagogic tricks, half-baked theories, novel programs dead aborning, scores of assessment devices, unfulfilled hopes, frustrations, name calling, and nearly all of it unrelieved by clearly demonstrable progress, consensus, understanding, or even healthy humor. Curricula emphasizing "whole word" versus "phonetic" or "linguistic" approaches vie for the educators attention, with proponents of each often claiming that it alone represents a satisfactory theory of the reading process. Similarly, diagnostic categories abound, each often stressing defects in some hypothesized underlying component of the reading process. Some theorists stress the role of motivation, pointing to how little evidence there is to differentiate the various teaching methods in terms of success, and thereby drawing the conclusion that success or failure lies wholly in the domain of motivation. Occasionally, such elements as dialectical variation, nutritional factors, or just plain uninspired teaching have been proposed as causes of reading failure. The list goes on: failure to appreciate individual differences, too much television, boring and/or irrelevant primers, etc. However, the laudatory goal of universal literacy not only remains unfulfilled, but has seemingly retreated with the failure of each new "solution."

There is something most impressive about all this. When so many intelligent, well-meaning, and insightful persons present so many cogent but divergent views, it is very likely that they all contain some particle of truth. Probably the most commonly proposed failure of existing programs and the one that, it seems to us, underlies all of the others, is not that the various reading curricula are "wrong" in any fundamental way, but rather that they spring from an overly specialized point of view with regard to the underlying component skills in reading and their relative importance during the acquisition of reading. The resulting tendency thus has been to focus too closely on one or two specific aspects of the reading process to the exclusion of others.

The thrust of this volume is that the reading process is not only more complex than previously assumed, but that like so many other cognitive and linguistic skills, the richness and depth of the complexity increases the more closely it is examined. This attitude has been recognized in other recent volumes (Gibson & Levin, 1975; Kavanagh & Mattingly, 1972; Levin & Williams, 1970) with the result that we are beginning to understand the reasons for past failures.

Each of the chapters in this volume not only focuses upon various aspects of the reading process but also provides for possible innovations and pedagogic developments that take into account these previously unrecognized components. The first two chapters coauthored by Gleitman and Rozin make this point effectively. In their first chapter they trace the historical evolution of writing systems and analyze the cognitive processes that are uniquely invoked by each. This historical analysis is an updating of the classic work of Gelb (1952), while the cognitive analysis is the first of its kind. What was missing from Gelb's essentially historical analysis was the specification of the kinds of cognitive operations recruited by different writing formats; logographies and alphabets make very different demands on the cognitive machinery of their readers. In their second chapter Rozin and Gleitman use their historical analysis as the foundation for a novel reading curriculum that is specifically built upon the evolution of writing systems from semasiographies to alphabets.

Brooks' chapter probes at yet another component of the reading process: the role of visual patterning. His arguments are particularly important because, until recently, little effort has been expended toward applying the work in pattern perception to questions of orthography, grapheme-to-phoneme correspondences, and abstraction processes. The strong implication of this research is that by controlling the orthography in ways that his experiments suggest we may lessen the burden on the beginning reader.

The cognitive processes underlying the reading skill of the fluent adult reader probably differ substantially from those of the beginning reader. However, by viewing these adult skills as a goal toward which the beginning reader must move, some problems in this transition may come into sharper focus. The two chapters of this volume dealing with the fluent reader enlarge upon the complexities of the cognitive processes discussed by those which deal with the early reader. Rayner and McConkie review their recent work on eye movements during reading. Aided by sophisticated computer techniques they are able to achieve control over the visual field as a function of the reader's saccades. The result is, again, a growing appreciation of the elaborate and complex relationship between the eye and the brain of a fluent reader and further insight into the intricate skills that an emergent reader must acquire.

Kintsch's contribution explores the question of how sophisticated readers extract meaningful information from prose passages. Beginning with his theory (Kintsch, 1974) that meaningful material is memorially represented by a propositional structure, he presents the results from several experiments which show how fluent readers extract information from printed text by building up propositional hierarchies. Kintsch's chapter is an example of how cognitive psychologists are beginning to "back door" their way into the study of reading by utilizing theory and technique originally developed for other domains.

Liberman, Shankweiler, Liberman, Fowler, and Fischer present, in their contribution, an analysis that supports again what many have suspected, that phonological patterning is an essential element in the acquisition of reading an alphabetic script. But they also show that the underlying mechanisms and the attendant requisite skills are exceedingly complex and compel the conclusion that most extant reading programs are not germane to teaching these skills.

Williams' chapter presents, first, a strong critique of existing reading programs, showing in detail why various past curricula have failed in teaching reading effectively. The essence of her arguments is that they were constructed around hypotheses about reading that were insensitive to the elaborate cognitive demands made upon the emergent reader. In this sense her work reflects the issues raised by the other authors. Further, she presents some preliminary data on a new curriculum that was developed in response to these demands.

Finally, according to Calfee, we do not really understand, as yet, how to assess even the skills that we do manage to teach. He argues that current assessment procedures do not reflect the nuances of the reading process and hence are neither particularly good explicators of what a child has managed to learn nor useful as diagnostic instruments for further instruction. His recommendation is to design assessment tools that evaluate independently the several skills that underlie reading, and he presents recent work toward that goal.

Taken as a whole the contents of the volume produced in us equal parts of optimism and despair. Obviously no genuine progress with complex behaviors is possible if we delude ourselves in thinking that they are simple. So there is hope in the growing awareness of the difficulties and in the reintroduction of careful experimentation.

The contributions to this volume are based upon presentations at two conferences held at the City University of New York in the Spring of 1974. The first was held at Brooklyn College and was sponsored by a delightfully informal organization of psychologists, linguists, and educators known as the Eastern Verbal Investigators League (or, as they prefer, EVIL). The second was held in May at the Graduate School and University Center and run under the auspices of the Center for Research in Cognition and Affect (CRCA). We thank both of these organizations for the opportunity to juxtapose their meetings and to coordinate the focus. John B. Carroll served as reviewer, critic, and discussant of the papers during the conferences. Although his words do not appear in this volume, we owe him a special debt for providing critical insights that aided our task as editors of the manuscripts.

Brooklyn College and the Graduate School provided the funds and the physical facilities. We would also like to thank John Antrobus, the Director of CRCA, for his help and add a special word of appreciation to the administrators of CUNY who somehow managed to find financial support when seemingly none existed. The royalties from the sale of this volume will be returned to the City University of New York to ensure that similar conferences will be held in the future.

ARTHUR S. REBER
DON L. SCARBOROUGH

References

Gelb, I. J. *A study of writing: the foundations of grammatology.* Chicago: University of Chicago Press, 1952.

Gibson, E. J., & Levin, H. *The psychology of reading.* Cambridge, Mass.: MIT Press, 1975.

Kavanagh, J. F., & Mattingly, I. G. (Eds.) *Language by ear and by eye.* Cambridge, Mass.: MIT Press, 1972.

Kintsch, W. *The representation of meaning in memory.* Hillsdale, N.J.: Lawrence Erlbaum Associates, 1974.

Levin, H., & Williams, J. P. (Eds.) *Basic studies in reading.* N.Y.: Basic Books, 1970.

TOWARD A PSYCHOLOGY OF READING
The Proceedings of the CUNY Conferences

1
The Structure and Acquisition of Reading I: Relations between Orthographies and the Structure of Language

Lila R. Gleitman
Paul Rozin

University of Pennsylvania

1 INTRODUCTION

1.1 Learning to Speak and Learning to Read

If meanings could be directly conveyed—in whatever form these are represented in the head—from one human to another, there would be little mystery in language acquisition, and precious little in the acquisition of reading. Problems arise both for listening and for reading because, to convey our ideas, we have encoded them onto a physical medium (a sound wave, a squiggle on paper); to apprehend, we must map heard or seen representations of ideas back onto mental representations. The past two decades of investigation in linguistics and psycholinguistics have enhanced our appreciation of the complexity of the encodings (roughly, semantic, syntactic, and phonological) that mediate between meaning and its physical realization in the sound-stream. In fact, so complex and indirect are the relations between meanings and sounds that the acquisition of language by the child seems an incredible accomplishment, at least in terms of the explanatory concepts available within psychology to account for learning. Yet, whatever the mechanisms, it must be acknowledged that each normal child readily learns the mappings between his thoughts and the sound stream of speech.

Is the case the same for reading? At first, the parallel between learning to speak and understand and learning to write and read does seem close. Written language becomes for many of us second nature, requiring no more effort or will to deploy than hearing or speaking. Even very young successful readers find it difficult to look at billboards without understanding "what they say." This state of affairs superficially seems a natural one—given that the spoken language has been learned—for written language appears to be a simple cipher on spoken language: each letter of the alphabet, roughly, is a visual analogue of some known sound category. In this view, the skill of reading reduces simply to learning a very small set of associations between the sounds of the spoken language and squiggles on a page of print. Yet if this is so, learning to read should be easy, for it involves little that is new to the prospective reader. The rich structures of syntax and semantics, and the relations between patterns here and the sound patterns of language, are already known in large part to the kindergartner. To read, it appears that we need "merely" transfer all of this knowledge of language to a visual modality whose symbols map onto it roughly one to one.

Then considering all that must be learned in order to speak and understand, beginning (as an infant) with no language in advance, acquiring one's native tongue should be a difficult and lengthy task. In contrast, learning to read should be simple. This follows from the parasitic relation between speaking and reading.

But the facts clearly violate these expectations. Significant numbers of individuals fail to learn to read even after years of lessons at school. To be sure, a few children learn to read almost overnight, but they are exceptions, and are sources of wonder to their proud parents. On the contrary, virtually no one fails to talk. Every normal individual comes to speak his native tongue in the ordinary context of events of the first years of life, and without the intervention of teachers and formal drill. The acquisition of speech proceeds successfully across broad ranges in intelligence and across vastly different cultures and child-rearing practices. Speech emerges more or less autonomously in response to a biologically determined maturational schedule that is immune to any but the most radical pathological or environmental interference (for a major statement, see Lenneberg, 1967). In contrast, except in special circumstances (Read, 1971), the acquisition of reading requires a long period of schooling, and varies in success and scope according to intelligence (Thorndike, 1971), motivational and cultural factors (Downing, 1973), and internal differences in the nature of the writing system that is to be acquired (Downing, 1973; Klima, 1972; Leong, 1973).

What account can be given for the fact that what appears to be the more general and complex task (learning to speak and understand) is less difficult and less variable than what appears to be a trivial derivative of this (learning to read and write)? In our view, the difference has only indirectly to do with the visual modality itself. In fact, writing systems whose symbols are words or "meanings" present no special problem for initial acquisition (Rozin, Poritsky, & Sotsky,

1971; Gleitman & Rozin, 1973a). The problem of reading has to do with the *cognitive prerequisites* to understanding alphabetic systems: properties of these orthographies require their users to become aware of and to focus attention on the phonological substratum of speech. Failure to achieve this fundamental insight about the nature of alphabets characterizes the preponderant number of normal individuals who do not achieve literacy (Rozin & Gleitman, this volume).

There seems to be something of a paradox here. Surely hearing and understanding presuppose decomposition and analysis of utterances into their sound properties, else how could we know the difference between such utterances as "The sow bit the cat" and "The cow bit the rat"? This analysis of the sound stream by the ear is carried out below the level of consciousness by an evolutionarily old and highly adapted mechanism for speech and hearing (A. M. Liberman, 1970; Lieberman, 1973). To be sure, reading and writing also appear to require decomposition and analysis: evidently one must analyze a sequence of alphabetic letters by eye "as if" the letters reproduced properties of the sound stream. But why should this be so much harder? Surely it is not the sheer visual aspect of reading (discriminating the visual forms of letters and letter sequences) that creates the difficulty. More likely visual decoding must be carried out at a *higher level of awareness* than acoustic decoding: reading is a comparatively new and arbitrary human ability for which specific biological adaptations do not, so far as we know, exist. One must quite consciously learn to carry out the analysis of visual symbols on a page "in the same way" one naturally analyzes speech signals without insight and without learning. In this derived sense only, the visual modality is implicated in the difficulty of learning to read. The problem with reading is not a visual perception problem; the problem is rather that the eye is not biologically adapted to language.

In sum, learning to read requires a rather explicit and conscious discovery and building from what one already knows implicitly for the sake of speech: the structure of one's language and, particularly, the sound structure of one's language.[1] To the extent that this is so, it is small wonder that the psychology of learning (and the practice of education) provides little guide to how to teach reading. Current theories of learning can scarcely distinguish between acquiring new and arbitrary behaviors—such as memorizing the Pledge of Allegiance and

---

[1] This position is a controversial one, in a field notable for its controversies (for an earlier statement along similar lines, see Gleitman & Rozin, 1973b; for a more general discussion of "metalinguistic" awareness, see Gleitman, Gleitman, & Shipley, 1972; for a more general discussion of the concept of accessibility, see Rozin, 1975). A number of investigators have similarly proposed that the requirement of explicit awareness of phonology is the fundamental cognitive barrier to the acquisition of alphabetic reading (Mattingly, 1972; Downing, 1973; Cazden, 1973; and I. Y. Liberman, 1970), but many investigators take a radically different view of the reading problem (see particularly Smith, 1971; Goodman, 1969, 1973; and discussion of their position in Rozin & Gleitman, this volume).

using a decimal notation—and becoming aware of knowledge already in the head—as in learning to parse English sentences and following a proof of the Pythagorean Theorem (at least according to Plato).

The present authors do not know any better than anyone else, for the purpose of teaching reading, how to make use of the fact that the child who is learning to read already "knows" that his own language consists of the sentences and words and sounds that he is encountering anew, in a visual analogue, on the printed page. We will argue in this chapter, in terms of facts about the history and conceptual nature of writing systems, and in the following chapter, in terms of facts about novice and fluent readers, that certain levels of language encoding are easier to bring to awareness than others, and thus easier to deploy in the service of the cognitive act of reading. Specifically, we maintain that it is easier to become aware of meaning than of syntax, easier to become aware of words than of sounds, and easier to become aware of syllabic segments than phonemic segments of speech. To the extent that this is so, we claim, the acquisition of reading will be made more coherent for the learner if the task is dissected in terms of successively more abstract encodings of meaning, beginning with relatively concrete visual representations (of words) and progressing by steps toward the phonological representations that underlie alphabetic writing.

In this presentation, we try to describe the constraints on reading acquisition that derive from the nature of alphabetic units and the way these could be perceived; primarily, we describe the categories *morpheme, syllable, phoneme,* and *phone.* After some definitional comments (Section 1), we sketch the history of writing systems in human culture (Section 2). From our point of view, the historical development of orthographies is conceptually orderly, for it reflects a step-by-step increase in the abstractness of the explicit knowledge required of the learner; that is, primitive scripts allow the learner to focus his attention on concrete linguistic categories (morpheme and syllable) while alphabets require him to focus on the abstract phoneme and phone. After outlining the history of writing, we provide in Section 3 a more detailed discussion of the English alphabetic system and the relations of this orthography to the sound patterns of language. In Section 4, we discuss those aspects of speech production and perception mechanisms that correspond to units of writing systems. In a final comment (Section 5), we relate the historical strands of evidence to the descriptive linguistic and perceptual facts, and make a suggestion about teaching reading.

Elsewhere (Rozin & Gleitman, this volume) we take up in detail facts about fluent and novice readers that give further empirical substance to the claims made here on the basis of historical and descriptive facts about scripts. We demonstrate there that the fluent reader makes use of the many levels of linguistic representation available in alphabetic writing, in terms of a rapid and critically integrated sequence of information manipulations. Further, we claim that the prereading child, in the normal course of his language development, becomes increasingly aware of successively more abstract linguistic levels and categories. In this sense, we maintain, the child's metalinguistic history (explicit knowledge of language) mirrors a cultural history seen in the evolution of scripts. We therefore finally propose and report on an approach to teaching reading that recapitulates in many respects the historical development of writing: we begin (as did paleolithic Man) with pictorial representations of words, and proceed through rebuses and syllabic scripts before introducing the highly abstract alphabetic notation of modern English writing.

1.2 On Defining Literacy

What is reading? An old story concerns an illiterate Greek who had an American friend who could decipher the Greek alphabetic notation, but did not understand the language. When mail arrived from Greece, the American would render the words aloud with fine incomprehension, while the Greek listened and understood. Does either of these men read Greek? But an act of reading took place.

This story highlights some difficulties in defining literacy. It points as well to some interlocking questions about what and how to teach children in a reading class; since this second issue is addressed in the accompanying chapter, we leave it aside here. It is hard to find a serious definition of reading that will encompass both protagonists in the apocryphal tale above. But a preliminary step can perhaps be taken by defining literacy in the terms of some test procedure: one who can perform competently in the test will be called a reader, and it is his performance we will subsequently try to describe. What is an appropriate test for literacy?

One possibility is a direct test for certain concepts underlying the script: for example, one might require the subject to read nonsense syllables aloud at a reasonable clip. This test would capture whatever skill the hypothetical American brings to reading Greek, a skill called "decoding" print into sound in the education literature. This test has some evident validity with respect to reading, but it is inadequate to engage some obvious skills of fluent readers of a known language. Clearly, the activities of a skilled reader reading a language he understands are guided, in part, by attention to syntactic and semantic constraints in the text. This accounts for the fact that while readers can recite nonsense text at the rate of about 100 word-like items per minute, their oral reading speed with real English text is more like 250 words per minute (Rozin & Gleitman, this volume). Even if the fluent reader does some "sounding out" or decoding of words, he also makes judicious guesses from context. A nonsense-reading test cannot recruit whatever skills are involved here.

An alternative is the reading-comprehension test. This requires the subject to answer questions about the meanings in a text rather than merely to reconstruct its sound. This plausible procedure has its own flaws. The reading-comprehension test is contaminated by matters external to conceivable reading skills, and rather more so than the nonsense-reading test just rejected. That is, vast differences in comprehension arise that do not involve the printed page in any way. Consider the differences in comprehension among college students listening to the same lecture, or the differences within an individual who is asked to read either *Finnegan's Wake* or *The Little Prince.* The reading comprehension score confounds the ability to read with the ability to understand. The confounding increases as the complexity of the test materials increases. Clearly, such a test confuses verbal intelligence and reading skill. Many so-called standardized tests of reading used in our schools are contaminated in just this way. This is one of the reasons why the correlation between IQ and reading achievement rises substantially between early and late elementary school (Singer, 1974).

What is required in a literacy test is measurement of some confluence of skills, separate in part from understanding complicated meanings but tapping the squiggle-to-meaning mapping, that relates to the difference between a reader and an illiterate, with intelligence equated. This dictates that an appropriate test for literacy consist of (1) meaningful and grammatical material, so that the proficient reader can manifest his various skills, and (2) content we know the reader could understand if he were to hear it rather than read it. It follows that an appropriate test is most properly a comparison of what a person can apprehend from a tape recording with what he can apprehend from a transcript of that recording. (The practical development of such a test is of course complicated immensely when we ask how to define "equal exposure time" to the two conditions, etc.)

At the beginning of reading instruction, the pupil understands spoken materials at some level, while he understands the same materials in print not at all. At the opposite extreme, many educated people seem to acquire information at least as easily from books as from lectures. We will define the individual as fluent when he performs about equally in both tasks. This definition is the sense of literacy we have in mind throughout this and the accompanying chapter. A reasonable goal for education, in reading instruction, is to narrow the original gap between oral comprehension scores and reading comprehension scores. Barring some basement cases, then, the absolute level of performance in the listening-to-looking comparison is of no moment in teaching or testing reading skill in an individual: one may be literate and clever or literate and dull. Of course, for the purposes of cognitive psychologists investigating the components of literacy (as opposed to those who test individual literacy for school purposes), there is much to be learned from measuring absolute performance with nonsense materials, with conceptually complex text, and the like. The point here is merely that the sources of differential performance under these paradigms are too complex to permit either one to stand alone as a definition of "reading" or as the sole evaluative tool in measuring individual literacy. Consequently, we define reading as the skill of extracting meaning from print to the same degree that one extracts it from the sound stream.

2 THE EVOLUTION OF WRITING

We now turn to the origins of writing in human culture, introducing each script (*orthography*) in the order in which it appeared in human society. This historical overview may appear to be tangential to a description of the cognitively ordered sequence of conceptualizations involved in reading acquisition. After all, why should the history of writing reflect psychological complexity and thus—even more derivatively and less securely—a teaching sequence? It is quite possible to suppose that the various orthographies used in different societies at different times arose quasi-independently of each other (and of principles of cognitive organization) in consequence of haphazard invention or local cultural need. If so, the historical record would provide no guide to issues of learning and using *our* alphabetic script. But a careful reading of the history of writing reveals a conceptually orderly progression. Orthographic convention proceeds, almost uninterruptedly over time, in a single direction: *at every advance, the number of symbols in the script decreases; concurrently, and as a direct consequence, the abstractness of the relations between the written symbols and the meanings increases.*

In retrospect, it is easy to see why the pictures of objects that appeared in primitive writings (see Fig. 1) were so useful: they immediately evoke meaningful interpretation. But it is also clear that since there are very many meanings, there will have to be very many symbols in a script that renders these so directly. Unless all scribes are realistic artists who can render nature veridically, and unless each picture reliably evokes a unique meaning interpretation from all viewers, the learner of a picture script (*pictography*) will have to commit an enormous number of picture-to-meaning pairs to memory. Obviously, if the number of symbols in the script can be reduced, learning will be easier and broader.

But how can the number of written signs be decreased if the writing system must continue to convey everything one wishes to write? The solution is to render language visually in terms of more abstract levels of linguistic representation, which contain fewer units. There are more meanings than words, more words than syllables, and more syllables than speech sounds (phonemes or phones). If, then, a writing system provides only a symbol for each phoneme—describing syllables and words and meanings only as compositions of phonemes—it will increase efficiency for the learner. But there is a cost to decreasing the number of symbols. If the writing system abstracts away from the meanings it conveys, the decipherer will have to recover the meanings from the now encoded form in which they have been rendered. And of course the prospective inventor of a script will have to notice and symbolize these more abstract units. The abstract analytic writing systems were invented later, were reinvented less frequently in different cultures (Gelb, 1952), and pose considerably greater learning problems for many individuals than do the primitive scripts (Rozin *et al.*, 1971; Gleitman & Rozin, 1973a). All of these facts suggest that some guidance for the issue of how to teach reading may come from the natural history of writing.

The observed orderliness in the successive invention of scripts is not surprising or fortuitous because writing did not develop through independent—or evidently very conscious—"invention" (here a syllabary, there a hieroglyph, somewhere else, perhaps, an alphabet). On the contrary, each orthography arose as a gradual refinement and generalization of resources already implicitly available in its predecessors, as though the early scripts formed the necessary conceptual building blocks required for further development. We regard it as very interesting, from the point of view of a possible teaching sequence, that the old conceptualizations did not disappear from later orthographies but were typically retained and embedded within them. For example, English orthography continues to represent words (see Section 3), as did primitive orthographies, but it of course represents abstract sound structure as well. In this sense, the primitive orthographic concepts are proper parts of the alphabetic writing system. That is, modern alphabetic writing is reasonably viewed as consisting of a set of layered concepts, only some of which were deployed systematically in primitive writing.

On these grounds, one can build a plausibility case (though only that) for organizing reading instruction in terms of a similar accumulation of conceptions: perhaps ontogeny recapitulates cultural evolution. The next chapter (Rozin & Gleitman, this volume) provides facts about the learning and use of alphabets that bolster this case considerably. Here we rest content to claim that the evolutionary context and many internal descriptive facts about the historical scripts are suggestive enough that they ought to be looked at, if the concern is to develop a conceptually orderly curriculum for teaching reading.

As we have implied, it misrepresents the historical facts to suppose that successively more analytic writing systems arose discretely, or that each overwhelmed and supplanted its immediate predecessor. To the contrary, orthographies tend to rigidify under the influence of conservative religious, ethnocentric, and possibly conceptual forces. Writing systems are rarely much changed within the society in which they originally emerge (Gelb, 1952). Advance comes primarily when one society gets hold of the system used in another, and improves it in the course of adapting it to the new language. By such successive borrowings with change, new and more efficient orthographies were adopted over time, without hurt nor leave of psychologists and professional educators, culminating in almost world-wide conquest by the Greek alphabet. After we have surveyed the writing systems that have had their day in the historical laboratory, we will describe how modern English writing fits into this picture.

2.1 Semasiography (the Writing of Concepts or Meanings)

It is not logically required that writing be based on the sounds or words of language. Concepts can sometimes be rendered directly without the mediation of spoken language; a general idea (*sememe*), rather than a sequence of words in a sentence, can be expressed. *Semasiography,* in this sense, is attested from rock paintings and inscriptions dating back at least as far as 20,000 B.C. (Diringer, 1962; Jensen, 1969). If we do not demand that writing consist of permanently scratched or painted signs, we can infer a yet earlier beginning that left no trace. Many preliterate societies employ a kind of "object writing" for communicative purposes; Gelb (1952) cites this instance of rudimentary object writing by the Yoruba, a tribe of Nigeria:

> During an attack of a king of Dahomey upon a city of the Yoruba one of the natives was taken captive and, anxious to inform his wife of his plight, sent her a stone, coal, pepper, corn, and a rag, conveying the following message: the stone indicated 'health', meaning 'as the stone is hard, so my body is hardy, strong'; the coal indicated 'gloom', meaning 'as the coal is black, so are my prospects dark and gloomy'; the pepper indicated 'heat', meaning 'as the pepper is hot, so is my mind heated, burning on account of the gloomy prospect'; the corn indicated 'leanness', meaning 'as the corn is dried up by parching, so my body is dried and become lean through the heat of my affliction and suffering'; and, finally, the rag indicated 'worn out', meaning 'as the rag is, so is my cloth cover worn and torn to a rag [Gollmer, 1885; as quoted by Gelb, 1952, p. 5].*

The objects do not convey particular words of the Yoruba language, and have no direct relation to these. Instead, through arousing semantic associations, the objects have the effect of putting across a meaning or concept. The North American Indian bead writing (*wampum*) apparently served a similar function. Yet it is apparent that this must be a sometime device, subject to rampant ambiguity and vagueness of interpretation.

The most widespread of semasiographic devices is the use of pictorial representations to refer to meanings, attested from upper Paleolithic times and in widely dispersed cultures. Since ideas (not the words of language) are directly expressed in these drawings, it is often possible to reconstruct something of the intent of the writer without knowledge of the language. An example is shown in Fig. 1 (from Jensen, 1969), from the Pasiega cave in Northern Spain. Jensen reconstructs, at the left, cave dwellings, at center a pair of footprints, and to the right, possibly a prohibition sign. We might render the idea, then, as *No Trespassing in Our Caves!* but the signs presumably do not stand for a sequence of concrete words ("no–feet–caves") in the protolanguage of the scribe. A further example is shown in Fig. 2 (adapted from Gelb, 1952), which depicts proverbs of the Ewe tribe of Togo. The first proverb, as the caption states, is literally "The thread

---

*From I. J. Gelb, *A Study of Writing.* Chicago: University of Chicago Press, 1952. Copyright © 1952 by The University of Chicago Press.

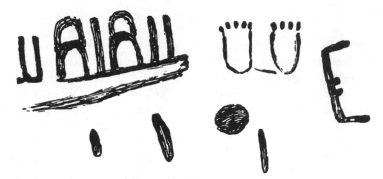

FIG. 1. The first *No Trespassing* sign: semasiographic writing from the Pasiega Cave, Northern Spain. (From Jensen, 1969, p. 40.)

follows the needle," which Gelb interprets as something like our "The apple doesn't fall far from the tree" or a "chip off the old block." The second is "Two opponents cannot last" meaning essentially that one disputant must give way. Notice, particularly in this second instance, that the literal words of the proverb are not rendered: the picture is of two warriors, neither of whom is shown yielding. The picture simply "brings to mind" the previously known proverb, rather than writing its words. Pictures used for these identifying mnemonic purposes may become abstract (*diagrammatic*), as in the circle that represents "the world" in the third panel of Fig. 2. Even so, if a concept as opposed to a word of the language is what is directly expressed, this diagrammatic representation is still properly called a *semasiogram,* as opposed to the *logograms* that we will presently discuss (Gelb, 1952).

So far as is known, semasiography was always severely restricted in use, being employed primarily to record stereotyped, culturally familiar material, such as

FIG. 2. Semasiographic writing: Proverbs of the Ewe tribe of Togo. The left-hand panel represents the proverb, "The thread follows the needle." The center panel reads, "Two warriors cannot stand" (see text). The right-hand panel reads, "The world is like a baobab tree," that is, so great that it is impossible to embrace it. This is expressed, as Gelb notes, by the picture of a man trying in vain to stretch his arms between the tree and a circle symbolizing the world. (From I. J. Gelb, *A Study of Writing.* Chicago: University of Chicago Press, 1952, p. 49. Copyright © 1952 by The University of Chicago Press.)

ritual celebrations and wise sayings. There is no evidence of an exhaustive system of this type—one that can render all items in the conceptual or linguistic domain. This is not surprising, for the variety of concepts available even in stone age societies must be very large, and then the number of diagrammatic indicators needed for unpicturable items would ultimately be crushing.

The historical decision to abandon semasiographies and to base writing on the words and sounds of the spoken language represents an implicit recognition that within human language infinite expressiveness is derived from finite means. Each subsequent system used a language unit with fewer elements than the last. All observed change is in this direction.

2.2 Logography (the Writing of Words or Morphemes)

The use of written signs to express the words of the spoken language is a device that cropped up independently in a large number of cultures, for example, the Mayan, the Egyptian, and the Chinese. The oldest writings we have evidence for appear on vessels of the First Dynasty of Egypt—about the fourth millenium B. C. The signs appear to represent root forms of substantives and verbs (so-called *morphemes:* roughly, minimal meaning-bearing elements of the language), the "grammatical" terms being ignored. Thus, as an example from English, the item *wanted* consists of two morphemes (*want + ed;* that is, verb + tense marker); in a primitive script, the sentence *I wanted to go* would be represented as *I want go,* the tense-marking and mood-marking elements of the verb being ignored.

The physical shapes of early logograms relate in obvious ways to the embryonic ideas of semasiography; chiefly, the signs derive from four simple bases (Gelb, 1952):

Pictograms: Concrete actions and objects are represented by pictures.

Diagrams: Arbitrary geometric signs are created for unpicturable words.

Ideograms: Semantic associates of pictograms are represented by the same sign; for example, if a picture of the sun originally signified *sun,* then the same sign might be used to express *bright* and *day,* with the results that less easily picturable words can be represented and that excessive proliferation of the set of signs is avoided; however, the signs consequently become ambiguous with respect to the set of words. It is important to realize that the logographic sign is meant to express a single particular word, not the general idea that subsumes *bright, sun,* and *day.* The ancient scribe often went to a good deal of trouble to disambiguate his use of these ideograms, using semantic complements as described below, and also contextual clues when these were available (Gelb, 1952).

Semantic complements: Additional, *unpronounced,* signs are appended to word signs to signify the superordinate semantic category to which the sign (in some particular occurrence) refers, especially where ambiguity arises among ideograms. An example from Gelb (1952) is the cuneiform writing of *Aššur,* the name both of a city and of a deity. A further sign, either 'deity' or 'city', is customarily appended to the *Aššur* sign; thus, ^{deity}Aššur, or else ^{city}*Aššur*. In either case, the sign is to be read "Aššur," (not "Aššur city" or "the God Aššur") but now the reader also knows the sense which is intended. In many ancient orthographies, the unpronounced complement came to be inserted habitually at each occurrence of the appropriate semantic category, even if no ambiguity arose.

Logography appears to be a useful kind of writing. Indeed it is sufficiently useful that one of the world's major languages, Chinese, is written essentially in logographic form today (see Fig. 3 and discussion in Section 2.3). While there are a great many words, and thus a great many signs to be memorized separately in learning a logography, yet the set of meaningful words is finite and changes its membership quite slowly. At least on a commonsensical view, there are many more concepts than words, for new concepts can generally be expressed by combinations of old words. In this sense, word writing seems to be more efficient than idea writing. However, this argument collapses when the case of new proper names is considered: these are incorporated frequently and freely into language usage, and are unpicturable. Since proper names are a good deal of

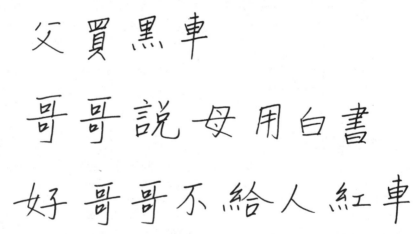

FIG. 3. Logographic writing: a few sentences in modern Chinese. These three sentences were among those read by second-grade subjects in an experiment by Rozin, Poritsky, and Sotsky (1971). Reading across from left to right, these sentences can be translated as: *top:* father buys (a) black car; *middle:* older-brother says mother uses (the) white book; *bottom:* good older-brother (would) not give (the) man a red car. Note the one-to-one mapping of English words to unitary Chinese characters (words in the translation that are not directly represented in the Chinese characters are included in parentheses). The principle of a phonetic complement is illustrated by the sign for *red,* the penultimate character on the bottom line. This character is a compound of two characters: the element on the left signifies *silk,* and the element on the right, which looks like I, is pronounced *ung.* The pronunciation of the word *red* in Mandarin Chinese is *hung.* Thus, *ung* is a phonetic clue for the proper reading of this character.

what the ancients wanted to write (in the commercial early uses of writing, ownership was a major topic), the resources of logography were insufficient. The stage was set for a further advance.

2.3 Phonography (the Writing of Sounds)

A description of orthographic history would be materially simplified if there had been a gradual and uniform development, in each society, from the simple logographic origins. However, the fact is that in some cultures, development proceeds no further (for example, the Mayan and Aztec scripts reveal only a few marginal instances of sound writing). For the case of Chinese, development proceeds to the use of "hints" for pronunciation, as we shall describe. On the other hand, the widespread use of phonological (sound-stream) devices dates from very early records in the case of Egyptian and other Near and Middle Eastern scripts. It is true that the earliest preserved writings are semasiographic and that the latest-invented writing is alphabetic; it is also true that no society moves backward from, say, alphabet to logography. But it is not clear, since the origins of writing are often shrouded, that each culture begins with the most primitive kind of writing and then proceeds unerringly to analytic, sound-stream scripts.

We can clearly observe, however, an orderly evolution of just this sort in the forms of the signs themselves; these become more extensive and highly conventionalized within a culture, with the passage of time. Figure 4 (from Gelb, 1952) shows early and later forms of some cuneiform signs, revealing the loss of pictorial clarity over time. The loss of the pictorial mnemonic, and the need to express unpicturable proper names, no doubt are related to the increasing tendency to represent sound properties of the language in the script. Two main devices developed to supplement the logographies with phonological information:

a. Phonetic complements. A phonetic complement is the sound-stream analogue of the semantic complement we previously discussed. Recall that the semantic complement gave a clue to a semantic range, such as "name of a city" or "name of a kind of cereal." Like the semantic complement, the phonetic conplement is a sign appended to the logogram, and is unpronounced: it gives a clue to the pronunciation of the logogram. For example, if English were written this way, the logogram for *river* would be accompanied by an additional sign interpretable as "sounds like *rover*" or, perhaps, "sounds like *liver*."

The large majority of the 50,000 or so Chinese characters are *phonetic compound signs* formed of a semantic complement (an ideogram, often called a *radical*) indicating the general semantic field to which the intended word belongs; and a phonetic complement (another ideogram, of a word similar in sound to the intended word). The pair, taken together, give—at least theoretically—sufficient information to isolate a particular spoken word of the

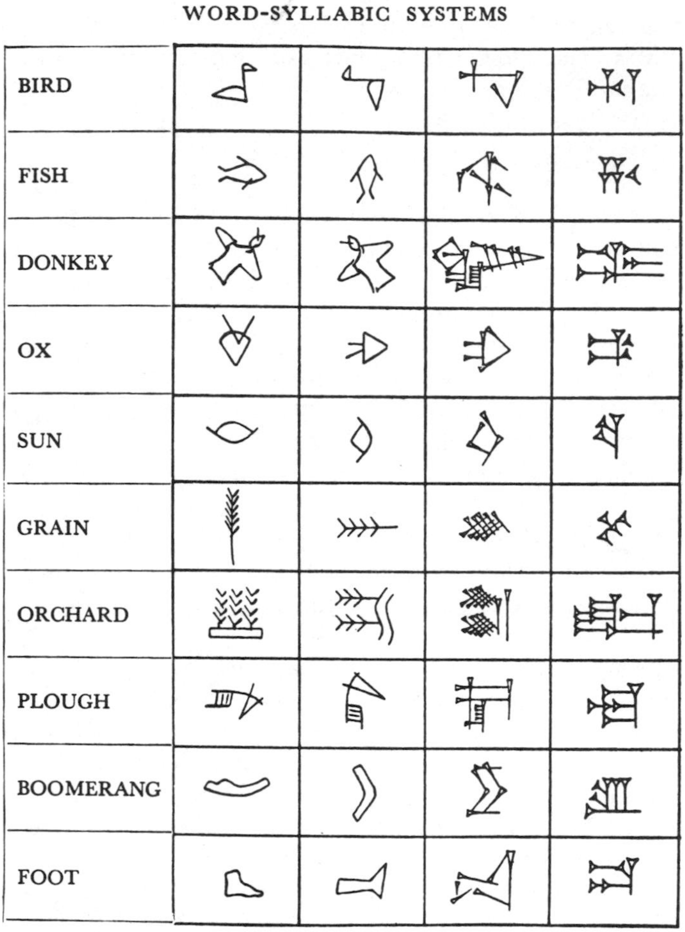

WORD-SYLLABIC SYSTEMS

FIG. 4. Pictorial origins of ten cuneiform signs. (From I. J. Gelb, *A Study of Writing:* Chicago: University of Chicago Press, 1952. Copyright © 1952 by The University of Chicago Press.)

language; hence, the whole two-part character is a logogram. Thus, for example, a Chinese style logogram for English *river* would read, literally, "a body of water that sounds like *liver*," while *creek* would read "a body of water that sounds like *crack.*" On the face of it, it would seem that one would have to decipher rather than read novel items in a script of this kind. Not only are there many spoken words to search, given the superordinate "body of water," but the phonetic clue may be a rhyme, a relative with one vowel difference, etc. (see Fig. 3, bottom line and caption, for an example from modern Chinese). Matters are further complicated by the fact that the semantic and phonological elements are not spatially ordered in the compound sign. Worse, the phonetic and semantic portions may physically merge and become unanalyzable as the sign is conventionalized and simplified over time (Martin, 1972; Chao, 1968). Even more confusing: since there is obviously a choice among items to use as the phonetic clue, the Chinese prefer to use a phonetic relative that also has some semantic relation to the meaning which is expressed by the radical. Thus a decoding act for a previously unlearned item would take on difficulties akin to those of word puzzles in which part of the problem is to decide which segment of the clue is definition, which an anagram on the solution. In practice, it seems that while the semantic and phonological components of a Chinese phonetic compound sign are worth telling the learner as a mnemonic for memorization, one reads Chinese logographically, as though each whole character was an indivisible symbol for a word in the spoken language (Leong, 1973; Chao, 1968).

The major conceptual fact about phonetic complements is that they are not directly "writings of sounds." They do include information about sounds, but merely as unpronounced clues. The Chinese use a further phonographic device, the rebus, mainly to render foreign loan words; but ordinarily they use the logographic characters. The Near and Middle Eastern scripts, however, increasingly incorporated the rebus principle, a concept which is much closer to modern sound writing than is the phonetic complement.

b. The rebus. The rebus concept is the true precursor of sound writing: essentially the notion is that two words that sound the same can be written with the same sign, regardless of meaning differences. Once this idea was conceived, it was theoretically no longer necessary to invent an arbitrary diagrammatic sign for each new unpicturable word; an already available picture sign, related in sound, could represent it. For example, *I* can be spelled 👁 , *deer* can be spelled 🦌 , and then *idea* can be spelled 👁 + 🦌 , at least for New Yorkers. Now the sound is rendered directly, and the meaning only by mediation of the sound. Notice that while the phonetic complement similarly indicates a rough sound value, it does so as an *additive* to a meaning sign. It does not, like the rebus, insert the sound value *in place of* the meaning value. Two main types of sound writing (phonography) developed from the logographic systems by development and extension of the rebus principle: *syllabary* and *alphabet.*

2.3.1 Syllabaries

Every word in every language can be written as an integral sequence of syllables; roughly, a syllable is a single vowel or diphthong, which may be preceded and/or followed by one or more consonants (see Section 4 for discussion of the syllable unit). Writing notations based on the syllable unit have appeared recurrently, by independent invention, and in different parts of the world; in Africa, North America (among the Cherokee, see Walker, 1969), the Far and Middle East, and in the Aegean. For the case of the Near and Middle Eastern scripts, where the surviving historical record is fairly rich and covers a great time depth, it is clear that the syllable signs evolved immediately from word signs and the rebus idea;

but now a phonographic concept becomes explicit: the syllable signs no longer represent morphemes or words directly, but solely phonological entities.

Suppose, for example, that a number of spoken words include an identically pronounced subpart, such as English "man," "manuscript," "Manhattan," "emancipate." Each of these would require a different logogram, since they are distinct words and since the overlapping portion "man" does not represent the same elemental idea in all these words. The sign for one of them, say, 木 = *man,* may be designated as the sign uniformly representing that pronunciation, regardless of the meaning of the word in which it is used. For example, "mandate" can be written:

man   +   date

If the script uniformly embodies this concept, the sign 木 is no longer a logogram, even when used to designate the word *man.* It represents this meaning through mediation of the sound properties. When a script includes a codified set of signs of this phonographic type, and when the unit size of each is the syllable, the system itself is called a syllabary.

Discovery of this syllabic–phonological principle did not necessarily or entirely lead to the dismantling of the logography that preceded it. Table 1 (from Gelb, 1952) compares the number of syllable signs and logograms coexisting in various scripts. Generally it is the foreign adapters of scripts, not the native users, who dispose of some of the residue from past systems. Logographic and syllabic systems may coexist for many centuries (Japanese writing still includes several thousand logograms, beside a full syllabary). The easy coexistence of varying conceptual principles within a script is one more indication of the relative lack of analyticity with which writing systems are invented and apprehended.

Since the number of syllables is for many languages vastly smaller than the number of differently pronounced words, adoption of a syllabic system can effect great economy of signs. However, this efficiency varies for different languages. Insofar as the language is largely monosyllabic (as Classical Chinese: Chao, 1968), the number of syllables approaches the number of words, and a

TABLE 1
Relationship of Word Signs to Syllabic Signs in Word–Syllabic Writings

	Total number of signs	Syllabic signs
Sumerian	about 600	about 100–150
Egyptian	about 700	about 100
Hittite	about 450 +	about 60
Chinese	about 50,000	[62 in fan-ch'ieh] .

syllabary yields no advantage over a logography.[2] The efficiency of syllabaries depends also on internal features of the individual syllables in the language. Ideally suited to a syllabary are those languages which allow only a few syllable types, either V (vowel alone) or CV (consonant + vowel), and nothing else. Japanese is such a language, and it can be represented adequately with a vocabulary of about 50 syllabic signs (see Fig. 5). English, at the other extreme, allows certain consonant clusters to a limit of four in syllable-final position (as in *lengths*) and also allows consonants in both syllable-initial and syllable-final position. Thus, among others, there are syllable types CCV, CCVC, CCVCC, CCCV, CCCVCCCC; examples are *spy, spied, spend, stray, strengths*.[3] In English, then, there are several thousand different spoken syllables. Moreover, since consonants occur at both the end and beginning of English syllables, the problem of segmenting polysyllabic words is theoretically and practically difficult, if not arbitrary (is it *fa-ster, fas-ter,* or *fast-er*?). Not surprisingly, syllabaries were invented and adopted within societies whose language had a simple syllable structure. These syllabic forms of writing have sometimes persisted to this day (as in Japanese), for an alphabet will hardly reduce the number of symbols in the script for a language with a highly constrained syllable stock.

A true syllabary, if conceptually consistent, has a separate sign whenever there is either a different consonant within the syllable (e.g., a sign for "pa" and a sign for "ba") or a different vowel (e.g., a sign for "ba" and a sign for "be"). But in practice the ancient syllabaries did not make all these distinctions.

For example, a single sign might be used for two syllables that are identical except for the voicing (vocal cord vibration) of a single consonant. Thus, the sign ∠ might represent both the syllable "nōz" and the syllable "nōs." And then ∠ + ⬚ might be a fit writing for "nostrum" (the unvoiced S is rendered by voiced Z; the unvoiced T is rendered by voiced D). A more important smudging of distinctions among syllables, for the subsequent development of writing, was the use of a single sign to represent all syllables sharing the same consonant, even

---

[2] As noted earlier, a syllabic notation is used in Chinese under conditions where it would be most effective: to render polysyllabic loan words. The Japanese similarly use their *Katakana* syllabary to transcribe Western loans. For example, Chao reports that *Katakana* syllables are used for the sequence *chi-ya-i-na-ta-u-n* on the sign of the "Chinatown" nightclub in Kyoto. It is worth noting that modern Chinese, unlike classical Chinese, cannot be characterized as simply monosyllabic in morpheme or word structure (Chao, 1968). It is also worth mentioning, with only the most timid implication of cause and effect, that the Chinese are now moving toward adoption of a phonographic script.

[3] Of course the *th* in *lengths* and in *strengths* transcribes a single phoneme, not a sequence of two phonemes. English writing uses a number of such digraphs, such as *th, sh, ph*. There are various historical reasons for this, discussion of which would carry us too far afield; it is also true that such writings are not descriptively irrelevant to the current phonological system (notice that all the sounds rendered by these digraphs with H share a feature of aspiration), but again we must ignore this detail. It is important here simply to realize that although five-consonant letter sequences appear in English words, these refer maximally to four-consonant spoken sequences.

Hiragana

a	ka	sa	ta	na	ha	ma	ya	ra	wa	ga	za	da	ba	pa
i	ki	si	ti,(tsi)	ni	hi	mi		ri	wi	gi	zi	di	bi	pi
u	ku	su	tu,(tsu)	nu	hu	mu	yu	ru		gu	zu	du	bu	pu
e	ke	se	te	ne	he	me	ye	re	we (e)	ge	ze	de	be	pe
o	ko	so	to	no	ho	mo	yo	ro	wo	go	zo	do	bo	po

n (n)

FIG. 5. The Japanese Hiragana syllabary. This syllabic system has a separate symbol for each vowel-alone syllable (the first column) and for each consonant + vowel syllable. Since no other syllabic types appear in the spoken Japanese language, it can be transcribed in terms of this small set of syllabic symbols. But notice that the fact that, e.g., *ka, ki,* and *ku* or *ka, sa,* and *ta* are phonologically related in the spoken language is not acknowledged in this script; from the symbols themselves one can glean only that there are 74 phonological entities, apparently unrelated to each other. (From I. J. Gelb, *A Study of Writing.* Chicago: University of Chicago Press, 1952, p. 161. Copyright © 1952 by The University of Chicago Press.)

though the vowel differed (for example, the Hebrew character *Beth* would represent, indifferently, "be," "bi," "bo," "bu," "ba").

In a way, representations of this sort appear (in hindsight) to *be* the alphabetic principle, lacking only separate signs for the vowels. Certainly the decision to write all consonant-identical syllables with the same sign is a major step toward an alphabet. Notice that the Japanese syllabary (Fig. 5), which did not evolve toward an alphabet, represents consonant-identical syllables differently; that is, five separate signs correspond to "ba," "be," "bi," "bo," "bu" in the Hiragana notation. On the contrary, one Hebrew sign stands for all five. In short, the first consonant of the name of the syllable (e.g., *Beth*) comes to be used as the sound value (e.g., "B") that sign takes in the script. This *acronymic* principle is essentially the same as the one that yields spoken English "radar" from the phrase "*ra*dio *d*etecting *a*nd *r*anging"). But it is important to state that this move toward the idea of phonemes (letter sounds) did not emerge self-consciously, as an analytic notion that was then readily generalized. On the contrary, it seems that the users of early syllabic scripts were unclear about whether the symbols of the script represented syllables or just the consonants of those syllables, and their usage was inconsistent in this respect (Chao, 1968).

The vagueness of the ancient writers concerning the alphabetic notions already manifest in their orthography is more understandable when considered in terms of the Semitic language which supplied the context for these writing advances. In many Semitic languages, consonants play a primary role in distinguishing the root forms, while vowels often render grammatical functions. As stated earlier, the ancient writers usually did not transcribe the grammatical functions such as tense markers, plural markers, and the like. Then if vowels render grammatical functions in the spoken Semitic language, and grammatical functions are not rendered in writing, vowels will tend not to be written or, perhaps, even noticed. The idea of a vowel within a syllable seems not to have been recognized explicitly, however odd this seems in retrospect. In essence, the Semitic writer tolerated a single sign for words with different vowels (as an example from English, a single writing would be possible for *goose* and *geese*) but not for words with different consonants (for instance, English *grief* and *grieve* would have to be written differently).[4]

Even though the insufficiency of vowel representation in Semitic syllabaries seems acceptable in terms of the language structure, it did yield some ambiguity of interpretation, and did so much more radically when the system was borrowed through cultural diffusion by the Greeks. This problem was relevant to the evolution of the syllabaries into an alphabet.

2.3.2 The Alphabet

To counter the ambiguity of consonant-syllabic representation, the practice of appending vocalic phonetic complements (see Section 2.3) to these signs gradually developed. At first, this added vowel mark was just a clue to the pronunciation of the ambiguous syllable, rather than an explicit writing of vowel letters. In this sense, the writing looks essentially alphabetic; only the "idea" of an alphabet is missing. As an example of what was probably going on conceptually at this stage, consider a hypothetical syllabary which has signs for whole CV syllables—but the sign is the same, regardless of the vowel in that syllable, and signs for vowel-alone syllables (*a, i,* etc.). Then to disambiguate a written syllable, one of the vowel syllables can be appended to it as a clue. Thus suppose we wanted to render the hypothetical polysyllabic spoken word "okoki" in this syllabary; assume we have the syllable signs:

---

[4] If these spelling notions seem odd or undecipherable, it may help to notice that conventional English spelling frequently, though inconsistently, makes similar compromise with the representation of sound, a problem to which we will return at length (Section 3). Yet there is little problem of decipherment. Consider the word *read* in English, which is pronounced like "reed" (in a present-tense interpretation) and like "red" (in a past-tense interpretation). The writing here is reminiscent of the Semitic. The root meaning of *read* ("apprehend language from a codified visual representation . . .") is represented by the consonants, that is, *r—d*. The grammatical form (tense) is rendered by a particular vowel change in speech, but the vowel alternation is unmarked in the print. Another case is the single writing *house* for the meaning "dwelling," rendered in speech with a final S sound, and for the meaning "to provide a dwelling for," rendered in speech with a final Z sound; again, grammatical function (noun versus verb) is here ignored in the script, with little consequent confusion.

\# = any of the syllables *ko, ki, ka, ke, ku*
o = the syllable consisting of the vowel O alone
i = the syllable consisting of the vowel I alone.

Then we could write o − \# − \#, but this could be read *okoki, okiki, okiko, okuka,* and so on. By using the vowel syllabics in an additional role, we can write unambiguously: o − \# − o − \# −i or, quite literally, o ("the syllable O") − \#−o ("I mean the \# with an O-sound") − \# − i ("I mean the \# with an I-sound"). But if this vocalic phonetic complement is used at every instance, then it can be interpreted as providing a redundant transcription of the vowel. That is, if the syllable *ko* is written \#, and the syllable *o* is written *o*, then the *o* in the \# = *ko* must be a vowel, O, and the residue, K, is a consonant. Now reinterpreting \# as a consonant sign, we derive the alphabetic o\#o\#i, *okoki.*

Was the "invention" of the alphabet from a transitional consonant-syllabic script really an analytic step of this sort, a conscious insight? Apparently it is better described as a quasi-artistic development and extension. Bolstering this view is a reconstruction of the way the Greeks came to derive symbols for vowel letters from the syllabary they borrowed from the Phoenicians. The "discovery" of the vowel letters (possibly the crowning post-Phoenician step in the history of the alphabet) was really something of an accident. Because of a limitation on the Greek phonological resources, they simply misheard the names of the Phoenician signs for syllables beginning with laryngal consonants (consonants produced by constricting the larynx): failing to perceive the initial consonantal sound, they heard these syllables as vowels alone. (The nature of such systematic "mishearings" between two linguistic communities is discussed in Section 3; see particularly Footnote 9). Since, by the acronymic principle, the initial sound of a syllable was taken as its sound value in the script, the vowels as well as the consonants could now be symbolized directly within CV syllables (H. M. Hoenigswald, personal communication; Jeffery, 1961).

A full alphabet, marking vowel as well as consonant phonemes, developed over a period of about 200 years during the first millenium B.C. in Greece (Kroeber, 1948). It did not arise whole cloth, as a single insight with fully generalizable consequences like, say, the idea of the internal combustion engine. But once the alphabet was designed, it spread across the ancient world by direct borrowing and adaptation with surprising rapidity. It was never reinvented in a separate cultural development. Our own alphabet is a descendant from this same source.

The fuzziness of the inferential line from syllable to alphabet may explain why it was invented only once. Perhaps the obscurity of the alphabetic principle is relevant, as well, to the question of why it is hard for many six-year-olds to acquire English reading. The consonantal segments of syllables are hard to analyze out of the syllabic context in which they (must) always be embedded (for a discussion of the speech-production and perception facts here, see Section 4). Whether individual users of modern alphabets must rediscover and extract the subsyllabic (phonemic) unit in order to achieve fluency is a question we take up elsewhere (Gleitman & Rozin, 1973b; Rozin & Gleitman, this volume).

2.4 Summary

The history of writing, as we have sketched it, involves the use of successively more analytic units of language to correspond to the squiggles on the page (or rock). Change has always been in this direction: from the representation of ideas or meanings, to the representation of words and morphemes, thence to syllables, and then to the yet smaller alphabetic units of vowels and consonants (so far undefined) popularly called phonemes. No revisionists are recorded in history. Nostalgia for bygone scripts and more global units has been absent from the history of writing until the most modern times when professional educators and psychologists—faced with the difficulty of achieving mass literacy—in effect began to resurrect the past. True, no one has come along who wishes literally to impress wedge-shaped marks in clay or paint hieroglyphs on papyrus. Except for a few aberrant cases, revisionists are content to leave The Library of Congress intact. Yet they often argue that the concepts underlying the letter forms can be ignored and that the method for learning and using English writing look back to more halcyon times. There are serious advocates of a return to paleolithic semasiographies, those who suggest that children should—and that adults literally do—learn to read meanings directly off the printed page (Smith, 1971; Goodman, 1969). Another group proposes that children should learn the whole words embodied in Chinese and early Egyptian hieroglyph for, purportedly, fluent adults read whole words (Huey, 1908). We ourselves have suggested a crucial role for the syllable in learning to read English orthography (Gleitman & Rozin, 1973a). In addition, the most diverse theoretical opponents claim to be champions of the alphabet (Bloomfield, 1933; C. Chomsky, 1970).

We believe that the alphabet is a useful invention, and that learning its principles is an essential component of English-language literacy. The alphabet is a highly analytic representation of language that took some two millenia to work out from word–syllabic origins. We cannot give the novice reader this leisure, but we believe that an encapsulation of the evolution of scripts will help the learner achieve the ultimate alphabetic insights. This is because all the conceptions and units of earlier orthographies are proper subparts of the conceptions and units embodied in the alphabet.

In light of this declaration, it is of some interest to ask how modern English writing fits into the history of writing. After all, it does seem at first glance that English and other European orthographies represent a certain backsliding from the alphabetic principle. Certainly that is the view of the persistent reformers of *alfabetic notashun* such as G. B. Shaw (1965) who would return to verities muddied in our script. This position misinterprets the ways alphabets could represent language, a problem to which we now turn.

3 MODERN ENGLISH ORTHOGRAPHY

It is well known that English orthography poses serious difficulties for some would-be learners. Often, it is supposed that the major problem lies in the irregularity of English spelling; that is, in its partially nonalphabetic character. *Psychology* begins with an S sound, but it is spelled with a P. The items *cough, through, though, trough,* and *tough* seem to show only the most haphazard spelling-to-sound correspondences. Although there is some dispute about the extent to which there is a rule-governed basis for much of this irregularity (N. Chomsky, 1970; Francis, 1970), we believe this issue is peripheral to the initial problem of learning to read. The major difficulty of the poor reader is not the inability to read *cough* or similar monstrosities. The poor reader has trouble reading *off* long before the case of *cough* arises so the irregularity of English spelling cannot fully explain why it is hard to learn to read English.

We will show that the major initial difficulty in reading is posed by the regular alphabetic principle itself: the relation between spoken "mat" and the spelling M-A-T (a conspicuously regular case) is highly abstract. The spelling system is related to sound only through the mediation of complex encodings that take place at various stages in the linguistic process:

1. there is a complex relation between the *phoneme* (a cognitive–perceptual category) and the *phone* (a perceptual category), and
2. there is a complex relation between the *phone* and the *acoustic stimulus.*

The preliterate individual must have some access to the nature of these encodings if he is to construct an interpretation of how alphabetic symbols relate to the spoken language. Unless he does this, he will not learn to read.[5]

3.1   From Phoneme to Phone

The alphabetic principle embodies a strong claim about language organization: that perceived speech consists of temporally linear sequences of minimal segments of sound, smaller than a syllable. Thus "pat" consists of three segments; "tap" and "apt" are rearrangements of the same three segments. It will be shown later on (Section 4) that there is no simple discrete analogue of these units of spelling in the acoustic wave; nevertheless, perception seems to yield up units of about this size. Let us call these units *phonemes.* If the phoneme can be defined for the spoken language, then alphabetic notation (in some hypothetical pure form) can be understood as a simple cipher on this unit: a squiggle is assigned to

---

[5] Many excellent discussions of the relations of generative phonology to hypothetical and real writing systems have appeared in recent years; the reader is referred particularly to Klima (1972), Venezky (1970), C. Chomsky (1970), N. Chomsky (1970), and Smith (1971).

each phoneme. In brief, the perceived sound "puh" would be written P, "duh" would be written D, and so on.

Discussed below are attempts to define and enumerate the set of phonemes as perceptual classes that have simple acoustic correlates (Section 3.1.1), as in the formulations of the descriptive linguists (see especially Bloch, 1941; Bloomfield, 1933; Chao, 1934, and Harris, 1951). In discussing the difficulties with this formulation, we follow an argument by N. Chomsky (1964). Of necessity, the version here is much abbreviated and many technical issues are left unstated. Next, we sketch the alternative generative–transformational formulation (N. Chomsky & Halle, 1968), in which the phoneme is defined as an abstract perceptual–cognitive category (Section 3.1.2).

Psychologists and educators approaching this material, which is tangled and highly inferential, may wish to throw in the towel in favor of a rough-and-ready alphabetic unit, on the grounds that Phoenicians or Greeks and seven-year-old readers of English required no great technicalities in inventing the alphabet and learning to read. But without a clear definition of the basic phonemic unit, one must give up hope of accounting for much of the broad range of behavioral language phenomena. A unit approximating the phoneme is the basis of the rhyme of "bat" and "cat" and the alliteration of "bat" and "bag." A unit of this approximate scope is involved in the account of tongue twisters such as "Peter Piper picked a peck of pickled peppers..." A unit of about phoneme size disappears from speech at the time in linguistic history that *knight, knee,* and *knickers* came to be pronounced "nite," "nee," and "nikkers." Substitutions of sound in young children's speech ("I wiv at Six, Wantern Wane . . .") are at this same approximate level. Finally, the phoneme is the unit selected by many to represent language visually.

The description of phonemes as relevant to the discussion of reading an alphabet proceeds in two steps:

1. the definition of a phoneme is shown to require information from the morphemic (word-structure) level above and the phonetic (sound-structure) level below; and

2. many regular conventions of everyday English spelling, as well as a large set of apparently irregular spelling conventions, are shown to follow once the phoneme is defined as a cognitive category.

3.1.1 Is the Phoneme a Simple Perceptual Category?

How shall we classify the many sounds that occur in the course of speaking? The reasonable first assumption made by the descriptive linguists was that the sounds of language could and should be described quite independently of meaning, syntax, or any other global level of linguistic representation:

Assumption (1) The *phoneme* is autonomous in the sense that it is a unit of the sound structure of language; information about the relation of sound differences to meaning or syntax differences is for this purpose beside the point.

The next obvious assumption is that the phoneme must be defined as a perceptual class or set of sounds; that is, the linguists agreed to disregard all differences among speech segments that are not discriminated by the hearer, for obviously such differences play no role in the use of language. There is much variation of pronunciation in real speech, both within and across individual speakers, and yet mutual intelligibility is maintained. Clearly many little variations go unnoticed, either because the ear cannot distinguish them or because after suitable training (learning the language) the individual comes to disregard them. The separate speech sounds are termed *phones*. Each collection of phones, all of which are regarded for purposes of language use as "the same" by speakers of that language, is called a *phoneme*.[6] The phonemes are the exhaustive set of *perceived* sound distinctions in a language:

Assumption (2)   Two phones are regarded as belonging to two separate phonemes if and only if the speakers of the language in question habitually make and hear a distinction between them in the context of speech.

A "good" alphabet will render phonemes rather than phones, for the differences among phones of the same phoneme are irrelevant to meaning distinctions.

The classical phonemicists developed an apparently straightforward method for isolating the phonemes of the language: find words that differ only by having a single perceived difference in one of the putative segments, *a minimal pair*. For example, the pair *bit/pit* establishes the phonemes B/P under Assumption (2).[7] This assumption and its associated minimal pair test turns out to have considerable power in isolating a perceptual unit very like the one usually symbolized in our alphabet. Some apparently difficult cases turn out to have manageable explanations under this scheme.

[6] The set of phonemes so defined varies somewhat from language to language, and even from dialect to dialect. Speakers of one dialect find it difficult to hear and pronounce distinctions readily made in another. For example, many New Yorkers have a pronunciation of voiced *th* in "these" and "those" that sounds to other English speakers exactly like D ("dese" and "dose"). Yet the New Yorkers in question reliably distinguish between their own pronunciations of "those" and "doze" ("sleep"). That is, some sounds that New Yorkers discriminate among (assign to different phonemes) are variants of a single phoneme (that is, are phones of a single phoneme) in other dialects of the English language.

[7] This is only an informal test, in the practice of the linguists. Whether it can be converted to a psychophysical procedure is not really clear. At any rate, even in its own terms, the test must be refined considerably. Subject reactions tell us only that *pit/bit* differ, but do not tell us exactly where this difference resides. Presumably, a number of further pairs must be compared (*bit/pit; pit/pat; bit/bid*) before we can converge on the initial consonant segment as the source of the difference judgment. For a detailed description of this method, see Harris (1951).

An example of the usefulness of this analysis, often discussed in the linguistic literature, compares the t sound in a word like *grate* (to scrape harshly") with the t sound in *grater* ("one who scrapes harshly"). With a bit of coaxing, speakers of most dialects of American English can be brought to the realization that these two sounds are different. The articulation of "t" in *grate* involves, roughly, placing the tip of the tongue on the ridge behind the teeth, thus momentarily stopping the air column on its way out of the mouth (hence, "t" is called a *stop* consonant).[8] In the articulation of "t" in *grater,* the tongue is allowed to flap against the ridge, and the consequent sound is perceptibly different from the "t" in *grate* (let us symbolize this flapping noise as ϕ). Since American speakers can be cajoled into noticing the t/ϕ distinction, and since they reliably produce these sounds during speech, Assumptions (1) and (2) might seem to require that we recognize t and ϕ as representing two separate phonemes.

This result would be disappointing on two grounds: (a) the speaker (and reader) of English still has the strong feeling that t and ϕ sound very much alike, and (b) the word *grater* seems to be simply the word *grate* with *er* ("one who") added at the end—how much less satisfying to say that the word *grater* is the word *grate* with the t removed, a ϕ inserted for the t, and *er* added at the end. The linguists' account already has enough definitional apparatus to maintain the simpler description; luckily, the minimal-pair test cannot be carried out in the case of t and ϕ. No two words of English differ solely in having t or ϕ in the same place. That is, the environments (of surrounding phones) in which these sounds occur are always different; in the usual linguistic terminology, the relative distributions of t and ϕ are entirely *complementary*. Restating this fact:

Assumption (3)   Two phones, even if reliably discriminable by speakers of the language, are assigned to the same phoneme if they are in complementary distribution (i.e., if there is no minimal pair involving these two phones in the language).

A direct parallel to the t/ϕ case exists for the voiced consonant "d." The "d" sound in *grade* ("a level or degree") and the "d" sound in *grader* ("one who puts things in levels or degrees") differ; The "d" of *grade* is a stop, and the "d" of *grader* is a flap (which we will symbolize as ϕ'), but there is no minimal pair of English words differing solely in this respect. Thus d and its flap ϕ' are assigned

[8] The pronunciation of the consonants (under a partial fiction useful at this point in the discussion) is accomplished by making several articulatory gestures in parallel. If the gestures include one that fully stops the air column, the sound is called a *stop* (e.g., P, T, B, G). If the vocal cords are allowed to vibrate rhythmically, the sound is said to be *voiced* (e.g., B, D, G, Z); if this vibrating is delayed, the sound is said to be *unvoiced* (e.g., P, T, K, S). A third dimension is the place of articulation (closure): T and D are *dental* (tip of the tongue behind front teeth), B and P are *bilabial* (the two lips close), and so on. Thus T is an unvoiced dental stop; D is a voiced dental stop; and B is a voiced bilabial stop.

to a single D phoneme. By this quite unexceptional route, linguists arrived at a simple description of the relations between *grate/grater* and grade/grader, under this analysis:

Phonemes	Component phones
T	t, ϕ
D	d, ϕ'

Unfortunately, this analysis is about to collapse. Could it be that the flaps of *grater* and *grader* are physically identical to each other (that $\phi = \phi'$)? In fact, for most dialects of American English, the medial consonants in these two words are indistinguishable, while their initial vowels differ.[9] However, the definitions of the phoneme so far accepted will not allow a statement of the facts in this simple way, for in what sense could the "same sound" refer to two different phonemes? That is, the same sound (the phone $\phi = \phi'$) cannot be assigned both to the phoneme D and the phoneme T, for this would violate Assumption (2). Neither can we claim that the phone $\phi = \phi'$ is an instance of a new and separate phoneme $\emptyset$, for the phone $\phi = \phi'$ is in complementary distribution with both d and t: no spoken English word differs from "graϕer" solely by having d or t where this word has ϕ. Then by Assumption (3), $\phi = \phi'$ must be assigned either to D or T, but by (2), it cannot be assigned to both at once. This complication generated extensive discussion within classical phonemics: how is the choice to be made? Agreeing that there is but one ϕ, let us arbitrarily assign it to D, and

---

[9] Some readers will have great difficulty agreeing (1) that the flap sounds in *grater/grader* are identical and (2) that the initial vowels in these words differ in duration. Though these are the physical (phonetic) facts, they will turn out not to be the phonemic (cognitive–perceptual) facts, as is the point of this whole discussion. Evidently, one systematically "hears" the sounds in words on the basis of prior language knowledge rather than simply, in terms of sheer physical distinction. We have remarked already on this fact (see Footnote 6). This feature of language organization is massively demonstrated in the systematic misunderstandings among speakers of different languages and of different dialects of the same language. The resulting confusion is the major vehicle for language change in a nonhomogeneous linguistic community (see, for discussion, Bloomfield, 1933; Hoenigswald, 1960). Shaw's comedy, *Pygmalion,* turns on this problem. While Eliza Doolittle believes she is distinguishing between initial H (in, e.g., "Hartford") and initial vowel (in, e.g., "owl")—and perhaps she is—the trained phonetician Henry Higgins, whose dialect is different, in effect hears H when it isn't there in her speech and hears no H when it is until, with great difficulty, she acquires productive use of a new subphonemic (phonetic) distinction. Earlier in our discussion (see Section 2.3.2) we mentioned that the Greeks failed to hear the Phoenician laryngal consonants, and assumed that certain words—here the words for Phoenician laryngal-syllable names—began with a vowel, a lucky misapprehension that led to the vowel-letter concept. So powerful are the conceptual organizing principles here that we have no optimism that all readers of the present chapter will now agree that the medial consonants of *grater/grader* are "the same" and their initial vowels "different." Further discussion is designed in large part to convince the reader that such an analysis applies to his own speech.

see how things turn out:

Phonemes	Component phones
T	t
D	d, ϕ

The next step is to recognize that *grater/grader* form a minimal pair. We already know that they do not differ in their medial consonant (both have ϕ, now claimed to be a phone of D). Since the two nevertheless can reliably be distinguished in pronunciation, a physical difference must lie elsewhere. Fortunate for sanity, it does: The "a" of *grater* is perceptibly shorter in duration than the "a" of *grader*. Symbolizing short a as Ă and long a as Ā, we now have a more complete phonemic inventory:

Phonemes	Component phones
T	t
D	d, ϕ
Ā	ā
Ă	ă

The ā and ă are, under this analysis, assigned to separate phonemes because they distinguish the minimal pair *grater/grader* (and many others, e.g., *traitor/trader, waiting/wading*). English spelling now seems to be incorrect, for it assigns the difference in *grater/grader* to the fourth (T/D consonant) segment, while the present phonemic analysis assigns the difference to the third (Ă/Ā vowel) segment.

Common sense rejects this outcome on the grounds that (a) the assignment of ϕ to D rather than to T—or to T rather than D—is wholly arbitrary and asymmetrical; and (b) the real ("perceived" or, better, "conceived") difference between *grater* and *grader* is in the D/T segment, just as the conventional spelling system claims. But notice that in order to refute the outcome of the analysis so far, one must give up the claim that the phoneme is a physically definable class; the domain of psychophysics cannot handle the desire to assign a single physical event (ϕ) to two different categories. That is, psychophysics provides no excuse for violating Assumption (2).

Before going on to the alternative view of the phoneme as a more complex cognitive category, let us simply show the effect, in the words *grade/grader* and *grate/grater*, of the perceptual definition of the phoneme. As is clear from Table 2, for the case of *grate/grater*, the morphological and meaning relation is obscured by the writing *grăt/grāder*. Notice that a decision to write phonetically (in terms of phones) rather than phonemically (in terms of phonemes) would just as surely obscure the same morphological relations (*grate* would be written *grăt* and *grater* would be written *grāϕer*). This state of affairs was viewed as

TABLE 2
Effect of the Perceptual Definition of the Phoneme

English spelling		"Phonemic" spelling[a]	
Word in isolation	Word with "er" added	Word in isolation	Word with "er" added
grade	grader	grād	grāder
grate	grater	grăt	grăder

[a]Read the symbol "a" in all cases as the vowel in *maid, date,* etc.

acceptable by some linguists despite its apparent descriptive asymmetries (Bloch, 1941). However, it is inadequate on a variety of psychological grounds.

3.1.2   The Phoneme Is a Cognitive–Perceptual Category

The concept of a phoneme must be rehabilitated to account for rhyme, alliteration, tongue twisters, language change, baby talk, and the invention and learnability of an alphabet. The particular ways that these phenomena are manifested in English (or any other language) can be understood only by looking to a set of general *phonological processes,* presumed to be part of each individual's mental apparatus (for discussion see N. Chomsky, 1964). For the examples we have been looking at (*grate/grater, grade/grader*), the particular process that is relevant is a regular increase of vowel length with voicing of the consonant that follows. That is, all vowels are long before a voiced consonant, and all vowels are short before an unvoiced consonant. (Compare the vowel duration in *rib/rip, maze/mace, save/safe, bag/back, wig/wick,* etc.) This "rule" is regularly honored by native American speakers (indeed, failure to observe this constraint in appropriate circumstances will lead speakers to identify accents in foreigners). A description of the sound system that cannot capture this generalization is inadequate. Yet the perceptual definition of the phone fails to capture it: our phonemic writing of *grater* was *grăder* (a counterinstance of the voiced consonant D being preceded by the short vowel Ă).

The generative–transformational description (attributable to N. Chomsky & Halle, 1968, and their co-workers) asserts that the phoneme is not *a perception of a pronunciation* in any direct way, but rather *an abstract internal representation* related to pronunciation only indirectly, through the mediation of a sequence of phonological processes (rules) that take the abstract representations as their inputs. Each morpheme is said to have a *phonological representation* in the mental lexicon (stored dictionary entries) in terms of a sequence of *systematic phonemes* or *lexical representations;* The systematic phonemes in turn are encoded into the *surface phones* through the application of mentally stored phonological rules. Finally, the surface phones are converted into the various articulatory gestures that yield pronunciations.

At the cost of postulating these unobservable internal representations, not

TABLE 3
Successive Representations of Example Words as Phonological Rules Are Applied

Steps from systematic phoneme to phonetic representation	grate	grater	grade	grader[a]
The presumed phonological representation in the mental lexicon	grat	grater	grad	grader
The outcome of postulated phonological Rule 1: lengthen vowels before voiced consonants	grat	grater	grād	grāder
The outcome of postulated phonological Rule 2: convert dental stops preceding unstressed V(C) syllables to flaps	grat	graφer	grād	grāφer

[a]Read "a" as the vowel sound in *grate, maid, may,* etc.

directly manifest in pronunciation, the generative grammarians can describe the perceived phonemes (as given by intuition and rendered directly by conventional spelling in our example cases) which are the inputs to the also unobservable phonological rules. They can also describe the perceived phones (perceptibly different sound segments) now described as the output of the phonological rules. The problem with the previous definitions was that these two levels of representation got mixed together, with chaotic results.

For the examples we have been working with, the results of the cognitive approach can be stated informally as shown in Table 3. Notice that the English spelling is very close to the systematic phonemic spelling presumed to appear in the mental lexicon. After application of relevant phonological rules (only two of which are sketched in Table 3), the representation is of the pronounced form. Thus, this kind of analysis allows us to preserve a single representation for a single morpheme in the presumed internal lexicon; to describe the intuition of native speakers about the perceptual–cognitive systematic phonemes; and to describe the surface phonetic (sound) properties of English utterances, even when these phonetic properties are in conflict with phonemic representations.[10]

Now we have shown what was only asserted to begin with: the phoneme can be defined and described only by looking at more global levels of analysis (the

[10] It is important to note that neither this analysis, nor the traditional phonemic analysis that preceded, can be carried out without taking into account even more global facts about the structure of the language. The domain of all the phonological processes described above is the word; these "rules" do not operate across word boundaries. That is, the flap is not substituted if the following V(C) unstressed syllable lies in the next word. For example, the following sentences do not receive the φ phone at the relevant point: "I often wri*te* *er*roneous essays," and "I often ri*de* *er*ratic horses."

morpheme and word) as well as more molecular levels (the phone). The phoneme is a perceptual–cognitive entity which cannot be defined autonomously by considering speech sounds alone.

One further note will become important in a later discussion of speech perception and production. Even the very informal remarks above about English phonological rules have been stated by referring to attributes or *features* of the sound segments rather than to whole phonemes and phones. In order to say that "all vowels" behave in such and such a way, or that "all voiced consonants" behave in such and such a way, we obviously conceived each segment as a simultaneous bundle of (binary) features such as *+voiced/–voiced, +vocalic/–vocalic,* and so on. Clearly this is no place to describe the set of all features and their linguistic–articulatory specifications. (See, for description, Jakobson, Fant, & Halle, 1963; N. Chomsky & Halle, 1968.) Two examples will suffice to show that the features cross classify the phonemic and phonetic segments in a number of ways. The segments T and D are *–continuant* while F and V are *+continuant*; that is, the articulation of T and D completely stop, or block, the air stream momentarily so that one cannot hold (continue saying) the consonant, while F and V allow a little air through, so one can continue this articulation (you can say 'ffffff' but not "bbbbbb"). At the same time, T and F are *–voiced* while D and V are *+voiced.* That is, during D and V, the vocal cords begin vibrating about 25 msec earlier than they do for T and F. On one dimension, then, T is classed with D; on another, it is classed with F. In sum, the classification is

	T	D	F	V
voiced	−	+	−	+
continuant	−	−	+	+

At the systematic phonemic level, the features can be interpreted as a classification; at the phone level, they are the direct inputs to the neural machinery that will trigger gestures of the vocal apparatus. That is, each feature has reference to an aspect of articulation (the features may not be strictly binary at this level). Not surprisingly, then, such matters as the acquisition of the sound system and sound change in language are best expressed in terms of these features, for they are the units closest to the articulation of real speech.[11] The

[11] The question arises whether a script based on features would be more efficient than one based on whole phones or phonemes, since this is apparently the "deeper" phonological unit. In a script of this sort, letters like *b, d, g* would share some visual features (a mark representing voicing; a mark representing stop; etc.). Whether such a notation would aid processing of visual language is problematical. But scripts employing this concept are not entirely unknown. Chao (1968) reports that the Korean *Han-gul* visually analyzes phonemes in terms of subphonemic features. "For example, the symbols for the tense consonant phonemes are made of doublets of the symbols for the corresponding non-tense consonants, such as ʎ for ordinary *s,* ʎʎ for tense *s. . .*" (Chao, 1968, p. 107).

extensive psychological and educational literature on confusability among the sound segments also is stated in featural terms. The notions *phoneme* and *phone,* then, have no real systematic import within the linguistic description. They are cover names (labels) for certain recurrent (classificatory and articulatory) bundles of features in the language in question. Different languages choose differently from the possible bundles of features. At the level of feature bundles, linguistic theory leaves off, bequeathing the speech and hearing apparatus to the psychologists.

3.2 English Orthography Often Represents Aspects of Systematic Phonemics

We have shown that English writing is phonemic rather than phonetic for instances such as *grater/grader.* Restated: the writing system frequently renders just the *unpredictable* (item-specific) facts about the sound of each word; it leaves unstated the *predictable* (rule-determined) facts that follow once the item-specific facts are known. Phonetic facts follow from the application of internalized phonological rules to the phonemic facts. Insofar as the orthography adopts this stance, it is useable only by a knower of the language, for he putatively has stored the phonological rules and will supply their effects automatically, recovering correct pronunciations. Reviewed below is one more well-known example of phonemic representation in English spelling, to show that the instance of *grater/grader* is not an isolated effect in the spelling system. In short, a broad look at the English writing system reveals that many apparently haphazard spelling conventions can be reinterpreted more charitably as transcriptions of systematic phonemes.

One important case is the tendency in English spelling not to mark changes in vowel quality that are totally predictable consequences of the stress on the syllable in which the vowel appears. To understand this phenomenon, consider the pronunciation of the boldface vowels in the following words: *te' le graph; Ca' na da; con' tract.* All these vowels sound different. All occur within stressed syllables. When suffixes are added to these words, their stress shifts to the next-right syllable as *te le' graph y; Ca na' di an; con trac' tu al,* a common effect for many thousands of English words. Now notice that the vowel sounds in boldface are different from what they were in the unsuffixed forms. While they were all different before, they now all sound alike. All now sound like a brief "uh" (usually symbolized ə).[12]

Is this ə a new phoneme and, consequently, should a proper phonemic alphabet, unlike our conventional one, render these words as *tə le' graph y; Cə na' di an; cən trac' tu al*? For the classical phonemicists the answer was yes, at

---

[12] The second vowels in *telegraphy* and *Canadian* also change in the suffixed form, for partly similar reasons; but the description of this fact is more complicated (see N. Chomsky & Halle, 1968).

least for the sake of describing the language system presumably known by speakers (Bloch, 1941). Such a solution would describe, at the required level of exactness, the actual sounds that are uttered. But notice that for these three words (and many thousands of English words that have this moving stress), this formulation requires two phonemic writings of each word in the lexicon.

Is it plausible to suppose that the speaker stores all these double entries in his mental lexicon? This seems a cumbersome method for the language user to adopt, especially since a single unifying "rule" will describe all these thousands of alternations: "Pronounce all vowels as ə when they occur in unstressed syllables." The grammarians hypothesize that speakers have acquired the rule instead of the double entries as part of their language knowledge: speakers implicitly know that ə is just the neutralized form of many vowel phonemes. Perhaps the best indication of the correctness of this psychological claim is that the writing system—a natural product, developed by nonlinguists—embodies an identical claim. The ə is assumed in conventional spelling not to be a separate phoneme, that is, there is no symbol for it in the script. The writing system thus implies that, since the speaker—reader has internalized the rule neutralizing unstressed vowels, he will supply the effects of that rule (ə insertion) automatically when his task is to recover pronunciations. Writing ə, on the other hand, would add phonetic detail to written words for which the speaker—reader has no need (as would, in the *grater/grader* example, writing φ instead of t or d). Much worse, the surface phonetic writing would wipe out distinctions that the speaker—reader needs in order to recover meanings from the script (such as the information that *grater* is *grate + er,* while *grader* is *grade + er*). Thus the linguistic description supports the rationality of the writing system. But, much more importantly, facts embodied in the conventional writing system support the psychological validity of the linguists' description.

The assumption that different sounds may map onto a single phoneme (e.g., t and φ may both map onto T and ə and e may both map onto E) materially simplifies the formal description of relations between morphemes and sounds; alphabetic writing often embodies the same assumption. Symmetrically, the same sound may map onto more than one phoneme (e.g., φ maps onto T and D, and ə maps onto a variety of vowel phonemes); this assumption is also manifest in English writing. In effect, then, the writing system often transcribes a level of organization somewhere between the meaning structure (*morphology*) and the sound structure (*phonology*); it is to this extent a *morphophonemic* writing. It follows that similarities in spelling are partly predictable on the basis of similarities in sound; for example, the two suffixes *est* and ist, which have different meanings, are spelled similarly because they sound similar. It follows as well that identity of sound does not uniformly predict identity of spelling; for example, the suffixes *est* and *ist* sound identical in the words *purest* and *purist,* but they are spelled differently to represent the different morphemes. In fact, we can confidently predict different spellings for the same pronunciation, even for new (invented) words, if these have a recognizable morphemic substructure. For example, suppose that *Mesabrate* is the name given to a new nation, created by redrawing some political boundaries in the Balkans, a not unlikely circumstance. Suppose also that there is a verb *to mesabrate* meaning the newly observed action "to kiss one's elbow." It follows, given English morphology and spelling convention, that a man from Mesabrate is a *Mesabratian* while an act of kissing one's elbow is *mesabration*. In short, spellings in English optimally have both morphological and phonological coherence.

It has been demonstrated that morphophonemic writings have a basis in the cognitive–linguistic organization of fluent speakers. But, obviously, so do phonetic writings. Then would a surface phonetic script also serve the purposes of a reader? Evidently not: to the extent that morphology and surface phonetics are complexly related through a series of intricate recodings, a surface phonetic script would have the effect of obscuring the meanings to be conveyed. Would it really help the reader if, for example, *know* and *no, comintern* and *Common Tern, nitrate* and *night rate, homonym* and *hominem,* or *too, to, two,* and *Thieu* were spelled the same? Indeed this might help the learner, who then has but a single (surface phonetic) principle to acquire. But different spellings for the same sound ultimately act to keep different morphemes apart for the reader, while in the spoken language, intonation and junctural cues, pauses, repetitions, and arm waving are available instead to mitigate the massive ambiguity in the sound stream. Chao (1968) provides a nice example from French displaying the confusion that might result from a phonetic writing. For the expression "If six hundred and six saws saw six hundred and six cypresses. . ." French orthographic convention yields *Si six cents six scies scient six cents six cyprès. . .* while a surface French orthography would yield instead *Si si sā si si si si sā si sipre. . .*

In sum, morphophonemic writing reflects the language organization of its users. Nevertheless, it is unclear whether a script embodying these principles is easy to learn or use. This is an empirical question that cannot be answered solely by pointing to the simplicity of the script with respect to the spoken language. Further, although we have demonstrated that English spelling sometimes reflects deep phonological and morphological facts about the spoken language, we have not shown that it always or nearly always does so. This latter claim has been made by N. Chomsky (1970) who asserts that English spelling convention is near optimal when interpreted as a transcription of systematic phonemics. In our view, it is more straightforward to assume that English writing intermixes a number of levels of linguistic representation, and some arbitrary features.

3.3 English Orthography Represents Many Levels of Language Structure

Although phonologically natural spellings characterize much of English writing, there is evidently not a one-to-one correspondence between letter and systematic phoneme. For example, consider the variety of letters and letter sequences that represent the sound "ay" in *by, buy, bite,* and *bind.* Not all refer to different systematic phonemes. Similarly, the letter A corresponds to a variety of phonemes in *bad, ball, wad,* and *radio.* Procrustean maneuvers would be required to relate these apparent diversities to the phonology of English.

The problem here, in some further detail, is whether we can relate each particular fact of conventional spelling to a morphophonemic fact in the spoken language. The concept of deep phonological representations in the mental lexicon arises as an account of the "best fit" between the sounds (surface phones) and the units of meaning (morphemes): the unobservable deep representations are hypothesized as descriptions that simplify the relationships between these observed levels. If conventional writing neatly transcribes at this intermediate level of organization, it follows that there must be an account in deep phonology of why, for example, we have the differing spellings *lute* and *loot* for two morphemes that sound identical (in most American English dialects). Let us assume, for the sake of the argument, that we do have an analysis of morphemes and their phonemic representations that rationalizes these two spellings for a single sound. But then the same analysis ought to account for the pair *chute* and *shoot,* or it is hopelessly ad hoc with respect to the spelling system. That is, in the proposed analysis, *lute* must be to *loot* as *chute* is to *shoot.* It is hard to conceive of any morphological analysis that would achieve this end (for none of these words has any meaningful relation to any of the others); it is harder yet to suppose that the language user has tacitly internalized such a relationship. The problem is exacerbated when we notice that the pair *route* and *root,* which again sound identical in many dialects, introduce yet another spelling variant, and for no obvious reason of word or sound structure. Worst of all, *mute* and *moot* (which sound quite different) show the same spelling relations as *chute* and *shoot* (which sound the same). Then there are *beaut* and *boot, cute* and *coot,* and so on. The most straightforward analysis, in light of the number of inexplicable variations, acknowledges that English spelling is only a loose transcription of English phonology.

It is important to acknowledge also that a "pure" phonemic or morphophonemic script may not really be feasible because of individual and developmental differences among users. If the deep phonological description most simply connects the morphemes to their pronunciations, then the individual's deep phonological organization depends on the richness and completeness of the etymological relations he notices among his own vocabulary items. That is, if the speaker does not implicitly realize that spoken "bomb" and "bombardier" or "hymn" and "hymnal" are meaningfully related, then the final B of "bomb" and N of "hymn" would not appear in his deep lexical representations; and then conventional spelling would seem to him irrational—as it does to many whom we would call normal adults. N. Chomsky (1970) seems to assume that all adults share enough vocabulary that their organization would tend to be the same, but some counterarguments seem plausible (for further discussion, see Francis,

1970). However this may be, it is certainly clear that the young child's phonological organization is quite different from that of adults (Moskowitz, 1973; Read, 1971). If the child's phonological analyses are different from our own, and if it is the child we must teach to read, then certain of the deep phonological analyses projected for adult competencies would be worse than useless as a basis for initial reading acquisition.

Summarizing, there is evidently no unique level of phonological analysis that accounts simply for all the byways of English spelling, and will also support the acquisition of reading in young children. The writing system is a hybrid, sometimes representing deep phonological and morphological facts, sometimes the facts of a more surface phonetics, and sometimes a fossilized historical process (as in the K of *knight* and *knee*). How can this hybrid system be characterized?

Despite rampant irregularity, redundancy, and downright misrepresentation, English writing is at bottom phonographic: it is an alphabet. Only a tiny fraction of words are represented as true logograms, lacking any phonological information (mainly, these are the numbers and assorted signs of weight and quantity such as %, $, #, and +). Aside from these, each spelled word contains guides to pronunciation; that is, if a word starts with a "buh" sound, it generally begins with the letter B. The historical move from logography to phonographies like our own has a clear basis in efficiency of the script for acquisition, and for the recognition of rare and novel items: there are about 50,000 words in the speaker's vocabulary, as well as a proliferation of proper names. There is no practical way to memorize 50,000 unrelated visual representations of these items. The alphabet provides a phonological mnemonic to reduce the burden on memory. Although we acknowledge that the alphabetic system does not reduce memorization to 26 items—it is not a simple cipher on the systematic phonemes—it probably does reduce memorization to a mere several hundred or at worst a few thousand items (see Rozin & Gleitman, this volume, for a general discussion of the efficiency of phonographic scripts).

Although the script has phonological coherence, it is just as clear that its representations are not solely or simply phonological, else why would *know* and *no, pain* and *pane,* and *in* and *inn* be spelled differently? Each of these writings does give guidance for pronunciation but—at the cost of muddying the clues to sound—each gives meaning information as well. If this meaning information were given systematically for all cases, as it is for the particular classes of examples described in Section 3.2, we would conclude that English writing is strictly morphophonemic, that it represents directly the phonology of mentally stored lexical items. But we have now shown that morphological information is represented inconsistently, even haphazardly, for many words in conventional spelling. This *item-specific* representation of an individual meaning by means of a unique orthographic configuration is the same principle that appears in stone-age scripts: English orthographic representations are partly logographic.

Is this mix of phonographic and logographic information a barrier to English readers? Quite the contrary, we hold that the multileveled representations are efficient for the fluent reader's purposes. Many aspects of the reader's performance suggest that he monitors visual language at many levels in a rapid and critically integrated series of information manipulations (Rozin & Gleitman, this volume). Fluent readers do not proceed solely by "sounding out" or solely by recognizing "whole meanings" of words. A script that represents meanings only (a logography) cannot ultimately serve the purpose of effortless recognition of rare or novel items. And on the other hand, a script that represents sounds only (a phonography) poses problems for the rapid reconstruction of meanings from text (see Fig. 6).[13]

A final comment. We have asserted that English writing usefully intermixes a number of levels of language representation. Surely this system did not get to be the way it is by conscious decisions to represent the sound structure here, the morphological structure somewhere else. Rather, like the ancient scripts, the English writing system comes down to us in its present form through errors by semiliterates, conditional sound changes, printers' preferences, grammarians' strictures, and the like. But then—in light of the traditionalism of the current spelling—is it not likely that the script will become less and less phonologically relevant with the passage of time? Of course this is possible in theory, but it does not seem likely. Rigid as the writing system now is, it does seem to succumb to reform just when the representations stray so far from current phonology as to become useless at that level. The most grotesque feature of current English

---

[13] The Japanese writing system, from this point of view, seems ideal. We have already mentioned that the Japanese employ a syllabary of about 50 items (see Section 2 and Fig. 5). In fact, they have two syllabaries, which appear intermixed on the page. Mainly grammatical elements (suffixes, and the like) are written in the *Hiragana* syllabary, while borrowings from Western languages are written in the *Katakana* syllabary. Notice, then, that two subcategories of the morphological stock are picked apart visually in terms of two separate sets of visual symbols (see Fig. 6). Further, most meaningful words (nouns, verbs, and the like) are written in a third notation (*Kanji*), in borrowed Chinese characters; this system is purely logographic. Theoretically, every Japanese word can be written in either of the syllabaries. Why are two syllabaries and a logography maintained? Doubtless some of the answers have to do with tradition rather than cognition. But the system is undeniably effective. Our theoretical sympathies with Japanese writing have occasioned incredulity in some quarters (Goodman, 1973; see also Gleitman & Rozin, 1973b) for, whatever one's view of the "best" writing system, it does seem unlikely on the face of it that the best one is three different ones—unless, of course, one assumes that linguistic information processing might be complex! If efficient readers monitor many levels of language representation in rapid succession—even, perhaps, in parallel—to extract meaning from the printed page, then a system that formally makes explicit the appropriate level to be sampled does not seem so strange. About 1800 of the most familiar, frequently recurring substantives appear in *Kanji* (logographic) form; for these words, it may be most efficient to take in the sought-for meaning "direct" without recourse to phonological intervention. But for words that are rare, relational, or external to the morphophonemic system (foreignisms), a more analytic decipherment might be indicated. Our claim is that English writing, by hook and accidental crook, has evolved into an informal representation of the same mixed character as Japanese.

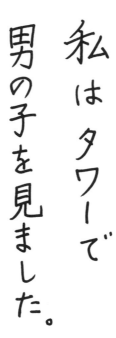

FIG. 6. Japanese orthography; three different scripts are used intermixed on the page in Japanese; the *Hiragana* and *Katakana* syllabaries and the logographic *Kanji.* The writing is read from the upper right corner down. In the illustrative example here, the English sentence, *I saw a boy at the tower,* is shown as it would be written when translated into Japanese. The three different scripts are all used within this sentence, as is usual in Japanese, for each script tends to be used for specific types of items (see the discussion in Footnote 13). The first symbol at the upper right is a Kanji for the first person. The symbol underneath it is a particle indicating the case (in this case, nominative). It is a Hiragana syllable, and is pronounced following the saying of the first person. These two symbols together thus constitute *I.* The following three symbols represent the English word *tower.* Japanese has borrowed this word from English, with essentially equivalent pronunciation. As a foreign loan word, it is written in Katakana. The first symbol (looking like a crossed seven) stands ·for "tau," and the second for "wa." The third symbol, a vertical line, indicates that the "wa" is lengthened. The final symbol in the first column is the syllable meaning *at,* and this is represented by a Hiragana syllable. The second column begins with the word *boy,* represented by three symbols. The first is a Kanji for *man,* and the third is a Kanji for *child,* with a Hiragana syllable sandwiched in between. The last four symbols represent *saw.* The first is a Kanji for the meaning *see,* and the last three, in Hiragana, represent the pronunciation indicating the past tense (the three syllables "ma-shi-ta"). Notice, then, that substantives and verbs are generally represented in Kanji, grammatical formatives in Hiragana, and loan words from other languages in Katakana.

writing is in the series with final *gh* and *ght.* Just these oddities have been subjected to spelling reform, at least in informal settings. Thus we find, ever more frequently, the spellings *thru, tho, nite,* and so on.

Summarizing, the particular orthographic forms of language that are learned by English readers have, simultaneously, morphological and phonological coherence in some complicated mixture. This mixture is not consistent from word to word and cannot—without unnatural stretching and squeezing—be described satisfactorily on any one unifying language principle or set of categories. The internal inconsistency is a result of the "natural" or unprofessional sources of spelling conventions. As long as the script maintains a loose but perceptible relation to language organization, there is little pressure for reform. On the contrary, the system works by providing meaning and sound information in a manner efficient for the judiciously sampling and constructing reader.

3.4 Problems of Acquiring the Phonemic Aspect of English Orthography

The phonographic aspect of the writing system poses a formidable conceptual problem for the six-year-old. Somehow the child must come to realize that the alphabetic characters and sequences are related to the language he brings to school. But how is a teacher to communicate that the alphabet is related to such conceptual categories as systematic phonemes and morphemes of the language? The learner has no clear idea of the meaning of such metalinguistic terms as *word* or *sentence* or *speech sound.* Much less is he aware of the abstractness of the relationships between speech sounds and phonemes, nor has he any vocabulary for discussing such matters.

In practice, teachers who wish to make explicit for the learner relations between alphabetic writing and phonology usually do so by attempting to relate each discrete letter to the utterance of a discrete surface phone. Thus a teacher may say, "The letter T here stands for the sound at the beginning of *tap."* A problem must eventually arise because the letter T does not really correspond to the spoken language at the level of one sound to one letter of the alphabet: T corresponds to quite different sounds in *tap, grater, creation, often,* and *think.* Some educators consider the possibility of misunderstanding here to be so serious that they counsel against teaching letter-to-sound correspondences, even as rough and ready first approximations for the learner.[14] Others, ourselves included, believe that the child is well served in initial acquisition stages by

---

[14] In particular, some educators (Goodman, 1973; Huey, 1908) suggest finessing the alphabetic principle by falling back on reference-making units the child will more readily recognize; that is, one might teach whole words or meanings. But then the huge number of items to be learned eventually imposes an overwhelming burden on the child's memory for arbitrary visual displays, a problem recognized six millenia ago by the Egyptians. It appears, then, that the teacher has no direct apparatus available for presenting the deep phonological units in a way that the child can grasp, and at the same time the whole game is lost if the phonological basis of writing is ignored. Some useful methods for introducing children to deep phonological concepts (and, hence, to the spelling pattern of English) have been suggested by C. Chomsky (1973). In her approach, children discuss morphological (meaningful) relations among items such as *sane* and *sanity* and so come to a realization of why they are spelled so similarly. But these techniques are useable only later in the course of literacy acquisition than the stage on which we focus.

learning some simple phone-to-letter correspondences, even though a later shift to deeper phonological analysis will be necessary if literacy is to be achieved. After all, a major step toward literacy has been taken merely by recognizing that *tip, tap,* and *top* do—and should—begin with the same letter. This is an insight about surface phones and reading; no concepts of deep phonology need be invoked to achieve this first insight. Yet with the limited terminology shared in common by teacher and learner, it is often very difficult to teach even these rudiments of "decoding." The teacher may talk about "the first sound in *tap*" or may give an instance of this sound (that is, "tuh"), but there is no reason to expect the learner to know how to refer these remarks to the appropriate firing patterns in his nervous system. The child does not (at least consciously) conceive speech as a sequence of phone-sized units such as "t" strung along in time on the speech wave like beads on a string. This is the issue to which we now turn: how is the phone "t," or any other, realized as a physical event, as an articulatory gesture and a consequent acoustic wave? The complexity of this problem goes some way toward explaining why it is hard for children to achieve the initial alphabetic insights.

4   FROM PHONE TO ACOUSTIC STIMULUS: THE PROBLEM OF SEGMENTATION

We have seen that the output of a linguistic description (Section 3.1.2) is a set of sequences of phones, described as bundles of features, which are related to the articulatory gestures involved in speech. The symbols of the alphabet refer in part to these phones, in part to phonemes. The concrete link between the alphabetic symbols and the phones is presumably provided by the physically real sound stream of speech. That is, the teacher of reading can hardly refer the learner to generative phonology for an understanding of the nature of alphabetic writing. He can only try to establish contact between the two available physically realized entities: the visible alphabetic symbols and the audible stream of speech. Here arises what we take to be the fundamental conceptual problem in early reading acquisition: the alphabetic signs (and their referents, the set of phones and phonemes) are discrete units, while speech itself does not consist of physically segmentable discrete units, but is a continuous, gradually varying event. Examination of the sound pattern that leads to the perception of a phone sequence shows no trace of segmentation. For example, Fig. 7 demonstrates the continuous complex pattern of acoustic energy emitted in uttering the word "bag." (See also the bottom of Fig. 9 for an idealized computer-generated sound pattern which is heard as "bag.") There is no way a physicist looking at such spectrograms could infer segmental components. The segmentation we perceive comes from within the head. As much for prereaders as for readers, there is surely a representation of language in the head in terms of discrete phones and

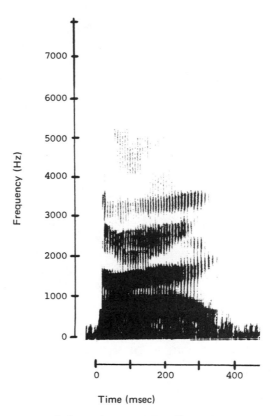

FIG. 7. Sound spectrogram of the spoken word "bag." The darker an area or point, the more acoustic energy is present at that frequency and time. The bands of energy which are relatively consistent over time are called formants. The lower two formants are sufficient to produce the perception of "bag." The computer-generated sound spectrogram of "bag" at the bottom of Fig. 9 represents only the two lowest formants.

phonemes. (Otherwise, as Savin, 1972 has observed, how could a little child "know enough" to get mixed up when saying tongue twisters?) However, since the circuitry of this system is internal, it cannot be physically manipulated for pedagogical purposes, nor is there any guarantee that it will be accessible to introspection. That is, the child is faced with an orthography that refers to a discrete representation of language that cannot be pointed to in speech. There is no clear time at which B ends and A begins in spoken "bag," only in written *bag*.

How is the teacher to refer to an internalized level of the language system at which the continuous stream of speech is segmented and discrete? The problems in giving the child contact with this level of organization are complicated enormously by the fact that the teacher cannot pronounce the three parts of "bag" separately for instructional purposes. The sequence of phones that is the output of the phonological system has been converted into an utterance in the form of a continuously varying wave. We discuss below the relations between phone perception and production and properties of the continuous speech wave. The discussion follows, for the most part, the positions set forward by the Haskins Laboratory group of investigators (A. M. Liberman, Cooper, Shankweiler, & Studdert-Kennedy, 1967; A. M. Liberman, 1970; Cooper, 1972; See also Stevens & House, 1972; Cole & Scott, 1974). The evidence from this very important work, and from related findings in the perception of running speech, points generally to the syllable as the basic unit of speech perception. From this, there is good reason to suppose that the kind of access to molecular levels of linguistic representation required to learn to read is simpler for the syllable unit than for the phone or phoneme unit (see also I. Y. Liberman et al., this volume). Reconstituting the sequential phone from the encoding in which it is embedded in real speech is a difficult cognitive act, not easy to elicit from prereaders.

4.1 Are the Phones Manifest in the Speech Wave?

The simplest hypothesis for understanding what the alphabetic letters refer to (or for understanding how we perceive speech in discrete terms) would be that there exist discrete and invariant acoustic patterns in the speech wave that are directly associated with the perception of the sequential phones. Each letter of the alphabet, approximately, would "stand for" a linguistically significant sound pattern; the alphabet would then bear a simple relation to sequential properties of the speech wave. In fact, such a characterization of the acoustic properties related to phone identification can be made fairly reliably for the case of nondiphthongized vowels. In utterances of such vowels, the energy that is emitted over a period of approximately 150 msec is largely concentrated in restricted frequency regions. The spectrographic display of Fig. 7 shows those characteristic vocalic energy bands (*formants*). The relationship of the frequencies of the first two (lowest) formants is closely related to the perception of various simple vowels. Spectrographic patterns consisting solely of the first two formants are sufficient to synthesize the simple vowels so that they are recognizable to human listeners. At least for these vowels, then, the relation between the phones of linguistic description and the speech wave appears to be straightforward: in A. M. Liberman's (1970) terms, a cipher or one-to-one mapping. The relative simplicity of this mapping can be seen in the synthetically produced spectrograms in Fig. 8 (from A. M. Liberman et al., 1967) where the perceived vowel can easily be referred to the relation between the first two formants.

Invariant properties of the acoustic wave yield information about consonant perception as well. For example, A. M. Liberman, Delattre, and Cooper (1952) showed, using synthetically produced speech, that very high-frequency bursts (about 3240 Hz) of about 15 msec duration were uniformly interpreted as T before various vowels, while low-frequency bursts (about 360 Hz) were interpreted as P before the same vowels. Frequency of an initial burst, then, is an

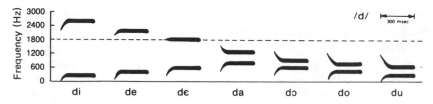

FIG. 8. Synthetic, computer-generated sound spectrograms sufficient to produce perceptions of various D + vowel syllables. The dashed line at 1800 Hz shows the locus for D (A. M. Liberman, Cooper, Shankweiler, & Studdert-Kennedy, 1967, p. 436. Copyright © 1967 by the American Psychological Association. Reproduced by permission.)

invariant (context-free) cue to the distinction between P and T (see Cole & Scott, 1974, for a review of the literature on invariant cues to consonant perception).

If, in all instances, invariant cues to the perception of each phone could be found in the acoustic wave, the perception of discrete phones in the continuous sound wave would be easier to understand. However, invariances in the acoustic wave are insufficient to allow unique identification of all consonants. For example, A. M. Liberman et al. (1952) also showed that a single synthetically produced burst of noise at 1800 Hz was understood as P before I and U, but as K before A. Thus the identification of consonants is in part context dependent: the same physical object can correspond to alphabetic writings of both P and K, for these are writings of perceptions, not writings of acoustic patterns.

Figure 8 further demonstrates the nature of this problem. The figure shows spectrographic patterns sufficient for the synthesis of various D + vowel syllables. The steady-state formants occupying all but the first 50 msec of each syllable are sufficient for the synthesis of the various vowels. That is, when we clip off the first 50 msec of these syllables and play back the remainder, subjects reliably report hearing the appropriate vowels. Then, obviously, the rapid frequency modulations (*transitions*) of the first 50 msec are somehow responsible for the perception of the consonant D. Yet inspection shows that these portions of the displays differ radically: for the syllable DI, the second formant is rising rapidly from about 2000 to 2500 Hz; for DE, the second formant is flat at 1800 Hz; for DU, the second formant is falling rapidly from about 1200 to 600 Hz. In short, the patterns of acoustic energy over time differ radically for D before various vowels. Yet in all cases the hearer reports a recognizable D. We have previously seen that the same physical event can represent two different perceived phones (a burst of energy at 1800 Hz is perceived as P before I, but as K before A). We now see that many different physical events can represent one perceived phone (D is realized differently before various vowels). The simple view of "one sound, one perceived phone" is obviously inadequate. On the same grounds, the view of "one sound, one symbol" for the alphabet is also inadequate. The complexity in the relations between these two levels of language organization is reminiscent of the complexity between the phone and phoneme levels (see Section 3).

A further understanding of the complexity at this level comes from the realization that the consonantal portion of the patterns in Fig. 8 cannot be segmented and recovered at all. While the vocalic portions of these patterns can be identified correctly in isolation, the consonantal patterns, clipped from these patterns and played in isolation, sound to the hearer like a chirping noise. Not only does the listener not hear D; he does not recognize a speech event (A. M. Liberman et al., 1967). Clearly, then, even if a teacher could pronounce the referents of the alphabetic symbols in isolation for the child (which he cannot, as we later show), the child could not hear them. Thus, a practical problem in teaching reading is that a word like "go" cannot be taken apart and pronounced and heard as "g" + "o." One cannot produce (as teacher) or hear (as learner) the elements of the system to be learned. This is the oft-mentioned "puh-ah-tuh" problem: the child is asked to hear, identify, and later *blend* three items that the teacher instances as three syllables. The reduced vowel (ə) is an obligatory part of any isolated utterance of a stop consonant, and yet no such vowel appears in "pat." Teachers' exhortations to pupils to blend by saying "puh-ah-tuh" very fast thus are quite misleading. The child's real task (approximately) is to identify three phones that appear within the teacher's three spoken syllables, and then to pronounce the three-phone monosyllabic outcome (see I. Y. Liberman et al., this volume).

We have shown that a variety of grossly different physical events all represent one phone in different vocalic contexts; symmetrically, the same physical event represents different phones, again depending on the vocalic context. There is no simple mapping between phone and acoustic event; the relation between the two levels of representation is highly complex and context dependent. The various representations of D in Fig. 8 do nevertheless have something in common: a somewhat hypothetical starting point. Notice that the initial transient portion of the second formant for each syllable seems to be aiming backward in time toward a fixed frequency, at about 1800 Hz. [No initial energy is actually emitted *at* 1800 Hz; that is, approximately 15 msec of relative silence precedes the onset of energy emission for all these syllables. This period of silence is, in fact, a context-free cue to the set of stop consonants; if it is removed, the perception is not of a stop consonant (Delattre, A. M. Liberman, & Cooper, 1955).] Thus 1800 Hz is said to be the *locus* for D (A. M. Liberman, Delattre, & Cooper, 1955; A. M. Liberman et al., 1967). What the D syllables seem to have in common, then, is a common starting point that is not physically represented in the speech wave.

The perceived invariance of all the D syllables appears to derive from a common articulation; the articulators are in a fairly uniform position (tip of tongue at alveolar ridge, etc.) as the D syllable begins. Our ear (mind?) has no trouble noting this invariance, although it is well disguised in the sound signal.

The invariance is more simply describable in terms of motor-speech acts than in terms of the acoustic events. These relationships have suggested to some (A. M. Liberman et al., 1967; Stevens & House, 1972), that the process of speech perception is related to the process of speech production, and that speech is recognized in some way by a process of analysis by synthesis: by determining what motor program or command phone matrix could produce the perceived signal. The full implications of such models are too complex for us to deal with here, but they clearly do point to fundamental relationships between alphabetic units and analysis of the wave by referring to its articulatory origins.

4.2   The Production of Speech Sound Is Related to the Letters of the Alphabet

The description of phones as bundles of component features (Section 3.1.2) is a convenient starting place for the description of speech production. If the phone is conceived in the speech production machinery, as in phonological theory, as if it began its journey from the nervous system to the mouth as a set of articulatory features, the facts of speech are easier to understand. We assume here, again following the formulations of the Haskins Laboratory group, that the phonetic features of the linguistic system are represented physiologically as neural commands that ultimately will control speech. We accept the simplifying hypothesis that the abstract linguistic features relate more or less directly to components of pronunciations. The neural commands are still remote from speech. The speech-production machinery converts the simultaneous discrete features into unit phones (Section 4.2.1) and the discrete sequences of phones into a smooth continuous flow (Section 4.2.2). A significant restructuring takes place as the commands to produce phone sequences are carried out simultaneously and become integrated into syllabic units (A. M. Liberman, 1970). One consequence of this restructuring is that it is difficult to achieve the alphabetic insights.

4.2.1   The Simultaneous Production of Features Yields the Unit Phone

There are no remarks in the linguistic account about how the feature bundles are to be realized as coordinated movements by the various articulators (the bone and muscle complexes of the articulatory apparatus—tongue, lips, pharynx, etc.). Because the articulators are essentially independent and can move at different rates, the accomplishment of an overall single phonic act evidently requires cooperative activities of the musculature; for example, to say "m," one vibrates the vocal cords, moves the tongue, lips, and so on, all at one time. We know that the smooth production of all these gestural elements of the phone by integration of the component gestures into larger-unit gestures is in part learned and highly automatized in the adult, since the feature bundles of different languages are partly different and since relearning by adults is difficult. Although all languages choose from the same list of possible features and overlap considerably, the simultaneous bundles differ. (Thus, for example, certain notorious French vowels are difficult for English speakers to utter and are rarely acquired perfectly by adult learners. These vowels may differ from English vowels only in a single feature, indeed in a feature that English speakers can easily pronounce within a different simultaneous bundle. Thus we can approximate the French vowel under such articulatory directions as, "Try to say 'ee' as in 'meet,' while holding the lips in the rounded position you would use for 'u,' as in 'soup.' ") The requirement to produce the component gestures of a phone smoothly and in parallel may involve a restructuring of each underlying gesture. That is, a feature may be realized differently by the musculature depending on its context of simultaneous features. At any rate, it is clear that the simultaneous bundle, or phone, is highly practiced, overlearned, and relatively immune to change by adulthood. Adults rarely acquire perfectly the bundles of a second language—they speak with an accent.

The letter-size unit in alphabetic writing must refer in part to these singular gesture chunks.[15] To the extent that we can identify and isolate psychologically relevant levels of linguistic representation, it is natural to view "the whole phone" as an operative unit in the articulartory system: it is the habitual, unitary, smoothed pronunciation of a bundle of features. From this point of view, it would seem that *the alphabetic notation makes contact with perception at the level of the neural command to produce the phone chunk, a language-specific compositional unit of pronunciation.* The featural substratum seems to be beneath the level of awareness, inaccessible in most circumstances (Cooper, 1972).

4.2.2 The Shingling of Sequential Phones Yields the Unit Syllable

A significant restructuring of the representation of speech takes place because we articulate "whole syllables" as opposed to discrete phones. The phone-chunks we have just recognized as articulatory organizations of the feature bundles are in turn swallowed up into a larger unit. The transmission of phone sequences up to about the level of syllables takes place in a partly parallel or overlapping fashion, thus further complicating the relation between articulatory gesture and acoustic outcome. Figure 9 (from A. M. Liberman, 1970) is a schematization of the pronunciation of "bag." Information in the sound stream related to the medial vowel (AE) is shown to overlap the transmission both of

---

[15] Of course we know this is not the whole story. An additional encoding has been recognized between phone and phoneme (Section 3.1). Moreover, even the identification of phonemes is highly dependent on yet more global analyses in terms of morphemes, syntax, and meaning. But part of the perception that there is a correspondence between letters and the "individual sounds" of the language derives, in our view, from access to some level of the program for integrated articulatory movements.

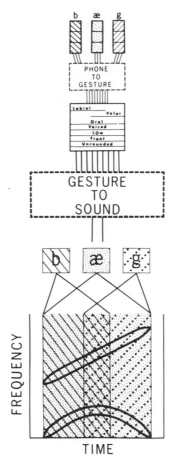

FIG. 9. Schematic model of speech production as formulated by the Haskins group. The figure shows production of the word "bag" in two stages: a conversion from phone to articulatory gesture, and from articulatory gesture to sound. (From A. M. Liberman, 1970, p. 314.)

the initial B and final G consonantal portions of the syllable. This parallel transmission is a consequence of the fact that the articulators respond relatively sluggishly, so that the command for certain muscles to contract arrives while previous commands are still being carried out. Further, the gestures are different depending on the position of the vocal apparatus just prior to and following the position for the gesture in question, so that the transitions between phones (the rapid frequency modulations described earlier; see Fig. 8) contain much of the useful information in the acoustic wave. The articulatory gestures and, hence, the sound pattern, will be influenced by what the vocal apparatus *was* and *will be* doing during the saying of the whole syllable. If this is so, we can understand why the pronunciation of the individual phones cannot be invariant: the pronunciation of each is dependent on the context of phones in which it occurs.

The net effect of the conversion of sequential phone commands to articulatory movements and sounds is that in the sound stream the phones are *shingled,* much in the sense of overlapping roof shingles (A. M. Liberman et al., 1967). Then the transition (frequency glide) between adjacent consonant and vowel gives information about both surrounding phones at once. It follows that there is no discrete sequential analogue of the phone in the wave-form.

A direct consequence of these facts is that it is impossible to utter most context-dependent phones in isolation, for they are realized in articulation shingled across the whole syllable. For the case of the stop consonants, there is silence at the time the articulators are in the required position (at the locus, as described in Section 4.1). Energy is emitted after the onset of the vocalic segment. Thus a teacher cannot utter D (or B, G, K, P, T) in isolation for the learner. He must add an artifactual vowel sound. For other sounds, a more satisfactory degree of isolation can be attained, although in normal speech there is a gradual, continuous shift from one phone to another.

Given the Haskins group's powerful demonstrations and explanation of the context dependence of realizations of phones, the relations between the presumed high-level neural commands (corresponding to the discrete features and phones) and articulatory movements must be complex. That is, as Stevens (1972) and Stevens and House (1972) have pointed out, the high-level command must program an articulatory goal or target (e.g., "move the tongue to a midpalatal position") but the actual articulatory movement must depend heavily on where the tongue was prior to this point. The actual command to achieve the midpalatal target might result in forward or backward tongue movement, depending on where the tongue was when the initial command was received. The same phone, differently approximated in the musculature, is invariant with respect to the initial command: invariant phone commands leading to various movements *toward* an articulatory target are heard as equivalent. On the contrary, the articulatory endpoints are not neatly related to the underlying phone command because of context dependence and shingling owing to sluggishness in the motor system.

Summarizing, the actual production of speech is not in terms of discrete phone chunks produced in a temporal row. A longer unit, approximately the length of a syllable, is preplanned so as to produce in a smoothed flow the set of gestures called for by each phone command in the sequence. The result shows simultaneous interactions among all parts of the syllable. The smoothed whole-syllable gestures, like the whole-phone gestures above them in the hierarchy, must be partially learned. (For example, Spanish words never begin with ST consonant clusters. Adult Spanish learners of English can often be heard to produce a vocalic context for the initial S of this cluster, thus relegating it to a separate syllable, one that occurs in Spanish. They do this because, presumably, the new ST syllable is hard to produce; for them, "stake" is more easily pronounced "es-take," making use of whole-syllable vocal gestures learned in childhood.) The discrete phone stratum above the whole syllable may be largely inaccessible, this level, like the featural components of the phones, residing only in the motor and perceptual systems (Cooper, 1972).

We have argued that the component features of a phone become a habitual unitary act and that the sequence of phones in a syllable become inextricably bound together. One may ask: how far can this game go? After all, one must learn to organize whole polysyllabic words, whole phrases, even whole lectures. Higher level preplanning of units at least as large as the sentence must be assumed, for otherwise it would be difficult to understand how prosodic features (stress and intonation) are inserted at the right times and places (see Cole & Scott, 1974, for a discussion of "envelope features" of the sound stream). The segmentation issue arises for these molar units too: pauses do not regularly appear at syllable, word, or phrase boundaries in real speech. (For some speakers we know, pauses cannot be shown to occur at a lower than whole-lecture boundary.) Thus the concept of chunking cannot by itself explain the fact that notions like syllable, word, and sentence seen to be relatively accessible to consciousness, while the notions of phone and phoneme are relatively inaccessible. Nevertheless, units more molecular than the syllable have been shown to share one property that complicates the process of learning to read: they are in varying degrees, in relation to their context dependence, difficult for the speaker to pronounce in isolation or for the listener to isolate from the sound stream.

4.3   The Syllable Is the Basic Unit of Speech Perception and Production

The fact that transitional cues are required for unique identification of certain consonants in certain environments is the central argument (A. M. Liberman, 1970) for the claim that the syllable represents the lower bound as a unit of speech perception (Cole & Scott, 1974, make a rather different argument for the same conclusion). In general, syllables are the smallest coherent units of speech: they tend to be physically undissectable, they are the smallest separately pronounceable units of speech, and they may be produced in preplanned units.

There is additional evidence for the primacy of the syllable in the speech processing of adults. The syllable maintains a salient position in perception, even for practiced adult readers of English phonemic writing. Adults can identify syllabic targets (e.g., BA) in running speech more rapidly than initial phonemes (e.g., B) of that same target (Savin & Bever, 1970; Warren, 1971). "Sounding out" by fluent readers seems to be organized around syllables when the material to be read is novel. Adults characteristically break an unfamiliar word into pronounceable syllables, e.g., *malagasy* would be broken down into *ma-la-ga-sy* on route to a pronunciation, not into *muh-a-luh-a-* and so on, despite years of experience with phonemic writing systems.

These findings about perception and characteristic organization in reading dovetail with the general Haskins findings. We have noted earlier (Section 2) that syllabic systems were the first phonographies to appear historically and that, unlike alphabets, they recurred by independent invention. We show elsewhere (Rozin & Gleitman, this volume) that the syllabic unit is accessible earlier in individual development than the phonemic unit and that syllabary scripts are easier for young children to acquire than phonemic scripts. We believe these effects derive from the fact that the syllable is the smallest independently perceivable unit of speech: "before" is physically quite close to a quick rendition of "be" + "fore." On the contrary, there is no physical basis for building "be" from "buh" + "e."

If the syllable represents the lower bound as a unit of real-time speech perception, what is the upper limit? It was mentioned earlier that speech production will require, at least for appropriate representation of prosodic features, preplanning of units as large as the sentence. Cooper (1972) points out that limits on the sophistication of auditory analysis and also on short-term memory must set a stringent upper bound on the perceptual processing unit; he concludes that minimal units of about syllable, word or short phrase length are about right because of these constraints on a possible auditory process.

It is important to notice that, even if the syllable has primacy as a unit in real-time speech processing, as we have asserted, it is a relatively superficial unit in terms of its relations to the underlying linguistic organization of word and syntactic form. Relations to this underlying system at the syllabic level have been obscured in the considerable recoding that takes place for the purpose of speaking and hearing. Most natural language mechanisms, such as language acquisition and language change, are conveniently describable only in terms of the underlying phonological units of phoneme and phone. Reading, however, is not a natural part of language organization, and it appears only under special circumstances of environment and careful training. Fluency does not emerge in response to quite automatic language-acquiring predispositions in humans. Our view is that, for such highly derived skills as learning to read an alphabet, the encoded speech signal must be unpeeled through quite conscious attention to its obscured underlying origins in tacit language organization. The syllabic unit may have special usefulness in this process of becoming aware because it is the smallest physically realized unit in real speech.

5 SUMMARY

The evolution of writing is orderly on the following analysis: each succeeding script required fewer different visual symbols to transcribe the spoken language than did the script before, thus reducing the burden on long-term memory for visual items required of learners and users; but in consequence, each new script represented language in terms of units more remote from meaning than the units of the preceding script, thus posing new problems for learning and decipherment. The alphabet (phonemic writing) was the latest script to be invented.

The nature of the phonological concepts embodied in modern English writing throws some light on why alphabetic scripts are hard to invent or learn: the relations between the cognitive–perceptual alphabetic units (phonemes and morphophonemes) and the perceived sounds of speech (syllables and phones) are very abstract, mediated through a set of covert rules whose operations are essentially closed to consciousness. That is, the meanings (morphemes) are encoded onto phonological representations in terms of a complex, context-dependent conversion.

An even more fundamental barrier to reading acquisition is the problem of segmenting the speech wave in discrete terms: the reader of an alphabet must relate the continuously varying acoustic wave of speech to a writing system that represents this in terms of a linear array of discrete symbols. Some of the difficulty in acquiring alphabets is therefore understandable through an analysis of speech production and perception. The perceived speech sounds (phones) are encoded onto syllables in the sound wave in terms of a complex, context-dependent conversion. The encoding of the phone onto the syllable in speech may account for why syllabic scripts were so much easier to invent than phonemic scripts, and why they are so much easier to learn.

The child's natural history of explicit language knowledge proceeds in a sequence similar to the evolution of writing. The young child first becomes explicitly aware of meaning units, and only later becomes aware of the syntactic and phonological substrata of language. Thus it is easy for the young child to learn the principles of a script that tracks meanings directly and hard for him to acquire a script that tracks the sound system. These parallels suggest an approach to teaching reading which we will expand upon in the next chapter (Rozin & Gleitman, this volume). It might be useful for the child to be introduced to visual language as a logography. Thereafter we suggest that the syllabic unit, which maintains its shape and sequential integrity in speech perception and production, may be useful for introducing the learner of an alphabet to the general class of phonographic scripts. In this approach, the abstract phonemic (alphabetic) concepts would be introduced to the learner relatively late. Summarizing, we propose that an initial reading curriculum that essentially recapitulates the historical evolution of writing will mirror the metalinguistic development of the child.

ACKNOWLEDGMENTS

The preparation of this paper was supported by NIH Grant No. 23505. We had the advantage of critical readings of earlier drafts of this manuscript by R. Gelman, E. Gallistel, and E. Newport. We thank H. Hoenigswald who made substantive contributions to our description of the history of writing and other sections of this paper. We also thank Ms. Mutsumi Ishida for invaluable assistance in preparing Fig. 6. And we particularly wish to thank Henry Gleitman, whose mediation between the print and the meaning of this and the accompanying chapter was crucial at all stages.

REFERENCES

Bloch, B. Phonemic overlapping. In M. Joos (Ed.), *Readings in linguistics: The development of descriptive linguistics in America since 1925* (2nd ed.). New York: American Council of Learned Societies, 1958. (Originally published in *American Speech,* 1941, *16,* 278–284.)

Bloomfield, L. *Language.* New York: Henry Holt, 1933.

Cazden, C. *Play with language and metalinguistic awareness: one dimension of language experience.* Paper presented at The Second Lucy Sprague Mitchell Memorial Conference, "Dimensions of Language Experience," Bank Street College of Education, May 19, 1973.

Chao, Y-R. The non-uniqueness of phonemic solutions of phonetic systems. In M. Joos (Ed.), *Readings in linguistics: The development of descriptive linguistics in America since 1925* (2nd ed.). New York: American Council of Learned Societies, 1958. (Originally published in *Bulletin of the Institute of History and Philology, Academia Sinica,* 1934, *4,* 363–397.)

Chao, Y-R. *Language and symbolic systems.* London: Cambridge University Press, 1968.

Chomsky, C. Reading, writing, and phonology. *Harvard Educational Review,* 1970, *40,* 287–309.

Chomsky, C. *Beginning reading through invented spelling.* Selected papers from New England Kindergarten Conference. Boston, November 30, 1973.

Chomsky, N. *Current issues in linguistic theory.* The Hague: Mouton, 1964.

Chomsky, N. Phonology and reading. In H. Levin & J. P. Williams (Eds.), *Basic studies on reading.* New York: Basic Books, 1970.

Chomsky, N., & Halle, M. *The sound pattern of English.* New York: Harper & Row, 1968.

Cole, R. A., & Scott, B. Toward a theory of speech perception. *Psychological Review,* 1974, *81,* 348–374.

Cooper, F. S. How is language conveyed by speech? In J. F. Kavanagh & I. G. Mattingly (Eds.), *Language by ear and by eye: The relationships between speech and reading.* Cambridge, Mass.: MIT Press, 1972.

Delattre, P. C., Liberman, A. M., & Cooper, F. S. Acoustic loci and transitional cues for consonants. *Journal of the Acoustical Society of America,* 1955, *27,* 769–773.

Diringer, D. *Writing.* New York: Frederick A. Praeger, 1962.

Downing, J. (Ed.). *Comparative reading: Cross-national studies of behavior and processes in reading and writing.* New York: Macmillan, 1973.

Francis, W. N. Linguistics and reading: A commentary on chapters 1 to 3. In H. Levin & J. P. Williams (Eds.), *Basic studies on reading.* New York: Basic Books, 1970.

Gelb, I. J. *A study of writing: the foundations of grammatology.* Chicago: University of Chicago Press, 1952.

Gleitman, L. R., Gleitman, H., & Shipley, E. The emergence of the child as grammarian. *Cognition,* 1972, *1,* 137–164.

Gleitman, L. R., & Rozin, P. Teaching reading by use of a syllabary. *Reading Research Quarterly,* 1973, *8,* 447–483. (a)

Gleitman, L. R., & Rozin, P. Phoenician go home? (A response to Goodman). *Reading Research Quarterly,* 1973, *8,* 494–501. (b)

Gollmer, C. A. On African symbolic messages. *The Journal of the (Royal) Anthropological Institute of Great Britain and Ireland,* 1885, *14,* 169–181 as cited by I. G. Gelb, *A study of writing; the foundations of grammatology.* Chicago: University of Chicago Press, 1952, p. 5.

Goodman, K. Reading: A psycholinguistic guessing game. In K. S. Goodman & J. Fleming (Eds.), *Selected papers from the IRA Pre-Convention Institute,* Boston, April 1968. Newark, Del.: International Reading Association, 1969.

Goodman, K. The 13th easy way to make learning to read difficult: A reaction to Gleitman and Rozin. *Reading Research Quarterly,* 1973, *8,* 484–493,

Harris, Z. S. *Methods in structural linguistics.* Chicago: University of Chicago Press, 1951.

Hoenigswald, H. M. *Language change and linguistic reconstruction.* Chicago: University of Chicago Press, 1960.

Huey, E. B. *The psychology and pedagogy of reading* (1908). Cambridge, Mass.: MIT Press, 1968.

Jakobson, R., Fant, C. G. M., & Halle, M. *Preliminaries to speech analysis.* Cambridge, Mass.: MIT Press, 1963.

Jeffery, L. H. *The local scripts of archaic Greece.* Oxford: Clarendon Press, 1961.

Jensen, H. *Sign, symbol and script* (3rd rev. ed.). New York: G. P. Putnam's Sons, 1969. (First American edition translated by George Allen & Unwin, Ltd.)

Klima, E. S. How alphabets might reflect language. In J. F. Kavanagh & I. G. Mattingly (Eds.), *Language by ear and by eye: The relationships between speech and reading.* Cambridge, Mass.: MIT Press, 1972.

Kroeber, A. L. *Anthropology: Race, language, culture, psychology, prehistory* (new ed., rev.). New York: Harcourt, Brace, 1948.

Lenneberg, E. H. *Biological foundations of language.* New York: Wiley, 1967.

Leong, C. K. Hong Kong. In J. Downing (Ed.), *Comparative reading: Cross-national studies of behavior and processes in reading and writing.* New York: Macmillan, 1973.

Liberman, A. M. The grammars of speech and language. *Cognitive Psychology,* 1970, *1,* 301–323.

Liberman, A. M., Cooper, F. S., Shankweiler, D. P., & Studdert-Kennedy, M. Perception of the speech code. *Psychological Review,* 1967, *74,* 431–461.

Liberman, A. M., Delattre, P. C., & Cooper, F. S. The role of selected stimulus variables in the perception of the unvoiced stop consonants. *American Journal of Psychology,* 1952, *65,* 497–516.

Liberman, A. M., Delattre, P. C., & Cooper, F. S. Acoustic loci and transitional cues for consonants. *Journal of the Acoustical Society of America,* 1955, *27,* 769–773.

Liberman, I. Y. Segmentation of the spoken word and reading acquisition. *Bulletin of The Orton Society,* 1970, *23,* 65–77.

Lieberman, P. On the evolution of language: A unified view. *Cognition,* 1973, *2,* 59–94.

Martin, S. E. Nonalphabetic writing systems: Some observations. In J. F. Kavanagh & I. G. Mattingly (Eds.), *Language by ear and by eye: The relationships between speech and reading.* Cambridge, Mass.: MIT Press, 1972.

Mattingly, I. G. Reading, the linguistic process, and linguistic awareness. In J. F. Kavanagh & I. G. Mattingly (Eds.), *Language by ear and by eye: The relationships between speech and reading.* Cambridge, Mass.: MIT Press, 1972.

Moskowitz, B. A. On the status of vowel shift in English. In T. E. Moore (Ed.), *Cognitive development and the acquisition of language.* New York: Academic Press, 1973.

Read, C. Pre-school children's knowledge of English phonology. *Harvard Educational Review,* 1971, *41,* 1–34.

Rozin, P. The evolution of intelligence and access to the cognitive unconscious. In J. Sprague & A. N. Epstein (Eds.), *Progress in psychobiology and physiological psychology,* Vol. 6. New York: Academic Press, 1975.

Rozin, P., Poritsky, S., & Sotsky, R. American children with reading problems can easily learn to read English represented by Chinese characters. *Science,* 1971, *171,* 1264–1267.

Savin, H. B. What the child knows about speech when he starts to read. In J. F. Kavanagh & I. G. Mattingly (Eds.), *Language by ear and by eye: The relationships between speech and reading.* Cambridge, Mass.: MIT Press, 1972.

Savin, H. B., & Bever, T. G. The nonperceptual reality of the phoneme. *Journal of Verbal Learning and Verbal Behavior,* 1970, *9,* 295–302.

Shaw, G. B. *Selection of his wit and wisdom.* (Compiled by C. T. Harnsberger.) New York: Follett, 1965.

Singer, H. IQ is and is not related to reading. In S. Wanat (Ed.), *Intelligence and reading.* Newark, Del.: International Reading Association, 1974.

Smith, F. *Understanding reading.* New York: Holt, Rinehart and Winston, 1971.

Stevens, K. N. Segments, features, and analysis by synthesis. In J. F. Kavanagh & I. G. Mattingly (Eds.), *Language by ear and by eye: The relationships between speech and reading.* Cambridge, Mass.: MIT Press, 1972.

Stevens, K. N., & House, A. S. Speech perception. In J. Tobias (Ed.), *Foundations of modern auditory theory,* Vol. 2. New York: Academic Press, 1972.

Thorndike, W. E. Reading as reasoning: A study of mistakes in paragraph reading. *Journal of Educational Psychology,* 1971, *8,* 323–332. (Also in *Reading Research Quarterly,* 1970–1971, *6,* 425–434.)

Venezky, R. L. Regularity in reading and spelling. In H. Levin & J. P. Williams (Eds.), *Basic studies on reading.* New York: Basic Books, 1970.

Walker, W. Notes on native writing systems and the design of native literacy programs. *Anthropological Linguistics,* 1969, *11,* 148–166.

Warren, R. M. Identification times for phonemic components of graded complexity and for spelling of speech. *Perception & Psychophysics,* 1971, *9,* 345–349.

2

The Structure and Acquisition of Reading II: The Reading Process and the Acquisition of the Alphabetic Principle

Paul Rozin
Lila R. Gleitman

University of Pennsylvania

1 INTRODUCTION

Human linguistic communication undoubtedly was originally by ear and by mouth, but men began to communicate with each other also by eye and by hand at least 20 millenia ago. The visual route of communication apparently developed on its own hook for some time, as men drew pictures representing their ideas, on rocks and walls of caves. This protowriting was based on man's natural ability to interpret the visual world meaningfully; it probably involved little or no reliance on concepts from the spoken language. Users of this kind of visual communication were perforce limited by artistic talent and ingenuity in representing all possible notions. Probably in consequence of this inherent limitation, "idea writing" eventually gave way to the representation of words of the spoken language itself; here an infinity of notions could be represented with finite means. But still, the number and variety of words, while finite, is very large, and it is not a trivial matter to think up and memorize a picture for each item. Eventually, writing systems that represented the sounds of speech were invented and came into wide use. Since all utterances can be represented in terms of relatively few speech-sound units, it now became easier to render by eye all those meanings originally conveyed by ear. The usual units of speech transcribed were syllables (as in the Mesopotamian cuneiform scripts). Only very recently, during the first millenium B.C., was the alphabet (a transcription of abstract phonemes) invented. The clear trend in this history, then, has been away from attempts to transcribe meanings directly, and toward the transcription of meaning mediated by sound. Further, the trend has been toward representation in terms of successively more molecular and abstract units of speech sound (from syllable to phoneme). This history is described in an accompanying paper (Gleitman & Rozin, this volume).

Why should evolution have been in this direction? Clearly those who were responsible for the successive modifications of writing were already in possession of a rich spoken language. To represent visually each of the, say, 50,000 words of such a language, both inventor and reader must come up with 50,000 essentially new encodings. But suppose the inventor and learner can, instead, parasitize their own speech in terms of its 500 or so spoken syllables, or its 50 or so phonemes; the long-term difficulty in memorization now drops precipitously.

But what is good for inventor and fluent user is not necessarily good for the learner, especially if he is a young child. Each advance in the development of writing was a step away from the very natural human capacity to recognize meaningful representations of the visual world. Anyone can understand something from cave pictographs, but almost no one (why be modest: no one at all) can interpret, without a substantial period of experience or instruction, the 26 geometric symbols that render "all the sounds" of a spoken language. In short, the increased reliance on speech as a mediator between written symbols and meanings required increased awareness of the sound stream of speech and its segmentation. In consequence, while writing systems have become more efficient for fluent adults, they have come also to make greater conceptual demands on aspiring learners. The very early stages of reading acquisition—in which one must come to terms with the principles behind the system—changed from transparent to opaque. The earlier stages of reading acquisition became more difficult as the sophistication of writing increased; in compensation, the later stages became easier (there were very few items to memorize).

What is so difficult about learning the principles behind the alphabet? We believe the difficulty arises because the alphabet is based on a segmentation of the sound stream in terms of highly abstract units, phonemes, which are represented only indirectly in the acoustic wave. The ear, brain, and articulatory apparatus form a highly specialized system, adapted over tens of thousands of years of evolution, to extract this unit from the sound stream and to assemble such units into coherent speech. But that some part of the brain accomplishes this segmentation and synthesis does not imply that humans are aware of *how* this is done, or even *that* it is done. The speech-processing programs in the brain seem to be tightly wired into auditory and articulatory systems and are *inaccessible,* or unavailable to other systems. This is hardly surprising; until recently in evolutionary time, phonological processing was related only to the ear and the articulatory system. Why should the language circuitry be connected to other processing systems in the brain? But the use of an alphabet requires, in our view, gaining access to the machinery in the head which analyzes and produces sound segments.

How can we give the prospective reader access to the phonemic segmentation of speech so that he can begin to understand the referents of the letters of the alphabet? Clues come from a number of distinct domains. We have discussed elsewhere (Gleitman & Rozin, this volume) some constraints on reading acquisition that derive from properties of the orthography itself. We ask here what information average fluent readers use in processing print. We argue that while readers interact with print at many linguistic and cognitive levels, alphabetic and syllabic principles and phonological representations continue to play a central role in fluent processing of print into meaning. If this is so, part of learning to read is learning to make use of these same phonological principles. We next discuss the language skills and knowledge the preliterate child brings into the reading acquisition task. The problem here is to isolate from the complex and poorly understood adult reading process what must actually be taught to the novice—what he does not know and probably will not acquire from mere exposure and practice. Our belief is that the stumbling block is access to phonology: while the young child can focus on and manipulate linguistic meaning, he does not in any conscious way realize that his speech is literally composed of sequences of sounds. To the limited extent that the young child is aware of phonological properties of his language, he has greater access to syllabic segmentation than to phonemic segmentation. This is essentially because syllables map linearly onto the sound stream, while phonemes are highly encoded in the sound stream.

The structure of this argument leads to some suggestions for how to teach children to read. The analogy between the child's developing explicit knowledge of (access to) his language and the historical evolution of scripts is suggestively close. Ancient scripts tracked meanings, not sounds; the young child can focus his attention on meanings, but not on sounds. In this sense, developmental history recapitulates cultural history. Taking as a clue this match between child and adult, we developed a reading curriculum that virtually recapitulates the historical development of scripts. We recognize the alphabetic insight as the critical event in this sequence. But since we do not know how to teach this directly, the historically oriented curriculum proceeds by isolating it—by teaching everything else about the writing system first, including the fact that it maps the sound of language.

Thus the curriculum moves by steps from meaning toward sound, as did the writing systems that appeared successively in Man's history. The curriculum then gives center stage for a lengthy period to syllable writing as a transitional mode, as did ancient Man. We are by no means the first to propose that understanding syllables may help a prospective reader to understand alphabetic writing. Preserved practice materials of the ancient Etruscans show syllables written side by side with the alphabetic letters. Quintilian in ancient Rome and Pascal (Sainte-Beuve, 1955) writing in 17th century France on the education of youth suggest teaching alphabetic concepts in terms of syllables. The idea crops up again in modern tracts on reading (Gleitman & Rozin, 1973a; Savin, 1972; Rosner, 1971;

Liberman, Shankweiler, Liberman, Fowler, & Fischer, this volume), incidentally showing us how far reading curricula have advanced in three millenia. To our knowledge, our curriculum is unique only in that it traces the whole range of the history of writing rather explicitly. In our historical curriculum, the alphabet is introduced to the child as the last step, reflecting its late—and single—cultural appearance and development.

Thus the sequence of teaching steps is an attempt to disentangle for the novice the layers of abstract concepts embodied in modern English writing. Despite many conceptual jumps that must be made to draw from the historical record and the nature of fluent reading a plausible curriculum, we have designed and tested such a program and we report on its fate here. Both our successes and difficulties with this approach confirm the view that the weak link in early reading acquisition is between syllable and phoneme. We do not know how to bridge this gap for all children. What is remarkable is that this great advance in writing, accomplished only once by the ancient Phoenicians and Greeks, is accomplished by most six- or seven-year-olds in the ordinary context of school instruction.

2 THE AVERAGE ADULT READER

Many people, even after years of schooling, fail to use the printed page as a ready means of communication. More than 10% of American adults are "functionally illiterate." That is, they read below the expected fourth-grade level. If this substantial segment of the population could be brought up to the present average, "the reading problem" would be solved, for the *average* adult reader can use the written word as an effective medium for communication and learning. There will always be better and poorer readers, but among the average and above-average readers in the present distribution, the limiting factors are in intelligence (i.e., the ability to comprehend complex materials; see Thorndike, 1971; Singer, 1974) and not in basic reading skills. The fact that the reading rates of such average and above-average individuals could probably be increased by special training will not be of concern to us, since they already read about as fast as they can listen to, and comprehend, speech (at the rate of about 250 words per min). On the other hand, the poorest readers are limited by the chore of reading itself. They are much more efficient at extracting meaning from speech than from the written page. The primary goal of reading instruction is to erase this difference. In terms of the scope of this chapter, then, we limit our account of adult reading approximately to the activities of the average successful reader, insofar as these are known. Readers whose rates are in the range of 500 words per minute (wpm) or greater may not be fully describable in terms of the mechanisms that we will try to discuss.

If the average reader is an average speaker, we can assume that he has an active vocabulary of about 50,000 items. Since he is an efficient "decoder," he can recognize approximately all of these items in print and can give consensual pronunciations to innumerably more new written items such as proper names seen for the first time and pseudowords (meaningless items which conform to common English orthographic patterns, such as *grap, tabe,* and the like). If he has about a 12th grade education, he will have a silent reading rate of about 250 wpm; his rate with adequate comprehension will vary between 200 and 300 wpm with the usual test materials, depending on their difficulty (Harris, 1970). This performance represents a reasonable goal for education, and it is this performance that we now try to describe.

2.1 Two Views of the Reader: Plodder or Explorer?

Psychologists and educators are a long way from being able to formulate a model of the average reading performance, or the mechanism by which this performance might be realized. At present, there exist only rather vague conceptions of the overall structure of fluent reading. Reasonable people, in possession of the same observations and experimental findings, adopt either of two disparate and opposing views (with all conceivable intermediate positions represented by other, also reasonable, people). At one pole stand those who claim that the reader is a *plodder.* He literally ploughs through text a letter at a time, building the words and sentences out of the individually identified phone-sized squiggles on the page; he converts the letters to sounds, which are then formed into phonological representations, which in turn contact the previously learned meanings. This plodder view is essentially a speeded-up, smoothed-out version of what the stumbling first-grader seems to do in "sounding out" the words of his primer. It is probably the common-sense view of any Phoenician on the Street. Because, on this account, meaning is derived through the systematic combination of minimal elements, the plodder view can be described as a "bottom up" approach. At the opposite extreme stand those romantics who view the reader as an *explorer* of the printed page. They suppose the fluent reader (including the average reader whose performance concerns us here) looks at the printed page as he does at other aspects of the visual world, sampling selectively from among many available cues, developing expectations for words or meanings, seeking confirmation of these guesses and, in general, bringing to bear at all levels his considerable linguistic, intellectual, and perceptual skills. On this view, then, reading is more problem solving than plodding through phonology. Because the reader is here conceived as arriving at the details of the printed message after deriving its meaning, the explorer view can be characterized as a "top down" approach.

Various problems of feasibility, in terms of human information-handling procedures, arise for both plodder and explorer positions. The plodder must face the task of building up meanings through a hierarchically organized sequence of information manipulations at a rate fast enough and accurate enough to account for normal reading. The explorer (who gets the required high-level units "immediately" from the print) has to explain how the practically infinite number of high-level units (such as sentences and other "whole meaning" units) could be stored and retrieved from memory, with the required accuracy and rapidity. Thus a concretely specified model, in either of these extreme terms, is not easy to come by.

What we *can* show with some ease is that the reader gets enough sheer visual information from the printed page to account for his performances, on either a plodder or explorer supposition. At the earliest levels of processing, the reader is exposed to about three or four glimpses of the printed page each second, each lasting for about ¼ sec. At normal reading distances of about 12 inches, with average-sized type faces, about 10 letters appear on the fovea on each fixation. This is enough visual information (about 500 wpm, on a conservative estimate) to account for reading rates faster than those normally observed. Probably other letters that appear near the fovea can also be seen clearly enough for identification. The question is how and to what extent the reader exploits the information he receives. Clearly, something other than the amount of visual information is limiting the processing, for an average reading rate is merely 250 wpm. If visual information "display" were the limiting factor, we would have trouble accounting for the sluggishness, not the speed, of normal reading.

It is likely that the large number of characters displayed four times a second on the retina tax the information-handling capacity of the brain. The characters can be seen, but probably not identified or sequenced at this rate. In order to optimize the amount of useable information, given limited capacity, humans must be selecting judiciously from the input array, and increasing processing efficiency (see Rayner & McConkie, this volume). Whatever the strategies used here, they must result eventually in the construction of those higher-order units (words, sentences, meanings) that are consciously available for report when the reading act is successfully completed. Summarized below are some of the information-handling strategies that have been recognized as contributing to a variety of cognitive acts in such diverse areas as memory, pattern recognition, and speech perception. We assume that these same strategies are involved as the reader constructs meanings from the visual displays.

2.1.1   Levels of Organization: The Phenomenon of Chunking

The nervous system seems to be organized in terms of levels. Higher levels of organization deal with the successively larger units that are the output of lower levels. This is well illustrated by the increasing complexity of single cells in the visual system as one ascends to the cortex, or by the increasing meaningfulness of the unit of motor function from muscle fiber to functional movement. Each level in these hierarchies seems to do some processing which reduces the information load of subsequent levels.

It is possible that the phenomena of chunking and organization in memory, and in various skilled performances such as reading, are realized in terms of a hierarchical arrangement of a similar sort. As early as 1899, Bryan and Harter argued that plateaus in the learning curves of apprentice telegraphers could be accounted for by postulating successively more complex levels of organization: they could first send and receive Morse letters, then words, then even phrases. Similarly, self directions to move the clutch, step on the accelerator, and turn the wheel are replaced in the consciousness of the skilled driver by such directions as "Off to grandmother's house." Apparently such mechanisms operate to increase the amount of material that can be held in consciousness at any one time: if we conceive a labile attention function which can focus on any of a number of levels, it would follow that the higher the level, the broader the span of "material" covered per unit time. Surely chunking starts to affect reading speed as soon as the diagrams (*th,* as in *think; sh* as in *ash*) come to be bound mentally together; this effect is observed in typing and Morse encoding as well. At higher levels, orthographic patterns (e.g., I before E, except after C) surely are also chunked. Whole words, even phrases, may also submit to this process for items that are highly frequent. Note, though, that for chunking to operate, there must be some lower-level units to chunk together at a later stage of acquisition.

2.1.2 Automatization

Interwoven with but not identical to the notion of chunking, is the notion of automatization (Bryan & Harter, 1897, 1899; LaBerge & Samuels, 1974). Processing at lower levels goes on, in highly skilled performers, without further participation of conscious attention; there is both a speeding up of processing and a release of attention for other matters. Thus a driver may have no conscious memory that he shifted gears and turned the wheel on the way to grandmother's house. In fact, low-level errors such as grinding of gears sometimes jar one back to attention to these ordinarily submerged activities. Athletes who drift from their considerable holistic motor skills, foreswearing automatization, "go back to fundamentals." The significance of automatization in reading was realized by Huey (1908) in his classic work: ". . .repetition progressively frees the mind from attention to details, makes facile the total act, shortens the time, and reduces the extent to which consciousness must concern itself with the processes." And so we have no awareness of the phonological underpinnings of our everyday reading behavior; and so develops the belief (Goodman, 1973; F. Smith, 1971) that we apprehend meanings "directly" from the printed page.

2.1.3 Parallel Processing

If the matter of reading is organized into various levels and sublevels through automatization and chunking, it is possible that processing can go on at a number of levels at once, even though we cannot attend to all levels. Thus we might perform letter identification and word identification simultaneously, at least to some degree. Similarly, processing in parallel may occur within a level;

for example, many letters may be identified simultaneously. Furthermore, the later stages of processing one letter may occur simultaneously with the earliest stages of processing the next letter.

Summarizing, we have claimed that the information-handling mechanisms acknowledged to be involved in a variety of linguistic, memorial, and visual performances are involved in reading as well. Clearly these strategies are so rich and can be used in such versatile ways by humans, that a number of extreme "plodder" or "explorer" models of reading can be supposed to be feasible by appeal to them. We must turn to the evidence from reading performance itself to determine the relative plausibility of some of these models. To do so, it is necessary to see at the outset that neither the plodder nor the explorer position is monolithic. If we investigate these views in further detail, we can break them down into a number of subclaims which are plausibly, but not necessarily, related (this is why it is quite possible to adopt an intelligible "mixed" view of reading along this dimension). Broadly, the two views can be decomposed into three different answers to partly separable questions:

a. Is there a phonological intermediary between print and meaning? The central component of a strict plodder view is an auditory (phonemic) representation as a part of alphabetic reading. The normal process, from this point of view, involves conversion of print to speech (presumably inner speech); the auditory representation of each item is combined with the representation produced by previous and subsequent items to "blend" into a word or syllable. Thus plodders go through an obligatory phonological intermediary between print and meaning. It follows from the supposition of molar units by the explorer proponents that there is a direct pathway from print to meaning, by-passing phonology. That is, although adults are surely capable of rendering a phonological representation of print (they can read out loud), this ability is not called upon in normal reading.

b. What are the mechanics for attacking the printed page? The bottom-up proponent holds that the reader moves through print in a step-by-step left-to-right fashion, as if he were viewing the printed page through a thin tube moving along the line of print, exposing a few letters at a time. In contrast, from a top-down point of view, the process of skilled reading is more jumpy and operates by judicious sampling. Selected pieces of information from the printed page are combined with prior linguistic knowledge and text-derived expectations in the construction of the meaning of the passage. The reader focusses on critical letters or words to confirm or disconfirm reasonable expectations, guided by minimal cues from peripheral vision and by selective hypothesis formation.

c. What are the units of reading? The essential unit of reading from the plodder, bottom-up point of view is the letter. Higher-order structures (words, meanings) are taken to be composed, in later processing, from the letter units. From the explorer point of view, units of print larger than letters are apprehended immediately, without in any sense being built from component letters.

Thus, for example, words could be identified without prior letter recognition and, in an extreme version (F. Smith, 1971), phrases and "meanings" could be identified without prior identification of words. (Information from individual letters or words might be used in some way, but these subunits would not be explicitly identified.)

Hopefully no one (if pushed) would unreservedly man the plodder or explorer barricades over the whole range of the three questions we have raised: in terms of unit, mode of scanning the printed page, and the issue of a phonological intermediary. Common sense and available evidence suggest that the truth lies at neither of these extremes; humans are very versatile and seem to make use of a variety of strategies in cognitive performances of all kinds. The same is likely to be true for reading performance. Phonological and higher-level organization are intertwined in acts of fluent reading, as we will show. The question to be asked is how, and in what degrees, do the bottom-up plodding and top-down exploring positions combine at various stages of the reading process to yield the phenomenon of average fluent reading.

2.2   The Role of a Phonological Intermediary in Fluent Reading

No one can doubt that the alphabet represents a major simplification and advance in the rendering of meanings in print (see Gleitman & Rozin, this volume). If sounds rather than meanings are symbolized on the page, than a relatively small number of symbols will serve to transcribe all the huge numbers of words in the spoken language. In theory, at least, this reduces the learner's task to acquiring just a small number of visual items by rote in order to know how to read everything. But does one who has had experience with the resulting system for very many years decipher each item in terms of the alphabetic algorithm? Does the fluent reader analyze a written word *phonologically* in the course of normal reading?

2.2.1   The Assertion that We Move Directly from Print to Meaning

Many observations seem to lend credence to a direct print-to-meaning conversion, without a phonological intermediary, and these are adduced very often in the educational literature. For example, fluent reading rates are rather fast; one might guess that working out the sound of each word from its sequential letters would occupy too much time to explain these rates. A related observation is that struggling first graders all too obviously are "sounding out"—and they are slow and inaccurate—while Evelyn Woods' graduates appear to be gamboling quickly and accurately across the pages with instant comprehension. Thus poor reading performance seems to involve phonology, and terrific reading performance seems not to involve it. Another observation is that some special populations almost certainly operate without recourse to a phonological intermediary. Chinese script, it is generally agreed, is read as a logography (for discussion, see Gleitman & Rozin, this volume). Surely we would not want to say that 600,000,000 Chinese adults are illiterate because they convert characters directly to word meanings without an intervening phonological step. The existence of congenitally deaf readers of English script would seem to argue the same point: if the deaf can read English, then it is at least *feasible* to go directly from print to meaning. Some investigators point to the awe-inspiring complexity of the relations between letter sounds and pronunciations of words as a further argument that at commonly observed reading rates the reader cannot be making this conversion.

There seems to be some initial plausibility, given these observations, for a direct conversion between print and meaning. However, in our view, these observations cut two ways, and in sum they probably strengthen the position that there is a phonological intermediary in the normal English reading process.

a. Reading rates.   A serious threat to the feasibility of plodder sounding out strategies comes from the argument that normal reading rates are faster than could be accounted for by a phonological conversion process. This argument is weak. Oral reading rates are in the same range as the silent reading rates that characterize the average adult (about 250–350 words per minute, wpm). Huey (1908) reports a maximum (not normal) oral reading rate in university students of 280 wpm, somewhat below the 340-wpm rate for silent reading in his population. But a somewhat slower oral than silent reading rate can be explained, consistent with the plodder who "hears the words in his head," on the simple assumption that the internal auditory representation can move more quickly than the muscles and bones of the articulatory tract (even leaving aside the fact that the oral reader must pause to breathe, but the silent reader may very well form auditory representations while he is breathing). Using known mechanisms from the information-processing literature and known processing times, it is quite possible to construct a model of reading which assumes a sequential conversion from letters to sounds, to build up a phonological representation of words that is consistent with normal reading rates (Gough, 1972).

Surprisingly, not only is the letter-to-sound view consistent with average reading rates, but it may not even be the limiting factor on speed. Reading rates are notoriously affected by the difficulty of the material. In fact, the reason that the normal reading rate is below the maximal rate is probably because not only the reader, but also the listener, cannot comprehend material of modest conceptual difficulty at rates faster than normal speech. In this regard, it is interesting that the rate of meaningful information transfer is approximately the same for Americans reading English, fluent Chinese readers reading Chinese logographs (Shen, 1927), and deaf people communicating with American Sign Language (Bellugi & Fischer, 1972). The same notion is supported by the fact that comprehension of compressed speech remains high until about 275 wpm and then falls off sharply (Foulke & Sticht, 1969). It can hardly be an accident that the maximum oral reading rate, normal silent reading rate, and the rate of intelligible compressed speech are all about the same.

A related finding is that explicit vocalization (e. g., moving the lips) during reading seems to occur more with difficult materials, as though phonological encoding at a more explicit level is an aid to comprehension. Hardyck and Petrinovich (1969) attempted to inhibit subvocalization by use of a behavior modification technique. Successful reading was maintained with easy materials but problems were encountered for more difficult materials. Extreme explorer theorists would claim triumphantly that these facts demonstrate that phonological encoding is a mere crutch. But there is much to be said in favor of crutches—they are exactly the kinds of mechanisms we are looking for. After all, turning on the lights is also a crutch for reading, but this does not diminish its relevance.

All of the above observations suggest that, at least to some extent, thought is akin to sequential language, so that the speed of thinking is a major determiner of the speed of reading. At any rate, a plodding view of reading emerges strengthened from a consideration of normal reading rates. It is probably not a coincidence that there is good agreement between vocalization rates and reading rates if we leave aside (and we shall) the much-vexed question of what Evelyn Woods' speed readers are doing with a page of print. These reading superstars—or, more likely, scanner–skippers—are beyond the scope of the average reading performance we have set out to describe.

b. Special cases: the Chinese and the deaf. The Chinese read a script that makes no readily usable reference to phonology. (Many Chinese compound characters include phonetic "clues" of a rather opaque sort, but the best guess is that these are not analyzed in fluent reading performance; see Chao, 1968, and Gleitman and Rozin, this volume.) We do not know whether the Chinese convert the characters to phonological representations when they read—whether they "say the words in their heads"—although some evidence from clinical neurology (Section 2.2.2) suggests that logographies are probably encoded differently from alphabets. If the Chinese can read without phonological analysis, why can't we? Each word could be apprehended as a visual whole, a hieroglyph for a word meaning (Goodman, 1973). A suggestion that we do not read as the Chinese do comes from noticing that there is a massive difference in written-word knowledge between fluent English and Chinese readers. The average English high-school student can read virtually every word he can utter and understand (about 50,000 items), and can approximately pronounce many pseudowords as well. A reasonable Chinese dictionary carries about 50,000 characters. Yet even Chinese scholars are estimated to know only about 4000 of these items; they have to look up the rest if they meet them in print (Martin, 1972; Leong, 1973). Learning just a few thousand items occupies many years of schooling and extensive drill.

How can we account for these large differences in orthographic knowledge between Chinese and English readers? Our expectations would be the contrary on purely visual grounds, for the Chinese symbols have more coherence and distinctiveness than our written words. Brooks (this volume) has shown that it is easier to learn to identify complex symbols than their spatially sequenced component parts. It is probably because of this visual distinctiveness that second-grade backward readers find it easier to assign spoken English words to Chinese characters than to written English words (Rozin, Poritsky, & Sotsky, 1971). Further, the Chinese symbols have some visual mnemonic value, as they derive very often from representational pictures (e.g., *tree* is written 木 ; *forest* (many trees) is written 森). But despite these advantages to Chinese calligraphy, we learn to read far more words than do the Chinese. This difference is most easily accounted for in terms of the conceptual difference between a logography and an alphabet. There is a mnemonic link between English spellings and previously mastered speech, in terms of sound. You may not be sure how to pronounce *guete* the first time you see it, but it certainly isn't "blog."

A different instance of phonological by-pass is reading in congenitally deaf people, who have virtually no spoken language. Surely, their reading performance cannot be described in terms of a phonological intermediary. But in fact these individuals usually have great difficulty learning to read, and they spend many years in the attempt (Furth, 1966). Very few congenitally deaf individuals get to college and even those who do read quite poorly (Conrad, 1972; Gibson, Shurcliff, & Yonas, 1970). The better deaf readers are those who acquire deafness after the onset of language learning (Lenneberg, 1967). Thus if all except access to phonology were equal between deaf and hearing populations—and assuredly all else is not equal—then comparative reading performances for the two populations would suggest a pervasive role for phonological processing in achieving literacy.

c. Complexity of the conversion from print to sound. It is sometimes supposed that phonology is by-passed in fluent reading on the grounds that the conversion from print to sound is "so complex" as to preclude learning or using the written code in accord with such rules (F. Smith, 1971). Indeed the rules for this conversion, insofar as these are known, *are* very complex (Gleitman & Rozin, this volume) and so we also marvel that they could be learned or used. But the fact is that even young successful readers can carry out this process, translating strings of nonsense words into consensually pronounced speech with great facility.[1] If readers can rapidly convert text to speech without semantic or syntactic support, one cannot very well deny that this could not occur because it

---

[1] Some question arises as to whether an average reader could do such processing quickly enough to account for his reading rate. A lower bound on the reader's competency along these lines can be determined by the oral reading rate for pseudowords (meaningless strings of letters that honor English pronunciation rules, such as *doke, zean*). On the basis of our informal measurements on college students, we estimate this rate to be about 100 wpm.

is too complex. It does occur. One might as well say that the relations between the retina and the occipital cortex are so complex that no one could see. We do see.

Extreme instances where print is converted to sound in the absence of meaning are observed in children taught to chant church ritual in languages they do not understand. This has been common in American Hebrew instruction. A well documented example of an Ethiopian population that learns reading through chanting text in an uncomprehended language is given by Ferguson (1971). Certainly, then, it is *feasible* to move from print to sound in normal reading, whether or not this is the ordinary route.

Incidentally, the sound-to-meaning conversion, following a print-to-sound conversion, is probably simpler than it first seems. Much of the complexity in orthography-to-phonology mapping is in getting the *final* pronunciation precise enough for recognition. A general rough schema is clearly cued in the spelling system (recall that "blog" would never be spelled *guete*). After all, the reader already knows the pronunciation of most of the words he reads; his only job is to match the orthographic representation with some known pronunciation (unless he is reading a novel by Dostoevski). If he generates a rough pronunciation, for example, "dray-gun" while reading a story about Chinese monsters, he can make a good semantic guess, guided by partial phonological decoding, that the item is *dragon*. Notice that if he guesses *unicorn,* he reads badly (though, to be sure, he means well).

2.2.2 The Case for a Phonological Intermediary

We have seen that the usual plausibility arguments that phonology is by-passed in fluent reading, when looked at in detail, point to the feasibility of a print-to-sound intermediate step. But showing that this conversion is feasible by no means indicates that it is really part of the normal reading process. We describe here a variety of arguments from common sense and experimental outcomes that provide positive evidence for a phonological stage in reading. The most obvious issue concerns the fact that novelty—of items, overall substance, even of typeface—is the rule, not the exception, in encounters with print. Further, observed phonological errors both in short-term memory performance and in reading performance must somehow be accounted for. A third support for a phonological component in reading comes from findings in clinical neurology.

a. The problem of novelty.

It is obvious that when the child is learning to read, he meets many printed words for the first time. For example, examination of the first six books in an Australian elementary reading series (for first and second grades) showed that 41% of 2747 different words occurred only once, and 73% occurred fewer than five times (Firth, 1972). (Notice that an Australian second grader is reasonably expected to recognize nearly as many words as a

Chinese scholar acquires in a lifetime.) Since these items are almost invariably in the child's spoken vocabulary, the natural route to recognition of the printed page would be via production of the appropriate sounds. In this respect, at least, letter-to-sound translations would be very useful. The question is whether a similar effect plausibly holds for fluent adults.

Fifty words account for about half the tokens used in spoken language (F. Smith, 1971), while there are about 50,000 words in the average English speaker's spoken vocabulary. It is not surprising that a great many rather familiar spoken words occur quite rarely in print (less than once per million words for 3000 words in the Thorndike–Lorge (1944) count, including such items as *wormy, yodel, abrasive, backache, strangler, soccer, terrifically,* and *waiver*). If we assume that a (voracious) reader reads 1½ hr a day at 300 words per minute, this comes to 9 million words a year. Clearly, many words he reads will not have been seen during the past year, and some probably never before. Many new proper names and technical terms enter the general vocabulary every year. Although context surely helps in guessing these from minimal clues, a certain amount of straight decoding must occur. Given the numbers we have cited, this must happen rather frequently within a typical newspaper passage. However, it is true that after a small number of exposures to a new word, a direct visual-to-meaning pathway may have been laid down (for some experimental support for this idea, see Brooks, this volume).

We will argue later that visual learning of written items is possible on a large scale only because of the prelearning of an underlying phonological mnemonic. Surely, for words seen infrequently, the phonological basis of the script must be consulted rather often, although possibly only for partial cues to supplement contextual information. At the extreme, we have already shown that readers of an alphabet can pronounce foreign text and nonsense text with fair facility. A logographic ("whole word") reader is stopped cold if the item is new, unless the symbol is pictorially suggestive (which writings in English never are) or unless there is extensive contextual support. The extent of contextual support in real reading performance is strictly limited by the *purpose* of reading. That is, one reads the newspaper in order to be surprised; if one knows what it says in advance, it is as stale as yesterday's newspaper. In this sense, one avoids reading whatever can plausibly be known from guessing and reasonable expectation.

b. Reading errors. Phonologically interpretable errors frequently occur in reading, though for good readers they are not as common as semantically interpretable errors. A complicated instance of phonological error is the well known "proofreader effect": we often fail to notice misspellings in text. In part, this fact shows a syntactic–semantic override of phonology in fluent reading, but in part it also shows that the reader does not rely fully on a learned visual rendition of a word. A rendition that preserves some of the phonological or orthographic properties of the correct writing is sufficient. Suppose it is claimed, for the sake of argument, that the *presence* of the proofreader effect (failure to notice misspellings in context) is an argument *for* phonological by-pass. In that case, the frequent *absence* of the proofreader effect (evidenced by the fact that we hire proofreaders, which would surely not be done if they always displayed the proofreader effect) must then be an argument *against* phonological by-pass. In general, demonstrations that deformed text can be deciphered with good comprehension cut in both these ways. A similar example is Miller and Friedman's demonstration (1957) that fluent readers can comprehend text with the vowels removed. This finding argues for phonological by-pass (one has no vowels to read, yet one reads words that have vowels normally) and against phonological bypass (phonological cues among the consonants tell one which words are being read).

In oral reading, where phonological errors are frequent and easy to observe, one might claim that mispronunciations are introduced after processing of the meaning is complete; that is, on the output side. However, it is well known from findings in information processing that alphabetic–linguistic visual stimuli are typically processed through a phonological intermediary, so that even when written or nonverbal outputs are demanded, errors interpretable on phonological grounds are very frequent (Conrad, 1972). Thus, if the subject is *shown* the letter E together with other letters and asked to recall it, then if he errs, he is much more likely to give C or D—which sound similar in their alphabetic names—than F, which is visually similar. In fact, in many quarters, phonological as opposed to semantic errors are taken as an index that the item is in the short-term store rather than the long-term store (Neisser, 1967).

c. Evidence from oriental clinical neurology. Modern-day Japanese writing is of particular interest to reading research, since the Japanese use an extensive logographic system (*Kanji*) and two phonological syllabary systems (*Katakana* and *Hiragana*). These systems are intermixed on the page in Japanese writing and sometimes the same item can be written either in Kanji or in a syllabary notation (see Gleitman & Rozin, this volume). Sasanuma and Fujimura (1971; 1972) have done a number of studies to determine how aphasic disorders affect these separate components of the writing system. For example, they asked normal and aphasic Japanese subjects to write down words suggested to them by pictures they were shown (that is, a picture of a familiar object was to be followed by writing of its name). For some of the pictures, where this was orthographically possible, they were asked to write both the Kanji and Katakana versions. Both normals and aphasics made modest numbers of errors using the Kanji (logograph) and these errors, for both groups, were classifiable as visual confusions on the written forms. Katakana (syllabary) errors were very rare in normals. They were extremely common in aphasics with speech apraxia (i.e., involvement of the phonological system in the disorder), while Kanji errors were no more common in such aphasics than in nonspeech apraxic patients. Furthermore, there was no correlation between the frequency of errors on any given word in Kanji vs. Katakana form. These results suggest a direct phonological involvement, for fluent adults, in processing the syllabary components. A good guess is that people make use of anything available in complex performances where speed is an issue. If you have learned a phonological script, you make use of its phonological properties (as well as all its other properties) in deciphering it. Then if this possibility is removed due to organic disorder, performance will suffer.

2.2.3 Some Good Evidence for Bypassing Phonology

It is as implausible to suppose that skilled humans would adopt a single phonetic strategy, ignoring all other available cues, as to suppose that they would make no use of this cue if it were readily available in the external stimulus (the printed page).

Some investigations, particularly on performance with homonyms (two word meanings with a single pronunciation) and homographs (two word meanings with a single written form), suggest that phonological processing cannot be the whole story. Baron (1973) performed an experiment showing that homonyms that are not homographs (e.g., *knot/not, scene/seen, sun/son*) do not confuse fluent readers. He asked subjects to read phrases, some of which were meaningful both as written and as they would be pronounced (e.g., *Tie the knot*), some of which were meaningful as they would be pronounced but which were meaningless as written (e.g., *Tie the not*) and some of which were meaningless in either case (e.g., *Ill him* in comparison to the meaningful *Kill him*). Reaction times for judgments of "not meaningful" were the same for items like *Tie the not* as for items like *Ill him*. If the subject had converted the message to a phonological form on the way to meaning, we would expect him to hear (in his head) *Tie the not* as meaningful, and then either to make the wrong judgment or to take an extra few milliseconds to notice and respond in terms of the spelling convention. The latter expectation was disconfirmed (although subjects did make a few more errors in judging the meaningfulness of items like *Tie the not*). A radical print-to-sound-to-meaning conversion cannot account for this outcome.

Baron's results are supported by common experience. If words are spelled wrong, they are often hard to decipher, as in the example of *Chute hymn inn the haul* which sounds like a plausible (if unpleasant) message when pronounced aloud. It is palpably harder to decipher than *Shoot him in the hall,* even though it has a quite regular phonological writing, and should be easy if comprehension proceeded entirely through conversion to inner speech. Note again that one can nevertheless read it after reflection: English orthography is not logographic. Bower (1970) tested a related notion by inserting Greek letters, with sounds approximating English sounds, into English text, which was then read by Greek–English bilinguals. Even though the passages were phonetically equivalent in the mixed orthography, reading rate was slowed considerably. Apparently, an ortho-graphic representation is learned for which phonetically equivalent substitutions cannot be made without performance decrements.

A finding by Szumski and Brooks (cited by Brooks, this volume) indicates rapid learning of orthographic or calligraphic patterns. If a subject learns a meaning for a *spoken* pseudoword (e.g., "doke" = *spoon*), he takes longer to interpret that meaning when the pseudoword appears for the first time in written form in a sentence than if he had previously learned the association as a *written* pseudoword/word association. However, this difference in speed of judgment is erased after a few practice trials with the written pseudowords. This outcome suggests that it is possible to establish direct connections between print and meaning efficiently and to learn these quite rapidly, at least if the visual representations are phonologically sensible and if the number of items is rela-tively small.

2.2.4 Summary Comments on the Role of Phonology in Fluent Reading Performance

The upshot of various observations is to suggest a clear role for a phonological component in reading. But we have also shown clear evidence of phonological by-pass. One way of reconciling these facts is on a kind of developmental hypothesis. After all, the beginner's sounding out strategy is clearly phono-logical, while the gyrations of Evelyn Woods graduates are hard to conceive as phonological. Then perhaps phonological involvement comes about primarily in "primitive" reading performances. In support of this view, we have seen that as the adult is forced back toward earlier reading rates and earlier comprehension levels (by distortion of the text as in Bower's example, or by making it conceptually difficult as in the Hardyck and Petrinovich situation), he shows evidence of returning to an explicit phonological strategy: he moves his lips and mumbles.

In sum, there seems to be a shift, with increasing fluency, away from reliance on straight decoding at the level of letter-to-sound correspondence. But we also know this shift is never fully made, and that therefore the "developmental" hypothesis (that moves from sound to direct-meaning decoding with growth of fluency) cannot be the whole story. Why, if it were, would the Japanese aphasics lose contact with their syllabary script as they lost functional contact with their speech apparatus? Why would fluent readers of English still make phonological errors? The facts, in total, are ill described if we assume that fluent readers have stored each word (or phrase, or sentence) as a visual whole, without internal phonological structure. The facts are best accommodated by supposing that the units for fluent reading are phonological—orthographic units at a level at least a step removed from correspondences between letters and phonetic entities. We reserve discussion of the units of processing until somewhat later (Sec-tion 2.4).

2.3   Do We Read Every Letter or Word or Do We Sample the Text?

Humans often have optional ways of performing the same task. They bring past experience and a variety of processing procedures to bear on the task of the moment. They frequently can "construct" much of a stimulus array by sampling from it in accordance with prior expectations about what could be present and important, returning for further sampling when there is a violation of expectations, and otherwise passing on to the next scene, problem, or line of print (Neisser, 1967). In the case of reading, redundant information from the topic of the text, meaning of the sentence, and syntax, as well as from letter arrangements (orthographic patterns), may be sampled judiciously. Thus reading speed is probably enhanced simply by not looking at, or attending to, all available information.

Hochberg (1970) has considered two submechanisms by which a reader could sample from the printed page rather than reading every letter, every word, or even every sentence. *Peripheral search guidance* would guide the next saccade (eye movement) to the most informative part of the page by picking up information from peripheral vision. *Cognitive search guidance* allows selective hypothesis formation to operate on the material in view at any glance. In general, Hochberg's conception is that the reader looks at the page as he looks at the scenes in the real world: scanning, picking up some information, constructing the remainder, and testing tentative suppositions. Such assumptions have led to the description of the adult reader as a player in a "psycholinguistic guessing game" (Goodman, 1969). Notice that on Hochberg's formulation, this matter need not get out of hand. After all, the explorer looking for what he expects to find might autocratically override the writer's intention (i.e., he might read everything he believes, rather than the other way round). Thus a constant monitoring at visual and cognitive levels by the trusty plodder is a necessary component of any reasonable sampling view. "Active-organism" models of the kind Hochberg envisages are supported also by data from visual perception and speech perception (e.g., Bever, 1970), so their application to the reading process is quite reasonable.

Evidence for sampling–constructive tendencies of the type suggested by Hochberg is extensive. As reading skill develops, the number of eye fixations per line of print drops. This seems to result from an increased ability to sample and construct meanings from the visual display rather than from an increased ability to apprehend more visual material per se. The notion of peripheral search guidance is strengthened by Hochberg's demonstration that placing X's in the white spaces between words slows down reading. Presumably, the spaces are important cues to the sampler since, by mechanisms of peripheral guidance, they may tell the eye where to look next; usually the letters at the beginnings of words carry the greatest amount of information. The fact that placing X's in the white spaces produces a relatively greater reading decrement in fifth and sixth graders, as opposed to first and second graders, argues for its involvement in a higher-level process (Hochberg, 1970).

There is also strong evidence for high-level cognitive guidance. The oral errors of fluent readers are usually syntactically and semantically appropriate; such errors predominate over phonological errors (Goodman, 1969; Kolers, 1970). They appear even in first-grade readers (Weber, 1970). Kolers (1970) also reports syntactic–semantic guidance in the reading of bilingually mixed texts by bilingual readers. Thus if the text says: *a la porte of his cell,* the reader may say "a la porte de sa cell," showing what might be called a high-level override.

Further evidence for high-level cognitive guidance may come from the phenomenon of the *eye–voice span,* although this phenomenon is subject to varying interpretations. It has been known for some time that, in oral reading, the reader has assimilated information from the text in advance of the portion he is articulating at any instant. This fact alone is consistent with either a step-by-step or sampling view, for it demonstrates only that the eye is quicker than the mouth. However, the span (measured by turning off the lights while someone is reading a passage aloud) tends to extend to a reasonable syntactic boundary rather than to a certain absolute number of letters or words ahead (Levin & Kaplan, 1970). This suggests reading phrase-by-phrase rather than letter-by-letter. However, this effect might well occur at the time of report; it is possible that halves and quarters of phrases are insufficiently processed to allow report and are thus lost. This alternative view receives much support from studies in sentence perception. For example, Johnson (1965), has shown a similar effect in the recall of spoken sentences: if part of a phrase is reported correctly, the rest of the phrase tends to be reported correctly as well. The likelihood of error rises significantly at phrase boundaries. In this case, the subject certainly heard the whole sentence during training, but cannot recall or report "halves of phrases" very reliably.

We can conclude that both step-by-step and sampling strategies are employed by the normal reader, depending on the circumstances of his interaction with the text. Sampling—at least, successful sampling—and phonological by-pass almost never proceed so far that the reader blithely comprehends a word or phrase all of whose letters are scrambled. Yet he appears not to be reading letter-by-letter over the whole text.

2.4   What Are the Units for Processing the Printed Page?

The common-sense view of the units of reading is that, as a first step, the letters on the page are identified and sequenced. The argument for a phonological component in reading also suggests that a unit of approximately letter size functions in reading performances. On this same view, more molar units such as the word can be assumed to function in reading, derived from the letter molecule by such mechanisms as automatization and chunking. Thus neither the plodder (only letter units) nor explorer (only larger-than-letter units) extremes can be expected to be wholly correct in defining the units of reading. On the contrary, for this issue the evidence runs entirely counter to the view that there is a unique, exclusive unit in terms of which the reading process is organized. Nevertheless, especially for pedagogical purposes to which we will shortly turn, there is some real interest in knowing whether the molar units of reading are constructed and then chunked by automated processes from initial letter detection, or whether this level could be bypassed entirely. After all, it is logically possible that words are detected as visual wholes: we have pointed to such a process in Chinese. We will show below that this whole-word view, while logically possible, is probably wrong. Further, some have supposed that units of even larger size than words are detected visually without separate identification of their parts. We will show that this is more than unlikely; it is not a logical possibility.

2.4.1 Are There Letterlike Units?

Many good arguments can be made that units of larger-than-letter size are constructed during reading. However, the only argument against individual letter identification as a stage in this process is that, putatively, this procedure might be too slow to account for normal reading rates. But in fact the rate of average reading can be accounted for in a model that assumes an initial letter-identification stage.

The average college student (an above-average reader) reading at about 280 wpm shows about nine fixations for every ten words. We know from the work of Sperling (1960) and others that when a display of nine or more unrelated letters is briefly exposed (for a fraction of the time of a fixation), subjects can report about five. This would amount to 15–20 letters per sec, or about 180 wpm, a little slower than the required rate. But note that Sperling required the subject to report verbally on the letters, and that they were unrelated. At the level of automatic processing, Sperling, Budiansky, Spivak, and Johnson (1971) calculate that letters can be *scanned* (though not necessarily identified individually) during a fixation at rates of about 10 msec each (100 letters per sec) which would easily allow more than enough characters per unit time to account for the normal reading rate. Gough (1972) has shown that the normal reading rate can be explained with a model like the one we are here considering (plodding through, letter by letter) by using well established findings from the information-processing literature. In general it seems quite reasonable to account for processing just a bit more than one word per fixation with known simple read-off and pronunciation mechanisms. Of course parallel processing must be assumed in the sense that letter identification of material in the sensory store is going on at the same time that previously identified letters are converted to phonological (or other) form.

2.4.2 Are There "Whole-Word" Units? Some Theoretical Questions

Letter identification and phonological conversion are certainly feasible, as we have shown. Nevertheless, a case is sometimes made that letter units do not enter into normal reading. One line of evidence comes from the clinical syndrome sometimes called *letter blindness* (Benson & Geschwind, 1969; Marshall & Newcombe, 1973), in which letter identification is poor but some familiar words can be read quite well. This suggests recognition of words as visual wholes, but it is also compatible with the interpretation that letter identification occurs but that the results of this stage are inaccessible to consciousness.

We have already seen that whole visual recognition of a few thousand characters is acquired regularly by a huge population of Chinese readers. It is possible that the English reader also acquires a sizable stock of visual wholes for the most frequent words. The only problem, a fundamental one, is to account for his huge reading vocabulary (including nonsense items) as a process of visually recognizing whole words. Nevertheless, the notion that words are identified as wholes—by their shapes—is worth investigating for sheer feasibility. In principle, one could imagine sets of visual features which would uniquely specify each word. Thus *dead* might be stored as "tall on both ends, low in the middle" and so on. The feature complexes would be learned through repeated exposures to these items.

A reasonable model of this sort would have to take into account variations in typeface, including cursive writing. But how could it account for the fact that subjects can read text in alternating upper and lower case quite rapidly (e. g., *PaRt* or *pArT*) with letter size equated (F. Smith, Lott, & Cronnell, 1969)? After all, since the subject has never seen *pArT* before, he could not have learned a total visual-feature set for it. So on the whole-word visual account, performance would be expected to deteriorate under these conditions. However, it is always possible, model-building being what it is, to doctor the proposed processor to handle any one problem of this kind. As soon as one such model is shot down, another arises to take its place. We cannot, therefore, once and for all show that a model involving a letter-detection preprocessor is simpler and more natural than any inventable visual-feature model. What we can do instead is to discuss in detail the most plausible current proposal for a whole-word recognition device, that of F. Smith (1971). It is suggested, by use of this exemplar, that the general class of visual-feature models is cumbersome and ad hoc. But this discussion will leave open the logical possibility that yet another feature program can be devised to handle the particular objections to Smith's model.

F. Smith's letter-by-pass model seems at first glance to account for the fact that subjects successfully read text written in alternating case. Smith supposes that instead of whole-shape or "Gestalt" cues, words are identified by a collection of features of each of the letters in sequence. Thus *dead* might be specified by a list such as "vertical in first position, curve in second, closed and open curve in third, vertical in fourth." He correctly points out that English words could be uniquely specified by such a list with fewer features than would be necessary to identify each letter of each word, and thus less information per word would be needed. If one further assumed that critical features were available for both upper- and lower-case letters then, in principle, a mixed-case word could be identified through this set, even though this particular calligraphic representation was novel: when features of *d* are entered into the criterial-feature list, features of *D* are entered also.

The Smith model has severe difficulties. Note that different features of a particular letter will be important in different words. For example, the critical feature of the initial *p* in *prop* might be the existence of a vertical on the left side which would differentiate *prop* from other possible words with different letters in the first position (*crop, drop*). On the other hand, the critical feature of the same initial *p* in *past* might be a closed loop, since this (and not left vertical) differentiates *past* from other possibilities (*cast, fast, last, mast*). The visual processor could not know which features of *p* to extract in these different circumstances, for it does not know which word it is getting until the whole feature complex has been extracted. Under the circumstances, the visual processor must extract all features in all cases, and thus it saves nothing at the initial stages.

According to the Smith model, for recognition of a word in lower-case print, the fully extracted feature set would have to be compared with feature sets of all the words in memory (or some subset if a sequenced search process is envisaged) along the lines of models like Pandemonium (Selfridge, 1959) or EPAM (Feigenbaum, 1963). A similar search would be required for a letter-identification model after the letters in the target word were identified. However, in the Smith model, in order to recognize the same word handwritten, or in mixed-case printed letters, large numbers of alternate features lists would have to be formed. For example, there are 16 versions of each 4-letter word in mixed case. The whole argument in favor of letter by-pass was to save processing time or space; yet this scheme vastly multiplies the number of items in the store. Note that Smith's idea that when a word is entered (usually in lower-case form), features are simultaneously entered for the upper-case letters at each position, will not markedly reduce this load. There is no obvious way in which the perceiver would know which features of the upper-case letter would be criterial in defining the word uniquely; it is certainly not a trivial problem to discover which characteristics of *D* in *Dark* should be entered. Would they be the same defining features as in *DARK* or *DaRK*? How would they relate to the defining features of *d* in *dark*? If the model is extended to the recognition of handwritten words, this matter becomes frighteningly complex.

The alternative plodder model does require one processing stage unneeded in the Smith model: the identification of the letters. But letter identification would drastically reduce the storage and retrieval problem: there is only one representation, the letters D-A-R-K for *dark, DaRk,* and so on, not a large number of sets of equivalent features. The "extra" stage, letter identification, that we propose to be part of normal word recognition, is independently known to exist, and in a highly practiced and automated form. In particular, the conversion of different forms of the same letter (e. g., upper and lower case) into a single underlying representation is a well documented process in readers (Posner, 1969). Such a mechanism makes it easy to explain the recognition of mixed case or handwritten items and cuts the postulated memory and retrieval load.

Perhaps it pays to remark once more that we have not delivered a general or formal blow to all featural models that by-pass letter identification. No doubt yet another model lurks unpublished and thus unchallenged in another information processor's head. (For example, suppose the initial and final letters along with word shape and possibly other cues were used?) But such proposals seem to us, as a class, artificial and unnecessarily complex. Why all this torture to avoid noticing 26 inoffensive little squiggles?

Summarizing, known whole-word visual detection models appear to place an inordinate burden on a system that must recognize tens of thousands of items rapidly and accurately, while the assumption of a letter-recognition preprocessor handles these requirements adequately.

2.4.3 Are There Whole-Word Units? The Word-Superiority Effect

In light of the somewhat labyrinthine nature of whole-word recognition devices, and in light of what we know of the massive reading vocabulary of adults, one might wonder why it is ever assumed that we do read in terms of whole words. Probably the major impetus for the whole-word view comes from the curious "word-superiority effect."

In 1885, Cattell reported a finding that is often discussed in the context of reading: readers can identify words in brief exposures more accurately than they can identify individual letters. This general finding is an instance of the word-superiority effect. A number of investigators (Reicher, 1969; Wheeler, 1970; Johnston & McClelland, 1973) have used a forced-choice procedure to show that this effect of context in apprehending briefly flashed stimuli is not merely a response bias, a result of guessing judiciously from incomplete visual information. The following kinds of stimuli are shown to the subject, briefly flashed: four-letter words (e. g., PART or PORT), single letters (e. g., A or O), and unrelated letter strings (e. g., APTR). In all cases, the subjects are asked which of two letters (A or O) appeared in the stimulus. Subjects perform more accurately, within the same exposure time, with the four-letter-word stimuli than with the isolated or unrelated letters; thus, in this example, it is easier to identify A in PART than A alone, or A in APTR. It is not the case that A could have been guessed from the context P-RT, for O would have made an acceptable word too.[2]

An effect of a similar sort appears in various tasks: subjects can identify distorted or mutilated words more easily than equivalently mutilated unrelated letter strings; they can respond more quickly in letter-identification tasks for letters in words vs. letters in isolation or unrelated letter strings; they can make judgments more efficiently for pairs of words as opposed to pairs of unrelated letter strings (see Baron, 1975, for a review of this literature).

Some investigators have supposed that the word-superiority effect bears on the question of whether processing in normal reading is based on preliminary letter identification. The argument goes something like this: if it takes more time and/or is less accurate to apprehend a letter or unrelated letter string than a whole word, then it must be that written words are perceived as a whole, by their *shapes,* without prior identification of letters. However, we have already suggested that it is difficult to conceive of a whole-word visual recognition device that does not identify component letters on the way. Further, it is quite easy to reinterpret the word-superiority effect in terms of a letter-recognition device: if letters are identified on the way to word identification, but the subject has no conscious access to this early stage in processing, he will report on words sooner and more accurately than on letters. On this view, the *conscious* letter identification that allows report would result when the subjects works back from the word, or retrospectively scans the stimulus array if no word resulted from the letter-analysis stage.

Whatever the theoretical account, the "whole-word" hypothesis of reading is quite unable to handle a number of basic features of the word-superiority effect. McClelland (1976) has shown a word-superiority effect for stimuli in which upper- and lower-case letters were alternated, with letter size equated. Yet the alternating-case words are, from a visual (calligraphic) point of view, totally new arrays, new shapes that were never learned from prior experience as wholes.

Another kind of result is also difficult to understand on a whole-word model of reading: a substantial word-superiority effect is achieved for pseudowords such as *pide* or *nart* compared to unrelated letters (Miller, Bruner, & Postman, 1954; Gibson, Pick, Osser, & Hammond, 1962; Baron & Thurston, 1973; McClelland, 1976). The pseudowords follow English spelling patterns, but they have no status as morphemes (meaningful words). Since the pseudoword has never been seen before by the subject, in any calligraphic form, a whole-word

[2] Because of the startling nature of this phenomenon, great ingenuity has been devoted to modeling the effect, including a variety of highly sophisticated guessing hypotheses (e.g., Wheeler, 1970). However, equally sophisticated experiments (e.g., Johnston, 1974) have eliminated these kinds of explanations, essentially by showing that redundancy or constraints in letter possibilities cannot explain the effect. In general, it appears that the word superiority effect will not be explained in terms of puzzle solving that involves guessing. The subject does not end up with an incompletely identified array which he then figures out as he might an anagram or an incomplete picture.

superiority hypothesis cannot explain its superiority over an unrelated letter string: the overall shape of the pseudoword is entirely novel.

The evidence we have presented so far is easily interpretable only by claiming that the substructure of the items plays some role in their processing; the visual shapes are not perceived as wholes. A first guess, then, is that the phonological properties of the stimuli are implicated in their processing: pseudowords that have English phonological structure yield a substantial word-superiority effect. A number of further findings complicate this picture. For example, deaf subjects also show a word-superiority effect for real words and for pseudowords (Gibson et al., 1970). Thus it cannot be that the sound ("pronounceability") of the pseudowords wholly accounts for their superiority over unrelated letter strings. It must be that something about the internal orthographic patterns in the pseudowords is apprehended by readers.

Some investigators also report a more accurate perception of letters in real words than letters in pseudowords (McClelland, 1976). This advantage is maintained even with alternating typefaces, again weakening the interpretation of the effect in terms of a whole visual-shape detection effect. We will relate both the pseudoword superiority effect and the apparent superiority of words over pseudowords to the notion of *orthographic representations* that are bound both to the phonological representations below and to the morphological representations above (Section 2.4.5). It remains here to assert that the word-superiority data overall are best accommodated under the view that reading involves a preliminary highly automatized letter-identification stage that is not easy to access consciously, that disintegrates rapidly, and thus is not neatly tied to the output side, that is, to report.

We should point out, finally, that the experimental situation in which the word-superiority effect is found is not directly analogous to a reading situation, and so findings for these two domains require some caution in interpretation. The stimuli in a typical word-superiority experiment are flashed briefly, or are otherwise hard to see. The subject's eye movements are not under his control, since the flashes are too brief. The task is, in addition, dissimilar to a reader's task. The subject must usually make some sort of match, choice, or judgment, rather than determining meaning. In short, even if words were directly apprehended without letter identification in this experimental context, it would be overexuberant to relate such findings directly to characteristics of the reader. (On the other hand, as Baron, in preparation, has pointed out, it would be hard to explain the efficiency and rapidity of subjects' performances in this situation if it were not a highly practiced task.)

2.4.4 Are There Phrase or "Meaning" Units?

An argument is sometimes made that meanings might be apprehended "directly" from print. No doubt proponents of this extreme explorer view are impressed with the sense of immediate comprehension we have when reading, and the apparent great facility of exceptional readers. However, the arguments we have made that word units are not a feasible processing base for reading (essentially arguments based on memory load and information-handling capacity) become crushing when applied to putative higher-level units if these are taken to arise in reading performance without being composed from smaller units. In the "reading whole meanings" approach (Goodman, 1973; F. Smith, 1971), we are asked to believe that, on the basis of *visual* features, humans learn to discriminate among millions of different sentences, mapping each onto some meaning. These feature mappings must be learned in spite of the fact that most sentences occur only once in a lifetime: it is sobering to realize that identity of one long—or a few short—sentences in two manuscripts by different authors is grounds enough for suspicion of plagiarism. Worse, the visual feature similarity of sentences is only very weakly related to meaning. Consider, on the one hand, the visually similar but meaningfully distinct sentences:

(1) Wendy, please don't put your head in that puma's mouth.
(2) Wendy, please put your head in that puma's mouth.

On the other hand, consider the visually dissimilar but meaningfully similar:

(3) The puma chewed the girl.
(4) The immature human female was masticated by the cougar.

Our limited information-processing system is not able to handle anything like the memory store that would be required to distinguish among all sentence pairs that have the shape similarities of Sentences (1) and (2); that is, such a memory system would have to distinguish additional instances such as *Wendy, please don't put your head (ears, tail, life savings...) in the puma's (aardvark's, penguin's, Martian's...) mouth (eye, dinner plate, pocket...).* The same memory system would have to code overall *visual* relations between such sentences as (3) and (4), in order to relate their meanings. The most powerful tools of the information-processing system (chunking, automatizing, sampling) would be of little use in such a vision-to-meaning procedure. The complexity of this mapping is a simple consequence of the fact that, in natural language, the relation of sound to meaning is highly complex—a fact accounting for the continuing employment picture for linguists for three millenia, so far. Despite these self-evident facts, an influential view in some education circles is that children should not be taught about sound-to-print relations, but rather should be taught to read directly for meanings. At best, the whole meaning position could be employed in the recognition of a small number of highly frequent and familiar phrases.

Incidentally, in addition to the theoretical impossibility of this position, since it would require an almost infinite memory store, there is no compelling evidence for direct meaning identification. Feelings of instant comprehension can be explained on the basis of the usual inaccessibility of early stages of processing, just as in memory, pattern recognition, and so forth. The fact that people can often report on the meaning of a passage they have read without remembering the words verbatim is also irrelevant to this position. One need only conclude, invoking such notions as automatization, that subcomponent identification occurred below the level of awareness, and that the component information was subsequently lost from memory while the more highly processed meaning remained. The facts about spoken sentence perception are described in just this way (e.g., Fillenbaum, 1966; Sachs, 1967; Bransford & Franks, 1971). No one in this domain of inquiry argues that because one remembers the gist of what is said and forgets the exact words, that one goes directly from whole sound waves to meanings without phonological processing.

2.4.5   The Natural Units of Reading

We have given evidence both for and against phonological by-pass in this discussion, referring darkly from time to time to *orthographic representations* of print. We have stated *how* processing in terms of such units could proceed, invoking various concepts from information processing to account for its speed. But we have never defined the orthographic representations or showed the part they play in normal reading performance. We summarize here the facts about reading performance, all cited earlier, that are to be accounted for in terms of the postulated orthographic units. Similarly, we have referred in passing to the fact that the processing of novel materials involves a low-level decoding from print to meaning through sound. We will suggest that *superficial syllabic representations* are plausibly postulated to account for this feature of normal reading performance.

a.   Orthographic representations.   Abundant evidence has been cited to show that the sound structure of the language plays a major role in reading. Perhaps the least inscrutable demonstrations come from the Orient: it is evidently almost impossible to learn tens of thousands of items in the Chinese notation, which has no intimate ties to phonology. Further, loss of facility with a phonological script (Katakana) accompanies functional loss of the speech system. These facts, as well as the word-superiority effect for pseudowords over unrelated letter strings, suggest that phonological representation plays a role in fluent performance. This is not surprising, given what we know from the information-processing literature about phonological representation at early stages in memory.

On the other hand, there is some compelling evidence that the relation between reading and sheer *sound* representations is indirect. The strongest argument for initial representation of print above the level of sounds comes from the lack of influence of nonhomographic homonyms (same pronunciations that have different conventional spellings) on meaning apprehension. The word-superiority effects cannot necessarily be assigned directly to sound relations, in the sense of pronounceability, for word-superiority effects are achieved with deaf readers. Further, the word-superiority effects cannot be related directly to learned subsyllabic visual patterns of letter groups, since letter sequences which are unrelated to English phonology or orthography in total, but which contain high-frequency bigrams or even high-frequency trigrams (e. g., KTER) yield no clear word-superiority effect (McClelland & Johnston, unpublished manuscript, 1976). In sum, there are clear demonstrations from a variety of experimental situations that there is an operative unit in reading tied to the sound system. Yet this orthographic unit is at a higher systematic level than the speech sound.

The letter sequences in words are obviously far from random. Some sequences never occur (D never follows Q) while some recur frequently (D often follows A). Obviously, such pattern constraints do not arise by accident. Much of the orthographic regularity can be traced to parallel regularities in the phonological system (for a detailed discussion, see Gleitman & Rozin, this volume). For many words, orthographic and phonological representations are quite close, once we correct for the fact that speech is continuously varying, while alphabetic writing is discrete. For words like *car, pet, carpet,* and so on, there is a fairly straightforward representation of phones (speech sounds) in English orthography. As we suggested in the preceding paper, a yet more satisfactory correspondence between orthography and phonology results if systematic phonemes, rather than phones or surface phonemes, are taken to be the phonological units transcribed by the alphabetic letters. This, for example, includes the written consonant difference between *grater* and *grader* despite the fact that these consonants (as speech sounds) are pronounced just the same—with a flapping noise. In spoken-language organization, phonological and morphological facts interact in a complicated way and this process is evident in the orthographic representation of spoken words. For example, *purist* and *purest,* which sound exactly the same, are written slightly differently to represent two different meanings ("one who is pure or insists upon purity" and "most pure of all"). In this instance, then, the patterns and rules of English orthography represent a *morphophonemic* (morphological—phonemic) level of language organization which is also patterned and rule governed. Then the relation between sound and spelling can be quite indirect. But the fact that it is indirect does not mean it is not there. Virtually all English writings of words (even the writing *through*) are to some extent related to phonology. Although the sound "ist" can be written *est* or *ist,* it could never be written *zap* or *uk.*

Common sense and a variety of evidence we have given suggest that this phonological relevance of orthographic representations is deployed both in learning and in fluent reading performances. Baron and Strawson (1976) have shown that words that have high phonological coherence in their written form (e.g., *off*) are read more quickly than words that have low phonological coherence (e.g., *cough*), with word frequency equated. It is noncoincidental and clearly relevant, as we described in the previous chapter, that items with low phonological coherence (e.g., *though, night*) are subject to spelling reform (e.g., *tho, nite*) by the method of scribe errors. Recent studies by Brooks (this volume) on the acquisition of a vocabulary of words written in a new alphabet bear directly on this point. Adults learned to identify six words written in a new alphabet. For one group, there was a direct and explicit correspondence between letters from the new alphabet and the traditional letters, so that subjects could figure out any of the words from these correspondences. For the other group, seeing the same set of symbol sequences, there was no such correspondence. The surprising finding here was that after extended practice (400 trials on each word) and with only a small set of six words to learn, subjects were significantly faster at identifying the orthographically regular, phonologically based items. Evidently phonological coherence has a long-term effect in the performance of highly skilled individuals.

At the same time, it is undeniable that English orthographic representations are not always straightforward transcriptions of phonology. For example, there are some orthographic regularities that by no stretch of the imagination make phonological sense: the sequence *qu* as in *quit* is an acceptable orthographic sequence while *kw,kwit* is not—barring marginal instances (*kwazy kat*) which are metaorthographic jokes. Huge numbers of words and classes of words have a significant arbitrary component in their orthographic representations. For example, knowledge of the spoken language alone does not allow a prior decision on which of *chute* and *shoot* refers to marksmanship. (Admittedly, once this is known, there is some systematic morphophonemic regularity in the orthography; that is, *parachuting* is not quasi-marksmanship.) Thus some orthographic facts are unaccountable on a phonological hypothesis: the one sound "oot" is written in different ways (*shoot, chute, suit, newt, route*) and two different sounds are often written in the same way (*boot, foot; pint, mint; worm, form*). Since these items are learned and recognized by readers, and since they yield clear word-superiority effects—just as do the phonologically more coherent items—it follows that orthographic patterns can be learned on an extra-phonological basis.

Other evidence already suggests that orthographic structures can be learned and used without phonology to some extent; the word-superiority effect appears in congenitally deaf subjects. Furthermore, Reber (1967) has shown that subjects can utilize new orthographic "rules" that have no phonological semblance. Exposed to consonant sequences (e.g., MVTRLR) which are generated by sequential rules (e.g., R can be followed by L or R), subjects learn the rules implicitly. Although the subjects are often overtly unaware of the regularities, no less the rules, after exposure to a series of such items in what they think is a memory experiment, they are able to classify other consonant sequences as to whether they belong with the original set, that is, whether they follow the underlying orthographic rules. Since these effects occur quite rapidly, we can conclude that humans are quite good at detecting regularities in alphabet-like representations even in the absence of a phonological basis (see also Brooks, this volume).

What is the nature of the nonphonological sequential units that are formed, that is, how can one define a "well formed orthographic representation" of some word or pseudoword? This matter is rather obscure. We know that readers are not simply acquiring global recognition of frequent sequences, for letter strings like KTER (which contains the high-frequency trigram TER) yield no word-superiority effect. The pseudoword PIDE, on the contrary, does yield the word-superiority effect—and for deaf subjects too. It is tempting to suppose that the orthographic units correspond closely to phonology at the syllabic level (KTER is not a possible syllable or integral sequence of syllables); but this "explanation" throws no light on the word-superiority performance of congenitally deaf subjects. The reader evidently responds selectively to some overall "English-like" properties of a letter sequence that are only partly describable as its phonological properties. Having said this, we acknowledge that a definition of "orthographically English-like" is not easy to come by.

Summarizing, phonologically coherent properties of English words are analyzed and utilized by fluent readers (they read *off* faster than *cough*); they do not read English as though it were a logography. Yet explicit phonological decoding is often by-passed (*seen* is not unduly confused with *scene;* artificial orthographies without phonological bases can be learned readily). An orthographic unit is constructed on the basis of phonological principles (NIDE yields a word-superiority effect while KTER does not) and some other (unknown) principles of pattern recognition (the deaf have a word-superiority effect for NIDE).

b. Superficial syllabic representations. When the reader encounters new or unfamiliar words, he most certainly forms an explicit phonological representation (he can "read" pseudoword texts; he can read words in his spoken vocabulary the first time he sees them). The strong preference for phonological representation in short-term memory suggests that he will represent the word in phonological form for at least the time that it takes to go from the printed page to the nearest dictionary.

When the reader does opt for an explicit phonological representation, it seems natural to suppose that he does so in terms of the surface syllabic unit. We have argued (Gleitman & Rozin, this volume) that the syllable is the smallest concrete independently pronounceable unit of speech and that analysis of this unit into its component phones appears to add processing time even for sophisticated readers of alphabets (Savin & Bever, 1970).

Notice that the number of English syllables to be learned as wholes on this view (about 5000 by one estimate) is not too different from the number of whole units we know are learned by rote by *educated* Chinese readers (about 4000 by one estimate). The separate memorization of 5000 items would surely place an enormous burden on the young learner of English reading, just as it does for Chinese children. However, it is not unlikely that a fluent reader, after years of experience with the printed page, recognizes these items as orthographic units. Plausibility here is bolstered by the fact that the syllables need not be *learned* independently of the underlying phonological mnemonic; we hypothesize that they are learned with the support of their underlying phone–phoneme coherence. But introspection (as well as the Savin & Bever evidence) suggests that whole syllables come to be operative units for the fluent reader approaching novel materials. For example, try to pronounce the word ROBATALIFIC. It hardly seems necessary to try to blend together the R and the O ("rrrrr–ooooo; aha, RO!"). Quite the contrary, one seems to work syllable by syllable (roughly, RO–BA–TA–LI–FIC).[3]

2.5 What the Average Reader Does

On the basis of the various arguments and experimental findings we have cited in this review, it seems fair to conclude that the adult reader plods from the bottom up and explores from the top down in a highly automated and critically integrated series of information manipulations. Certainly, in view of memory load issues, we must assume that the reader makes low-level initial identification in terms of phonological–orthographic units. At the same time, it is just as clear that high-level expectations and context effects influence the letter-to-meaning sequential process by filling in and correcting letters and words, guiding future saccades, and interpreting ambiguity. Even these higher-level processes are often automatized, along with the letter–word–meaning pathway, freeing the mind for such gainful activities as enjoying novels–getting the big picture.

We hold that the fluent reader represents print in initial processing in accordance with well learned orthographic rules, based in large part on phonological (phonemic and syllabic) principles, but certainly including morphological principles as well. For items frequently encountered, it is unclear in detail how much direct phonological decoding continues to occur for fluent readers. For items that are new or relatively unfamiliar, we expect that explicit phonological representations are formed, based on superficial syllabic units. The normal English reader, in our view, never abandons the alphabet in favor of a logographic (whole-word) representation of print except, perhaps, for a small stock of highly frequent words. His speed, accuracy, and holistic interpretation in spite of the molecular nature of his processing units are accounted for in terms of versatile strategies of chunking, automatization, and parallel processing, the very

---

[3]Notice that the difficulty of absolute syllable segmentation is not relevant here. One could as easily say ROB-AT-AL-IF-IC. The difficulty and arbitrariness of syllable segmentation could become issues only if we try to describe the overall language organization in terms of this (or any other) superficial unit of pronunciation. But we are not suggesting describing English in terms of its syllable structure. We suggest merely that the superficial syllable is a useful heuristic in a strategy for recovering pronunciations of unknown printed sequences.

same processes that evidently enable listeners to construct meanings from minimal acoustic properties of the speech signal.

3   THE PRELITERATE CHILD

The foregoing analysis of the knowledge and behavior of fluent readers, even if correct and sufficient, can hardly tell us how to teach children to read. The relationships between performance goals and the type of teaching required for them is marvelously varied. In some cases, such as walking, explicit teaching is altogether unnecessary. For skills such as performing arithmetic calculations, formal instruction in principles and extensive direct practice are usually required. Sometimes what is appropriately taught may not be a detectable component of the final performance, but rather a means of getting into a position from which the final goal can be achieved, much as a scaffold functions for building construction. An example here is teaching snow plowing to novice skiers; this skill aids the novice in attaining balance and controlled movement, but it is not directly employed by the skilled skier except in cases where he is in unusual difficulty. In yet other cases, what must be taught may be a distinct, minor, but nevertheless critical component of a complex task. A driver receiving a new car may be unable to operate it simply because he cannot engage one of the newfangled ignition-linked safety belts; he can easily be taught this subtask which is critical, but hardly central, to the driving process. Consider as a final example a task analysis of bicycle riding. Surely many complex skills are involved here: steering, pedaling, balancing, and the like. But the novice bicycle rider is almost certainly a fluent tricycle rider. Taking this into account, the main focus of teaching should be on maintaining balance, and this skill is often attained not through instruction but mostly by spontaneous practice and hard scrapes.

The general point here is obvious but often overlooked in the literature of reading instruction: one cannot jump from an analysis of the final product to a program for teaching it. Adult task analysis is only a first step. For the case of reading, we first ask what the preliterate child brings to the task; surely this need not be taught. Similarly, we consider what the child will learn relevant to reading in the process of normal development during the school years, that results simply from becoming more sophisticated with language and with the experience of reading. It is only the residue that must be taught.

3.1   What the Preliterate Child Already Knows

Many children have only the dimmest notion of the specific nature of reading, of how adults go about extracting the stories they read aloud from books (Downing, 1970). Yet they bring to school a variety of perceptual and linguistic skills that will be relevant to the eventual acquisition of literacy.

3.1.1   Visual–Perceptual Skills and Visual–Auditory Translation Skills

Some children have great difficulty in recognizing, and especially naming, the letters of the alphabet (see Gibson, 1965, 1970; Harris, 1970, for discussions of this issue). This fact has sometimes led to the view that difficulties in visual detection or discrimination may be a critical weak link in reading acquisition. Certainly, as far as this deficit exists in first graders, it might be expected to interfere with learning to read. However, the variation in visual naming abilities that may exist does not seem adequate to explain the large variance in reading abilities. Most kindergartners have it within their capacity to discriminate visually the letters of the alphabet (Calfee, Chapman, & Venezky, 1972; Calfee; Williams; both this volume). In fact, children of this age are quite proficient at extracting information from the visual world in general. Presumably this involves sampling, making inferences from partial information, and the like. Sensibly enough, children are rarely given lessons in *looking* or *seeing* at school.

In the area of visual-to-auditory translation, a process clearly relevant to reading, most kindergartners are quite proficient. Were this not so, it would be hard to account for their extensive visual-recognition vocabularies, including the ability to name a large number of people and many objects by sight. It is not surprising, given the high correlation between IQ and reading ability, that those who will become better readers already possess a larger spoken vocabulary at five years of age than those less likely to become proficient readers. Yet even the least talented five-year-olds can name a very large number of objects and events. Surely visual–auditory translation differences cannot account for the inability of some children to discriminate and name the 26 letters of the alphabet.

Some experimental support for this view comes from a study by Rozin et al. (1971). They taught second graders with severe reading disability (characterized as the inability to read unfamiliar, regularly spelled, three-letter words) to identify 30 Chinese characters with the proper English words. After three to six hours of instruction, these subjects could read stories written in the Chinese notation with fair comprehension. (See Fig. 3 of Gleitman & Rozin, in this volume, for examples of some of the sentences these children were able to read.) We cannot say that skilled English readers might not have learned this new reading task even more quickly, but the relative efficiency with which this type of reading was acquired by very poor readers argues against strong rate-limiting effects of visual discrimination or visual–auditory translation capacities. Whatever difficulties these children were having with English reading, it does not seem to be describable primarily as a deficit in the abilities needed to detect and identify the 26 alphabetic squiggles.

The fact remains that for some children there is a significant problem with letter identification. Despite the small size of the letter set in comparison to the child's visual vocabulary, many do encounter modest difficulty in learning to name the letters. Our observation in kindergarten classrooms suggests that this problem is often a matter of visual–conceptual confusion or interference. Many children we have seen recognize the written letters as letters and know the set of letter names, but have trouble matching them accurately to each other. Some care in the timing and order of presentation of the 26 items may be expected to mitigate this problem.

3.1.2 Auditory–Perceptual Skills

Many five-year-olds have difficulty in naming the sounds that occur in words. This has sometimes led to the view that auditory discrimination difficulties are implicated in reading acquisition. An example of the issue here is the response pattern of young children to the Wepman Auditory Discrimination Test (Wepman, 1958), a reading-readiness test. Children are required to respond "same" or "different" to pairs of simple spoken words which are either identical or minimally phonologically distinct (that differ in one phonemic segment). Many five-year-olds fail to respond appropriately in this task, and difficulty in this regard correlates to some extent with reading difficulty in early stages. On the basis of these and similar findings, some educators advocate teaching children to "hear" the appropriate sound distinctions. However, difficulty in auditory discrimination skills is not really the explanation of these correlations. Blank (1968) has shown that children who do poorly in answering the same/different question of the Wepman test are entirely capable of *repeating* the various items correctly. That is, a child who reports that *pat* and *bat* are "the same" in the usual test condition, will make the appropriate distinction if asked instead simply to repeat each word after hearing it spoken by the tester. (This is not really surprising since, after all, five-year-olds are perfectly capable of understanding conversations about bats and rats and cats without confusion.) Thus there has been a misinterpretation of why children fail these tests. Evidently the child does have the appropriate acoustic–perceptual skills. He lacks either the ability to understand an instruction to answer "same/different" or to focus on "sound" in words as a basis for following such instructions. In either case, as we will later discuss, a correlation with later reading skill would be expected.

The facts of initial language acquisition make clear that auditory discrimination deficits for language materials cannot be a major source of reading difficulty. Eimas, Siqueland, Jusczyk, and Vigorito (1971) have shown that infants under one month of age—who give no evidence of understanding any meaningful words at all—can discriminate between physically similar syllables such as PA and BA. Further, three-year-olds can get mixed up saying tongue twisters, even though this fumbling depends logically on being victimized by delicate phonetic properties of one's language (e.g., the difficulty of *She sells sea shells . . .* is in the close similarity, but significant difference, between the phonemes S and SH). While some high-level morphophonemic processes may still be absent in the young prereader (Moskowitz, 1973) and while phonemic groupings may differ to some extent between young children and adults (Read, 1971), the child of three or four has mastered the preponderance of phonological distinctions and relations in his native tongue, both in speech and perception (Moskowitz, 1970; 1971). Perceptual problems with the sounds of speech thus cannot be assumed to play a major role in reading disability, except in rare individuals.

3.1.3 Syntactic and Semantic Skills

Poor readers have trouble understanding the meanings rendered on a page of print; they perform poorly on reading comprehension tests. This has sometimes led to the view that those with reading difficulty have deficient understanding of "meanings." But of course the individual scoring poorly on such a test may be having trouble decoding the print rather than having trouble with meanings. (A "listening comprehension test" would be one method for disentangling these issues; for discussion, see Gleitman & Rozin, this volume). Similarly, ill-formulated dialect biases have sometimes led to the view that knowledge of syntax is deficient in kindergartners who have trouble acquiring reading. That is, lower-class status and nonwhite race are predictors of reading difficulty and also form relatively distinct dialect groupings, and so it has sometimes been assumed that the "inadequate" syntax of nonstandard speech is implicated in reading difficulty. Labov (1970, 1973) has argued persuasively that the syntax of nonstandard speech is equivalent in logic, even if different, from that generally approved in the schools. There is nothing obvious in the syntactic properties of these dialects that would seem to account for poor early reading performance.

Virtually all kindergartners are reasonable speakers and understanders of their native tongue. A striking fact about language acquisition is its speed. The major milestones in this process are long passed in the five-year-old (Lenneberg, 1967; also see Dale, 1972, and Gleitman & Gleitman, 1970, for reviews of the relevant literature). Although some of the most complex aspects of language structure and interpretation are not apparent in five-year-olds (Chomsky, 1969; Osherson & Markman, 1975), *almost every kindergartner is capable of understanding utterances far more complex than anything he will be asked to read during the first few years of school.* Surely the ability to understand English is not limiting the progress of children through such masterpieces as "Run, Spot, run!" This same comprehension of speech of course secures the presence of adequate auditory perception and speech processing in young children.

3.2 What Is Not Known: The Problem of Access to Linguistic Knowledge

It is clear from the preceding sketch of the prereader's competence that he is in possession of visual and auditory perceptual skills and linguistic skills prerequisite to reading before he comes to school. Then what is missing that makes it so difficult to learn to read? Of course the child usually has no clear idea of the general framework, the dimensions and details of the task he faces (Downing,

1970). Further, some problems of setting and motivating the task are relevant to the initial solution; we reserve discussion of these facts for later (Section 4.2.1). We believe there is a cognitive problem as well: although children "know" the structure and content of their language in the weak sense of being able to use it effectively, they cannot necessarily *access* this knowledge toward the solution of further problems, such as reading. We believe that conscious awareness of, and access to, implicitly known language facts and processes are necessary for learning to read. We will argue that access to low-level ("surface") aspects of language is more difficult to come by than is access to high-level ("deep" or "underlying") aspects of language. Thus we claim that difficulty in understanding the phonological basis of alphabetic orthography (the child's insufficient access to the segmental nature of his own or another's speech) is the major cognitive barrier to initial progress in reading, and that this must be taught.

Everyday speech and understanding are evidently insufficient skills to guarantee literacy. The capacities required for reading are of a special sort and are not indicated by ordinary speech production and perception. While individual differences surely exist, virtually all children have the fundamental machinery for decoding speech input into meanings, and encoding meanings into a phonologically realized organization. But for reading to be learned, one must focus on features of language that are unattended in ordinary language use. This problem, in our view, is an instance of a more general psycholinguistic relationship: *The lower the level of the language feature that must be attended to and accessed for any languagelike activity beyond comprehension, the more individual differences we find in adults; further, the lower the level of the language feature, the later its accessibility to the language-learning child.* Semantics is easier to access than syntax, and syntax easier than phonology. Within phonology, again, global syllables are easier to access than are phonemes and phonetic features. It follows that it will be relatively hard to learn a script organized around the phoneme concept.

3.2.1 Access to High-Level Language Features

At first glance, it might seem that the high-level, meaningful aspects of language would be those that differ most among adults of differing linguistic capacities. After all, verbally talented people are those who have large vocabularies and who understand ornate poetry and complex prose. Yet at least for certain kinds of materials, we find striking *similarities* across adults in the ability to think about and comment on semantic novelty in language, but enormous *differences* in the ability to think about and comment on surface syntactic novelty. For example, Gleitman and Gleitman (1970) asked adults to paraphrase novel three-word nominal sequences. They found that two educational groups (clerical workers and Ph.D. candidates) could understand and paraphrase more or less equivalently such semantic oddities as *house foot-bird* ("a bird with large feet who lives in houses," or "a live-in livery bird"). On the contrary, only the highly educated group handled perceived syntactic oddity by changing the categorial assignment of words (e. g., *bird house-black* was paraphrased by an educated subject as "a blackener of houses who is a bird" and *eat house-bird* was paraphrased as "a house-bird who is very eat."). The response style of the clerical group was quite different. These subjects paraphrased syntactic oddities by ignoring, rather than manipulating, their syntactic properties. *Bird house-black* was typically paraphrased by this group as "a black bird who lives in the house"; *eat house-bird* was paraphrased as "everybody is eating up their pet birds." In short, when taxed, the average group focused on plausibility and meaning, while the highly educated group focused on the syntax, even when meaningfulness was thereby obscured (as it surely was in the response "a house-bird who is very eat."). Manipulation and puzzle solving with low-level syntactic features seem to be attributes of linguistically talented people. This difference is apparent even though one can show that the syntactic structures in question are handled adequately, for the sake of normal production and comprehension, by both populations. The only clear difference is in *focussing on* the syntactic features, *accessing* and manipulating tacit knowledge in a noncommunicative setting. On the contrary, everybody appears to be able to focus on questions of semantics and to comment about these outside a communicative setting. Surely this does not imply that adults are all equal in their ability to analyze complicated meanings in everyday life—not everyone can understand Kant or Joyce. But across a range broad enough to be of considerable psychological interest, all normal individuals can realize quite consciously that some expressions within their semantic compass (however limited this may be) are "meaningless" or "odd in meaning." Everyone knows there is something peculiar about the sentence *George frightened the color green* and can "fix it up" via some semantic change. But not everyone can focus on a syntactic anomaly and perform an appropriate syntactic manipulation to repair it, even if they are in productive control of the construction during ongoing conversational exchange. In this sense, "meaning" can be brought to conscious attention more readily and more broadly than can syntactic form. Apparently, descending to phonological levels, the facts are similar. Jotto, Scrabble, anagrams and cryptograms—all in part phonological puzzles—require skills that are unequally distributed in the population. Perhaps plays on words and puns are not the lowest form of humor after all.

Summarizing, differences in adult linguistic performances in a conversational setting are not especially dramatic; the differences among people seem to be more of quantity than of quality. But differences that are qualitative and sometimes categorical appear between populations when we ask people to think about language and to perform manipulations that do not directly serve communication. Such matters are surely relevant to the enjoyment of modern poetry or the writing of literary criticism. But can such exquisite distinctions among population groups, in restricted "metalinguistic" skills, be of relevance to widely distributed skills such as reading? We think so. While it is easy to learn and use language, it is hard to think about language, to submit one's own behavior to analysis, to recognize that arbitrary squiggles on a printed page can be thought of as "referring to" some analytic representation of speech.

The relation of metalinguistic awareness to questions of reading becomes clearer when it is noted that similar results are seen developmentally. Shatz (1972) and Gleitman, Gleitman, and Shipley (1972) asked children to detect and comment about anomalous sentences. The instructions were deliberately vague: "Tell me which of these sentences are good and which are silly." They found that children of five years typically recognized and commented on matters of semantics and plausibility (in the world) of the stimulus sentences. For example, *The men wait for the bus* was rejected by five-year-old suburbanites on the grounds that only children wait for busses. *The color green frightens George* was rejected on grounds that green can't stand up and go "Boo!" But violations of syntax that scarcely affected meaningfulness went unnoticed by these kindergartners (examples are *Claire and Eleanor is a sister; Morning makes the sun to shine*), even though these subjects did not make such "errors" in their own spontaneous speech. On the contrary, the seven-year-olds in these studies adopted a syntactic strategy in response to the same instructions that is similar to that adopted by adults asked to judge the "correctness" or "grammaticality" of sentences. The seven-year-olds usually accepted semantically odd or implausible sentences as "good" and not "silly." For example, a subject responded to *The color green frightens George* by saying "Doesn't frighten me, but it sounds OK." But these same subjects rejected meaningful but syntactically anomalous sentences. For example, in response to *Claire and Eleanor is a sister,* a seven-year-old commented "You can't use *is* there: Claire and Eleanor *are* sisters." Thus the surface structure anomaly is harder for the kindergartner to spot than the high-level meaning anomaly, while the syntactic anomaly becomes more salient to the seven-year-old in response to general and vague instructions about "good" sentences. It is of some interest in the same regard that most five-year-olds fail to understand constructional puns while seven-year-olds generally enjoy them.[4] Differences in the levels of linguistic analysis accessible to reflection at various ages contrast with the facts of speech acquisition: children learn to speak with adequate syntactic form well before they express very complex thoughts, but they come to *notice* oddities of thought (that are within

---

[4] Gleitman and Brill (see Brill, 1974) found that five-year-old children will indeed laugh at puns, but probes reveal that they understand only one side of the ambiguity involved. For example, in a typical joke, a genie told by his master, "Make me a milkshake!" responds, "Poof: you're a milkshake!" The younger subjects laugh, but explain the joke by saying that a milkshake isn't much of a wish. The seven-year-olds respond in terms of the difference between *Make a milkshake for me* and *Make me into a milkshake.* How, then, do the five-year-olds know enough to laugh? It turns out that the format: "Why did the X Y the Z? Because he was Q!" will get a (slightly forced) laugh from any self-respecting five-year-old who wants to make the social scene. Canned laughter on early-evening TV no doubt accelerates the acquisition of this strange propriety.

their compass) before oddities of syntax, even that syntax that they have under productive control.

When descending linguistic levels, the facts appear to be the same. Children of five can be taught the difference between the concepts "word" and "sentence" with little difficulty, but it is hard for them to distinguish among such concepts as "word," "syllable," and "sound" (Downing & Oliver 1973–1974). Children of five and six have some mild difficulty segmenting speech into words (Holden & MacGinitie, 1972), often failing to isolate connectives (such as *and*) and deter-miners (such as *the*) as separable words. They have greater difficulty in seg-menting words into syllables (Rosner, 1974; Liberman, Shankweiler, Fischer, & Carter, 1974; and Liberman et al., this volume). But they have the greatest difficulty of all in segmenting words or syllables into phonemes (Liberman et al., 1974; Rosner, 1972; Elkonin, 1973; Rosner & Simon, 1971). In sum, the lower the level of linguistic organization called for, the more difficult it is for young children to respond to noncommunicative linguistic activities in these terms.

We claim that a major cognitive problem in reading can be viewed as a subpart of the more general problem of linguistic, or "metalinguistic," awareness where large individual differences coexist with identical tacit linguistic knowledge. Accessing low-level (phonological) linguistic features is a central cognitive barrier to reading acquisition. We have stated this view elsewhere (Gleitman & Rozin, 1973a; Rozin, 1975). Related positions have been taken by Mattingly (1972), Shankweiler and Liberman (1972), Savin (1972), Downing, (1973), and Liber-man, et al. (1974). We now turn to documentation of this claim.

3.2.2 Access to Low-Level Language Features: Reading and Phonological Awareness

Many inner-city youngsters fail to understand a fundamental relationship between sound and writing: words that take longer to say are written with more letters (Rozin, Bressman, & Taft, 1974). Specifically, children were shown word pairs such as MOW and MOTORCYCLE and then told, "One of these words is *mow,* the other is *motorcycle.*" They were then asked: "Which one is *mow*?" Pairs always consisted of a very short word and a long word, such that the target word could easily be discriminated by spoken and written length.

Only 10% of inner-city kindergarten children satisfied a strict criterion of correct response in 7 out of 8 pairs, and ability to describe, even in the simplest terms, the relationship between lengths of spoken and written words. Only 48% of inner-city children who had completed first grade met this criterion. Only 60% of inner-city second graders met the criterion. In contrast, 43% of children in a suburban kindergarten met this criterion (Rozin et al., 1974). These population differences exist despite the fact that all these children can talk and understand.

It is certainly true that somewhere in every little brain the word *bag* is generated by three sequential commands, and that the difference between *bag* and *tag* is appreciated, and referred to different meanings, based on the difference in a single phoneme. Why, then, can some six- and seven-year-olds not appreciate the sound difference between *pat* and *bat* in the context of the Wepman Auditory Discrimination Test (see Section 3.1.2)? What is missing, we submit, is access to the speech machinery in the head for a task other than that for which the machinery was evolved: speech production and perception.

The machinery involved in speech production and perception, as described by A. M. Liberman and his colleagues (for a review, see Gleitman & Rozin, this volume), appears to be confined in most individuals to the left cerebral hemisphere, and in particular to those portions of this hemisphere that border on the Sylvian fissure. Isolation of this area from the rest of the brain, caused by severe brain damage, can result in a "speaking machine," a patient capable of accurately repeating everything heard, but with no contact of any of this material to other aspects of the self, intelligence, or meaning (Geschwind, Quadfasel, & Segarra, 1968). This pathology dramatically illustrates the physical existence of a mass of nervous tissue containing the relevant phonological encoding and decoding machinery. The process of reading an alphabet demands some access to this segmentation machinery (see Rozin, 1975, for further discussion of the notion of accessing). This is the only way that the existence of three segments in *bag* would make sense since, as we have pointed out, the physical stimulus is not so segmented. Access to the phonological system in the head can be conceived as a form of conscious or unconscious realization of the underlying principles of the operation of the system; the access required of the reading learner may be very crude, but it must be at least sufficient to make the alphabet-to-speech mapping coherent. If one cannot attend at all to sound properties of the language, even in the gross *mow–motorcycle* test, surely one cannot understand the alphabetic concept.

While five-year-olds do have the phonological capacities and tacit knowledge requisite to speech and comprehension, they lack useful access to this knowledge and thus fail to bring it to bear in the solution of tasks that logically require it. In a broad survey of the capacities of kindergartners that might reasonably be considered basic to early reading success, Calfee et al. (1972) found generally adequate performance in a variety of visual tasks, but inadequate performance on tasks involving acoustic–phonetic manipulations. Thus these children could not segment words into phonemes or establish sound–symbol relationships. Note again that absence of a relevant phonological unit in the head cannot be the explanation for such deficits—the children *can* hear the difference between *cat* and *bat*; but they are not aware that the difference is, on one level, the difference between C and B. Along similar lines, J. A. Smith (1974) found that it was quite easy to train kindergartners to discriminate which of three *written* letters in pairs of trigrams (e.g., *mit/mat*) differed; they could notice and respond to this visual difference. Yet these children could not extend this task to indicate which *spoken* segment differed in the same trigrams. In short, the children could not only see a difference between I and A; they could report on it. Yet, although we know they could also hear a difference between spoken I and A, they could not in this case report on it.

Children less than six years of age do not seem to be especially dependent on phonological encoding in short-term memory (Conrad, 1972). Conrad tested children of different ages for their ability to recall the position of particular pictures in a previously exposed picture array. Performance of children above six was poorer when the names of the pictures were phonologically confusing (e. g., bat, bag, cat). Recall by children less than six years old was unaffected by the phonological properties (names) of the visual stimuli. Thus even where organization in phonological units is damaging in terms of the task requirements, older populations could not avoid this. Conrad concludes that phonological encoding is the preferred mode in short-term memory for mature speakers. One might assert, somewhat differently, that the phonological awareness—explicit knowledge—of the mature speaker can hardly be suppressed, while it is hardly there in the very young speaker.

What we know about differing phonological awareness in younger and older individuals appears as well when we compare poor to good learners of reading. For example, Liberman, et al. (this volume) show that superior readers process *written* materials with more reliance on phonological features than do poor readers in the same grade. When presented tachistoscopically with either phonologically confusable or phonologically distinctive letter arrays, the superior readers show a greater relative error rate on the confusable strings. This is another case where, for just those individuals who are successful readers, phonological organization cannot be suppressed and ignored even when it interferes with performance in the task. One might guess, on the basis of such findings, that even if superior readers *could* read without phonological involvement, they would hardly be likely to do so.

Age is a factor in successful performance in the Wepman Auditory Discrimination Test, as we have stated, when the experimental question is a request for a phonological *judgment*. Similarly, performance on this test (as opposed to the condition where a *repetition*, as opposed to a judgment, is required) has value as a predictor of reading success. That is, good readers and poor readers differ not in their underlying phonological organization, but in their ability to make judgments based on this. Broad-based studies of kindergartners' performance on a variety of tasks indicate significant predictive value for measures of phonological awareness (see Dykstra, 1966, and DeHirsch, Jansky, & Langford, 1966, for a review of this literature). A study by Liberman, et al. (this volume) gives direct evidence on this point. They show that the relative success of five-year-old prereaders in a phonemic segmentation task strongly predicted achievement in the Wide Range Achievement Test (a word-recognition reading test) when measured at the beginning of second grade. Children who can understand what it might mean to break a word into phonological pieces have solved a major puzzle in reading before they ever see a printed page. They have identified, and can respond to, a cognitive–phonological unit in their heads that has no direct physical realization in the sound stream. While we have not logically established a unique status for cognitive–phonological factors (phonological awareness or accessibility) among predictors of reading disability, we believe that the general results stated here are sufficient to conclude that these factors are of major importance.

Specific involvement of phonological awareness as a factor in reading disability is also indicated by studies on the performance of elementary schoolers on the Auditory Analysis Test (AAT) (Rosner, 1972, 1973; see also Bruce, 1964). This test involves answering problems such as, "Say MAN. Now say it again, but don't say M."[5] For first and second graders, there were substantial correlations between these AAT scores and Stanford Achievement reading scores (correlations in the range of .37–.53). A replication of this study for children from the first through sixth grades in a suburban school yielded a maximum correlation of .84 between the AAT score and the Stanford Language Arts score for third graders, with correlation values dropping off on both sides of the third graders (Rosner & Simon, 1971). Also of substantial interest in the Rosner studies was evidence of rather poor performance on the AAT in suburban sixth graders. The mean score for these children was 29.9 correct out of 40 items, or far from complete competency with this rather simple phoneme deletion task (Rosner, 1972).

Working retrospectively, one can also look at the differences between successful and unsuccessful readers in the early grades to see how these populations differ in terms of fundamental capacities or acquired skill and, just as important, in what ways they are the same. Firth (1972), in an extremely important and well designed series of experiments, has shown that groups of third graders, matched for IQ (one group at about 100 and another at about 80) but differing in reading skills ("good" and "poor" readers, by teacher judgments), perform virtually identically in such semantic tasks as guessing plausible completions for incomplete orally presented sentences. Notice that this task is very close to what

[5] In some further detail, Rosner and Simon (1971) gave children of varying ages 40 problems of the form: "Say X (e.g., cowboy, belt)"; S responds; "Now say it again without Y (e.g., boy, /t/)." The test includes two two-syllable words with one syllable deleted, 28 three- to seven-letter words with one phoneme deleted, and 10 multisyllabic words with an intermediate syllable deleted (e.g., take out *ca* from lo*ca*tion). On the whole, the two-syllable words with one syllable deleted were the easiest, with 80% of kindergartners correctly reporting *birthday* with *day* eliminated, and 52% correct on *carpet* with *car* eliminated. The next-easiest category, according to the results of this test, consisted of six items with the deletion of the terminal consonant. Only 20% of kindergartners succeeded with this category. Performance was poorest on the deletion of intermediate syllables of polysyllabic words. However, these words tended to be difficult and unfamiliar, and of course, long. Thus, sixth graders, who scored 74% correct on the most difficult category of phoneme deletions (e. g., *skin* to *sin*), scored only 44.9% correct on the multisyllabic words. These seem to involve limiting factors beyond the basic unit blending.

the "explorer" theory regards as central for good reading: read part of the text and infer the remainder on the basis of syntactic–semantic redundancy. On the contrary, Firth found (with the same subject populations) that the ability to provide acceptable pronunciations for written nonsense words (a "surface" phonological task) appropriately classified his "good" and "poor" readers (by teacher judgment) in 98% of instances. Apparently, while the extraction of meaning from print is the ultimate goal of reading, decoding rather than syntactic–semantic abilities distinguish high-achieving from low-achieving beginning readers.

Notice, however, that because Firth equated for IQ in his investigations, he may well have factored out the capacity (whatever it is) that contributes to explorer tendencies in expert readers. We know that for advanced readers there is a substantial correlation between IQ and reading success. The difference here does seem to be in extracting meaning from print (that is, the usual context for investigating relative fluency among advanced readers is a timed reading–comprehension test). Perhaps, then, Firth finds little relation between high-level ("meaning") processing and fluency among young readers because he has extracted variance attributable to such factors by equating IQ. If so, his results are interpretable only more narrowly: the substantial difference in reading ability among young readers *with IQ equated* results primarily from "phonological awareness" differences. Yet some further findings allow broader interpretation in these same terms across a range of IQs.

Firth (1972) and also Shankweiler and Liberman (1972) have shown that tests of reading meaningful materials and tests of deciphering the individual words of such materials yield essentially the same ranking of young readers. Firth's groups were IQ equated, but Shankweiler and Liberman tested across a broad IQ range. We can conclude that a critical difference between young superior readers and their mediocre peers, across the range of normal IQ's, appears to be in the low-level ability to decode a single word and not in the high-level ability to derive meaning from texts. It is of particular importance that the ability to perform word-segmentation and construction tasks continues to distinguish successful from unsuccessful readers all the way through twelfth grade (Calfee, Lindamood, & Lindamood, 1973; Rosner, 1972). Thus even at advanced stages and over a broad IQ range, the ability to think about phonology is a trait characteristic of good readers of alphabets.

Summarizing the position thus far, there seems to be strong evidence that good and poor readers, as well as younger and older individuals, will respond similarly to meaning distinctions and meaningful contexts. At the other extreme, the ability to read word lists aloud distinguishes very reliably between good and poor readers (Firth, 1972; Shankweiler & Liberman, 1972); the ability to make explicit phonological distinctions distinguishes between younger and older individuals and between good and poor readers. Apparently, an inability to notice and cope with phonological aspects of the language poses a stumbling block to reading acquisition (although, to be sure, success at the decoding skills does not fully or immediately guarantee fluency, an issue to which we will return later). Perhaps most compellingly, disabled readers can acquire a logography with little difficulty even though its symbols are arbitrary and nonrepresentational (Rozin et al., 1971). Phonology, not meaning, is at the crux of the early reading problem. Since poor readers can be shown to have the requisite phonological organization in their heads, the quintessential difficulty for these individuals appears to be in explicitly accessing their own phonological machinery.

3.3   The Syllable Is a Readily Accessible Phonological Unit

Although lack of explicit knowledge of phonology has been implicated as the prime culprit in reading difficulty, the level at which this problem occurs has not been remarked on thus far. Most of the studies we have cited asked for explicit knowledge at the level of phones and phonemes. Is the difficulty the same at all levels of phonological organization? We think not. The general findings of the Haskins Laboratory group have established that the syllable is the smallest concrete unit of speech production and perception (Gleitman & Rozin, this volume). We now argue that the syllable unit, because it is easier to access than the phoneme, is a useful pedagogical tool for teaching the preliterate what he does not know and what he is unlikely to learn on his own: how to become aware of the phonological nature of speech and, specifically, how to extract the phonemic unit from its encoding in real speech. Syllables are accessed more readily by young children than are phonemes. Syllables maintain their cognitive–perceptual salience even in adults trained for many years in the use of a phonemically based script. Syllabary scripts are easier to invent than alphabets, and apparently are easier to learn; most centrally, there is preliminary evidence that syllabaries or syllabic segmentation may serve a useful transitional function on the way to the acquisition of alphabetic principles. Some documentation of these strong claims follows.

3.3.1   Early Appearance of the Syllabic Unit

We have alluded to the fact that the more atomic the phonological particles to be accessed, the more difficult the accessibility problem becomes: children are better at segmenting and reconstituting words than syllables (Holden & Mac-Ginitie, 1972), and better at segmenting and reconstituting syllables than phones or phonemes (Elkonin, 1973). Children can be taught to tap out the syllabic units in words more easily than they can be taught to tap out the phonemic units (Liberman, 1970; Liberman et al., this volume). In memory tasks, children who fail to recall particular words that had just been presented are aided much more by initial syllable prompts than by initial phoneme prompts (J. A. Smith, 1974). Kindergartners are better at blending two syllables than two phonemes (Brown, 1971), and are better at recognizing two-syllable spoken words when a pause is introduced at the syllable boundary (PA'–PER), than when a pause is introduced at the first phoneme boundary (PUH–A'PER), as shown by Allen, Rozin, and Gleitman (unpublished manuscript; results are reported in Gleitman & Rozin, 1973a). Rosner and Simon (1971) showed that syllables are easier to delete ("say carpet without car") than phonemes (say man without M"). Quite clearly, the syllabic unit becomes accessible earlier in development than does the phonemic unit. Perhaps, then, it may be easier to learn to read in terms of this unit.

3.3.2 Learnability of the Syllabic Unit

Given the complex encoding of the phone in the sound stream (Gleitman & Rozin, this volume) it is reasonable to suspect that what is highly encoded may be difficult to extract and manipulate. The reading teacher—again, because of the encoding of phonemes onto syllables in speech—cannot even exemplify many of the alphabetic (phone–phoneme) units in isolation for the benefit of the learner. The adult, in the Savin and Bever experiments (1970; see Section 2), seems to extract the phoneme from a more readily available syllable. The child of five has virtually no access to the atomic phone unit. All these facts suggest that a syllabary might be easier to learn than an alphabet. It is relevant here to recall that the syllable occupied center stage in the history of writing for some millennia (see Gleitman & Rozin in this volume, Section 2). The syllabary notion was reinvented several times while the alphabet was invented only once; further, the alphabet was derived directly from a preexisting syllabary.

Some cross-cultural evidence may be adduced to support the view that syllabaries are easier to discover and learn than alphabets (although we present such evidence with the caveats due: many cultural differences exist simultaneously with script differences, and these may be salient indeed). The Cherokee Indian, Sequoyah, invented a syllabic writing system for the Cherokee language in the last century. Its amazing success is indicated by the fact that the Cherokee were 90% literate in their native language, using the syllabary, during the 1830s (Walker, 1969). The Cherokee experience suggests that syllabic scripts may provide a useful transition into an alphabetic system since, by 1880, Walker (1969) reports that they had a higher level of English alphabetic literacy than the neighboring white populations. This evidence is weak by itself, for we cannot equate motivational and sociological factors across the cultures, but there are some supporting cases. Preschool children in Ethiopia learn to read by chanting a syllabic text in a church language they do not understand—hardly a motivating situation, but learning is quite successful (Ferguson, 1971).

More compelling evidence exists in the case of Japanese. The modern Japanese orthography is a mixture of systems, one logographic and two syllabic (Sakamoto & Makita, 1973). All are taught at school, but the syllabic component

(*Katakana*) is taken to be far simpler, and so almost everything is written in syllabary in the first primers, while the logographic (*Kanji*) characters are introduced and taught in slow succession during the first eight grades (Sakamoto & Makita, 1973). The belief among Japanese educators that the syllabary is "easier" than the logography has to be taken seriously: Sakamoto and Makita (1973) report that many Japanese children learn the Katakana syllabic component without formal instruction before they enter school. Only infrequently is our own alphabetic system acquired spontaneously. On the contrary, mastery of the logographic Kanji components, because of the high memory load, continues into adulthood. The ease of acquisition of the Katakana syllabaries is further attested by the fact that illiteracy and reading backwardness are extremely rare in Japan (Makita, 1968; Sakamoto & Makita, 1973). Still, such evidence, without appropriate cross-cultural control, cannot be interpreted too enthusiastically. Direct evidence for the relative ease of learning a syllabary comes from our own work. We have shown that kindergartners and first graders with poor prognosis for reading English acquire a limited English syllabary with minimal difficulty (Gleitman & Rozin, 1973a). This work will be taken up in detail later (Section 4).

3.4 Conclusions

We claimed (Gleitman & Rozin, in this volume) that logographic scripts are easy both to invent and to learn in principle; however, they eventually pose a burden because of limitations on rote memory for individual items. On the contrary, phonological scripts are more rarely invented, and introduce a problem for acquisition: it is hard for the inventor or learner to see through to the principles. Yet phonological scripts are easier to learn fully, if they can be learned at all, and more efficient, for they radically reduce the number of elements to be acquired by rote learning.

Within the phonological scripts, those that make use of the basic perceptual and productive unit, the syllable, are easier to invent and easier to learn than those that are organized around the more analytic phonemic unit. Yet, at least for English with its complex syllabic structure, the syllable unit would impose a great burden on memory, for the number of syllable items is in the thousands.

The requirement for a simple accessible principle that is to be the basis of learning conflicts with the requirement for a small number of items to be memorized. We will suggest that the syllabic unit represents a middle ground in this conflict: syllables have the phonological property necessary to reduce the number of symbols in the script, while being less encoded (and thus more accessible) to the learner than are phonemes. We will argue further that the specially complex nature of the English syllable requires eventual acquisition of the phonemic concept if literacy is to be acquired. Thus we conceive a transitional role for the syllabic unit in reading acquisition.

4 PROBLEMS IN ACHIEVING LITERACY

Discussion of the preliterate child and the beginning reader has centered on the problem of achieving phonological awareness, for this seems the least likely, among component reading skills, for the child to learn spontaneously, without instruction. However, understanding the concept of phoneticization is only one step on the road to literacy. The child must learn that there is meaning on the printed page, that the page is to be sampled quickly and judiciously, and that orthographic representations must be constructed on the basis of the deep phonological and morphological knowledge already in the head. There are many low-level facts and visual—auditory tasks to be learned along the way: that the page is to be scanned roughly from left to right, that it consists of letters whose visual properties are to be memorized, and that these letters have names and associated "sounds." (See Gibson, 1965, and Brooks, this volume, for analysis of some of these problems.) In short, one does not learn to read on the basis of one instantaneous insight but on the basis of many insights, many facts, and long, often dull, practice.

Usually the beginner enters this situation having little idea what reading is all about, why one should look at the page, why the telling of a story by one's mother requires *her* to look at a page or, in particular, why one should know that the sound of B is BUH or that *sit* and *pit* belong to the "IT family." These details of everyday school life, in which teachers make pupils do lots of odd, unconnected things, are often not tied palpably to the future pleasures of literacy. Significant motivational problems arise in this situation and they are not solved quickly and easily for many children. Some of these problems have nothing to do with the curriculum itself, but rather are related to the social interactions in a classroom. The child's background, the cooperation that comes from the home, and the general school atmosphere can be expected to be relevant to his achievement. Similarly, the teacher's attitude toward the child, toward social interaction in the classroom, and toward the curriculum itself can be expected to play major roles. Further, the individual needs of a child cannot wholly be dealt with while managing the needs of 30 other children, also special, all different. It is hardly surprising to discover, then, that variables related to the teacher, to the school, and to the individual account for more of the variance in reading acquisition than does the curriculum itself (Coleman, 1966). Most children learn to read by any reading method, and some fail with any reading method.

In this light, one wonders how much to worry about curriculum design in particular. But although the curriculum may be only a minor contributor to reading success, it is the only feature of the reading acquisition situation that we can easily manipulate. We can at least be hopeful. After all, the variance in agricultural productivity owing to technology was probably low before the invention of the plough. Further, common sense—as opposed to the results of "methods testing"—suggests that the curriculum structure must be relevant to the likelihood of reading success. Learning to read is a laborious long-term task with little intrinsic reward until the skill is highly developed. Since this is so, the motivational content of the initial reading curriculum must interact strongly with the major social and individual variables that are almost impossible to manipulate. In short, we are arguing that to the extent that an appropriately conceived and executed curriculum can make reading acquisition easy enough, perhaps it will be learned despite all the obvious political and social factors that impinge on classrooms.

4.1   Approaches to a Reading Curriculum

We turn now to a sketch of some overall curricular approaches, what they require the child to learn directly, and how they address the problems of motivating the novice to acquire a set of skills whose purpose he perceives only dimly, if at all.

4.1.1   Learning to Plod; Some Motivational Vices

Largely because the common-sense view of reading suggests a critical phonological encoding stage, a great many curricula based on the letter-to-sound-to-meaning conversion have been devised over the years. Existing studies comparing these various decoding curricula, or groups of such methods, do not clearly discriminate among them in terms of overall success (see Williams, this volume). All sound-stream-oriented approaches are moderately successful: most children learn by any of them, and a small but significant minority fails (Bond & Dykstra, 1967; see also Chall, 1967, for a major review).

Failures of all decoding approaches with some students is partly attributable to the extracurricular variables already acknowledged. But some of the problems may have to do with the decoding curriculum itself: how it deals with the conceptions and details behind alphabetic reading performance. These internal problems may be the source for an ultimate motivational stumbling block: the child learning to decode may not have his eye on the big picture—getting meaning from print—and therefore may cease to cooperate. It is also possible to suppose that teaching a child to decode is not the correct method at all for teaching him to read, that learning to decode is counterproductive for fluency. Ink has flowed on all these suppositions, so we must consider the facts.

Observation reveals that very early decoding acts sometimes do not lead the child to the meaning on the page. Until decoding skills become highly automated, at least, children often appear to expend so much effort and attention on decoding that they have trouble attending to the outcome—comprehensible sentences in the language of the decoder. Although the observer may hear the child correctly pronouncing each word of a simple written sentence, the young learner may report that he was "too busy reading" to understand what he just saw and uttered.

A further problem arises because the limited set of decoding strategies that can realistically be taught to a six-year-old involves inconsistencies across items, and lacks generality. A strategy that enables a child to read *try*, *by*, and cry will not automatically allow him to decipher *rye*, *buy*, and *sigh*. Even worse is the problem that even the most refined specifications for converting print into sound in many cases yield only a rough schema for pronunciation. One observes the learner giving agonizingly close renditions with, for instance, the vowel just slightly off target. He sees *dragon*, says "draygun," and is unable to derive spoken "dragon" from the context and this phonological hint. Decoding becomes maximally useful when the child learns to use the approximations this method yields to guess at similar-sounding words that are in his vocabulary and that plausibly fit the context. Development of such a strategy takes time and there is significant frustration along the way.

Despite all these problems, most children do plough through a large set of sound-to-letter correspondences during the first two years of school, with the outcome that they can read most "regularly" spelled short words—even pseudowords. Many poor readers cannot, however, read polysyllabic words. We have

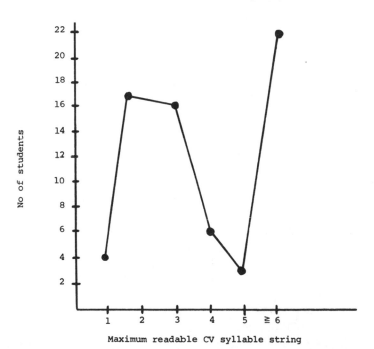

FIG. 1. Ability of inner-city junior high school students to read fluently a sequence of CV (consonant–vowel) syllables. All students contributing to this data were able to read individual syllables such as CA, GA, and FA without great difficulty. For each student, the score entered on the graph is the longest CV string that could be read fluently (e.g., an entry at 3 would indicate that a student could fluently read *la-fa-ra*, but not *va-na-za-ta*). (Data collected by Lisa Lyons, under our sponsorship.)

encountered inner-city junior-high-school students who could read simple syllables such as *ba* and *ga,* but could not generate fluent versions of pseudowords with more than two or three of these syllables, even when we marked the syllable boundaries with hyphens (e.g., *ba-ga-la*). While some students in the class we tested could fluently blend any number of syllables, others had great difficulty with strings longer than two or three (Fig. 1).

In sum, getting the insight that the alphabet represents sound structure does not result in knowing how to read soon, easily, or well. At the least, decoding must become mastered to the extent that polysyllabic words can be read with ease. In easy stages, there is failure of comprehension, confusion about the purpose of learning, and dull repetitious drill. The result in many cases must be failure to cooperate in the practice necessary for achieving the end point. That is, the problem of motivating the child through the period of detailed learning and extended drill that lead to automatization—freeing the mind for the pleasure of comprehension—interlocks with the likelihood of ever achieving that goal at all.

4.1.2   The Virtues of Learning to Plod

Recognition of the motivational difficulties in teaching decoding, as well as the potential endlessness of the set of decoding rules, has been a major impetus for devising reading curricula that initially by-pass the decoding task. If the child can be taught some whole-word-recognition skills, perhaps he can reap the fruits of the reading enterprise quickly enough so that he will want to continue learning. This push for quick comprehension has much to recommend it, but it has considerable danger if carelessly handled. If the child comes to believe that whole-word recognition is what reading is about, he may never achieve the alphabetic insights. This, for reasons lengthily stated already, is probably fatal to the achievement of literacy: one cannot read English fluently in terms of whole words.

Many aspects of the structure and content of reading suggest that the decoding issue should be faced early, despite the very real motivational problems this produces. Recall, for example, that of the 2757 different words in some Australian first- and second-grade readers, 41% occurred only once (Firth, 1972). Asking for an adult's help in recognizing such words at each instance would disrupt comprehension even more than struggling to decode. Perhaps a principal value of the alphabetic concept is that it allows the novice to re-present each item to himself, in the absence of a teacher and without prior comprehension. That is, a child who does not recognize *bat,* but who has some decoding skill, can derive it and then recognize it. He can do this again and again until he recognizes it by a more immediate, or at least faster, process. On the simplest learning assumptions, the fact that the alphabet makes unknown items systematically available for practice is enough excuse for having invented it and for pushing its adoption by learners. This is true even in the unlikely event that the fluent reader never refers to alphabetic concepts.

A decoding approach is likely to have its most consistent success at early stages of learning. For the beginning reader, newly encountered written words are almost always in his spoken vocabulary, so that deciphering them into pronunciations will in fact lead to comprehension. When an educated adult sees a new word in print (e.g., *ankylosis*), there is a good chance that, after decoding, he still will not understand it, for it is not in his lexicon. His recourse is guessing from context—a fallible procedure—or using the dictionary. At early stages, when the ratio of spoken-to-written vocabulary is greatest, decoding has the most to offer.

It is fair to note as well that the problem of decoding without understanding is often overdone. The puzzle-solving component of decoding is frequently self-reinforcing (so much so, that "Run, Spot, run!" becomes tolerable reading material). Moreover, for most children comprehension enters very early. Given the simple-minded nature of early reading materials, contextual cues serve as a ready aid to primitive decoding strategies. With some success at deciphering a few carefully drilled word classes, children begin to gain confidence that they can in general recognize words in this manner. They grow increasingly willing and able to vary pronunciations suggested by the written words to make them match known words that might fit the particular context. This heuristic becomes particularly important as the reader begins to encounter the complexities and irregularities of conventional spelling. For most youngsters, then, the decoding drills eventually lead to reading skill. Despite the motivational problems, sound-stream-oriented approaches yield superior results as opposed to whole-word approaches (Chall, 1967), and children who can segment and decode are the better readers (Shankweiler & Liberman, 1972; Firth, 1972; Calfee et al., 1973).

4.1.3 Learning to Explore the Page

We have noted that there may be a *motivational* argument for by-passing decoding as a step in reading acquisition. A *conceptual* argument for by-passing decoding is also sometimes made: it is alleged that decoding is not a component of fluent reading. A related but weaker claim is that *concentrating* on decoding will retard the acquisition of higher-level units. A number of the performances of beginning readers lend surface credence to these views for in many ways the beginning decoder acts just like the poor adult reader. He vocalizes, he runs his index finger across the page to keep his place, he sounds out words in a slow and often unproductive way, and loses track of the meaning of the text. Perhaps (some say) this is because he has been taught the wrong things, those step-by-step bottom-up procedures that must limit both rate and accuracy.

It is certainly true that many of the acts the novice performs have no place in fluent reading. Yet, as asserted earlier in discussion, these acts may serve a necessary function in building the higher-level rules used in the final performance. Scaffolds serve a clear function in building construction although, to be sure, the building is unfinished until the scaffold is dismantled. Vocalization and finger pointing may be examples of such necessary temporary structures.

Explicit conversion of print to speech by moving the lips and mumbling may serve as a mnemonic for acquiring the letter-sequence-to-meaning relations; it is well established that phonological encoding is the preferred mode for short-term information storage. Place keeping with the moving finger may help to establish the required saccades for scanning the printed page. Most important of all, whatever the status of direct phonological representation in fluent reading, we believe that the phonetic coherence of the alphabetic representations of words explains why we can learn so many of them. Learning the phonetic under-pinnings of the writing system establishes the mnemonic for acquisition (prob-ably of many thousands of superficial syllabic segments). And as the next and crucial step, the pronounced syllabic segments are in turn the mnemonic base for establishing those tens of thousands of orthographic representations known to fluent readers. Summarizing, the reader must learn a number of "plodding" activities: these will help him learn to explore; then he may discard some of the plodding acts.

Symmetrically, many of the acts of a fluent reader should be avoided by the novice, for he will trip over them. For example, we must often urge the beginner *not* to guess from context and minimal cues, because he makes too many mistakes. [Although poor readers are no worse at guessing from context than better readers in the same IQ range (Firth, 1972), they usually have insufficient contextual cues, else they would not be poor readers]. For similar reasons, we coach beginners to move across the line of print from left to right even though jumping around and sampling in the text may be the appropriate skilled performance under some circumstances. Without highly overlearned procedures for getting back to the right place, and sampling wisely, these explorer pro-cedures will merely mislead the novice.

Many of the explorer mechanisms we have described that contribute to adult reading performance (Section 2) appear to result—we know not how—from repeated practice of low-level acts. In a variety of domains, automatization and chunking, with the consequence of the formation of high-level units, come about through the sequential repetition of component acts. On the contrary, specific instructions to automate, to use high-level units, have no such effect. A well known example from Lashley (1951) is the learning of "whole arpeggios" by skilled piano players, essentially from practice in moving one finger after another. Lashley pointed out that the speed of a skilled pianist's arpeggio could not be described in terms of each finger movement serving as the cue for the next finger to move, given the constraints imposed by the time required for the nerve impulse to proceed from finger to brain and back to the next finger. Yet, evidently, one learns to perform an arpeggio by numerous repetitions in just such terms, one finger and then the next. The piano teacher cannot simply tell the novice to "play an integrated arpeggio." We believe the analogy to reading is very close. Rapid identification and sequencing of letters, words, and phrases may not be described directly as mere speeding up of the plodder's acts. Fluent performance may take place in terms of larger units. But, if so, the only way to achieve the high-level units is through the practice of components that will eventually be merged into larger unitary chunks. Telling a child to read whole meanings will not do the job.

It is necessary to acknowledge that highly automated explorer tendencies do not emerge equally in all readers. Even among the top half of adult readers, we see very large differences in performance. It may well be that practice is not enough and that specific instruction, as in speed-reading courses, may contribute to the most acrobatic levels of reading performance. Further, there is no doubt that the advanced skills will differ for those of differing verbal capacity. By about the fourth grade, for that majority of children we call successful learners, automatization and chunking have to some extent taken place, as evidenced by the appearance of a substantial word-superiority effect (Krueger, Keen, & Rublevich, 1974). At about this time for the average child, reading skill becomes comparable to listening skill and may exceed it. High-level cognitive factors of the sort measured on IQ tests, now become the prime determiners of success (Singer, 1974; Thorndike, 1973–1974). Between the early and late elementary school years the correlation between IQ and reading achievement rises substantially (Singer, 1974). (Surely what makes Immanuel Kant harder than Mickey Spillane is not a matter of decoding.)

These facts are very often misinterpreted in the educational literature to suggest that decoding is not important in learning to read. After all, since the majority of children do learn to decode, this skill ceases to have the major effect on test scores after the first few years of schooling, whatever the original method of reading instruction. But of course this must be so, for advanced reading-achievement tests are reading comprehension tests! The lingering effects of decoding deficits on understanding complex text, for the minority of children, may be submerged and masked by the massive effects of verbal-capacity differences across the whole range of children (but see Calfee et al., 1973, who show that in a manipulative decoding task there are still wide variations even among junior-high-school children).

For the average and above-average child, the various explorer techniques seem to come to the fore without explicit training. Evidence for peripheral search guidance and cognitive guidance appears as readers advance in age: the number of words read in a single fixation increases, the number of regressions in eye movements decreases, and the overall rate of reading increases (Harris, 1970). To our knowledge, these improvements do not come about by teaching; they just happen. Many, such as the use of contextual cues, are apparent in first graders (Weber, 1970) and are probably transferred from other areas of experience, such as looking at the world. Our view is that if you can teach the child to decode, the exploring will, to an adequate degree, take care of itself. We are naturally explorers of the world, and eventually of the printed page. But if you cannot teach the child to decode, he will never achieve full literacy.

4.1.4 Some Problems of Finding Out; General Problems in Testing Curricula and Their Users

Whatever the real merits of various curricula, they are very hard to discern in practice. If we had a curriculum that reduced the number of reading failures by, say, 10 or 20%, we might never discover this from normal testing and measurement procedures.

The most significant difficulty to be surmounted in evaluating a curriculum is the control, or at least measurement, of the many and powerful extracurricular variables that we have already acknowledged. But even if we could control or measure the influence of teacher, child, home environment, and the like, serious problems would remain because these factors interact in complicated ways. For example, imagine an ideal test for the relative effectiveness of two very different curricula in meeting the same goals. Even if we could procure identical twin teachers (a paired design) to instruct classes of identical children of known mental capacity, reared in isolation in a germ-free school, we would still have serious problems. To illustrate these, we consider below just those problems related to the teacher, leaving all other factors aside.

In the usual school setting, the curriculum contacts the pupil through the medium of the teacher. Therefore, the teacher's conception of the curriculum is a powerful determinant of what children are exposed to. For example, if a teacher believes that phonemic decoding is fundamental to reading acquisition, he will spend considerable time on those segmentation illustrations and exercises the curriculum provides; on the contrary, a teacher who adopts a reading-for-meaning or "language-experience" approach will deemphasize these analytic components of the curriculum. Thus neither the goals nor the priorities of a single curriculum are represented in the same way by all teachers; teachers are often very ingenious at interpreting any curriculum as an embodiment of their own preferred theory and method. In our own study of the Syllabary Curriculum (Section 4.3), some teachers emphasized syllabic "blending" (basically a decoding approach) while others emphasized rote memorization of meaningful whole syllables (basically a whole-word approach). Some teachers religiously avoided talking about the B sound as "buh" in initial instruction, while others slipped back into this familiar habit. These extreme variations occurred in fine disregard of the curriculum materials themselves, of *our* conception of the program, of the exhortations of our field workers, and of explicit instructions in the teacher's manual for use of the program.

The sources of these reinterpretations are many: the teacher may misunderstand the program or understand it all too well—and disagree with its approach for all or some of the pupils. The teacher's attempts to improve the curriculum may be helpful to learning or the opposite. In the absence of a tried and proven theory of reading and a curriculum known to embody this theory optimally, there is no educational reason to be too distressed about the teacher's manipulation of the formal curriculum. Teachers may know more about teaching reading than curriculum developers. However, from the point of view of the tester, this problem is extremely serious.

Whatever the conception the teacher grafts onto a curriculum, the general style and manner of dealing with children can be critical and may interact with the curriculum itself. For example, the teacher may contract or expand the amount of self-initiated work prescribed in the curriculum materials. Further, the teacher's view of the centrality of reading acquisition in first-grade education will affect how much time is devoted to reading instruction, rather than to nature study or arithmetic. Even if this time variation could be measured, it is close to impossible to measure how much time teachers spend on the reading issue outside explicit reading-instruction sessions. For example, in our own project, a few teachers enthusiastically applied the child's early ability to read simple English syllables to the arithmetic lession: instruction for arithmetic work was written in syllabary notation. In general, the teacher's enthusiasm for a curriculum, manifested in many subtle and some not so subtle ways, strongly influences the likelihood of success.

This last point brings us head-on to the "Hawthorne" effect, the finding that anything new has an effect simply because it *is* new, and not necessarily because it is better or worse than what went before. It is commonly stated that new curricula tend to succeed because they are new and presumably recruit enthusiastic support from all involved. This is a clear possibility, one that can be evaluated by waiting for the curriculum to become old hat. But there is an opposing possibility that may be immune to evaluation. Perhaps many curricula die aborning because their novelty falls on deaf or unenthusiastic ears. If a curriculum fails on these grounds, it will be subverted in use and probably ejected from the school before, by long acquaintance, its ideas come to seem less radical. Our own curriculum, in conception and format, is rather radically different from its predecessors. We observed teacher responses at both extremes. Some teachers clung to tried and well known methods, displaying a marked suspicion of the new and different-looking curriculum. Other teachers embraced the curriculum just because it was "innovative." Both responses occurred in schools with prior high success in teaching reading and in schools where failure has been rampant. Evidently Hawthorne effects here can represent complex interactions between type of teacher, type of class, and novelty of curriculum. Extracting and measuring these factors and interactions in a real school setting will be close to impossible.

Summarizing the position, we have tried to show that teacher-related variables make it very difficult to evaluate the relative effectiveness of two proposed curricula. But this issue is only one of many: child variables, school and home variables, and so on, can be shown by similar analysis to introduce yet further issues which in turn will interact with each other and with the teacher variables. Thus explicit testing of methods and curricula are costly, time consuming, and probably inconclusive. But the problem for practical educational research is even worse than this. Assuming, through a miracle, a clear determination of the superiority of curriculum A over curriculum B, another problem remains to be tackled. Which components of the better curriculum (or interactions of this curriculum with extracurricular variables) were critical to its success? This fundamental issue is almost impossible to formulate, no less resolve, because real reading programs for real children are not merely theoretical conceptions. A reading curriculum consists of a variety of detailed procedures, bolstered by practice materials, all of these handled in distinctive ways by particular teachers. This is because little children and their teachers require things to do every moment of the school day: circle the M, draw a picture of the D-O-G, paste your vowels in the workbook, color S-P-O-T brown. To which of these "activities" shall we attribute our success, or is it, rather, the "underlying concept" of the program that works, as we should prefer to believe?

Even in the presence of a "good" and a "bad" curriculum, with matched students and teachers, and the time and money to test all components of the competing curricula, one could not gain acceptance for objectively measured results because there is no generally agreed-upon definition of reading in the educational community. More important, the test outcomes would tell us very little about mechanisms involved in the achievement of literacy, for there is no generally agreed-upon measure of partial attainment of literacy goals. For instance, if one learner can recall and pronounce 1000 words that he has been drilled on, while another learner can read only the pitiful 8 or 10 members of the IT-family—but also can read three pseudo-IT-family words, RIT, DIT, and JIT—then which learner is closer to being a reader? There is room for disagreement among reasonable people. If one child always reads the correct line of print because he runs his finger from word to word, while another frequently is on the wrong line but keeps his hands to himself, then which is closer to being a good reader? The first, because he recognizes a relevant visual problem, or the second because he is attempting to do without a "crutch?" This implies that we will have to decide also on an optimal moment for testing reading performance: one curriculum may move the child faster to partial reading goals, accomplished more slowly with another curriculum; yet the second curriculum may get the child further in the long run. How shall we decide when the "long run" has arrived? Should we test fourth graders or eighth graders?

All of these caveats would pale inso insignificance in the presence of the perfect method of teaching reading: if all children learned quickly, there would be no evaluation problem. Even the most suspicious and neophobic teachers would be converted, for they all wish their pupils to learn to read. But the facts are that this has never happened because there has never been a curriculum so remarkably effective.

We are left in a puzzling situation. A curriculum can logically be validated in one of three ways: best of all, it produces superior results in a variety of classrooms, overwhelming other variables, even if the reasons for this are unknown in detail. This outcome has eluded all existing methods. Next best, it produces clear-cut superior effects in a controlled experimental situation; this can be achieved but the results may not apply to a classroom situation. Third, we might simply opt for a curriculum or components of a curriculum that have a sound basis in some reasonable theory of the reading process itself. This kind of validation is perhaps the best we can hope for at this moment. Armed, but hardly forewarned, with this last and weakest supposition, we have attempted to validate our own curriculum in the classroom; we turn now to an account of this adventure.

4.2 A Historical Approach to Teaching Reading

The discovery of the alphabet required millenia to accomplish. Early man was able to convey some limited ideas with pictorial representations that would "remind" the viewer of some meaning already known (such as a wise saying of the tribe). Later, in some societies, writing progressed to tracking the syntactic formatives of language (words and morphemes) by the use of logographic characters. This method was enriched by the discovery that abstract diagrams could be used to represent relatively unpicturable words. Later still, some cultures developed writing systems based on concrete ("utterable") features of the sound system, the syllables, thus reducing the number of characters to be learned. Finally, but only once, a great economy of representation was achieved by analyzing the concrete syllables into their conceptual atoms, the phones (or phonemes, or morphophonemes) of the language.

We have seen from the review of the competence of young children (Section 3) that the units and processes required for reading any script are available in the head from late infancy. However, we noted that some of these units and organizational principles are not accessible to consciousness in early life. The developing child seems to traverse, in his conscious discovery of properties of his own speech, the road traveled in historical time by those who designed successive writing systems. First, the most global meaning properties of language become accessible; second, gross properties of syntax, the arrangement of words and morphemes, can be manipulated; third, the child becomes able to access concrete syllabic sound units; last, the abstract phoneme and morphophoneme concepts become understandable. The likelihood of discovery and manipulation of abstract linguistic units and processes is also linked to individual differences in verbal capacity. Everyone can think to some extent about meaning, and everyone can learn a logographic or semasiographic script. Fewer individuals can reflect about phonology, and some individuals will not acquire an alphabet. Differences, just as in development, are with respect to abstract surface properties of the language.

The performance of "functional illiterates" and very poor readers is consistent with the assumption that they have approached English script as though it were a logography: they acquire a few hundred frequent items, and the learning curve

FIG. 2. Conceptual outline of the syllabary curriculum.

	SEMASIOGRAPHY	LOGOGRAPHY	PHONETICIZATION	SYLLABARY	INTRODUCTION TO THE ALPHABET
DESCRIPTION	Reading for meaning through pictures	Mapping between spoken words and visual symbols	Focusing on sound rather than meaning by developing awareness of sound segmentation	Constructing and segmenting meaningful words and sentences in terms of syllables	Segmenting and blending initial consonant sounds
ACTIVITIES	Interpretation of pictures	Reading material of the form: 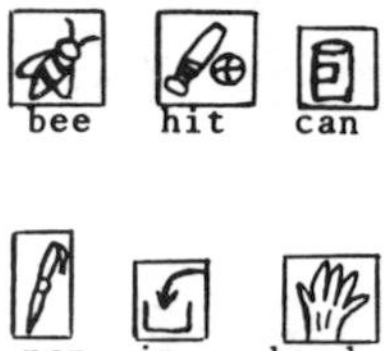 bee hit can / pen in hand	"Speaking slowly" game / Nonsense noise game  / goo la la la goo / Rebus homonyms  / man can saw can / Concrete blends 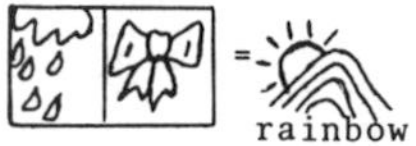 / = rainbow	Basic blends of meaningful syllables  / = sandwich / sand witch / Addition of meaningless syllables (e.g., terminal y, er, ing) 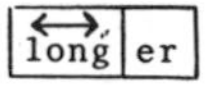 / long er / Partial fading of segmentation cues  / bee•ing	Blends using initial consonant sounds: / s•ing / s•and

tails off very rapidly as the number of items in memory becomes large, apparently at about the fourth-grade level of reading competence. The performance of skilled readers, who can pronounce nonsense materials with some rapidity, can be accounted for only by assuming that they have acquired a generative procedure for processing print.

Summarizing, history, individual development, and individual differences in language awareness and reading all show the same order of *accessibility* of the language features *available* to everyone: from global to atomic, and from concrete to abstract. All these facts suggest that if we follow the order of invention of scripts in the process of teaching them, we will mirror individual skill and concept development as well.

Traditional approaches to teaching decoding, in a typical school setting, encapsulate the discoveries of thousands of years in a few complicated remarks to the beleaguered beginner. The issues of visual renditions of meaning, phoneticization, "blending," and unit size (i.e., phoneme rather than, say, syllable or word) are all introduced in a single step. The result is often that the pupil has no idea of what the teacher is talking about. As an example, consider what is taken for granted when the teacher points to a page and says, "This is *bat*. The first sound in 'bat' is 'buh,' the second is 'ah,' and so on." What is intended, approximately is: "Represented on this page in terms of visual squiggles is something about the language you speak. In particular, the unitary abstractions underlying your perception and production of speech are represented. The particular abstractions of concern are the letter phones, which I have just given you instances of. The first of these in *bat* is 'buh' (by which I don't mean 'first in time,' for we know the B is shingled onto the subsequent vowel, but ignore that). Ignore also the 'uh' in 'buh' for this appeared merely as an artifact of constraints on my articulatory apparatus. Of course, if the word were *but*, the second 'uh' would be a vowel, not an artifact. OK? Now, the next sound is 'ah'. . ." One might hope that the teacher who says, instead, "There is a B sound in 'bear' and 'bat' " has avoided some of these difficulties, but he has not. There is a similarity in both these words, all right, but that similarity is cognitive–perceptual, not physical in any direct way. Perceiving the similarity consciously is tantamount to having the alphabetic insight, not a sure way of teaching it.

In our historical approach, we try to unravel the components of decoding, presenting them in an order from easy to hard, from earlier to later historical appearance. A sequential outline of the curriculum appears in Fig. 2:

1. We teach the child that meaning can be represented visually, by various semasiographic devices.
2. We assign to each word its own logographic representation.
3. We teach phoneticization notions: that spoken words are segmentable in terms of sounds and that written symbols can represent these sounds (hence, in particular, that words that sound alike can be written with the same character).

4. We give each utterable sound, each syllable, a unique writing and show that these syllables recombine and blend to form new words.

5. We try to teach the learner that each syllable can be dissected into integral parts, phones, that approximately correspond to alphabetic symbols.

The easy parts of writing are introduced first so that the child will gain a feeling for the idea of writing and the fun of reading before he is taxed with complexities. He can extract meaning from primitive scripts before coming to the cruncher: the unspeakable phoneme. Thus we achieve early comprehension without deluding the learner than the alphabet in particular is a direct transcription of meaning into visual arrays. If the learner gets even as far as the syllable in this sequence, he has acquired a generative device for reading words never seen before, although doubtless he will have trouble memorizing the many thousands of these that appear in English. If he can proceed further, he will be introduced to the phonemes at a point when they can be incorporated immediately into meaningful text, building on the prior syllabic base. He need not memorize the "sound" and visual shape of each of these hard, sometimes physically ficticious, items all at once before reading stories.

Summarizing, the historical approach teaches first what we know how to teach and what is easy to learn. It reserves the hardest step for last. It is hoped that what has been learned along the way will aid in taking the last step. If not, it can be used on its own terms. We now review this curriculum, which tries to embody this order of teaching and these conceptions.

4.2.1 Elements of a Historically Oriented Curriculum

The syllabary curriculum has developed gradually over the past five years. It began as a small-scale attempt to validate the theoretical views expressed in this and the previous chapter through informal attempts to teach a few first graders and kindergartners to read through the gradual stages described above. The scope and the depth of the enterprise gradually expanded: informal teaching materials became a formal curriculum with workbooks and readers, a few children became more than ten city classes, and the instructors became regular classroom teachers. This change was motivated by our faith in the underlying justification of this program, and our naïveté with respect to the uncontrollable and powerful variables described in the previous section. We believed throughout that we could validate our ideas by skipping over intermediate experimental or highly controlled studies, and simply teach a group of children with poor reading prognosis to read in a relatively brief period of time.

The Syllabary Curriculum (Rozin & Gleitman, 1974) moves through five historical–conceptual stages: semasiographic, logographic, phonographic, syllabic, and phonemic. (These steps in the evolution of writing are described in the previous chapter). It has been used over the past few years in kindergarten and first-grade classrooms, with modifications each year, and is still undergoing change. In all versions, the syllable stage occupies by far the greatest share of time and this is where we have developed most of the classroom materials. A complete program would require development of an extensive phonemic component with associated materials; however, there are in existence many reasonable programs which can in any case handle this last step.

4.2.2 Semasiography (the Reading of Meanings)

Children are first exposed to the notion that meaning can be extracted from a number of kinds of visual displays and real objects. They are read to. They try to figure out the messages in pictures that "tell a story." They play communication games in which one player must convey information to the others without speaking, using only paper and pencil or the blackboard. For instance, the teacher or pupil is asked to indicate where an object is hidden in the room; he may draw a map, a picture of the object under which the target object is hidden, and so on. In the best tradition of primitive writing, children make up personal inventories of their possessions by drawing pictures (see Fig. 2 to follow the sequence of events in the curriculum).

4.2.3 Logography (Reading Word Sequences)

Children are introduced to the idea that visual representations can track the words of a sentence. They play with a set of cards or other materials that show a picture of some word that represents an object, action, or relation (see Fig. 2). Teacher and pupils try to construct sentences with the cards (e. g., *man hit bee;* see Fig. 3) and discuss their meanings. Notice, then, that the child is not only

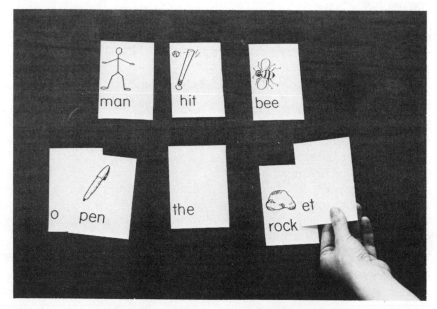

FIG. 3. Syllable cards in use in the syllabary curriculum.

reading but "writing" in the sense that he constructs messages by placing cards in sequence. Neither the semasiographic nor logographic segment of the curriculum presents any learning problem for any population we have studied.

4.2.4 Phoneticization

This is the first component of the program at which minimal difficulty may be experienced. Its purpose is to get the child to attend to the sound stream of speech, to become aware that speech can be segmented and represented visually. Awareness of segmentation is encouraged in a "speaking slowly" game, in which the teacher and later the children pronounce familiar polysyllabic words with explicit breaks at syllable boundaries (e.g., HOS-PI-TAL). The listener is to guess the word, thus in effect "blending" the syllables back together. A "nonsense noise" game introduces the notion that any sound can be represented visually. Children are asked to invent noises (a most motivating task) and a nonsense figure is assigned by mutual consent to each noise. The figures are then written out in rows on the blackboard and read off in quick sequence, with ensuing hilarity (see Fig. 2). Not surprisingly, while syllable blending and segmentation require explicit drill for some learners, the nonsense sequences come naturally.

At this point we step forward to the concept of the rebus, which involves using homographs (same writings) for homonyms (same sounds). Thus, for example, the *can* word card introduced during the logographic segment of the curriculum is now used both to represent the tin can which appears as the pictorial hint and also the auxiliary verb (e.g., *man can saw can*; see Fig. 2). This conceptual leap seems to require little or no explicit teaching; at least appropriate performance appears immediately (see Gleitman & Rozin, 1973a). The rebus represents the child's first explicit clue that the orthography maps sound and does not map meaning directly.

The pictorial representations on the cards serve a number of purposes.

1. If a picture of a can represents both the meaning referred to by the picture and also the meaningfully unrelated auxilliary verb, then it is the sound, not the meaning, of these two words that links them orthographically. This is an essential conception necessary for reading any phonography.

2. The pictorial hint is a useful mnemonic for acquiring the English orthographic form printed directly below it (evidence that this purpose was in fact served is given below; see Section 4.3.3).

3. The pictorial representation of word meanings makes reading of sentences easy by speeding up the identification of individual items.

This same pictorial approach to the introduction of reading has been used with some success in another program (the Peabody Rebus Reading Program: Woodcock, 1968; Woodcock, Clark, & Davies, 1968). The picture clue enables the child to represent to himself, without teacher aid, the required paired associates (the sound and the written form).[6] In this stage, children also play a game in which they combine pictures representing one-syllable words (e. g., *sand* and *witch; rain* and *bow*) to make new words (*sandwitch; rainbow;* see Fig. 2). In these combinations, the pictures are used for their sound value; there is no sand in sandwitch (beach-parties excepted).

4.2.5 Syllabary (Reading Syllable Sequences)

We now extend this blending exercise by introducing a larger number of syllables, written in English orthography and accompanied by a picture (see Fig. 3). In traditional programs, blending is introduced at the phone level ("BUH-AH-TUH"), where it has least physical reality. Our aim is to get the blending concept across first in terms of the concrete, physically real, syllabic segments. The syllable-blending concept, like the rebus concept, is learned with fair facility even by populations that show significant failure with alphabetic reading, though, to be sure, acquisition even of syllable blending takes some time and effort (experimental evidence of acquisition of the syllabary is presented in Section 4.3.3 and also in Gleitman & Rozin, 1973a).

In some further detail, this component of the curriculum is designed to teach the child a system of writing that is phonographic, but syllabic rather than phonemic. Between 45 and 77 syllable elements, depending on the version of the curriculum, are introduced a few at a time. The children learn to read these and then to combine them with previously learned elements to form new words and sentences, especially by manipulating syllable cards (Fig. 3). Graded readers and workbooks support these activities (Figs. 4 and 5). Most of the syllables introduced early have a word meaning (e.g., *sand* and *can*). Later, semimeaning-less or "grammatical" elements are introduced (e.g., *ing, er,* and terminal *y*). Most of the meaningful syllables are written with the picture hint above, while the meaningless syllables have (could have) no accompanying picture. The format is such that the pictures can be covered with a strip of paper while the English orthography is exposed; in this way, one can peek at the pictures only when stumped (Figs. 3, 4, 6). Some of the pictorial hints are rather abstract (e.g., & is the symbol for *and,* ▨☐ is the symbol for *side*). These hints have surprising mnemonic value, nevertheless, in part because the pictures usually do have some direct representational significance and in part because they are relatively simple and coherent visual wholes (Brooks, this volume; Rozin et al.,

---

[6] In our program, the long-term goal is not to teach large numbers of whole words or even whole-syllable representations. We believe that the mass of English written words can be learned only through realization of the phoneme concept. We use the syllable only as an interim device to ease the acquisition of the phoneme principle. We teach 77 "whole syllables" simply so that the child has some items to manipulate while learning the concept. Therefore, nothing is lost by giving him memorial assistance in acquiring items that, it is hoped, he will relearn in a more efficient way later on. The picture hints help him to store a number of units that he can manipulate with respect to the conceptions under study, reading with comprehension in these interim terms.

FIG. 4.   A page from one of the first books in the syllabary curriculum (Rozin & Gleitman, 1974).

1971). In some versions of the program, the pictorial hints were gradually "faded out" a few at a time at later stages of training. Specific exercises in matching pictorial hints with the corresponding word were provided. The convention for blending (i.e., for representing a bisyllabic word, as opposed to representing a sequence of two monosyllabic words) in this orthography is continuity of the pair of syllable cards or, on the printed page, immediately adjoined boxes (see Figs. 3 and 4). Later in training, a less obtrusive dot replaces the boxed syllables (Fig. 6). Later yet, a dot-eating monster gobbles up the dots, and explicit segmentation of polysyllables disappears (as in Fig. 7; Fig. 8 shows the dot-eating monster at work). It is fair to note that disappearance of the explicit syllable segmentation created great difficulty for children. The study did not allow us to test whether long-term problems were involved at this step.[7]

---

[7] In the most recent versions, we have decided to retain explicit syllable segmentation with the dot throughout the curriculum. Since syllable segmentation of written words creates a long-term problem for many readers trained by traditional methods, we would guess that it is worth spending considerable time and effort on instruction on this issue. Whether it is desirable to do so at an early stage of acquisition remains an open question.

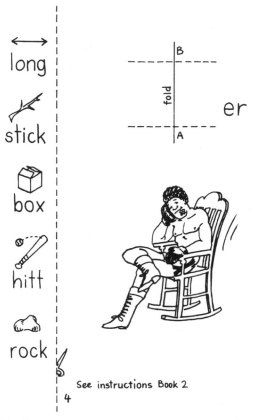

FIG. 5. A syllabic blending exercise from an early portion of the curriculum. Children cut out a strip of words and also cut along the dotted lines near *er*. The paper strip is then inserted through cuts A and B so that one syllable at a time appears next to *er* (Rozin & Gleitman, 1974).

A primary emphasis of the syllabic stage of training is the fun of reading. With pictorial hints and explicit syllable segmentation, the children can eventually read stories that use over 200 words, based on minimal phonographic insights and memorization of a maximum of 77 syllable elements. After one or two weeks of training, most children can read simple stories employing logograph and rebus without teacher aid. Children are encouraged to take the "books" home and read them with their parents. Within days to months, fluent blending and reading of multisyllabic words appears. Thus comprehension in syllabary notation, even including syllable blending, proceeds rather quickly. Rather surprisingly, the real sticking point with low-achieving populations is the rote memorization of items, not the syllabic concept. That is, items without picture aids, such as *get, the, is,* were difficult for low achievers to learn and held these learners back in spite of their progress with the phonographic concepts. In short, while this program was designed with conceptual issues in mind, it has the

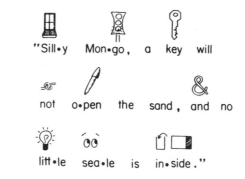

"Sill•y Mon•go, a key will

not o•pen the sand , and no

litt•le sea•le is in•side ."

FIG. 6. A page from an intermediate-level reader in the syllabary curriculum. Segmentation cues have shifted from boxes to dots. The page also illustrates the rebus drop-out procedure. The word *sand* was originally introduced with a pictorial hint (see Fig. 4), which has been eliminated by this stage (Rozin & Gleitman, 1974).

motivational virtue that its initial materials are very simple and the learner reads and comprehends very soon.

In order to construct a curriculum without the massive research that would be involved in testing each component item and determining its best form, we made many arbitrary decisions. There is no telling from what we have done whether the resulting curriculum is a particularly sound embodiment of the underlying conceptions. We tried to rely on common sense. The main problems were to decide on the number, type, and identity of the syllables we would teach.

The syllables were chosen with five criteria in mind.

1. It was obvious that the acquisition of items by visual memorization was rate limiting, for reasons that were conceptually irrelevant to the program, so we favored syllables for which we could concoct a workable pictorial hint.

2. We wanted the pupils to be able to read as many words as possible while memorizing as few items as possible, both for the purpose of displaying the

Sommy gets very fat, so

Sommy sits and rests.   5

FIG. 7. A page from an advanced syllabary book, incorporating a blending of the initial phonemes S, F, and R and the terminal phoneme S. The word *Sammy* is made up of the known syllables, *am(m)* and terminal *y* with initial *s* blended on. Similarly, *fat* is based on the known syllable *at*, and *rest* on the known syllable *est*. Terminal S is blended onto the known syllables *get*, *sit*, and *rest* (Rozin & Gleitman, 1974).

efficiency of a phonography and so that interesting stories could be written. Thus, for example, *long* and *er* were chosen for their combinability possibilities (e.g., *belong, along, longer, runner* . . .).

3. Some of the items had to be homonymous so as to display the rebus principle (e.g., *can, saw, fly, be(e)*).

4. Certain high-frequency words were necessary in the interest of smooth syntax and the sense of the stories (e.g., *it, the, get*).

5. Looking ahead to the alphabetic component of the curriculum, some of the items had to represent common English spelling patterns, rhyme relations, and the like (e.g., *and/sand/hand; it/sit/hit*).

The syllables chosen represent a composite of these criterial decisions.

A final note concerning spelling should be added. We sometimes violate English spelling conventions (e.g., *pensill*). The reason is obvious: we wanted to maximize the usefulness of a few items in constructing a lot of words, to teach syllable blending. Yet there are dangers to this course. For one thing, it upsets

FIG. 8. A workbook exercise introducing children to the elimination of dot-segmentation cues (Rozin & Gleitman, 1974).

teachers and parents. Also, we recognize that orthographic representations are the hoped for long-run output of a reading program, and not phonetic spellings. On these grounds, we made every effort to minimize misspellings while maximizing the use of each syllable within polysyllabic words. Misspellings were accepted only when the conventional spelling was relatively unsystematic with respect to the deep phonological representation of these words. On the contrary, where the conventional spelling has generality in the written language, especially where this mirrors phonological organization, we preserve it. For example, many English words double their final consonant before *er, y,* and *ing* (as *running, runner, sunny*), and it would hardly do to delude the learner on this matter. Therefore, two syllable cards were created for the initial syllables of these words (e.g., *sun* and *sunn; run* and *runn*). Both had the same pictorial hint, but the teacher was instructed to use the correct one in writing exercises (whether teachers did this, considering the considerable difficulty in finding the right card when you are looking for it, is another question) and the story books followed this convention. Rarely did a child remark on this dual representation. Summarizing, on conceptual grounds we would be delighted if, for example, our beginning pupils "erred" by spelling *syllable* as *sill-a-bull.*

4.2.6 Alphabet (Reading Phone–Phoneme Sequences)

An ideal version of this program, with ideal learners, would yield the surface phone concept as a logical extraction from the syllable concept. After all, the pupils now should know that meaning can be rendered visually, that like sounds should be written alike, and that sounds are segmentable and recombinable by blending. All they need to learn is that these procedures can be carried out conceptually in terms of the letter phonemes as well as in syllabic terms. But we know no more than anyone else about how to get readers to accomplish this last leap. In practice, our ideal learners (an upper-middle-class first-grade suburban group) made the jump with little help at the conclusion of just about a month of syllabic training. But of course we cannot say with certainty that these children would not have read fluently if taught by other methods without formal drill. Some of our urban children, in contrast, failed to learn to deal satisfactorily with alphabetic–phonemic units during the first grade (see Section 4.3.3 for discussion).

Conceptually, the program continues by introducing one phoneme unit at a time after syllabary training is complete. The idea is that these units, intractable if introduced initially, might now be understandable due to prior learning of the syllabic-blending concepts. The phonemes are to be blended onto syllables already learned at the stage before (see Figs. 7 and 9); at this juncture, the program is very similar to some of the "linguistic" methods. Notice than that as (if) each phoneme unit is learned it can be incorporated directly into meaningful text. In this sense, there is a motivational advantage to teaching syllables first. The child does not have to learn a large number of phoneme–letter correspondences all at once before being able to read and comprehend text.

Two devices were used to try to make the transition from syllable to phoneme more transparent. First, we included among the syllabary materials two syllables, *er* and *le* (as in *runner* and *little*) that lose their syllabic integrity in some words, becoming more like single phonemes (as in *beer*, from quickly pronounced BE+ER, and *whale*, from quickly pronounced WAY+LE). Moving from bisyllables like *runner* to monosyllables like *beer* was surprisingly easy for most of our pupils. A second device was to begin phoneme instruction with the continuant consonants F and S, which can be pronounced in isolation and thus can be physically blended in the sense these children were used to (SSS-AND = SAND).

4.2.7 Summary

The curriculum operates from the view that prior learning of primitive phonographic concepts will help learners get access to the phonemic principle. In this way, we try to reduce the number who fail to learn to read by traditional methods by making fewer assumptions about the knowledge they bring to the classroom; we spell out a number of prerequisite conceptions. We believe the

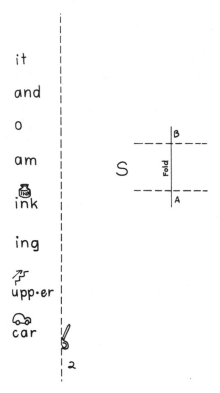

FIG. 9. An initial-phoneme blending exercise. Blending of initial S onto known syllables. Use of this activity is explained in Fig. 5 (Rozin & Gleitman, 1974).

program has advantages for high-achieving readers also, for it presents the reading issue in a way designed to give the learner insight into his own language organization and the way this may be reflected in writing systems.

4.3   The Historically Oriented Curriculum ("Syllabary") in Use

The curriculum we have described evolved over a three-year period, largely through informal use in kindergarten and first-grade classrooms. In 1973–1974, an attempt was made to provide some formal evaluation of its effects. The version of the curriculum used for testing emphasized the syllabic component of the program, with less formal emphasis on the earlier word-writing stages. The syllabary itself consisted of 77 items of which 51 had accompanying pictorial hints. During training, 30 of the pictorial hints were "faded out," 6 at a time, after fairly extensive drill in matching these pictures with their appropriate orthographic equivalents. Syllable segmentation cues were also faded out toward the end of the program (see Figs. 4, 6–8). Following mastery of the syllabary, a brief phonemic training period introduced blending of four initial letters (S, F, R, and B) and terminal S onto the known syllabic elements (see Figs. 7 and 9). Physically, the curriculum consisted of 20 graded readers (story books), 11 workbooks (graded practice exercises and games), and some additional activities. (Figures 3–9 represent materials from the 1973–1974 curriculum.)

This curriculum was used as the sole initial reading program in seven first-grade classrooms from three inner-city Philadelphia schools, all in the same school district. These schools ranged from about average (54th percentile) to well below average (24th percentile) on national norms for reading achievement (California Reading Achievement Tests). Scores of our subjects on pretests of reading readiness showed many of them to be lacking in some basic prereading skills.[8] For instance, when asked to identify the names and sounds of five common letters, the children as a group got less than half correct (the average score was 4.3 correct out of 10 items).

Problems of control and sampling were present throughout the training period, despite our best efforts. For example, the teachers were probably not a random sample of Philadelphia teachers; some of them were enthusiastic about the program, while others were suspicious. And in one case, a teacher left the school during the year and was replaced by an alternate untrained in the use of the curriculum. Further, teachers used the curriculum in various ways, emphasizing different aspects (e.g., blending versus item recognition), devoting differing amounts of time per day to reading instruction, using varying classroom styles (e.g., open versus traditional class), and differentially integrating the reading concepts into other activities. Again, despite much effort, the population of pupils was not well chosen. Although we specified heterogeneous classes, we obtained nonheterogeneous groupings in some instances (in one of the three schools, the bottom-achieving two of six first-grade classrooms were assigned to syllabary instruction).[9] The classes moved through the curriculum at very different paces. Whether this difference was due primarily to teacher style or to varying average abilities of the pupils we cannot tell. At any rate, children in five of the seven classrooms completed the program within the school year, while many children in the other two classes did not complete the phoneme-transition portion of the curriculum by the end of the year. (This contrasts with the use of similar curricula in suburban first grades where children finished the syllabary and progressed to phonics instruction in a period of at most a few months.)

[8] This reading-readiness test, of our own design, measured knowledge of letter names and sounds, rhyme, initial sounds, blending of syllables and phonemes, and the ability to read a few simple words or nonsense words.

[9] Even worse, students doing poorly in the traditional classes were in one instance, transferred to syllabary classes after about a month of instruction, while a few superior students in the syllabary classes were removed to the traditional program. This came about, apparently, because some members of the school staff viewed the syllabary as a remedial program.

Under these trying circumstances, it is difficult to glean too much information about the effects of this curriculum on learning to read. Overall, the program did not work like magic: those of our subjects with a poor prognosis for reading acquisition did not learn to read *well* during the first grade. To this extent, the program takes its place with other valiant attempts of the recent past. Although the curriculum was no panacea, overwhelming all other variables, children did make substantial progress in acquiring some hypothesized components of reading skill.

4.3.1   Learning Logographic Concepts

No child experienced significant difficulty in learning the "whole-word" initial component of the program. Thus the demonstration by Rozin et al. (1971) that children can learn a logographic script was replicated, this time using English orthographic items and group teaching as opposed to the one-on-one situation in the former experiment.[10]

4.3.2   Learning to Blend Syllables

Most of the pupils in these low-achieving populations learned to read the syllabary fluently during the school year. Even in the poorest of the classes (the bottom two first grades in a school whose entire second grade averaged in the 24th percentile on the California Reading Achievement Test norms) showed significant ability during testing to blend a new syllable they had just learned and hence had never blended before (Fig. 10C; see Fig. 10 for summary of other results). The 57 children tested in these two highly disadvantaged classes scored

[10] There were, of course, significant differences in the speed with which the 77 elements were memorized, but most children acquired most of them during the school year. Yet the fact that 77 items did take an entire year to learn for some children with a poor prognosis for reading suggests that a whole-word method is approximately hopeless even as a remedial device for acquiring literacy. It is of some interest that the pictorial hints were extremely useful for this component of the curriculum, which requires rote memorization. For most children, the most difficult aspect of the curriculum (phonemes aside) was learning to recognize those elements initially presented without pictorial hints (e.g., *the, get, but*). Some children were blending syllables fluently and reading eagerly well before they acquired these items. Children had an easier time learning the *orthographic* representation of words which were introduced with pictorial hints, whether or not this picture was later faded out. Recall that syllables whose pictures were to be faded out were first practiced in a "match-up" situation for some time so as to provide a transition from picture to orthography. No drill of this sort was presented if the picture was among those which would not be faded out. The syllabary mastery test administered toward the end of the school year included tests for the recognition of the orthographic form of two syllables whose pictures were retained, and two faded-out items that were introduced into the curriculum at about the same time. On a four-choice recognition test (Fig. 10A), children scored 82% correct on the faded-out items (25% is the chance expectation) which is not surprising in light of the drill, but also scored 63% correct on items always presented, before the test, with pictorial hints. Thus, children learn a substantial amount about the orthography associated with the pictures, and may have learned less about the orthography of items never pictured (e.g., *get*).

FIG. 10. Sample items from the test of competence with the syllabic components of the "syllabary" curriculum. Items of type A (top row of figure) test recognition of the meaning of a particular syllable. The child's task is to select the pictorial hint that has actually been used with the syllable in the curriculum (the use of *go* with its picture can be seen in Fig. 6). Children must select one of the four choices, all of which are pictorial representations used in the syllabary. The test included eight items of this type: six of the syllables tested had their pictorial cues faded out, while two had always appeared with pictorial hints. The 191 children in 7 classes scored an average of 6.1 correct out of 8. Items of type B (middle row of figure) test for the ability to recognize syllable blends already taught in the curriculum. Note that the negative choices were made as difficult as possible: one shares a common first syllable with the target word (*bull*) and another shares a common last syllable (*et*). The 191 first graders scored an average of 3.1 correct out of 5 items of this type. The items of type C (bottom line of figure) test the ability to read blends involving a new syllable element. Since the new element (*crack,* in this example) was taught just a moment before this item was presented, we can be confident that the child had not encountered *cracker* before. Again, the incorrect choices have some phonological resemblance to *cracker.* The 191 first graders scored an average 2.7 correct on 4 items of this type. Children from the two slowest classes scored an average 2.2 correct.

an average of 2.2 correct out of 4 new syllable blends, where 1 would be expected by chance guessing. That is, they could make some use of the concept of blending to decipher novel instances. What we know of this population suggests that these children would not have made comparable progress in acquiring alphabetic–phonemic materials. It is fair to conclude that teaching a syllabary is far easier than teaching an alphabet to populations with a poor prognosis for reading acquisition. It is our guess that, at least for those populations that find the phonemic concept intractable, a remedial syllabary approach will provide significant benefits. After all (and despite the large number of syllables in English), the number of words readable by blending new syllable combinations will increase increasingly faster than the number of syllables separately memorized (see Gleitman & Rozin, 1973a, for a discussion of this possibility).

4.3.3 Learning to Blend Phonemes

Despite successful acquisition of the syllabary, many of our subjects experienced great difficulty with the concept of initial phones. The hope was that concepts acquired during syllabary training would be transferred when the phonemic unit was introduced in the context of known syllables. (This hope, in fact, accounts for the paucity of phonics-drill materials in the curriculum as then conceived.) Significant learning of phoneme blends did occur as evidenced by children's ability to blend an initial letter onto a new (just learned) syllable to form a recognizable new word (Fig. 11B; see Fig. 11 for more details). However, our pupils seemed to be no better and no worse at understanding the phonemic concept than pupils in traditional phonics-oriented classrooms. This conclusion is derived from testing them at the end of the school year with a matched sample of comparable students from the same school district who had studied phonics concepts in traditional curricula for the whole school year. Before training began, we had administered a reading-readiness test[8] to a random sample of children entering syllabary classes and also to a somewhat larger number of

FIG. 11. Sample items from the test of competence with the initial phonemes introduced at the end of the syllabary curriculum. The general scheme employed is the same as that described in Fig. 10. Both sample items shown here involve blending of initial *r*. In items of type A, the blend (*ring* in this case) involves a syllable (*ing*) which was learned during the syllabary component. Children were actually exposed to these test words (e. g., *ring*) during the "phonemic" section of the curriculum. The 134 first graders who finished the curriculum (5 classes) scored an average of 3.2 correct out of 5 items of this type. The 57 children in the two slowest classes that did not get significant exposure to this last part of the curriculum scored an average of 1.3 correct, or approximately chance. Items of the type B (bottom row of figure) involve new blends. In the example, the syllable *ip* was introduced just before presentation of the test item, *rip*. On the 8 items of this type, the 134 children who completed the curriculum scored an impressive average of 6.3 correct, while the 57 children in the two slower classes averaged 3.5 correct, significantly above the chance level of 2 correct.

children in ten roughly equivalent traditional classes in the district. At the year's end, all children in the district took the California Achievement Test (reading–vocabulary), administered by the teacher. This test measures word recognition, letter recognition, and initial and final phone recognition skills. We matched 60 syllabary with 60 control children so that the pretest scores of members of each pair were at most one point apart. Looking at relative performances of members of each pair, the control child was superior in Achievement Test score in 31 cases, the syllabary child in 26 cases, with 3 ties. Clearly there is no difference on this measure between the groups. Neither method resulted in good reading skill during the first grade.

Is the syllabary method ineffective in teaching phonics skills? We do not know, for the fact is that the syllabary pupils knew as much about letter sounds (phonemes) after a few weeks of instruction in this matter as did control children who were so instructed for nine months. Would syllabary children acquire these skills rapidly now, and as a consequence of the prior syllabary training? Such a conclusion would require a good deal of optimism. It is adequate to conclude (although we do not, being optimists) that the differing nature of the two curricula had little to do with the likelihood of learning to read phonemically.

But notice that even if the program failed to solve the reading problem because of internal inadequacies (rather than because of variables we could not foresee, control, measure, or even recognize) there is still no acceptable way to evaluate the notions behind the syllabary approach from what we have done: the various games, workbooks, and so on, that physically represented the theory may or may not have been appropriate embodiments of the concepts under study. In fact, a quite different curriculum, employed with a different population, but embodying many of the same concepts as ours, apperas to have had even greater success (The Perceptual Skills Curriculum; Rosner, 1971, 1972, 1974). Rosner's method involves introducing children to the problem of phonological segmentation through speech rather than writing. But, like us, he moves from concrete to abstract, first teaching children to manipulate words (e.g., "Say, 'I see you' without the 'see' "), then syllables (e.g., " 'cowboy,' 'cow': What did I leave out?"), and finally phonemes (e.g., " 'slip,' 'sip': What did I leave out?"). He reports progress with preschoolers and first graders in auditory segmentation abilities consequent upon instruction with his curriculum. Moreover, he also acknowledges greater ease in teaching syllabic segmentation than phonemic segmentation.

4.3.4 Intangibles: Possible Motivational Advantage of the Syllabary

The most striking effect of the Syllabary Curriculum according to teachers' observations and our own, is in motivating the child to read. As a consequence of the pictorial hints which reduce memory load, and syllabic segmentation which is easy to acquire and use, our subjects can read books and identify new words (blends of familiar syllables) within the first few weeks of the school year. They clearly respond enthuasiastically to this success, as evidenced by extensive reading of syllabary books during "free" periods and requests to take the books home. Since disenchantment with reading is a major stumbling block to reading acquisition in later grades, this property of a syllabary—quick comprehension of meaningful stories within a very brief time—could be integrated into a larger total reading program. It is a widespread view that many children with reading difficulties would nevertheless eventually acquire the basic phonemic concepts if they could be kept at the task, rather than tuning out because of early failure or slow progress. Syllabary instruction may provide a motivational and cognitive background for slow learners: it appropriately focusses on phonological properties of the language and provides enthusiasm for continuing practice.

4.3.5 Summary

Early work introducing phonological segmentation through more readily accessible units shows some promise but is certainly inconclusive at this stage. The major justification for pursuing curriculum development from this point of view remains a theoretical one: the general method flows naturally from a plausible and coherent conception of the language and reading processes, and their acquisition.

5 SUMMARY AND CONCLUSIONS

The aim of this chapter has been to describe the early stages of reading acquisition and to suggest means for teaching initial reading skills. The problem of initial reading acquisition raises some fundamental cognitive—linguistic issues which we have tried to discuss. Moreover, on a practical level, it seems that just those problems in initial acquisition that perplex and confound the six-year-old are those that stand as long-term barriers to the acquisition of literacy. Even after many years of explicit reading instruction, many children who are fluent speakers of their native language still have significant difficulty reading simple materials. Apparently these individuals have failed to master a few early reading concepts or skills. Without these, reading remains a chore. With them, reading becomes self reinforcing and improves "spontaneously" with practice.

The average adult reader extracts information from print about as efficiently as he extracts information from speech. The curricular goal envisaged in this discussion has been the accomplishment of this average performance. To this end, we have analyzed the process of reading and its acquisition through examination of the literature in a number of domains plausibly related to these issues. In the preceding chapter (Gleitman & Rozin, this volume) we discussed the history of writing, the nature of English orthography, and human speech perception and production. The conclusions emphasized the abstractness of phonographies and of alphabets in particular. In this chapter, we discussed the cognitive–perceptual analysis of reading in the adult, and the cognitive, perceptual, and linguistic abilities brought to the reading task by the preliterate child. We believe that information from all these areas at minimum provides clues and constraints to curriculum developers, and at best provides specific direction for teaching reading. We suggested a curriculum design that grows directly out of such considerations.

The reader is ultimately constrained by the information and its manner of presentation in the script being read. We therefore first examined in the accompanying chapter the nature of the English alphabetic writing system. The alphabet is the last and most successful major writing system in a history spanning many thousands of years. Examination of this history reveals a clear and uniform movement toward representing fewer, but more abstract, elements in each successive script: a logography represents many of the endless number of concrete words with individual symbols, while an alphabet, at least a good alphabet, represents each of the small number of perceptual–cognitive sound categories (phonemes). The logographic principle of representing concrete words visually seems to be easy to acquire, but the items to be learned are so many as to impose a limit on vocabulary acquisition owing to memorial constraints. The principle of representing phonological distinctions usually reduces the memorial task almost to insignificance, but this principle itself is apparently hard to acquire. Thus almost every Chinese learns to read a few thousand Chinese logograms; on the contrary, a significant reading problem develops almost immediately for a minority of English children reading a phonological script. But on the other hand, the average Chinese adult is severely restricted in recognition vocabulary, while the average successful English reader can read about as many words as he understands. The forced abandonment of the phonological principle in reading acquisition by congenitally deaf individuals also results in poor adult reading performance.

Analysis of the English alphabet begins to reveal some of the reasons why acquiring the phonological principle behind reading is hard. The alphabet can and does represent the sounds of speech in a complex and variable way, sometimes tracking surface phonology (e.g., in the writing *hafta* or *wanna*), more often tracking a deeper cognitive–perceptual level of phonological organization (e.g., *have to, want to*), and frequently also tracking semantic, etymological, or morephemic features (e.g., *have to, have two, have too*). There is little doubt that the phonological basis of English writing at these many levels is the source of its efficiency, but the levels of representation to be apprehended in acquisition contribute to the failure of some individuals to learn.

Understanding of the problems underlying failure to learn an alphabetic script comes also in part from looking at the facts of speech perception. The discrete alphabetic units (letters) roughly correspond to discrete conceptual categories (phonemes). However, the concrete mediator of this correspondence is the sound wave of speech, which is continuous and not physically segmented; the phonemes are "shingled" together in their encoding for speech. This encoding essentially involves two transformations: one from phoneme to articulatory command (phone), and a second from articulatory command through movement of the articulators to the sound waves. The phonemes lose their individual physical identity under these transformations and cannot be physically recovered from the sound wave, that is, pronounced in isolation. Thus, in our view, the first major step in reading an alphabet is attained on the realization that the spoken word "bag" has three perceptual–cognitive segments. Many beginning readers do not understand this despite the fact that this segmentation surely exists in their heads and is manifest every time they say or understand the word.

Since the efficiency of alphabetic notation derives directly from its representation of segmental phonological facts about the language (the relation between *house* and *mouse* is manifest in the script) rather than morphological facts (the relation between *house* and *cottage* is not directly marked in the script), it is not surprising to discover that the average adult reader, reading at about 200–300 words per minute, does a substantial amount of phonological processing of the print, converting individual letters or letter sequences into some covert phonological form enroute to meaning. We describe this aspect of adult performance as *plodding* through print. In fluent reading, these alphabetic reading processes seem to be intermingled with more *explorative* processes including sampling from the page, inferring meaning from context, processing units larger than the letter, and sometimes by-passing the phonological step. Although these two aspects of the reader are hard to pick apart in his everyday performance, many experimental findings suggest that both are present. For the reading of new or relatively unfamiliar items, we suggest that the adult reader forms a roughly syllabic segmentation enroute to generating a pronunciation and then a meaning. For more familiar items, recognition may be mediated by a partly different knowledge of orthographic structure which has roots both in phonological and morphological considerations (e.g., there are phonological but also morphological clues to meaning, illustrated by the writing *chute* vs. *shoot* and Gre*cian* vs. inci*sion*). Most of the low-level processing (letter identification and application of phonological and orthographic rules) is highly automatized in the average adult reader, taking place for the most part below the level of consciousness. For this and similar reasons, introspection does not reveal their presence in the reading act.

This overall conception of what is represented in print and how the average adult processes this formed a starting point for the question of what must be taught to the beginning reader. It was acknowledged in particular that some adult reading skills need not be taught explicitly (e.g., scanning and guessing from context), while some transitional skills not employed by adult readers (e.g., subvocalizing and marking the place with a finger) might usefully be learned by the novice. We showed that the preliterate child approaches the learning of reading with a great many relevant skills and abilities already in place. Most significantly, the five-year-old hears phonological distinctions, and speaks and comprehends his native tongue; none of this has to be taught. Similarly, the ability to sample, guess from context, and the like (also crucial parts of adult performance) are already in place in the child and will, we claim, emerge spontaneously in his reading performance with exposure and practice. On the contrary, we believe that the major problem in early reading acquisition is the complex and abstract relationship between alphabetic writing and speech; we argued that understanding of this relationship is hard to come by, and ordinarily has to be taught explicitly.

In detail, we demonstrated that while tacit knowledge of the relevant categories (phonemes) can be shown from oral language use to exist in the head, this is insufficient to form the basis for reading acquisition: the prospective reader must achieve *phonological awareness,* or quite explicit *access* to the phonological mechanisms or principles at work in his speech system. We observed that, in general, access to linguistic functions is related to both age and verbal capacity. Further, and partly as a function of these age and capacity differences, meaning is easier to access than syntax, and syntax is easier to access than phonology. We also concluded, on the basis of evidence from speech perception, cross-cultural studies of reading, and other sources, that within phonology, syllables are easier to access (apprehend, talk about, manipulate) than are phonemes.

How can one teach a child something he already knows, but only in the restricted context of speech? The foregoing analysis of the reading acquisition process leaves us at an uncomfortable impasse in this regard. We claim that the basic barrier to initial progress is in the realization of the segmentation of speech. But this segmentation is produced, and perceived, in the brain; it is evidently quite inaccessible to awareness, "tightly wired" into those portions of the brain specifically devoted to speech and language.

This problem of teaching the child what he already knows is not specific to reading but arises also in other areas of learning, as, for example, in teaching the rules of grammar, which must in some sense be already "known" by every fluent speaker. We know of no systematic approaches to teaching what is already and deeply known in ways plausibly different from teaching what is unknown, or arbitrary (such as tables of measurement or The Pledge of Allegiance). The psychology of education or learning provides little guidance as to how we might make use of the fact that the child implicitly already knows what we now want to teach him to deploy in the service of reading.

Our own rough-and-ready approach to these issues was to develop a teaching method designed to minimize some of the most intractable conceptual difficulties in learning to read. This curriculum (*Syllabary*) essentially recapitulates the conceptual steps taken by inventors of writing systems. Most of the component items and conceptions of reading and writing can be exemplified concretely in the primitive scripts we teach before the alphabet is introduced. In particular, most traditional reading curricula confound four aspects of the alphabetic system and teach them all in an undifferentiated way at the same time:

1. the idea that meaning can be represented with visual symbols;
2. the idea that this can be accomplished by mapping the symbols onto already learned speech;
3. the idea that new meaningful elements can be generated by combining smaller elements for their sound values, that is, the notion of blending; and
4. that the elements used in alphabetic writing, in particular, are approximately the phonemes.

We have listed these four aspects in the order in which they were involved in inventing successively more analytic scripts, over cultural time; this is the same order that seems to be appropriate to teach them in the natural development of the young learner. In particular, the last step (segmentation and blending of the phonemic unit) is the most difficult. Hence, our historical curriculum (again consonant with the history of writing) spends much time at the syllabary stage. Syllabaries require learning the principle that sound patterns can be represented visually and can be blended. But they do not require reconstruction of an abstract unit from its encoding in the head. Syllables are concrete, pronounceable, and easily segmented from the continuous sound stream. In our terminology, syllables are more accessible than phonemes.

Results of teaching with this curriculum support some assertions made also on conceptual grounds. In practice as well as in theory, it turns out to be easier to teach a logography (word writing) than to teach a syllabary (syllable-sound writing), and easier to teach a syllabary than to teach an alphabet (phoneme-sound writing). In fact, children whose prognosis for learning to read an alphabet is very poor do acquire the principles of a syllabic script, can use its concepts to decipher new materials, and can read syllabary notation smoothly and with good comprehension.

Yet it was shown that the step from syllabary to alphabet is not easy to take except for those children (fortunately, the majority of children) who will learn to read by almost any method of instruction, no matter how remote from the conceptual base of the system. In part, the outcome that most children learn with any system of instruction, while a minority fails even with a theoretically coherent system of instruction, can be interpreted, and often is in the educational literature, to support the view that the nature of the curriculum itself, in its conceptual aspects, has little practical effect. Yet our discussion of the complications and difficulties involved in testing suggest that the effects of differences among curricula may simply be too hard to measure without exposing subjects to possible long-term dislocation. In general terms, then, we suggest that curriculum proposals—since none of them now does the job for all the children—must be evaluated in terms of their theoretical coherence with respect to the task.

The evidence is good, in fact, that the most important thing to teach the aspiring reader is the conceptual basis of the alphabet, at minimum the notion that English is written with a phonologically based script. In defiance of the very good evidence as well as theoretical sense of this view, a powerful belief and practice has arisen among many educators and psycholinguists to the effect that reading should be taught as though the writing system consisted of meaningful hieroglyphs. These educators thus teach reading at its most global extreme, exhorting learners to grasp at whole meanings without explicit reference to the phonological underpinnings of the writing system. In brief, they see the reading acquisition problem in terms of high-level sampling and guessing strategies and thus they urge the learner to explore even before he can plod. This dichotomy of approach between sound-oriented and meaning-oriented teachers, curriculum developers, and theorists lies at the heart of what Chall (1967) aptly calls the "Great Debate" in reading instruction. We have tried to present the available evidence in a way that gives substance to the common-sense stand on this matter: the alphabet, a useful invention, relates visual arrays to meanings through the mediation of the phonological system in the head; the straightforward way to teach reading is by activating that system in a new way, making it accessible to reflection and manipulation.

ACKNOWLEDGMENTS

The preparation of this presentation and some of the research reported in it were supported by NIH Grant #23505 and NSF Grant GB8013. We thank Henry Gleitman for helping us to clarify in our own minds many of the issues raised here, through both discussion and comment on the manuscript. We thank J. Baron, F. Gallistel, R. Gelman, H. Hoenigswald, and E. Newport for valuable comments on the manuscript, and Raoul Garnier for calling Pascal's utilization of a syllabary to our attention.

The development of the curriculum discussed in Section 4.2.1 would not have been possible without the participation of a number of dedicated students, research assistants, and teachers. We would like particularly to acknowledge major contributions by Margaret Allen, Barbara Chaddock, July Buchanan, and Muffy Siegel for the earlier versions, and Ivy Kuhn and Muffy Siegel for the more recent versions. The more recent versions (1973–1975) have been supported by Curriculum Development Associates. Dr. Morton Botel has provided valuable advice and Lisa Esser has provided excellent artistic support. The early versions of the curriculum (1973 and before) were in part supported by NIH Grant MH 20041 to Lila Gleitman and NSF Grant GB 8013 to Paul Rozin.

With respect to Section 4.3, we thank Dr. Thomas Minter, Superintendent of School District 7 in Philadelphia, for helping to arrange the basic evaluation program in his district, and the members of his staff, school principals, and teachers who participated in the program.

REFERENCES

Allen, M. W., Rozin, P., & Gleitman, L. R. *A test of the blending abilities of kindergarten children using syllable and phoneme segments,* (unpublished manuscript, University of Pennsylvania, 1972).

Baron, J. Phonemic stage not necessary for reading. *Quarterly Journal of Experimental Psychology,* 1973, *25,* 241–246.

Baron, J. The word-superiority effect. In W. K. Estes (Ed.), *Handbook of learning and cognitive processes.* Hillsdale, N.J.: Lawrence Erlbaum Press, in preparation.

Baron, J., & Strawson, C. Use of orthographic and word-specific knowledge in reading words aloud. *Journal of Experimental Psychology,* Human Perception & Performance, 1976 (in press).

Baron, J., & Thurston, I. An analysis of the word-superiority effect. *Cognitive Psychology,* 1973, *4,* 207–228.

Bellugi, U., & Fischer, S. A comparison of sign language and spoken language. *Cognition.* 1972, *1,* 173–200.

Benson, F., & Geschwind, N. The alexias. In P. J. Vinken & G. W. Bruyn (Eds.), *Handbook of clinical neurology,* Vol. 4. New York: American Elsevier, 1969.

Bever, T. G. Cognitive basis for linguistic structure. In J. R. Hayes (Ed.), *Cognition and the development of language.* New York: Wiley, 1970.

Blank, M. Cognitive processes in auditory discrimination in normal and retarded readers. *Child Development,* 1968, *39,* 1091–1101.

Bond, G. L., & Dykstra, R. *Coordinating center for first-grade reading instruction programs,* Final Report, Project No. X-001, U. S. Office of Education. Minneapolis: University of Minnesota, 1967.

Bower, T. G. R. Reading by eye. In H. Levin & J. P. Williams (Eds.), *Basic studies on reading.* New York: Basic Books, 1970.

Bransford, J. D., & Franks, J. J. The abstraction of linguistic ideas. *Cognitive Psychology,* 1971, *2,* 331–350.

Brill, L. *"What's so funny?" Children's understanding of puns.* Unpublished manuscript, University of Pennsylvania, 1974.

Brown, D. L. Some linguistic dimensions in auditory blending. In F. Green (Ed.), *Reading: the right to participate. Yearbook of the National Reading Conference,* 1971, *20,* 227–236.

Bruce, D. J. The analysis of word sounds by children. *British Journal of Educational Psychology,* 1964, *34,* 158–170.

Bryan, W. L., & Harter, N. Studies on the physiology and psychology of the telegraphic language. *Psychological Review,* 1897, *4,* 27–53.

Bryan, W. L., & Harter, N. Studies on the telegraphic language. The acquisition of a hierarchy of habits. *Psychological Review,* 1899, *6,* 345–375.

Calfee, R. C., Chapman, R., & Venezky, R. How a child needs to think to learn to read. In L. W. Gregg (Ed.), *Cognition and learning in memory.* New York: Wiley, 1972.

Calfee, R. C., Lindamood, P., & Lindamood, C. Acoustic–phonetic skills and reading–kindergarten through twelfth grade. *Journal of Educational Psychology,* 1973, *64,* 293–298.

Cattell, J. McK. Über der Zeit der Erkennung und Benennung von Schriftzeichen, Bildern, und Farben. *Philosophische Studien,* 1885, *2,* 635–650.

Chall, J. *Learning to read: The great debate.* New York: McGraw-Hill, 1967.

Chao, Y-R. *Language and symbolic systems.* London: Cambridge University Press, 1968.

Chomsky, C. Reading, writing, and phonology. *Harvard Educational Review,* 1970, *40,* 287–309.

Chomsky, C. *The acquisition of syntax in children from 5 go 10.* Cambridge, Mass.: MIT Press, 1969.

Coleman, J. S. *Equality of educational opportunity.* Washington, D. C.: U. S. Office of Education, 1966.

Conrad, R. Speech and reading. In J. F. Kavanagh & I. G. Mattingly (Eds.), *Language by ear and by eye: The relationships between speech and reading.* Cambridge, Mass.: MIT Press, 1972.

Dale, P. S. *Language development: structure and function.* Hinsdale, Illinois: Dryden Press, 1972.

deHirsch, K., Jansky, J. J., & Langford, W. S. *Predicting reading failure: A preliminary study of reading, writing, and spelling disabilities in preschool children.* New York: Harper & Row, 1966.

Downing, J. Children's concepts of language in learning to read. *Educational Research,* 1970, *12* 106–112.

Downing, J. (Ed.). *Comparative reading: Cross-national studies of behavior and processes in reading and writing.* New York: Macmillan, 1973.

Downing, J., & Oliver P. The child's conception of "a word." *Reading Research Quarterly,* 1973–1974, *9,* 568–582.

Dykstra, R. Auditory discrimination abilities and beginning reading achievement. *Reading Research Quarterly,* 1966, *1,* 5–34.

Eimas, P. D., Siqueland, E. R., Jusczyk, P., & Vigorito, J. Speech perception in infants. *Science,* 1971, *171,* 303–306.

Elkonin, D. B. (USSR). Trans. by R. Raeder & J. Downing in J. Downing (Ed.), *Comparative reading: Cross-national studies of behavior and processes in reading and writing.* New York: Macmillan, 1973.

Feigenbaum, E. A. The simulation of verbal learning behavior. In E. A. Feigenbaum & J. Feldman (Eds.), *Computers and thought.* New York: McGraw-Hill, 1963.

Ferguson, C. A. Contrasting patterns of literacy acquisition in a multilingual nation. In W. H. Whiteley (Ed.), *Language use and social change.* London: Oxford University Press, 1971.

Fillenbaum, S. Memory for gist: Some relevant variables. *Language and Speech,* 1966, *9,* 217–227.

Firth, I. *Components of reading disability.* Unpublished doctoral differtation, University of New South Wales, Kensington, N. S. W., Australia, 1972.

Foulke, E., & Sticht, T. G. Review of research on the intelligibility and compression of accelerated speech. *Psychological Bulletin,* 1969, *72,* 50–62.

Furth, H. G. *Thinking without language: Psychological implications of deafness.* New York: Free Press, 1966.

Geschwind, N., Quadfasel, F. A., & Segarra, J. M. Isolation of the speech area. *Neuropsychologia,* 1968, *6,* 327–340.

Gibson, E. J. Learning to read. *Science,* 1965, *148,* 1066–1072.

Gibson, E. J. The ontogeny of reading. *American Psychologist,* 1970, *25,* 136–143.

Gibson, E. J., Pick, A., Osser, H., & Hammond, M. The role of grapheme-phoneme correspondence in the perception of words. *American Journal of Psychology,* 1962, *75,* 554–570.

Gibson, E. J., Shurcliff, A., & Yonas, A. Utilization of spelling patterns by deaf and hearing subjects. In H. Levin & J. P. Williams (Eds.), *Basic studies on reading.* New York: Basic Books, 1970.

Gleitman, L. R., & Gleitman, H. *Phrase and paraphrase: Some innovative uses of language.* New York: W. W. Norton Co., Inc., 1970.

Gleitman, L. R., Gleitman, H., & Shipley, E. The emergence of the child as grammarian. *Cognition*, 1972, *1*, 137–164.

Gleitman, L. R., & Rozin, P. Teaching reading by use of a syllabary. *Reading Research Quarterly*, 1973, *8*, 447–483. (a)

Gleitman, L. R., & Rozin, P. Phoenician go home? (A response to Goodman). *Reading Research Quarterly*, 1973, *8*, 494–501. (b)

Goodman, K. Reading: A psycholinguistic guessing game. In K. S. Goodman & J. Fleming (Eds.), *Selected papers from the IRA Preconvention Institute*, Boston, April 1968. Newark, Del.: International Reading Association, 1969.

Goodman, K. The 13th easy way to make learning to read difficult: A reaction to Gleitman and Rozin. *Reading Research Quarterly*, 1973, *8*, 484–493.

Gough, P. B. One second of reading. In J. F. Kavanagh & I. G. Mattingly (Eds.), *Language by ear and by eye: The relationships between speech and reading*. Cambridge, Mass.: MIT Press, 1972.

Hardyck, C. D., & Petrinovich, L. F. Treatment of subvocal speech during reading. *Journal of Reading*, 1969, *12*, 361–368.

Harris, A. J. *How to increase reading ability*. (5th ed.) New York: David McKay, 1970.

Hochberg, J. Components of literacy: Speculations and exploratory research. In H. Levin & J. P. Williams (Eds.), *Basic studies on reading*. New York: Basic Books, 1970.

Holden, M. H., & MacGinitie, W. H. Children's conceptions of word boundaries in speech and print. *Journal of Educational Psychology*, 1972, *63*, 551–557.

Huey, E. B. *The psychology and pedagogy of reading* (1908). Cambridge, Mass.: MIT Press, 1968.

Johnson, N. F. The psychological reality of phrase-structure rules. *Journal of Verbal Learning and Verbal Behavior*, 1965, *4*, 469–475.

Johnston, J. C. *The role of contextual constraint in the perception of letters in words*. Unpublished doctoral dissertation. University of Pennsylvania, Philadelphia, Pa., 1974.

Johnston, J. C., & McClelland, J. L. Visual factors in word perception. *Perception and Psychophysics*, 1973, *14*, 365–370.

Kolers, P. Three stages of reading. In H. Levin & J. P. Williams (Eds.), *Basic studies on reading*. New York: Basic Books, 1970.

Krueger, L. E., Keen, R. H., & Rublevich, B. Letter search through words and nonwords by adults and fourth-grade children. *Journal of Experimental Psychology*, 1974, *5*, 845–849.

LaBerge, D., & Samuels, S. J. Toward a theory of automatic information processing in reading. *Cognitive Psychology*, 1974, *6*, 293–323.

Labov, W. *Study of nonstandard English* (rev. ed.). Urbana, Illinois: National Council of Teachers of English, 1970.

Labov, W. *Language in the inner city: Studies in the Black English vernacular*. Philadelphia, Pa.: University of Pennsylvania Press, 1973.

Lashley, K. S. The problem of serial order in behavior. In L. A. Jeffress (Ed.), *Cerebral mechanisms in behavior*. New York: Wiley, 1951.

Lenneberg, E. H. *Biological foundations of language*. New York: Wiley, 1967.

Leong, C. K. Hong Kong. In J. Downing (Ed.), *Comparative reading: Cross-national studies of behavior and processes in reading and writing*. New York: Macmillan, 1973.

Levin, H., & Kaplan, E. L. Grammatical structure and reading. In H. Levin & J. P. Williams (Eds.), *Basic studies on reading*. New York: Basic Books, 1970.

Liberman, I. Y. Segmentation of the spoken word and reading acquisition. *Bulletin of the Orton Society*, 1970, *23*, 65–77.

Liberman, I. Y., Shankweiler, D., Fischer, F. W., & Carter, B. Explicit syllable and phoneme segmentation in the young child. *Journal of Experimental Child Psychology*, 1974, *18*, 201–212.

Lieberman, P. *On the origin of language*. New York: Macmillan, 1975.

Makita, K. The rarity of reading disability in Japanese children. *American Journal of Orthopsychiatry,* 1968, *38,* 599–614.

Marshall, J. C., & Newcombe, F. Patterns of paralexia: A psycholinguistic approach. *Journal of Psycholinguistic Research,* 1973, *2,* 175–199.

Martin, S. E. Nonalphabetic writing systems: Some observations. In J. F. Kavanagh & I. G. Mattingly (Eds.), *Language by ear and by eye: The relationships between speech and reading.* Cambridge, Mass.: MIT Press, 1972.

Mattingly, I. G. Reading, the linguistic process, and linguistic awareness. In J. F. Kavanagh & I. G. Mattingly (Eds.), *Language by ear and by eye: The relationships between speech and reading.* Cambridge, Mass.: MIT Press, 1972.

McClelland, J. L. Preliminary letter identification in the perception of words and nonwords. *Journal of Experimental Psychology: Human Perception and Performance,* 1976, *2,* 80–91.

McClelland, J. L., & Johnston, J. C. *The role of familiar units in the perception of words and nonwords.* Unpublished manuscript. University of Pennsylvania, Philadelphia, 1976.

Miller, G. A., Bruner, J. S., & Postman, L. Familiarity of letter sequences and tachistoscopic identification. *Journal of General Psychology,* 1954, *50,* 129–139.

Miller, G. A., & Friedman, E. A. The recognition of mutilated English texts. *Information and Control,* 1957, *1,* 38–55.

Moskowitz, A. I. The two-year-old stage in the acquisition of English phonology. *Language,* 1970, *46,* 426–441.

Moskowitz, A. I. *The acquisition of phonology.* Unpublished doctoral dissertation. University of California, Berkeley, 1971.

Moskowitz, B. A. On the status of vowel shift in English. In T. E. Moore (Ed.), *Cognitive development and the acquisition of language.* New York: Academic Press, 1973.

Neisser, U. *Cognitive psychology.* New York: Appleton-Century-Crofts, 1967.

Osherson, D., & Markman, E. Language and the ability to evaluate contradictions and tautologies. *Cognition,* 1975, *3*(3), 213–226.

Posner, M. I. Representational systems for storing information in memory. In G. A. Talland & N. Waugh (Eds.), *The pathology of memory.* New York: Academic Press, 1969.

Quintilian, *The institutio oratoria of Quintilian,* Vol. 1. Translated by H. E. Butler. New York: G. P. Putnam's Sons, 1920.

Read, C. Preschool children's knowledge of English phonology. *Harvard Educational Review,* 1971, *41,* 1–34.

Reber, A. S. Implicit learning of artificial grammars. *Journal of Verbal Learning, Verbal Behavior,* 1967, *6,* 855–863.

Reicher, G. M. Perceptual recognition as a function of meaningfulness of stimulus material. *Journal of Experimental Psychology,* 1969, *81,* 275–280.

Rosner, J. Phonic analysis training and beginning reading skills. *Proceedings of American Psychological Association, 79th Annual Convention,* 1971, *6,* 533–534. (Also published in Learning Research and Development Center, University of Pittsburgh. Publication 1971/19.)

Rosner, J. *The development and validation of an individualized perceptual-skills curriculum.* Learning Research and Development Center, University of Pittsburgh. Publication 1972/7. 1972.

Rosner, J. Language arts and arithmetic achievement, and specifically related perceptual skills. *American Educational Research Journal,* 1973, *10,* 59–68.

Rosner, J. Auditory analysis training with prereaders. *The Reading Teacher,* 1974, *27,* 379–384.

Rosner, J., & Simon, D. P. *The auditory analysis test: An initial report.* Learning Research and Development Center, University of Pittsburgh. Publication 1971/3. 1971.

Rozin, P. The evolution of intelligence and access to the cognitive unconscious. In J.

Sprague & A. N. Epstein (Eds.), *Progress in psychobiology and physiological psychology*, Vol. 6. New York: Academic Press, 1975.

Rozin, P., Bressman, B., & Taft, M. Do children understand the basic relationship between speech and writing? The mow*n*motorcycle test. *Journal of Reading Behavior*, 1974, *6*, 327–334.

Rozin, P., & Gleitman, L. *Syllabary: An introductory reading curriculum.* Washington, D.C.: Curriculum Development Associates, 1974.

Rozin, P., Poritsky, S., & Sotsky, R. American children with reading problems can easily learn to read English represented by Chinese characters. *Science*, 1971, *171*, 1264–1267.

Sachs, J. S. Recognition memory for syntactic and semantic aspects of connected discourse. *Perception and Psychophysics*, 1967, *2*, 437–442.

Sainte-Beuve. *Port-Royal de Sainte-Beuve.* Paris, librairie Gallimard, NRF collection de la Pleiade, tome, II, 1955, p.454.

Sakamoto, T., & Makita, K. Japan. In J. Downing (Ed.), *Comparative reading: Cross-national studies of behavior and processes in reading and writing.* New York: Macmillan, 1973.

Sasanuma, S., & Fujimura, O. Selective impairment of phonetic nonphonetic transcription of words in Japanese aphasic patients: Kana vs. Kanji in visual recognition and writing. *Cortex*, 1971, 7, 1–18.

Sasanuma, S., & Fujimura, O. An analysis of writing errors in Japanese patients: Kanji versus Kana words. *Cortex*, 1972, *8*, 265–282.

Savin, H. B. What the child knows about speech when he starts to read. In J. F. Kavanagh & I. G. Mattingly (Eds.), *Language by ear and by eye: The relationships between speech and reading.* Cambridge, Mass.: MIT Press, 1972.

Savin, H. B., & Bever, T. G. The nonperceptual reality of the phoneme. *Journal of Verbal Learning and Verbal Behavior*, 1970, *9*, 295–302.

Selfridge, O. G. Pandemonium: A paradigm for learning. In *The mechanization of thought processes.* London: H. M. Stationery Office, 1959.

Shankweiler, D., & Liberman, I. Y. Misreading: A search for causes. In J. F. Kavanagh & I. G. Mattingly (Eds.), *Language by ear and by eye: The relationships between speech and reading.* Cambridge, Mass.: MIT Press, 1972.

Shatz, M. *Children's judgments of sentence acceptability.* Unpublished manuscript, 1972. (Available from Department of Psychology, University of Pennsylvania, Philadelphia, Pa.).

Shen, E. An analysis of eye movements in the reading of Chinese. *Journal of Experimental Psychology*, 1927, *10*, 158–183.

Singer, H. IQ is and is not related to reading. In S. Wanat (Ed.), *Intelligence and reading.* Newark, Del.: International Reading Association, 1974.

Smith, F. *Understanding reading; a psycholinguistic analysis of reading and learning to read.* New York: Holt, Rinehart & Winston, 1971.

Smith, F., Lott, D., & Cronnell, B. The effect of type size and case alternation on word identification. *American Journal of Psychology*, 1969, *82*, 248–253.

Smith, J. A. *The relationship between phonemic sensitivity and the effectiveness of phonemic retrieval cues in preliterate children.* Unpublished doctoral dissertation, University of Pennsylvania, 1974.

Sperling, G. The information available in brief visual presentations. *Psychological Monographs*, 1960, *74* (Whole No. 498), 1–29.

Sperling, G., Budiansky, J., Spivak, J. G., & Johnson, M. C. Extremely rapid visual search: The maximum rate of scanning letters in the presence of a numeral. *Science*, 1971, *174*, 307–311.

Thorndike, E. L., & Lorge, I. *The teacher's word book of 30,000 words.* New York: Columbia University Teachers College, Bureau of Publications, 1944.

Thorndike, R. L. Reading as reasoning. *Reading Research Quarterly,* 1973–1974, *9,* 135–147.

Thorndike, W. E. Reading as reasoning: A study of mistakes in paragraph reading. *Journal of Educational Psychology,* 1971, *8,* 323–332. (Also in *Reading Research Quarterly,* 1970–1971, *6,* 425–434.)

Walker, W. Notes on native writing systems and the design of native literacy programs. *Anthropological Linguistics,* 1969, *11,* 148–166.

Weber, R. First graders' use of grammatical context in reading. In H. Levin & J. P. Williams (Eds.), *Basic studies on reading.* New York: Basic Books, 1970.

Wepman, J. M. *Wepman auditory discrimination test.* Chicago: Language Research Associates, 1958.

Wheeler, D. D. Processes in word recognition. *Cognitive Psychology,* 1970, *1,* 59–85.

Woodcock, R. W. Rebus as a medium in beginning reading instruction. *IMRID Papers and Reports,* 1968, *5,* 1–34.

Woodcock, R. W., Clark, C. R., & Davies, C. O. *The Peabody rebus reading program.* Circle Pines, Minn.: American Guidance Service, 1968.

3
Visual Pattern in Fluent Word Identification

Lee Brooks

McMaster University

1   INTRODUCTION

Many of the important aspects of the reading process are frustratingly difficult to unravel. But in this sea of intangibles, there is at least one variable that we can easily manipulate: the visual form of words. By varying visual form we might be able to make words more discriminable, or common pronunciation patterns more salient. By varying visual form, then, we might be able to increase the speed with which people learn to identify words rapidly. In this chapter I would like to describe some experiments we have done to investigate the theoretical and potentially practical role of visual form in the acquisition of the ability to fluently identify words.

2   POSSIBLE VARIATIONS IN VISUAL FORM

Alphabetic writing can range from forms as lean as binary codes to those as lurid as advertising logos. Let us examine the variations that we could make on the standard typefaces and the reasons we might have for varying them.

2.1   Increase the Distinctiveness of Individual Letters

We could try to make individual letters more distinctive so that the reader could more easily translate from visual form into underlying letter identities or linguistic units. However, despite the notorious b, d, p, q confusions in most typefaces, the extremely thorough work on typographic legibility by Tinker and his associates (Tinker, 1965) does not provide much encouragement for this possibility. Either the visual form of individual letters is not particularly crucial for word identification or the standard typefaces of the English alphabet are already sufficiently legible to act as unit signals.

2.2 Add Arbitrary Distinctiveness to Whole Words

Advertisers spend an enormous amount every year to distort corporate names into distinctive shapes. Clearly they believe that these distortions gain more in memorability than they cost in legibility. If visual distinctiveness is in fact a dominant factor in learning to identify a word rapidly, then the material in Fig. 1 should be a considerable improvement over standard typefaces for beginning readers. The words are no less alphabetic for all the variation in their appearance, and repeated occurrences of a word, such as the word "a," are quite easy to pick out. Yet the normal typographies of the world's alphabetic languages seem remarkably regular in appearance, an impression that is particularly striking when looking at a page printed in an unfamiliar alphabet. The reason for this visual regularity could be strictly due to output problems; learning to write as in Fig. 1 would require a terrific amount of skill and specific learning, and the traditional typographical technology would be impossible. But more importantly, the arbitrary visual variation of Fig. 1 could be wrong in principle. If fluent readers normally transform the visual stimulus into underlying linguistic units as a means of identifying a word, then we probably could make their task easier by making each letter look the same each time it occurs. Later in this paper, evidence will be presented that suggests that whatever is effective about what advertisers do with their logos does not extend to high levels of fluency.

FIG. 1. Madison Avenue Typography. The shapes of individual letters change from word to word in order to increase the distinctiveness of the overall word. If word distinctiveness is an overriding consideration, then this typography ought to be excellent for helping a new reader to gain fluency. If interword transfer based on component letter groups is important, then this typography might hinder fluency.

2.3   Change Individual Letters to Produce Visual Interaction

The previous two alternatives vary between the extremes of not considering interletter patterns at all to considering only whole-word patterns. However, we might be able to gain some of the distinctiveness of advertising logos without paying the price of arbitrary variation of individual letters. Amina Miller and I designed the typeface shown in Fig. 2 with the objective of making the letters visually interact and thereby making word patterns clearly more than just a collection of letters. Most critically, we intended that words that differ by a single letter or solely in the sequence of their component letters should look quite different. Each letter is the same every time it occurs, but it is hoped that words differ from one another more strikingly than with conventional typefaces. All we want is to have our cake and eat it too.

2.4   Make Letters in Regular Pronunciation Patterns
Appear Related

In the example of Fig. 2, we also darkened the vowels to make them stand out as a group. The issue is not whether a beginner can decide whether a given letter is a vowel or a consonant, but whether the difference between them is so strikingly salient that he will quickly learn the patterns in which they occur. In this way we might be able to develop a typography that will train the inspection habits of

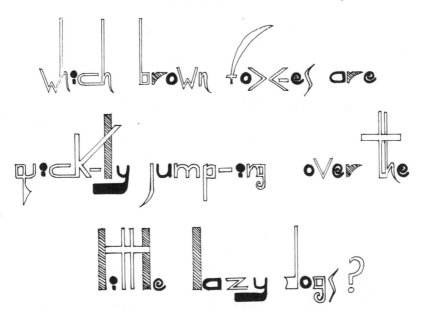

FIG. 2. Sound-correlated patterning. In this typography, letters are kept constant from word to word, but are designed to make words more distinctive and to make the normal pronunciation cues of English more salient.

a new reader to work with the spatially separated cues that are so important in English orthography. For example, one's best guess about the pronunciation of an O will change if it is followed immediately by another vowel, by a simple consonant and then a vowel, or by an L or an R (Venezky, 1967; Wijk, 1966). If a beginner were decoding from left to right and letter by letter, then he easily might make tentative guesses that would have to be corrected later, at a considerable cost in effort and confusion. As we shall see later, even adults in fact suffer this confusion when they attempt to read words written with unfamiliar letter forms. The pronunciation cues provided by subsequent and spatially separated letters are not obvious, and sampling them before guessing is certainly not automatically encouraged by the necessity of taking into account the left-to-right ordering of letters. Possibly by making the vowel–consonant groupings more salient, the necessary prepronunciation inspection habits would be easier to acquire. We can make comparable arguments for distinguishing L's and R's, for making the X look complex, and for indicating bound morphemes.

As a contrast to this type of pattern enhancement, let us look at two other systems that have been tried in initial reading instruction. Both the diacritical marking system (DMS) and the initial teaching alphabet (ITA) change the appearance of words in order to simplify pronunciation. The ITA (Fig. 3) accomplishes this by introducing new letters into the alphabet (Southgate & Warburton, 1969). Since each letter is consistently associated with a single sound, the process of pronunciation is simplified and the child presumably is

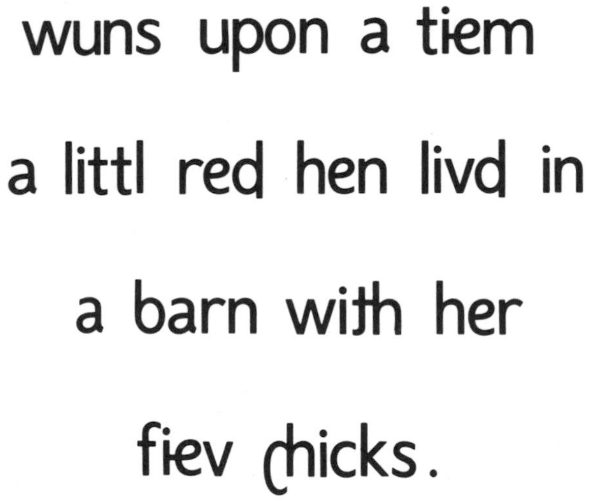

wuns upon a tiem

a littl red hen livd in

a barn with her

fiev chicks.

FIG. 3. Initial Teaching Alphabet. The orthography of English is changed to insure that every symbol has only one sound value. If the major difficulty for new readers is the principle of phonemic representation, then this system might be a good transition step. If the major difficulty is learning either the normal English orthography or the normal visual patterns, then I.T.A.'s advantages are not as clear.

free to get on with the other tasks and pleasures of reading. But the task of learning the visual appearance of words in traditional English orthography is obviously delayed, as is the task of learning the multiple letter groups that normally signal English sound units. If either of these tasks is a key stumbling block, then ITA is not the obvious prescription. The DMS (Fig. 4) simplifies pronunciation rules by adding marks that indicate the pronunciation of traditional English letters (Fry, 1964). For example, in the word "time" a bar is placed over the "i" to indicate the glided "i" pronunciation and the terminal "e" is slashed to indicate that it is not separately pronounced. This does preserve the traditional spelling of "time," but it might be directing the reader's attention away from one of the regular pronunciation signals in traditional spelling: the terminal "e." Further, it might be encouraging the wrong principle; namely, in order to pronounce a letter, look only at that letter itself.

Visual changes might be put to better use in increasing distinctiveness by caricaturing the normal features of English words and in enhancing the letter groupings that normally signal sound units. This was the intent, if not the effect, of the typography in Fig. 2. After the tasks of initial instruction were completed, these changes could be faded out along a physical dimension instead of the abrupt change necessitated by changing ITA to traditional orthography and typography. The important groups of visual features would still be there as would the vowel–consonant patterns to which attention had been drawn; more importantly, the knowledge of what to look for might also still be there. The calligraphy in Fig. 2 jars adult reading habits, but that is irrelevant to the issue at hand. Both the first impressions of adults and the work on legibility by Tinker (1965) in effect test the material for its compatibility with already established visual learning. The purpose of the material in Fig. 2 is to train inspection habits and support sight-word learning in a person who is in the process of learning standard English orthography and letter forms.

These possibilities are strictly conjectural. I have discussed them mainly to show why we are interested in research on the role of visual pattern in the

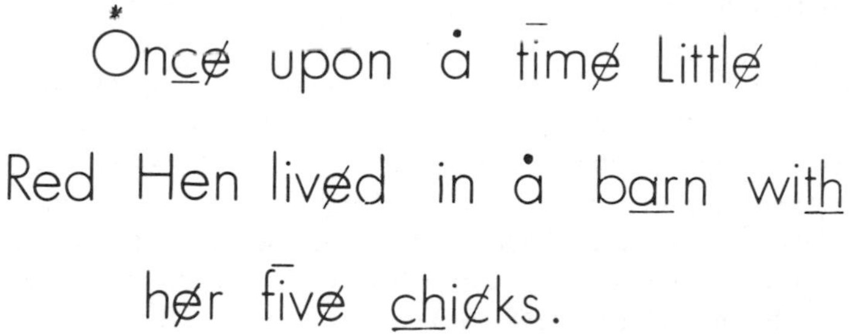

FIG. 4. Diacritical Marking System. The intent of this system is the same as that of I.T.A., but with the possible advantage of leaving the normal visual patterns of English intact. It is still true, however, that attention is not directed to the important orthographic cues of English.

acquisition of fluency. Visual distictiveness and the visual control of letter grouping are manipulable factors in reading, but we do not know enough about the normal role of visual pattern in word identification to know if they are worth changing.

3 THEORIES OF FLUENCY

Which variations in visual form we expect to be important depends in part on what we think happens in normal word identification. On the one hand, no one questions that knowledge of an alphabet helps a reader to identify novel words. On the other hand, advertisers leave us with little doubt that increasing the distinctiveness of a company trademark makes it easier to associate meaning with them. What is at question is how these two factors, sound reference and word distinctiveness, work together in the identification of very familiar words. To guide the discussion in this chapter, let us first distinguish two traditional positions on the nature of fluent word identification and what their relation is to the importance of visual pattern.

3.1 Specific-Stimulus Learning

According to this position, the sound-reference capabilities of the alphabet are used mainly to identify novel words. As a reader becomes familiar with a word, he learns what it looks like and identifies it with little reference to its sound or other linguistic properties. In other terms, he readdresses each word in his lexicon so that component sounds are bypassed, and the word is directly accessed from some aspects of its visual appearance. An early version of this position was championed in the "whole-word" approach to the teaching of reading. Advocates of this version claimed that fluent readers identify familiar words by their overall shape, possibly even their outlines. Clearly then, according to this notion, the visual characteristics of words ought to be very important.

Subsequently, information-processing analysis has made it clear that the several assumptions of the whole-word approach could be adopted separately, and it is the logical separateness of these assumptions that I would like to stress here. We could assume that the meanings of words in the lexicon were accessed directly, that is, without intermediate decisions about sound values or component letters, without also assuming that large visual patterns are important. As Smith (1971) has pointed out, a reader could as logically access words in his lexicon with a list of separate visual features as with a list of component letters or as with some characterization of an overall pattern. But direct access *does* imply that the reader has at least some specific-stimulus learning to do for each word that is accessed this way. Regardless of whether the reader is learning the overall pattern of the word or just the sets of visual features that are sufficient to sort out a word from contextually possible alternatives, he is still facing a formidable amount of learning about specific stimuli.

In this paper we will separately address the importance of visual pattern and the importance of specific-stimulus learning. Visual patterning is worth investigating because it is an immediately manipulable input to the reading process. Specific-stimulus learning is worth investigating because, as the early advocates of the whole-word method pointed out, it has profound implications for the teaching of reading. But demonstrating the importance of one does not imply the importance of the other.

3.2 Linguistic Translation

The alternative traditional position about the nature of fluency is that the reader normally makes very heavy use of information derived from his prior experience with words in speech. The economy of such a notion is obvious. With a relatively small amount of learning about the alphabet the learner might be able to immediately access words regardless of whether he has ever *seen* those particular words before. If something like this is happening at fluency, then it would be very sensible to do as the "phonic" school advocated: start reading instruction with a stress on regular letter-to-sound correspondences. With sufficient practice on the general system, one would expect very high transfer to new words.

Two influences have pushed psychology strongly in the direction of this position. One is the demonstrations that readers are sensitive to general linguistic regularities; for fluency, an example is the demonstration of faster tachistoscopic recognition of pronounceable nonwords than of unpronounceable letter strings (Baron & Thurston, 1973). The other is the demonstrations that fluent readers are incredibly resistant to distortions in form and orientation (Kolers, 1970; Neisser, 1967). In combination these demonstrations suggest that readers lessen their dependence on visual input and hence their vulnerability to visual distortion by using other forms of information, such as their knowledge of contextually possible linguistic units. This view, of course, does not encourage assigning a crucial role to visual pattern. However, the fact that linguistic compensation occurs under distorted or time-limited conditions does not demonstrate that it occurs in normal fast reading. When all conditions of stimulation are very familiar, the reader might tend toward the use of relatively unprocessed, highly specific information.

As with the whole-word school, subsequent analysis has underlined the fact that the several assumptions combined in the original phonic position do not necessarily belong together. For example, a model that stresses linguistic translation does not have to deny an important role to visual pattern; that is, multiletter spelling units could be assessed from visual patterns without an intervening translation to letter identities. Thus —ght could be evaluated as /t/ without first requiring separate identification of "g," "h," and "t." Or for another example of inferential independence, a model that assumes mandatory linguistic translation does not have to predict immediate high interword transfer in gaining fluency; a word in the lexicon may not be immediately recognizable even though it had been translated into speech-related units because the relative salience or the sequence in which the intermediate linguistic units were derived was different from that encountered in speech. If there is high interword transfer in gaining fluency, as the phonic school implied, then that is an important fact about learning to read; but it does not follow automatically from a demonstration that a reader derives intermediate linguistic units.

4 THE RESEARCH

My intent in the preceding section was to suggest that issues regarding the importance of visual pattern, of specific-stimulus learning, and of linguistic translation are more separate than has often been supposed. Consequently, we probably know less about the role of visual form than might be supposed. If we could conclude from studies showing the importance of linguistic processing that visual pattern was unimportant or even a distraction from the real business of reading, then we would already have a substantial pile of discouraging evidence. But since we cannot, the visual form variations mentioned earlier still seem to be live alternatives.

To investigate how visual pattern affects the interplay of specific-stimulus learning and linguistic translation at fluency, we need to ensure that the learner is given sufficient practice so that he could learn specific stimuli if they are useful and that he is cognitively capable of using an alphabet if it is useful. Both of these conditions are dramatically easier to achieve with adults, so we will now lapse into the time-honored tactic of looking for the wallet where the light is good. All of the work in this chapter was conducted with adults, generally learning artificial alphabets. This has allowed us to screen several notions about the ultimate competence that adults have achieved. With luck, it also will guide us in the more empirically difficult and ethically hazardous business of running long-term studies with children who are in the process of learning to read. In this section I will use the adult data to address six basic questions about fluency. Later, the usefulness of this strategy will be considered again.

4.1 Are Sound Properties Important at Fluency?

This is an important first point to establish. If we are so lucky as to find a conveniently available effect of sound, then we can test a variety of questions about the interaction between visual pattern and sound accessing. If we do not, then we will be nagged by the possibility that sound properties are normally important but we just have not found them yet—that we just did not give our subjects the right kind or amount of practice. The experiments reported in these first two sections are a result of a collaboration between Jon Baron of the University of Pennsylvania and myself. They are a true collaborative effort in that I am sure that neither of us would have done them if he hadn't had the other to argue with.

The basic plan of the experiments is simple. We asked adult subjects to learn associations between a small set of printed words and spoken responses. The words were printed in an artificial alphabet, shown in Fig. 5. In the orthographic condition each response can be derived from the stimulus by a cipher (one-to-one substitution) on the normal orthographic rules of English. In the paired-associate condition the responses are arbitrarily related to the stimuli. The question is whether or not the speeds of responding in these two conditions eventually become the same. If the orthographic condition is faster even after

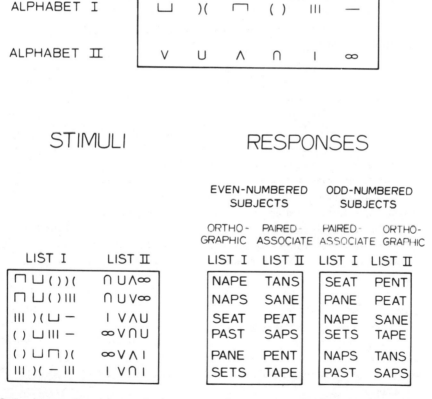

FIG. 5. An experiment to test the importance of an alphabet at fluency. For each subject, one list has a functional alphabet and one does not. Each subject is given 400 trials of practice naming the words in each of the two lists. Which list is orthographic (has a functional alphabet) is counterbalanced across even- and odd-numbered subjects.

extensive practice, we can conclude that something other than arbitrary association between the response and all or parts of the stimuli is important.

In more detail, we first gave the eight subjects in this within-subject experiment about 10 min of practice translating the artificial letters in their orthographic condition into traditional English letter names. We told the subjects that they were to read as rapidly as possible a set of six words printed in those letters, and gave them a card with the six stimulus words on it. After this first trial (omitted from the analysis) each trial consisted of presenting a new ordering of the six stimulus words and recording the time required to pronounce all six words. Following 20 trials in this condition, the subjects studied a card with the six paired-associate stimulus words and associated responses for five minutes. Twenty paired-associate trials were run, followed by 20 orthographic, and so on to the end of the experiment. At the end of each trial in either condition, the experimenter corrected any response that the subject had not spontaneously corrected himself. In fact, omitting the first trial in each condition, there was a trivial number of such corrections and more of them were required for the orthographic trials than for the paired-associate trials.

Let us examine the reasons why we might expect speed of naming in these two conditions to converge:

1. The whole-word position might be correct. With extensive practice on a very small number of words, the stimuli might be processed virtually as single, overall patterns. If we were using a list of several hundred stimuli, it would be less plausible that this result would occur. But with a very short list, some of the possible advantages of an alphabet seem less compelling.

2. Some less restrictive version of specific-stimulus learning might be correct. This experiment was designed so that the stimuli would give exactly the same amount of information about the responses in the paired-associate condition as in the orthographic condition. Even-numbered subjects were taught Alphabet I, which made List I possible to sound out. Odd-numbered subjects were taught Alphabet II, which made List II possible to sound out. The paired-associate condition for both groups was formed by rematching the stimuli and responses for the alternate list. This procedure, together with the obvious matching of spelling patterns, guarantees that the stimuli for both conditions are structurally the same. As a result, when averaged across subjects, each stimulus component in each position signals the same amount of information about the same set of responses in the orthographic and the paired-associate conditions. For example, the vertical line in the initial position of List II stimuli distinguishes between exactly two words for both conditions. Unless one refers to some property of the response other than its identity, the two conditions should converge to the same speed.

In fact, as shown in Fig. 6, the orthographic condition was clearly faster over the last 200 trials ($p < .001$). Something about having a functional alphabet is important for identifying even a small number of familiar words. We have no

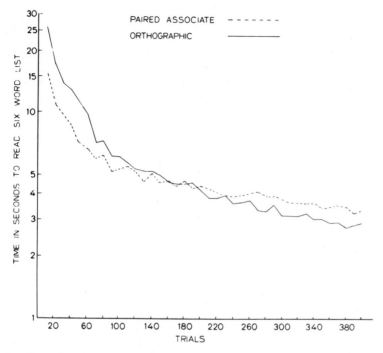

FIG. 6. Time taken in seconds (log scale) to read each of two sets of six words over 400 trials of practice. Rather than converging, as might be expected from a "whole-word" notion of fluency, the set with a functional orthography became faster with practice.

reason to say that this effect is at asymptote or that the two conditions wouldn't reconverge after even more practice, but we can say that the advantage of having a functional alphabet can be shown over a considerable range of practice. After the next experiment we will go into the possible interpretations of this effect.

The answer to our original question, then, is yes, sound properties are important at fluency. The surprise to me is that they are apparent with a six-word vocabulary in a strange alphabet. I started several talks that I gave on earlier phases of this project with the statement, "Obviously, we wouldn't have an alphabet if there were only 10 words in the written language; 10 distinctive symbols would do as well." Fortunately, I never mentioned six words.

4.2 Will Enhancing the Visual Pattern of a Word Help at Fluency? If So, Is It at the Cost of Using the Sound Properties?

The purpose of this chapter, however, is to investigate the effect of visual patterning. I would first like to describe visual form variations together with the reasons why we suspect that they increase the distinctiveness of words. Then these new forms will be run in a version of the experiment just described to see

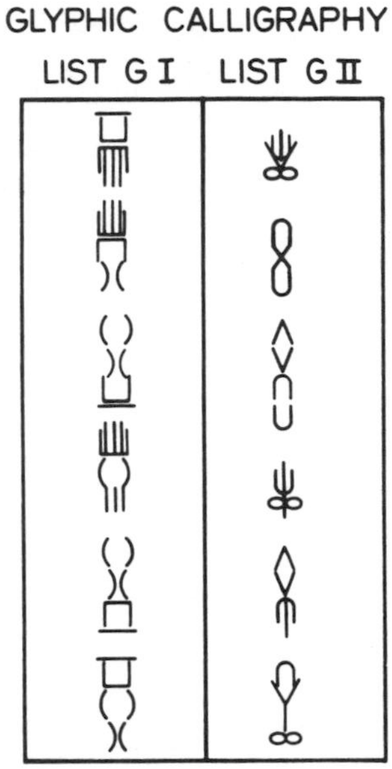

GLYPHIC CALLIGRAPHY		ORTHO- PAIRED- GRAPHIC ASSOC.		PAIRED- ORTHO- ASSOC. GRAPHIC.	
LIST G I	LIST G II	LIST GI	LIST GII	LIST GI	LIST GII
		TANS	NAPE	PENT	SEAT
		SANE	NAPS	PEAT	PANE
		PEAT	SEAT	SANE	NAPE
		SAPS	PAST	TAPE	SETS
		PENT	PANE	TANS	NAPS
		TAPE	SETS	SAPS	PAST

FIG. 7. Glyphic calligraphy. These stimuli are constructed from the same artificial letters used in Fig. 5. This glyphic type of stimulus and the discrete form shown in Fig. 5 were run in a four-condition, within-subjects experiment. For a given subject, one alphabet was functional for six glyphic and six discrete stimuli and the other alphabet was arbitrarily related to six glyphic and six discrete stimuli.

if increasing visual distinctiveness changes the reader's response to the sound properties of words.

The letter forms of Alphabets I and II can be combined in a way that increases their visual interaction without changing any of the letters themselves, as is shown in Fig. 7. This "glyphic" arrangement is very much in the spirit of the typography shown in Fig. 2; that is, we have attempted to increase the distinctiveness of the overall words without varying the component letters from word to word. Some feeling for the effectiveness of this manipulation can be gained by comparing the time taken to find the six pairs of duplications between the glyphic forms in Fig. 8 and those in Fig. 7 with the time taken to find the duplications between the "discrete" forms in Figs. 8 and 5. The usual result of this comparison is that the glyphic form is easier to scan than the discrete form even though they have the same component letters and therefore the same ability to signal alphabetic information. Since neither of these forms has any acoustic component signaling power for the adults that we tested on this initial scanning demonstration, we can assert that in some sense the glyphic form is visually easier to work with than is the discrete form.

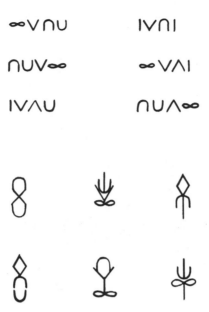

FIG. 8. Scanning demonstration for glyphic and discrete stimuli. The stimuli above are duplicates of the List II stimuli shown in Figs. 5 and 7. Time how long it takes you to match each of the discrete stimuli above with its duplicate in Fig. 5. Compare this with the time you take to compare the glyphic stimuli with those in Fig. 7. Although the two forms are composed of identical letters and therefore have the same possibility of signaling sound values, the glyphic form is usually easier to deal with in this type of visual short-term memory task.

A comparable demonstration can be made between the two typefaces in Fig. 9. This demonstration with traditional letters is tricky with adults, however, because in effect it is pitting a possible increase in distinctiveness against previously well established visual expectations, a problem avoided in the work in this section by use of the artificial discrete and glyphic alphabets. The problems with the demonstration in Fig. 9 underline the limitations inherent in doing any short-term screening with new typefaces as, in fact, Tinker (1965) and his associates did. However, it is exactly this type of short-term screening that we will be interested in when we get to the stage of developing a typeface for use with children. With the work on visual matching and visual scanning in mind (Beller, 1970; Eichelman, 1970; Krueger, 1970; Posner, Lewis, & Conrad, 1972), we pretested these two typographies with a small group of children in a visual matching task using a large number of pairs of words arrayed one above the other. The results of this pilot demonstration were positive, which is encouraging enough for the present purposes. Ultimately, we plan to use this visual matching task as a screening device to improve the distinctiveness of our experimental typefaces.

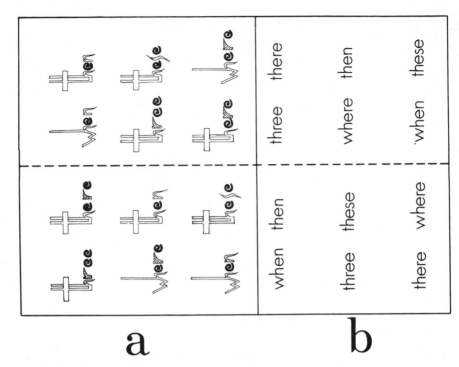

a   **b**

FIG. 9. Scanning demonstration. Without tilting your head, time how long it takes you to find the matches between the six words at the top of Panel a and the same six words at the bottom of Panel a. Compare this with the comparable scan of Panel b. This comparison of the scanning times for the two different typefaces is meant to demonstrate differences in visual distinctiveness, but with adults it is confounded with the opposing effect of familiarity. Tilting the words and averaging the effect across two or three trials are possible correctives for the effect of familiarity.

What is not clear from the glyphic—discrete scanning task in adults is whether this increase in visual distinctiveness or short-term memorability will be important when the subjects *are* able to use the alphabets. To test this, we ran essentially the same experiment described in the previous section with four conditions within subjects rather than two. That is, each of the eight subjects in this experiment alternated 20-trial blocks among the four conditions shown in Figs. 7 and 5. Note that the same letters are alphabetic in both the glyphic and the discrete forms. This design allows replication of the previous result and tests the effect of adding one kind of visual distinctiveness. (In fact, in this experiment we reassigned letter forms to letter names to make sure that the previous result was not an accident of letter assignment. To save space, however, I have shown the stimulus material for both experiments as if they were run with the same letter-form to letter-name assignments.)

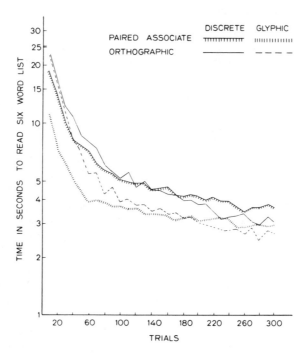

FIG. 10. Results of the glyphic–discrete experiment. The effect of a functional alphabet is significant over the last 100 trials for both the discrete and the glyphic calligraphies. The effect of visual patterning is significant and does not significantly interact with the presence of a functional alphabet.

Visual distinctiveness had a positive effect and did not grossly interfere with the effect of an alphabet, as can be seen in Fig. 10. Over the last 100 trials, the main effects of both visual form (discrete vs. glyphic) and orthography (paired-associate vs. orthographic) were significant ($p < .01$). The interaction between form and orthography was close to significance, but this is not crucial since the effect of orthography was significant on both levels of the visual form variable. Under these conditions, in any event, we do seem to be able to have our cake and eat it too.

These two experiments demonstrate that the advantages of a functional alphabet can be remarkably persistent. Let us look at two ways of interpreting this alphabetic effect:

1. Component correspondence: possibly the correspondence between some components of the stimulus, such as letters or visual features, and some components of the response, such as phonemes or acoustic features, is important in identifying familiar words. An extreme version of this view is that the same orthographic rules that allow a sounding out of unfamiliar words are also used

for fluent word identification. However, one also could hold that the rules changed somewhat (e.g., to the use of larger units) and still claim that correspondence between parts of the stimulus and parts of the response are important for fluent identification.

2. Similarity correspondence: one of the consequences of an alphabetic system is that, within broad limits, the more similar words are as stimuli the more similar they are as articulated responses. Possibly the correspondence between overall similarity of the stimuli and overall similarity of responses is important at fluency. We could imagine that the stimulus patterns formed by words were arrayed in a conceptual space according to their similarity to one another, such that the more similar two words were to one another, the closer together in space they would occur. We then could array the acoustic properties of words into an independent space. The effective relation between the stimuli and the responses might be that knowing the location of a word in the stimulus space would allow us to predict the relevant location in the response space. In this view, "pronunciation rules" would be dealt with in the manner of the distance models discussed by Shepard (1962a, b) and Reed (1972). Possibly these models could also treat the effect of visual patterning by the same mechanism.

Until other assumptions are specified we cannot say whether these two lines of explanation make different predictions. The purpose that they serve for us now is to prevent our thinking from locking onto the traditional rule terminology, a terminology that might be at least heuristically prejudicial. Let us now look at the pattern effect from these two viewpoints. We might ask, first, why the pattern variable is effective with both the discrete and the glyphic forms and, second, why the alphabetic superiority does not show until late for both forms. Several answers are possible from the rule (component correspondence) viewpoint; one is that the identity decision is based on both derived sound properties and visual pattern information (Meyer, Schvaneveldt, & Ruddy, 1974). The pattern information is evaluated independently of the sound properties and the decision is made when enough information from either source is available. Until the derivation of sound is fast enough to win the race on at least some trials, speed of processing will be determined mainly by the pattern information. After that point it could be determined by both. There are some problems in the early part of the curves with this explanation, such as the interaction between the form and the orthographic variable, but we probably cannot rule this type of explanation out without more specification.

From the similarity view, we could assume that there is an advantage with both the glyphic and the discrete forms in finding the relevant location in the response space, but this is easier to do with the glyphic form because it is easier to find one's location in the mental representation of the stimulus space. With both forms it might take a considerable amount of practice to establish either the general or the specific correspondences between the two spaces, which would mean that it would take a considerable amount of practice before the alphabetic superiority would appear. Heuristically, this line of explanation suggests the usefulness of thinking about stimulus generalization rather than explicit pronunciation rules for explaining performance.

Regardless of which type of explanation is used, however, we do have an answer to our original question: yes, visual pattern can help at fluency without necessarily eliminating the usefulness of the sound properties. This is the answer we need to sidestep some of the old "look–say" arguments about the necessarily distracting effect of visual pattern. We now would like to know what type of patterning will do this job.

4.3   Is Arbitrary Pattern Enhancement as Effective as Sound-Correlated Pattern Enhancement?

We increased visual patterning in the glyphic form by increasing visual inter-action between adjacent letters rather than by changing the letters themselves from word to word. As a result, the patterning is at least partly correlated with particular sounds. For example, if the initial letters "na" formed a particularly salient unit for a subject, then he would be using a unit that signaled the related "nā" or "nă" sounds. By contrast, when advertisers increase the distinctiveness of company logos, the patterning they add is usually arbitrary with respect to the sound of the words they are dealing with. What we do not know from the preceding study is whether this arbitrary type of patterning would have been just as effective as the sound-correlated patterning that we did use.

Amina Miller tested this in an honors project by changing the overall shape of a set of words in either a sound-correlated or an arbitrary manner. In the sound-correlated condition (see Fig. 11), the shape of the envelope signaled the vowel sound of the word; in the arbitrary condition, a different set of shapes was used that gave no information about the sound of the words; and in the discrete condition, a single shape of envelope was used for all eight words. Eight subjects were run in a within-subjects design in which the same functional alphabet and the same responses were used. The major variable, then, was whether or not the envelope of the word, as well as the letters themselves, signaled the vowel sound.

The results, shown in Fig. 12, are beautifully clear. There is a significant interaction, with both types of patterning being superior to discrete in the initial 40-trial segment but with only sound-correlated patterning being superior over the last 40 trials (all $p < .001$). This latter effect also is apparent in a transfer list consisting of four nonsense words. This study is not sufficient to conclusively demonstrate that the much less precise correlation between sound and glyphic patterning was an equally crucial factor in the previous study. But it certainly does indicate that sound correlation can be crucial, and it certainly does decrease our motivation to use arbitrary patterning for potential applications. But most important, it suggests that we could introduce patterning and profit for different

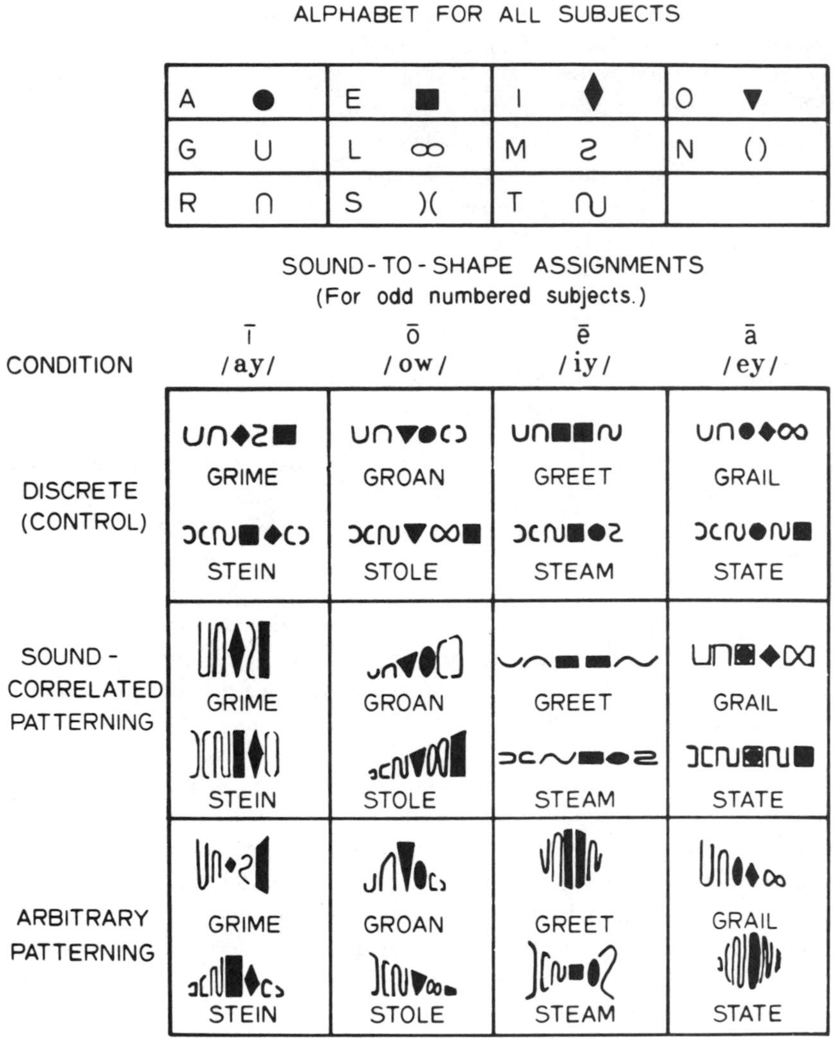

A	●	E	■	I	◆	O	▼
G	U	L	∞	M	ꙅ	N	()
R	∩	S	)(	T	∽		

SOUND-TO-SHAPE ASSIGNMENTS
(For odd numbered subjects.)

CONDITION	ī /ay/	ō /ow/	ē /iy/	ā /ey/
DISCRETE (CONTROL)	∪∩◆ꙅ■ GRIME)(∩■◆() STEIN	∪∩▼●() GROAN)(∩▼∞■ STOLE	∪∩■■∽ GREET)(∩■●ꙅ STEAM	∪∩●◆∞ GRAIL)(∩●∩■ STATE
SOUND-CORRELATED PATTERNING	∪∩◆ꙅ GRIME)(∩■◆() STEIN	∩▼●() GROAN ∩▼∞■ STOLE	～∩■■～ GREET)(～■●ꙅ STEAM	∪∩■◆∞ GRAIL)(∩■∩■ STATE
ARBITRARY PATTERNING	∪∩◆ꙅ GRIME ∩■◆() STEIN	∩▼●() GROAN)(∩▼∞■ STOLE	∩■■ GREET)(∩■●ꙅ STEAM	∪∩◆◆∞ GRAIL ∩■∩■ STATE

FIG. 11. An experiment to test the importance of sound-correlated patterning. For each subject, one set of word outlines signaled the vowel sound and another set of outlines increased word distinctiveness but did not signal anything about sound. The same alphabet was used for both of these conditions as well as for a control condition. Sound-to-shape assignments were counterbalanced across subjects so that there was no relationship between particular envelopes and particular vowels.

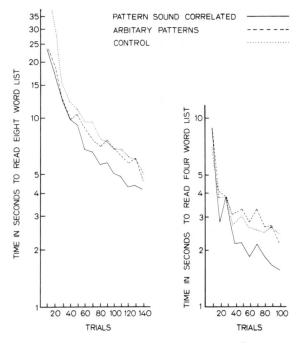

FIG. 12.   Results of arbitrary-pattern experiment. Both kinds of patterning are superior to the discrete-form control condition over the first 40 trials; only the sound-correlated patterning is superior in the last 40 and in the transfer list. Note that time is plotted on a log scale and that the transfer list has only 4 words.

reasons at different stages of practice. This could be the key to potential applications: we might be able to help with different problems by using the same material.

4.4   Does the Effect of Pattern Disappear with an Increase in Vocabulary?

We used lists of only eight, six, and four words in the preceding three studies to provide a hard test of the usefulness of alphabetic regularities. If a subject were ever going to rely solely on some kind of specific-stimulus direct access, he would surely do so when there were only six specific stimuli to learn. But when we are considering a visual pattern variable, we have to worry about the opposite problem; namely, that he would use patterns only when there were few words to learn. As the vocabulary increased beyond the list lengths that are convenient in paired-associate studies, he might lean ever more exclusively on some form of linguistic translation.

To test this we gave a group of six subjects 120 words to learn, 60 discrete and 60 glyphic. The words were introduced in lists of 12 each but then were

TABLE 1
Design and Results of First Large Vocabulary Experiment[a]

| Words[b]: | 1–24 | 25–48 | 1–48 | 49–72 | 1–72 | 73–96 | 1–96 | 97–120 | 1–120 |
| | D_1 | D_2 | $D_{1,2}$ | D_3 | D_{1-3} | D_4 | D_{1n4} | D_5 | D_{1-5} |
Lists[c]:	G_1	G_2	$G_{1,2}$	G_3	G_{1-3}	G_4	G_{1-4}	G_5	G_{1-5}
Discrete (D)	44.7	26.7	17.7	13.8	11.8	11.5	15.0	12.0	13.7
Glyphic (G)	21.5	20.1	13.2	16.5	9.8	10.7	10.8	7.8	10.3

[a]With one exception, glyphic lists are learned more rapidly to a criterion of one identification per second than are discrete lists. The effects of patterning, then, are not wiped out as the list length exceeds that used in most paired-associate experiments.

[b]Criterion is the ability to pronounce words at the rate of one word per second.

[c]See text for description of word distribution on lists.

cumulated with all previous words. The subjects' task, after learning the alphabet, was to work on each of the lists until they were able to say the words at the rate of one word per second. The order of conditions is shown in Table 1, with three subjects running through the conditions from top to bottom, left to right, and the other three from bottom to top, left to right. Words were always presented and timed six at a time, so that the trials to criterion would not depend on list length for mechanical reasons such as taking a breath or losing one's place. The alphabet consisted of 12 symbols and was the same for both the glyphic and discrete forms. The words averaged 4.4 letters in length and were not restricted to a small number of spelling patterns as was done in the studies described in the preceding subsection.

The glyphic form was superior throughout ($p < .001$). All six subjects required fewer total trials to learn the glyphic words and, most important, required fewer trials on the final 120 cumulation. Of course, if we had pushed the subjects to a larger vocabulary yet, the visual pattern variable might have wiped out. But, especially since these adult subjects were already sophisticated in the use of the principle of sound reference, this study does cover a fairly large chunk of an initial learning period. The least we can claim is that the advantage of patterning is not restricted to just the first few words.

We found an interesting sign of general learning in both this and the next experiment. After reaching criterion on the 120 words, each subject was asked to scan arrays of 24 words for 0, 1, or 2 occurrences of a target stimulus that was specified for that trial. The target and background items in a given array consisted of words in one of the six categories shown in Table 2. "Old" refers to the words that were among the 120 words just mastered; "new" refers to new words printed in the same artificial alphabet; "scrambled" refers to random rearrangements of the letters in the "new" words. The times in Table 2 are the means of two trials in each condition for each of the six subjects.

TABLE 2
Results of the Scanning Posttest

Type[b]	Mean time[a] (sec)		
	Old words	New words	Scrambled words
Discrete	7.8	8.9	10.2
Glyphic	6.2	7.5	8.4

[a]To scan 24-word array for targets that occur 0, 1, or 2 times.

[b]Item in array (both target and background).

The results were that each orthogonally adjacent pair of conditions shows a significant difference ($p < .05$). The difference between the discrete and the glyphic conditions replicates the same difference referred to in conjunction with Fig. 8. The difference between the new and the old conditions could be expected on a variety of grounds and is reminiscent of Krueger's (1970) work on scanning. But the difference between the new and scrambled conditions is interesting because it indicates that the subjects were being helped by something that they had learned about permissible sequences of letters. This result is another indication that the glyphic patterning is not obviously suppressing general learning.

Both the 120-word experiment just described and the following one were in fact the first experiments that we performed on patterning. At that time I had considerable doubts (understatement) that the orthography of the language played any detectable role in fluent performance, at least until the reader had years of experience with the particular system. By my view, most of the data in the literature could be explained as the combination of the orthography acting as a low-speed cuing device for relatively unfamiliar words, together with learning literal patterns and permissible sequences in the visual stimulus. In the sunny light of this bias, I thought that the effect of an orthography would show before the subject reached an identification rate of one word per second—if the effect were ever going to show. As a matter of fact, 1 sec per word is almost exactly the point at which the discrete curves cross over in both Figs. 6 and 10. After I had lost my bet with Jon Baron, as is graphically recorded in those two figures, I began to wonder why I had not picked a sensible criterion, such as 5/8 or 9/16 sec. Since then, I have been substantially more reluctant than have my subjects to stop an experiment. This is all by way of explaining why the next experiment will be described rather briefly.

We designed this experiment to assess the role in acquisition played by some obvious pattern and linguistic translation variables, illustrated in Fig. 13. Let us first look at the two pattern variables, one being the glyphic—discrete forms and the other being a respelling manipulation that roughly corresponds to an upper-

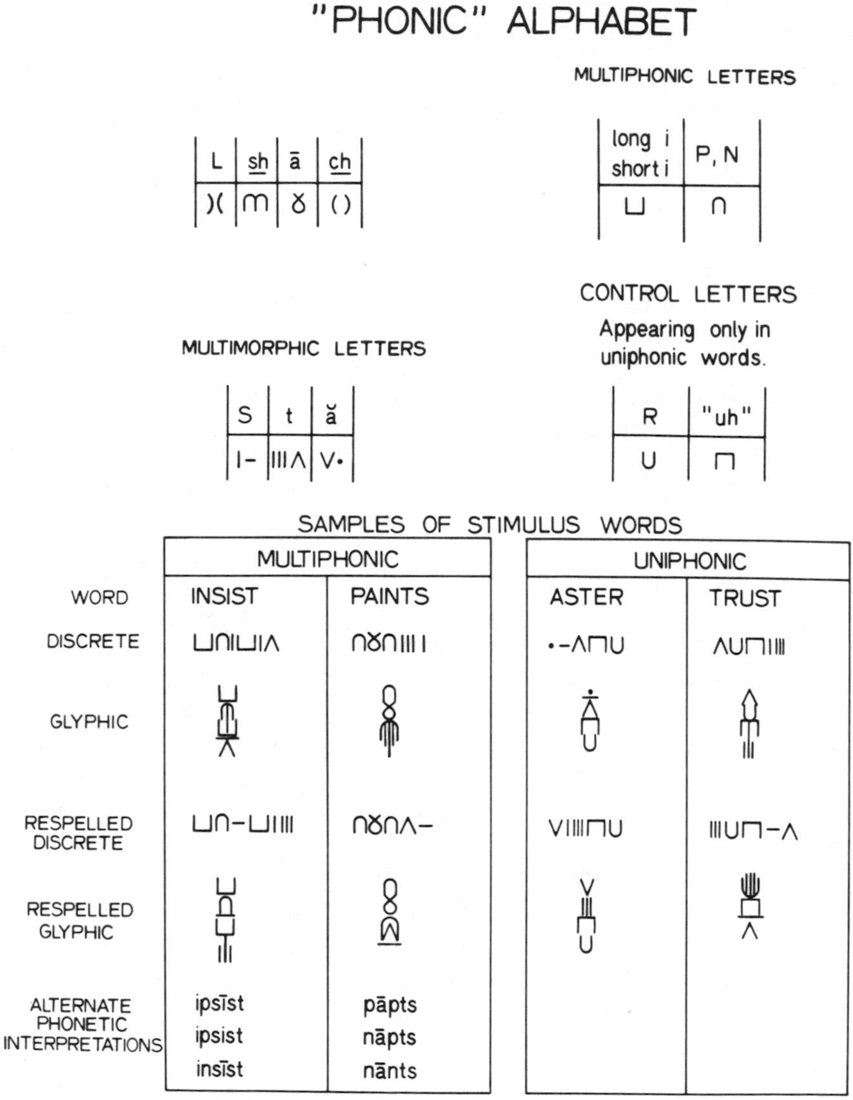

"PHONIC" ALPHABET

FIG. 13. Material for the second large-vocabulary study. Four variables were orthogonally varied. The two visual pattern variables were whether a word was printed in glyphic or discrete form and whether it occurred on different trials in both spellings or in only one. The two linguistic variables were whether the letters would contain multiphonic letters, and could therefore be sounded out in more than one way, and whether or not the responses were paired so that the subject could use an alphabet. This last variable was run between subjects, the other three within subjects.

case-to-lower-case variation. Three sounds were represented by either of two symbols (multimorphic letters) so that words could be spelled with either of two sets of symbols, as illustrated in the figure. Half of the words in the experiment were shown in each of two spellings (with an average of 2.3 symbol changes per word) and half were shown in only one spelling. The frequencies of both forms of the multimorphic letters were carefully balanced across the experiment so that any effect due to presenting a word in two different spellings could not be influenced by unfamiliarity with any of the component letters. But if part of the speed of identification is due to learning word-specific patterns or low-frequency-letter patterns, then the words with two spellings ought to be acquired more slowly.

The linguistic translation variables are the orthographic-paired-associate variable described in previous sections and the multiphonic variable illustrated in Fig. 13. The ambiguity of a multiphonic stimulus word (average of 2.4 multiphonic letters per word) could always be resolved because only one of the sound combinations was in fact an English word, as is illustrated in the examples. There was a total of 96 words in the experiment arranged in lists of 24. Half of the words in each list were multiphonic and, orthogonally varied, half were presented in each of two spellings. Getting separate times for all these categories of words required a complicated procedure, the description of which is more than the current space limitation justifies.

The major reason for mentioning this experiment is that it provides, under quite different circumstances, a rough confirmation of the trends apparent in Fig. 10 up to the one-per-second (6 sec per list) criterion. The ordering of the groups in trials to criterion is similar for the first two glyphic and discrete lists, as is shown in Table 3. As in the previous work, the glyphic-paired-associate condition is markedly better than the other three. An interesting comment on this result is provided by the fact that the orthographic subjects did not immediately realize that some of the words were being spelled in more than one way. They reported feeling some confusion when they were working on the respelled words, but could not for some time put their finger on what the

TABLE 3
Trials to Criterion for Each List in Second Large Vocabulary Experiment[a]

Lists:	Mean trials to criterion					
	D_1	G_1	D_2	G_2	D_{1+2}	G_{1+2}
Orthographic group	79.6	83.8	50.2	45.4	37.6	23.4
Paired-associate group	81.5	26.0	42.0	27.0	28.5	24.0

[a]The results for the first two glyphic and discrete lists are similar to the ordering apparent at the 6-sec mark (one identification/sec) in Fig. 10. In this experiment, however, having a functional alphabet was a between-subjects variable and the list length was 24 words.

difficulty was. In contrast, the paired-associate subjects immediately reported their outrage at having two stimuli for the same response. Something about laboring at the task of decoding seems to prevent full exploitation of the pattern. Breaking these results down to the subclasses of stimuli, we find that the original speed advantage of uniphonic words had been wiped out by the time the lists had reached criterion; whether it would have reappeared with continuation of the experiment we of course cannot tell (but would like to know). On the other hand, in a possible analogy with the glyphic–discrete difference, the respelling variable continued to have an effect right up to criterion (criterion was defined over the whole list, so it was still possible for a within-list variable to have an effect).

An interesting byproduct of this experiment was the indication of general learning by the paired-associate group. After completing the experiment, we gave this group a set of 48 glyphic and 48 discrete stimulus words that they had not seen before. Half of these stimuli spelled English words and half of them were scrambled versions of real words. The subjects were to sort them into words and nonwords. Since this group had learned arbitrary associates to the stimuli of the main experiment, they could not sound out these words and solve the task that way. But if they had implicitly learned sequencing rules, then they might have been able to say whether the new words "looked funny," that is, violated restrictions on what symbols could follow one another. This apparently was what they were able to do, as is shown in Table 4. Similar to the findings previously reported by Reber (1967), none of the subjects were able to report even an approximation of the cues on which they were basing their performance, but in all cases they sorted well above chance. Again, it is worth noting that this evidence is at least as compelling for glyphic as for discrete stimuli, further suggesting that general learning is not obviously suppressed by strong patterning.

TABLE 4
Results from the Word–Nonword Sorting Task[a]

| | Mean number of classifications | | | |
| | Discrete | | Glyphic | |
Stimulus called	W	NW	W	NW
Word (W)	19.3	8.0	18.6	5.8
Nonword (NW)	4.7	16.0	6.4	18.2

[a] All six members of the paired-associate group were given 24 new words and 24 scrambled strings to sort. All subjects did this above chance for both glyphic and discrete forms. This performance could not have been based on pronunciation, since this group at no stage had a functional alphabet.

Finally, these subjects were asked to learn two new paired-associate lists, half of the stimuli of which were words and half of which were nonwords. Despite the possibility of greater proactive interference for the word stimuli, the items with word stimuli were learned faster than those with nonword stimuli. This is the second piece of evidence suggesting that these subjects have learned something about the general structure of the stimuli.

The major reason for my interest in these two effects is because they demonstrate how results that could easily be attributed to the sound-reference properties of an alphabet might in fact be due to learning general stimulus patterns. Normally, visual patterns and sound patterns are confounded in words. But for this group of subjects, nonauditory patterns were the only information on which they could have based their performance. The fact that they did so well suggests that the symbol-sequencing aspect of an alphabetic system has to be taken as seriously as its sound-reference aspect. It was in fact this possibility that prompted J. Baron and me to use the response-reassignment technique that we did for the paired-associate control in the first two experiments in this paper. A comparison analogous to the one that I have just reported could have been obtained only if we had also included a condition in which the stimuli were scrambled arrangements of the same symbols.

4.5   Does Visual Enhancement of Normal Spelling Patterns Improve Speed of Word Identification?

Up to this point, we have not mentioned one surprising and consistent feature of the data: adults have a remarkably difficult time using a new alphabet. One dimension of this difficulty is shown in Figs. 6 and 10 where the subjects take longer in the orthographic condition than in the paired-associate condition for the first 80 or so trials. This result is not just due to the use of extremely short lists, complex English spelling, or within-subjects designs, as is shown in Table 3. These three comparisons between paired-associate and orthographic conditions, however, do not quite get at the feeling of frustration so strongly expressed by many of our subjects. As they tell the story, they often would have all the letters translated well before they could put together a full word. The peculiar thing about this, of course, is that these subjects are sophisticated in the use of at least one alphabetic system, and in some sense they already know the very spelling patterns that are being used. All they have to do is learn a simple six-letter cipher on the English alphabet.

Any temptation that I might have had to blame the difficulty on declining university admission standards was dispelled, for reasons of ego if nothing else, by my own performance on materials made up by Tom Anderson. In his experiments, the time taken to identify a new word was compared with the time taken to complete the cipher itself. That is, the time taken to identify a word was compared with the time taken to identify each of the letters in a comparable

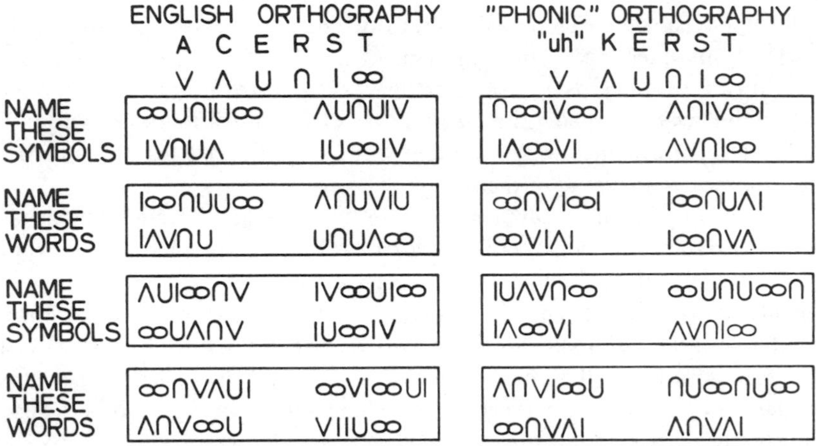

	ENGLISH ORTHOGRAPHY A C E R S T V ∧ U ∩ I ∞		"PHONIC" ORTHOGRAPHY "uh" K Ē R S T V ∧ U ∩ I ∞	
NAME THESE SYMBOLS	∞U∩IU∞ IV∩U∧	∧U∩UIV IU∞IV	∩∞IV∞I I∧∞VI	∧∩IV∞I ∧V∩I∞
NAME THESE WORDS	I∞∩UU∞ I∧V∩U	∧∩UVIU U∩U∧∞	∞∩VI∞I ∞VI∧I	I∞∩U∧I I∞∩V∧
NAME THESE SYMBOLS	∧UI∞∩V ∞U∧∩V	IV∞UI∞ IU∞IV	IU∧V∩∞ I∧∞VI	∞U∩U∞∩ ∧V∩I∞
NAME THESE WORDS	∞∩V∧UI ∧∩V∞U	∞VI∞UI VIIU∞	∧∩VI∞U ∞∩V∧I	∩U∞∩U∞ ∧∩V∧I

FIG. 14. Demonstration of sounding out. For either the English or the phonic orthography, first study the alphabet. Then practice the correspondences by naming symbols anywhere on the page, possibly in the other column right to left, bottom to top. When these can be done with fair facility, compare the times you take to do the two tasks in the column on which you started. Record your times for naming the symbols in each of the four strings in the top box. Then record your times for naming the *words* in the next box down.

string, a short demonstration of which is shown in Fig. 14. His subjects first practiced the basic alphabet (208 responses to each of eight symbols) and then were alternately timed on naming each of the component letters of a string and naming the word spelled by a matched letter string. Despite reasonable fluency in the alphabet, subjects took approximately 50% longer to name five-letter words and twice as long to name six-letter words than to translate each of the letters in matched five- and six-letter strings. In the course of producing these effects, a number of these adult subjects also showed the type of blocking that is often reported with children who are just beginning to read. On some occasions, people could correctly translate all the letters and not be able to come up with a correct pronunciation for an incredible period, the record being 5½ min. This effect seems to be associated with making an initial bad guess, but is still amazing in its persistence. On other occasions, people could come up with the correct pronunciation and not be able to recognize it as a meaningful English word. These effects are reminiscent of such phenomena as recall without recognition (Tulving & Thompson, 1973) and demonstrations of interaction between perceptual difficulty and memory (e.g., Rabbitt, 1968; Thurston, 1969). The large individual differences that we have observed suggest investigating a possible correlation with R. Day's language-bound, stimulus-bound distinction.

In other experiments in this series, Anderson has shown that the effect is about as strong with a phonic alphabet as with a cipher on the normal English alphabet. This suggests that the difficulty may be with using an alphabet, reminiscent of Rozin and Gleitman's work (this volume), rather than just with the complex orthography of English. There is also no obvious effect of word frequency, since the effect is present to about the same degree with nonsense words as with familiar English words. Finally, Anderson has shown that the effect is not an artifact of having interspersed 50% of the trials in which just the letters are named.

The picture that we get from these experiments is that many of the effects associated with early reading are not due solely to a failure to "understand the alphabetic principle." At least some of them can also be found with adults who surely in some sense understand the principle on which English orthography is based. But the habits which allow them to use this principle are obviously partly specific to the particular forms of English letters. By extension, possibly even adults would benefit from a visual emphasis of the spelling rules that they also in some sense know.

In another series of experiments, T. Anderson has also shown this to be the case. In these experiments the regular vowel patterns were emphasized by increasing the size of the vowels. This in essence is the same manipulation that we previously discussed in connection with Fig. 2. He gave a group of 10 subjects 10 trials on a list of 12 words which consisted of two examples of each of six vowel spelling patterns. The subjects were then transferred for four trials to a list of six unenhanced words consisting of one example of each of the same six spelling patterns. This procedure was repeated for two additional pairs of training and test lists that exemplified these six spelling patterns. If the subjects learned which visual symbols to look for to identify these regular English spellings, then we might expect to see a facilitation on the test lists. To assess this, the performance of this group was compared with a control group that received both the training and the test lists in unenhanced typography. To ensure that any difference between these groups was due to emphasis on vowel patterns and not just any sound-correlated units, a third group was run in which all occurrences of T, L, and A in the training lists were increased in size. Samples of these stimuli are shown in Fig. 15. Note that this TLA control group is not the arbitrary pattern control run in Amina Miller's experiment shown in Fig. 11. In the present case the T and the L are perfectly correlated with a unit of pronunciation, and the A is limited to the glided and the unglided A sounds. But there is no reason to believe that the subject will particularly benefit from having his attention drawn to these three letters. On the other hand, he might benefit from having the pattern of vowel letters drawn to his attention since these constitute a regular English pattern for signaling vowel sounds. If in fact the effect of this pattern manipulation is to establish a regular set of inspection habits, then it is necessary to use either the present between-groups design or the equally awkward procedure of using three separate alphabets. Using a between-subjects design vastly increases the amount of work, which accounts for the relatively small amount of practice given any one list in this experiment.

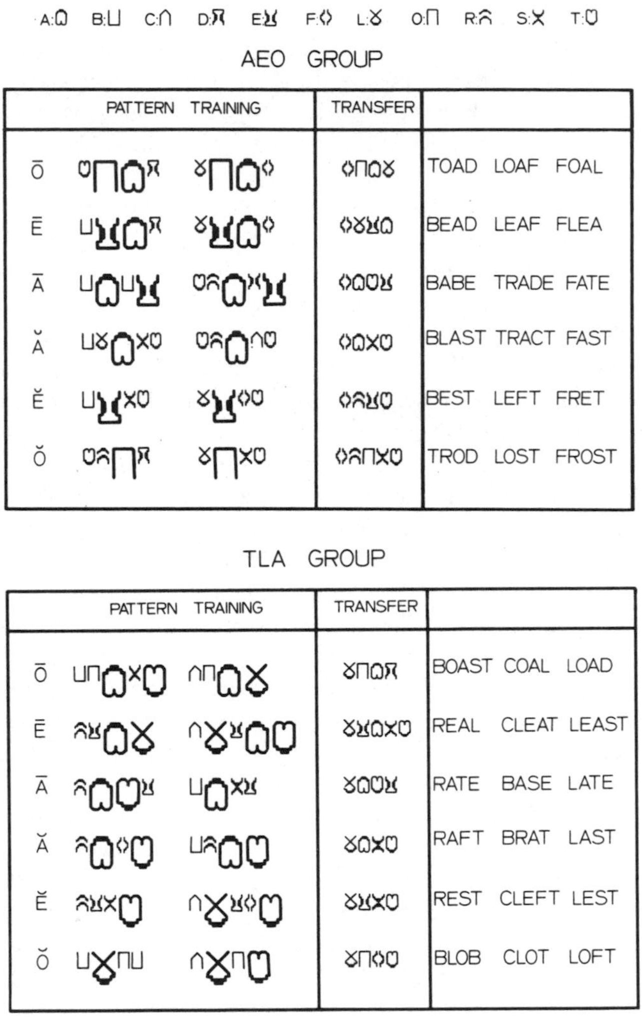

A:◌̣   B:⊔   C:∩   D:Ȓ   E:⋊   F:◇   L:⋆   O:∩   R:ȃ   S:✕   T:◌̇

AEO GROUP

	PATTERN TRAINING		TRANSFER	
ō	ᵒ∏◌̣ᴿ ⋆∏◌̣◇		◇∏◌̣⋆	TOAD LOAF FOAL
ē	⊔⋊◌̣ᴿ ⋆⋊◌̣◇		◇⋆⋊◌̣	BEAD LEAF FLEA
ā	⊔◌̣⋊⋊ ᵒȃ◌̣ˣ⋊		◇◌̣◌̣⋊	BABE TRADE FATE
ă	⊔⋆◌̣ˣᵒ ᵒȃ◌̣∩ᵒ		◇◌̣ˣᵒ	BLAST TRACT FAST
ĕ	⊔⋌ˣᵒ ⋆⋌◇ᵒ		◇ȃ⋊ᵒ	BEST LEFT FRET
ŏ	ᵒȃ∏ᴿ ⋆∏ˣᵒ		◇ȃ∏ˣᵒ	TROD LOST FROST

TLA GROUP

	PATTERN TRAINING		TRANSFER	
ō	⊔∏◌̣ˣᵒ ∩∏◌̣✕		⋆∏◌̣ȃ	BOAST COAL LOAD
ē	ȃ⋊◌̣✕ ∩✕⋊◌̣ᵒ		⋆⋊◌̣ˣᵒ	REAL CLEAT LEAST
ā	ȃ◌̣◌̣⋊ ⊔◌̣ˣ⋊		⋆◌̣◌̣⋊	RATE BASE LATE
ă	ȃ◌̣◇ᵒ ⊔ȃ◌̣ᵒ		⋆◌̣ˣᵒ	RAFT BRAT LAST
ĕ	ȃ⋊ˣᵒ ∩✕⋊◇ᵒ		⋆⋊ˣᵒ	REST CLEFT LEST
ŏ	⊔✕∏⊔ ∩✕∏ᵒ		⋆∏◇ᵒ	BLOB CLOT LOFT

FIG. 15. Materials for the vowel pattern experiment. In the AEO group all the vowels are increased in size. This emphasizes the vowel–consonant patterns that are important English signals for vowel sounds. In the TLA group, three letters are increased in size as a control. These letters are correlated with sound components of the response word, but do not constitute a natural orthographic group. The subjects in these two groups were transferred to lists printed in unenhanced form at various times in the experiment.

The results, shown in Fig. 16, are very encouraging for the notion of emphasizing vowel–consonant patterns. The vowel group is faster on both training and transfer lists than is the discrete control group; the TLA group is, if anything, worse than the discrete control. The difference between the vowel and the discrete control groups may be in the process of disappearing by the third transfer, since the difference is significant only when the last two trials are

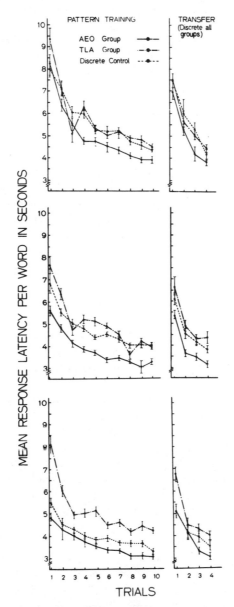

FIG. 16. Results of vowel-patterning experiment. The conditions were run in the order shown left to right, top to bottom. On the transfer tasks all three groups were run on a six word list printed in discrete (unenhanced) form. The vowel (AEO) group was overall faster on both training and transfer lists. This result is not due to pattern enhancement in itself, since the TLA group was, if anything, worse than the control group.

analyzed. However, even if the effect has in fact disappeared at this point, it is impressive that emphasis of such common spelling patterns is useful even that long for adults. To conjecture about possible applications, emphasis of these patterns might be perceptually useful for a substantially longer period with children, and in any event would make it easier for the teacher to talk about the necessary rules.

4.6   Is Visual-Pattern Learning Important with Traditional Typefaces?

Several experiments in this paper suggest that phonic translation becomes more important or at least more apparent with practice. If so, all of the effects of pattern and typography that we have been discussing might be solely transitional. That is, with enough experience, the effect of visual variables might indeed be reduced to matters of legibility and translational familiarity. If we could find the effects of visual pattern and specific visual learning with adults reading normal typography, we would have some assurance that we are dealing with more than a transient phenomenon. Two lines of evidence will be presented in this section that show visual effects with adults reading traditional typefaces.

Smith (1969) and Smith, Lott, and Cronnell (1969) found that adults suffered no deficit when orally reading and scanning connected prose in which the letters of all the words were printed in alternating upper and lower case, provided that the size of the upper case was reduced to prevent obscuring the lower case ascenders in letters such as t, l, and h. If this is a robust finding, then it indicates that no interletter features are crucial in practiced word identification and is obviously an ultimate limit that we would like to know about. Our first concern was that neither of the tasks that Smith and his colleagues used were as sensitive as we would have liked. Oral reading of prose has a response-speed limitation and gives contextual cues that might limit the subject's dependence on the stimuli; the scanning task was a rather slowly performed scan through prose for multiple targets. We hoped that a semantic scan through word lists might avoid response-speed limitations, force the subject to depend strongly on the stimulus, and yet still guarantee that he was accessing meanings. We still agree with Smith and his colleagues that the extent to which people adapt to pattern changes is extremely impressive; but to find a complete absence of any effect due to pattern variation is important for our research and deserves another look.

The specific task we designed is illustrated in Fig. 17. Subjects were asked to report whether a given set of 16 words had 3, 4, or 5 first names in it; or, for alternate subjects, whether that same set had 3, 4, or 5 place names in it. These lists were drawn from a vocabulary of 256 words, which meant that 16 sets were required to complete a trial; that is, 16 sets were required to run through the entire vocabulary in either the alternating or the lower case typography. Eight subjects were run in this task with every other set being lower case or al-

rObBeR   LiNdA   OyStEr   wAtErLoO   hEnRy   sWeDeN   lEaThEr   HaRnEsS

KeNyA   LeTtUcE   QuEeN   aNnE   NiGeRiA   MichAeL   pAlACE   aPpLe

gErMaNy   ClArInEt   ArTiSt   NeCtArInE   cEliA   VICToR   yEsTeRdAy   mAtThEw

PiStOn   KeTtLe   MeXiCo   eRiC   HeDgE   DaNCEr   scOtLaNd   viViAnNe

ohio   elbow   uncle   headlight   jewelry   douglas   waterloo   flag

peter   neil   manitoba   palace   paris   factory   oyster   gordon

FIG. 17. Materials to test for disruption or visual pattern. Subjects were asked to scan sets of 16 words to report the number of first names or, on other trials, the number of place names. The top two sets of 16 are printed in alternating lower and upper case with the size of the upper case decreased to prevent obscuring the relative height cues in the lower case. F. Smith and his colleagues had previously reported that this type of pattern disruption produced no performance decrement.

ternating. As is indicated in the left-hand panel of Fig. 18, subjects showed a highly significant deficit ($p < .001$) in the first two trials of scanning the alternating type. Finding a deficit due to alternating type is similar to a report by Coltheart and Freeman (1974) of a tachistoscopic recognition study.

This effect, however, does not prove that the subject is critically relying on interletter patterns for his highest rate of word access. He could be reacting cautiously to the novel typography in what are generally novel circumstances. At its limit this novelty explanation can amount to the same thing as saying that interletter cues are important; that is, each new word introduced in the new typography could be regarded as a novel stimulus and therefore a signal for caution. However, we can get rid of two less extreme versions. One is that the novel print is reacted to more slowly only when the whole task is unfamiliar; the other is that the subject simply has to adapt to ignoring interletter cues in favor of other, equally efficient cues. Coltheart and Freeman's answer to these possibilities was the observation that their subjects generally reported not noticing that a different typography had been used.

We addressed ourselves to these possibilities in a procedure which the subjects first followed until they met a criterion of 16 sets in which the average

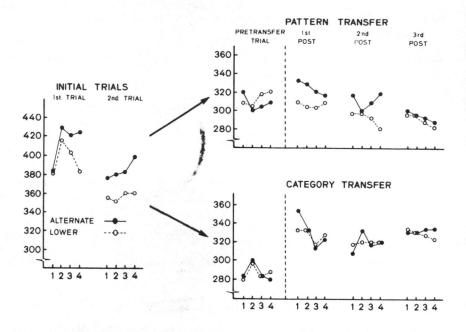

MSEC/WORD FOR EACH ¼ OF SELECTED TRIALS (256 WORDS/TRIAL)

FIG. 18. Results of the pattern-disruption experiment. Alternating upper and lower case did produce a decrement on this semantic scan task. This decrement returned when the same words were printed with the other alternation, but not when a nonpattern difficulty was introduced.

difference between the two typographies was zero. We then ran one additional trial to provide a free baseline and carried out (in balanced order) one of two transfer tasks for three trials and then switched to the other transfer task. For the pattern transfer, the subject was asked to scan for whatever category he had trained on (first names or place names) in lists in which the same vocabulary had been retyped. For example, if in his training lists he had searched for first names among words such as RoBbEr, lInDa, KeNyA, he would now search for first names among rObBeR, LiNdA, kEnYa. This transfer changes the appearance of the stimulus but leaves the vocabulary, task, and target category the same. In the category transfer the subject was to search for the other category in unchanged stimulus sets. So if he had been searching for first names, he was now to look for the place names that had been there in the same form all along. If the typographic difference is due to an interaction with a new task, it might show in this category transfer even though the stimulus itself remained unchanged.

As is illustrated in Fig. 18, the typography did have an effect for the first two trials ($p < .01$ on each trial) when the stimulus pattern was changed, but not when the search category was changed. The category transfer did significantly change the level of performance but did not interact with the typography. Evidently the typographic difference is controlled more by the visual stimulus than by the general difficulty of the task. This experiment indicates that visual patterns (interletter cues) are important for efficient performance of this task, but it does not tell us whether the effect is due to specific-word learning. The subject might be using the appearance of part or all of the specific word, in which case the revived effect would be due to changing that appearance. On the other hand, he might be translating to sound with multiletter units, in which case the revived effect would be due to meeting letter groups that had not been met in the original 256-word sample. If the latter case is the whole story, however, I am surprised that the size of the pattern-transfer effect is as large as it is, given the substantial number of letter combinations that must have become familiar with the training stimuli.

Jan Szumski (1974), how at the Ontario Institute for Studies in Education, has addressed himself to this point by producing a series of experiments that clearly points to the existence of some very specific stimulus learning in adult reading. To appreciate the design problems that he had to solve, let us first consider how we might demonstrate that a reader would require some visual experience with each word in order to respond to it at maximum rate. First we would have to be sure that the reader was sufficiently familiar with the typeface and the orthography used so that any deficit with a new word could not be interpreted as a *general* inability to read fluently. This is easy to establish with adults, but then we have the problem of finding words that he has not seen. Usually if an adult has not seen a word, then he is unfamiliar with the word in any sense, and that is not the question we wish to ask. In the morally fibrous days of yore, we might have entertained the notion that many subjects had a stock of highly familiar obscene words that they had not regularly seen in standard typefaces. In the world's current state of progress, however, we are forced to make up our own words, which is exactly what Szumski did.

His basic procedure was to run a series of trials in which he taught 20 one-word "definitions" such as HEN, GLOVE, COFFEE, as responses to a set of 20 nonsense stimulus words such as SPAG, DOKE, TESH. Half of these nonsense words were presented only auditorily and half were presented in normal printing as well. After learning all the associations, the subject was given four additional speed trials to consolidate the learning. He was then given a series of trials in which he was asked to judge whether one of the words in the list was an appropriate ending for a given sentence; for example, "Ann spilled a glass of . . . SPAG." This was the key task because the final word was always presented visually on a separate card. If, in fact, the subject's general experience with the typography and normal English orthography is sufficient to allow his highest rate of word identification, then he ought to identify the auditorily trained words as rapidly as the visually trained words. If, in addition to these general abilities, he needs some visual experience with each new word, then the visually trained words ought to be identified more rapidly.

However, there are other possible explanations for any difference that might be found; for example, the subject might have mentally spelled the word differently or he might be mildly surprised at seeing it in print—the novelty explanation again. To control for these possibilities, we preceded the meaning-training trials with 12 trials in which the subjects were asked to read aloud as rapidly as possible a list of nonsense words that included five words that would be used in visual training and five that would be used in auditory training. As a result of this training, the subjects had seen both classes of words in print and were exposed to their particular spellings. But what the subjects did not have with the auditorily trained words was experience in retrieving meaning from the visual stimulus, the task that was being tested in the final appropriateness-judgment trials. One more of these pronunciation trials was inserted between training and testing to refresh the subjects' memory of the spelling and general appearance of the words.

Reaction time on the final judgment trials is shown in Fig. 19a. There was a highly significant difference due to prior experience with retrieving meaning from the visual stimulus, (V vs. A), but no difference due to visual experience per se (V vs. V–N, A vs. A–N). Evidently, despite the tremendous amount of prior experience of these subjects with standard English orthography and typography, some additional specific-stimulus learning is necessary to attain the highest rate of retrieval. Given the speed with which this effect disappears, one additional control should be mentioned. On the test trials the words were introduced in subgroups so that the first trial of some words overlapped with the second trial of others and the first trial of a third subgroup overlapped with the second and third trials of the first two subgroups. This procedure was introduced, among other reasons, to avoid having all of the first trial measurements confounded with the introduction of the test procedure. The differences shown in Fig. 19 were found also among the words introduced later in the procedure.

Earlier in this paper we discussed the point that evidence of incomplete transfer to new words, as we have just found, does not necessarily imply either the presence or the absence of linguistic translation. To infer that linguistic translation is important or relatively unimportant, we would need additional evidence. Evidence that suggests that acoustic representations are relatively unimportant after specific visual retrieval experience was obtained in another of Szumski's experiments. In this case, half of the stimulus words were acoustically confusible, such as JIGHT, PITE, PAWPH, JAWF, NOFF, and half were not, such as DOKE, BARM, GOLP, LART, SPAG. As can be seen in Fig. 19b, acoustic confusibility made a big difference when the only prior retrieval experience was from auditorily presented words, but not when the prior experi-

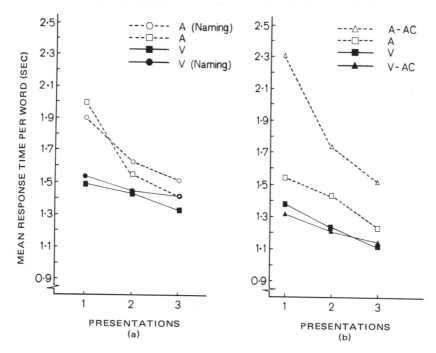

FIG. 19. Results of the specific visual-learning experiments. (a) Words that had not been seen during meaning training (auditory) were evaluated more slowly on the first presentation than those that had been seen (visual). This is despite the fact that some of the words (auditory-naming, visual-naming) had been seen before for purposes of rapid pronunciation. (b) High acoustic confusibility (AC) made a difference for words that had not been seen before (A–AC vs. A) but not for those that had (V–AC vs. V).

ence was with visual stimuli as well. Evidently, showing the stimuli allows the subject to bypass the most deleterious effects of acoustic confusibility.

In combination the two sets of experiments described in this section make a case that adults are still using some visual patterns and some stimulus-specific learning even after years of reading practice. We have no way of knowing what their relative importance is at this stage, but at least we do have evidence that they are still there. We cannot use the small differences in Fig. 19 to say that the visual contribution to retrieval is small since we cannot estimate what proportion of these response times is related to retrieval and what proportion is related to other activities such as semantic decision and response execution. Further, the fact that the effect disappears within two or three trials might mean, by analogy with the large vocabulary studies described above, that readers have learned how to learn visual patterns rapidly. Speed of visual learning, as well as speed of orthographic processing, may be the useful fruit of years of practice. In any event, the roles of specific-stimulus learning and visual patterning in acquisition of fluency cannot be taken lightly, given that they are still in evidence at this late stage of general practice.

5 CONCLUSIONS AND DISCUSSION

In summary:

1. An alphabet helps at fluency (Figs. 6 and 10), but so does a sound-correlated pattern (Figs. 10 and 12).

2. The effect of arbitrary distinctiveness disappears with practice (Fig. 12), but the effect of sound-correlated pattern is robust over increases in practice (Fig. 12), and vocabulary (Tables 1 and 3).

3. Adults have a surprisingly difficult time using an unfamiliar alphabet (Fig. 14), but at least one way of overcoming this difficulty is to visually enhance pronunciation groups (Fig. 16).

4. Visual patterns (Fig. 18) and specific visual learning (Fig. 19) apparently still play a role for adults using the traditional English alphabet.

5. Finally, there are signs of generalizable learning for subjects who are restricted to the visual stimulus, that is, who do not have access to a functional alphabet (Table 4).

All of the conclusions, of course, are subject to limitations imposed by the materials and subjects.

5.1 Limitations and Theoretical Implications

Before considering the limitations, let us look at the logical implications of the findings. The data clearly give us empirical reason for keeping separate the issues of visual pattern, specific learning, and linguistic translation. Early in practice the effects of sound-correlated pattern cannot be distinguished from the effects of patterning that is completely arbitrary and therefore must be specific to the particular word. Later in practice the sound-correlated pattern is superior, which indicates that the sound properties of the word are being taken into account; although, as we have previously discussed, this could be a result of similarity relations rather than linguistic translation in the more usual component correspondence sense. But further, even if the sound properties are ignored, the reader is not condemned completely to specific-stimulus learning. As we saw in the second large-vocabulary study, subjects who never had a functional alphabet still showed signs of generalizable learning, signs that under other conditions could have been mistaken for orthographic learning.

The most interesting general result for adult processes is that in four of the studies in this paper, sound referencing had an effect over and above that due to information transmission; that is, over and above that solely due to the elimination of possible response words. This conclusion is counter to the tenor of explanation in much of the tachistoscopic recognition work of the 1950s and 1960s. But it is also a conclusion that is subject to an important methodological limitation: the task in each of these studies was to overtly pronounce unordered series of words. We could easily imagine that the result would occur only with pronunciation or only when the anticipatory effects of interword context were removed. The only evidence in the current work relevant to this point is a follow-up to the first experiment reported in this chapter. Four of these subjects, the most patient four, continued for another 400 trials using the same stimuli but writing the arbitrarily assigned digits 2 through 7 as responses. The advantage of the orthographic items was smaller but still significant throughout, which suggests that overt pronunciation is not immediately crucial to the effect. Subjects reported initially using the original responses as mediators and evidently they continued to be affected by this prior experience. J. Baron and I are working on experiments that are more compelling than this, but they are hard to do and will clearly take more time. In the long run, we suspect that the fact that the alphabetic advantage is apparent with such a small number of words will speak a volume about fluent adult information processing. What is still at question is whether the effect is restricted solely to phonemic reference or whether it will extend to any reference system with interpretable components.

I personally am fascinated by the fact that adults show so many of the deficits associated with early reading problems. The blocking of blending and semantic retrieval shown in Anderson's experiments are intriguing dividends of this research. These parallels suggest that many of the phenomena that are being investigated with selected natural language materials can also be investigated with artificial materials. The advantage of this, of course, is that artificial materials can have any characteristics built into them, and can therefore be a useful source of supplementary evidence.

5.2 Reading Instruction

Ultimately the major payoff would be for this work to suggest ways of improving initial or remedial reading instruction. For this purpose, a different set of methodological cautions should be observed. Given the fact that we are looking to an early stage of reading, the limits placed by our current use of overt pronunciation and unordered lists is probably not crucial; the child does not read silently anyway, and reliance on context is relatively weak. By comparison a far more serious limitation is the fact that the child will not previously have learned the use of an alphabet as our adult subjects had. There is no way of investigating this factor except with children, and I cannot anticipate how it will come out. On the one hand our sound-correlated patterning could make acquisition of orthographic knowledge easier. On the other hand the increased visual distinctiveness could distract the child from even trying to acquire this knowledge, a fear similar to that voiced by the early phonic advocates.

Our plan for extension of this work to children has two initial stages. One is to use the visual matching task mentioned earlier (page 155) to increase the distinctiveness of the typography. The other is to use some traditional-letter version of Anderson's vowel-enhancement experiment to test for the influence on the use of sound properties. The important aspect of both these tasks is that they are cheap to run and are aimed at small, immediate results. This might help us to weed out a variety of errors without paying the enormous cost of implementing a full course of instruction.

In the long run, it is the variety of uses to which visual pattern can be put that gives me the greatest hope that something useful will come out of this work. Visual pattern could be introduced to speed up the word-specific learning that still seems to be found with adults in traditional typography. It could also be used to make it easier for teachers to describe pronunciation rules in explicit phonic instruction. Compare for yourself the relative ease of describing the rules for long and short vowel pronunciation in the material in Fig. 2 and that in traditional typefaces. Visual pattern can also be used to influence the segmentation and size of units learned about during sight training. It is this factor that might make sight training a more useful preparation for explicit instruction on phonic representation and that might allow the child to avoid some of the problems of alphabetic blending. If visual similarity has been correctly arranged, the child might more naturally generalize to similarly pronounced words and not have to deal as long with isolated letters. In essence, visual pattern could be used to reduce the load on explicit instruction and to guide implicit learning.

ACKNOWLEDGMENTS

I would like to thank Amina Miller and Nancy Nelson for their exceptionally constructive and intelligent assistance with the research reported here. This research was funded by the National Research Council of Canada.

REFERENCES

Baron, J., & Thurston, I. An analysis of the word superiority effect. *Cognitive Psychology,* 1973, *4,* 207–228.

Beller, H. K. Parallel and serial stages in matching. *Journal of Experimental Psychology,* 1970, *84,* 213–219.

Bower, T. G. R. Reading by eye. In H. Levin & J. P. Williams (Eds.), *Basic studies on reading.* New York: Basic Books, Inc., 1970.

Coltheart, M., & Freeman, R. Case alternation impairs word identification. *Bulletin of the Psychonomic Society,* 1974, *3,* 102–104.

Eichelman, W. H. Familiarity effects in the simultaneous matching task. *Journal of Experimental Psychology,* 1970, *86,* 275–282.

Fry, E. A diacritical marking system to aid beginning reading instruction. *Elementary English,* 1964, 526–529.

Kolers, P. A. Three stages of reading. In H. Levin and J. P. Williams, *Basic Studies in Reading.* New York: Harper & Row, 1970.

Krueger, L. E. Visual comparison in a redundant display. *Cognitive Psychology,* 1970, *1,* 341–357.

Meyer, D. E., Schvaneveldt, R. W., & Ruddy, M. G. Functions of graphemic and phonemic codes in visual word recognition. *Memory and Cognition,* 1974, 309–321.

Neisser, U. *Cognitive psychology.* New York: Appleton-Century-Crofts, 1967.

Posner, M. I., Lewis, J. Z., & Conrad, C. Component processes in reading. In J. Kavanaugh & I. Mattingly (Eds.), *Language by Ear and by Eye.* Cambridge, Massachusetts: MIT Press, 1972.

Rabbitt, P. M. A. Channel-capacity, intelligibility, and immediate memory. *Quarterly Journal of Experimental Psychology,* 1968, *20,* 241–248.

Reber, A. S. Implicit learning of artificial grammars. *Journal of Verbal Learning and Verbal Behavior,* 1967, *6,* 855–863.

Reed, S. K. Pattern recognition and categorization. *Cognitive Psychology,* 1972, *3,* 382–407.

Shepard, R. N. The analysis of proximities: multidimensional scaling with an unknown distance function. I. *Psychometrika,* 1962, *27,* 125–140 (a); II. *Psychometrika,* 1962, *27,* 219–246 (b).

Smith, F. The use of featural dependencies across letters in the visual identification of words. *Journal of Verbal Learning and Verbal Behavior,* 1969, *8,* 215–218.

Smith, F. *Understanding Reading.* New York: Holt, Rhinehart & Winston, 1971.

Smith, F., Lott, D., & Cronnell, B. The effect of type size and case alternation on word identification. *American Journal of Psychology,* 1969, *82,* 248–253.

Southgate, V., & Warburton, F. W. *I.T.A.: An independent evaluation.* London: J. Murray, 1969.

Szumski, J. M. The effects of specific visual experience on rapid visual word identification. Master's thesis, McMaster University, Hamilton 1974.

Thurston, I. M. The effects of difficult recognition on accuracy of recall: evidence for modality specific processing. Master's thesis, McMaster University, Hamilton 1969.

Tinker, M. A. *Bases for effective reading.* Minneapolis: University of Minnesota Press, 1965.

Tulving, E., & Thompson, D. M. Encoding specificity and retrieval processes in episodic memory. *Psychological Review,* 1973, *80,* 352–373.

Venezky, R. L. English orthography: its graphical structure and its relation to sound. *Reading Research Quarterly,* 1967, *2,* 75–106.

Wijk, A. *Rules of Pronunciation for the English Language.* London: Oxford University Press, 1966.

4

Perceptual Processes in Reading: The Perceptual Spans

Keith Rayner

University of Rochester

George W. McConkie

Cornell University

1 INTRODUCTION

The first question that we must confront in seeking to understand some phenomenon, such as reading, is how to conceptualize the phenomenon of interest. The nature of that conceptualization largely determines the questions that we will attempt to investigate in our research. One way to view reading is as a set of mental (cognitive) processes which the person carries out in order to gain certain information that is expressed in a text. From this point of view, our task is to be able to establish evidence about the types and sequences of processes which take place in the mind of the reader as he is engaged in reading, and about the products which result from this activity (for instance, the nature of the memory representation of information obtained from the text). The development of such a cognitive-processing theory of reading requires several steps:

1. assembling one's knowledge of characteristics of reading which are believed to be adequately supported by evidence;

2. specifying several alternative sets of processes which, if the person actually operated in that way, would give rise to reading behavior having the identified characteristics;

3. identifying critical differences among those different sets of processes which might be testable;

4. setting up an experiment, the data from which would provide evidence for or against the different models of reading that have been identified; and

5. refining the theory by repeatedly cycling through these steps.

Those sets of processes which are inconsistent with new information obtained from experiments can be discarded as serious contenders as theories of reading. In actuality, it generally requires a number of studies having some agreement to provide sufficient evidence to eliminate a possible theory of reading.

We have elected to take this approach to the study of fluent reading. This approach tends to give us several biases which need to be stated. First, we see ourselves as attempting to identify obvious or well-documented facts about the nature of reading, both as a basis for saying that certain possible theories or models of the reading process cannot be correct and as a stimulus for generating sets of processes which might still be serious contenders as processes actually involved in reading. Second, we tend to look at any information about reading, including results from experiments, in terms of what sorts of processes would be capable of producing such behavior. Information about reading is valued when it can help eliminate alternative possible models of the reading process. Information that eliminates only already-eliminated models or that is not useful in selecting among models is not valued. Finally, we are skeptical of whether conclusions based on experiments involving a task other than normal reading can be generalized to the reading task itself. It is clear that people are capable of selecting and using their cognitive processes in manners which attempt to maximize their performance in the task at hand. Therefore, we would prefer to study people actually involved in reading passages for the purpose of understanding them, rather than to study the same people as they identify isolated words, attempt to remember individual sentences, etc. Only by studying people who are actually reading can we be sure that the phenomena we observe in our research are characteristic of people as they read.

This last preference poses a difficulty for the researcher interested in reading. There is so little overt behavior to observe as a person is engaged in fluent, silent reading that it is difficult to know how to go about it. As a result, most of the "facts" about reading on which present theories are built come from three sources: data from tasks other than normal reading (tachistoscopic presentations of words or phrases, retention of individual disconnected sentences, etc.); data from tests given following reading (which may tell about the product of reading, the memory content, but which say little about the processes that yielded that product); and generally accepted conclusions about reading which result from the researcher's own experience (such as: people can change their way of reading according to their purpose). The most notable exception to this is the recording of eye movements which, of course, occur as reading is in process. So far eye-movement data have yielded little information about the processes involved in reading. Thus, we have few well-established facts about the nature of fluent reading, and even less good theory about the processes involved.

This chapter will describe our attempt to develop a way of answering one important question about fluent reading. The question studied concerned the size of the perceptual span: From how wide an area of text is visual information obtained during a fixation while reading? The method of study involved tracking the subject's eyes by computer and actually manipulating the text display as he was reading it. Both the question and the method used to study it require some additional comment.

2 THE PERCEPTUAL SPANS IN READING

In the development of a cognitive processing theory of reading, the question of the size of the perceptual span is extremely important. To take two extreme possibilities, the span may be very narrow, so the reader identifies little more than a single word during a fixation, or the span may be very broad, so the reader obtains visual information about a whole phrase of more on the line fixated and perhaps information from lines other than the one fixated. If the span were very narrow, the cognitive processes involved in reading could be much like those in hearing speech, gaining access to the text one word at a time, and handling the text generally in a linear order. If the span were extremely wide, the cognitive processes must be capable of storing and operating on a wide array of visual information at the same time, or they must be able to decide where in the array the useful information is and operate on that part of the total pattern. It would then seem possible for the mind to detect at once entire phrases or clauses or perhaps even more, and to detect information on the next line to assist in the interpretation of the line the person is presently reading. Thus, the structure of the rest of the theory will be greatly influenced by an answer to the perceptual-span question.

In reality, there is undoubtedly not a single perceptual span. Much visual detail is available to the person in a small area of central vision called the fovea. The fovea is about $2°$ of visual angle across: with newpaper print held at 18 in. from the eye, about 8–9 letters of a line would fall in the fovea. Beyond this is the parafoveal region (from $2°$ to $10°$ across the retina, according to Ditchburn, 1973), and finally the visual periphery. The further the stimulus pattern is from the fovea on the retina, the poorer the visual acuity or ability to discriminate shapes. Thus, it is probably true that certain characteristics of the text pattern are available only in the near-foveal region, such as the full detail of letters. Other more gross characteristics may be available further toward the periphery, such as word shape, word-length patterns, information about where sentences end and begin, etc. Thus, the perceptual spans for different aspects of the visual pattern will probably be different: visual detail necessary to identify letters in words may be obtained from a narrower range than visual information necessary to identify word shape or word length. For this reason we will frequently speak of the perceptual spans, in the plural.

2.1 Previous Research

Since late in the 19th century, when it was discovered that the eye does not move smoothly in reading but rather executes a series of rapid movements (saccades), each followed by a relatively long period during which time the eye is relatively stationary (fixation), there have been studies aimed at identifying the size of the region seen by the reader during a fixation. Most studies have involved tachistoscopic presentation: flashing a string of letters or words for a short period of time so the subject cannot fixate them more than once, and then testing to see how many of the items he can identify or recall (early studies are described by Huey, 1908). Subjects can generally report about three–four unconnected letters, two unconnected short words or four connected short words from a presentation of 1/100 sec. Knowing something about the words to be presented increases the amount that can be reported (Tulving & Gold, 1963; Morton, 1964; Marcel, 1974). Other studies have presented letters and words at different distances from the fovea, with the subjects attempting to identify them (Mackworth, 1965; Bouma, 1973). In this research, only four or five letters around the fixation point are generally identified with near-100% accuracy, and accuracy drops as the stimulus is presented farther from the fovea. These studies tell us what people are capable of seeing in a single stimulus presentation. However, what subjects are capable of seeing in this task may be quite different from what they actually see in reading, where they are making four fixations per second and not specifically attempting to name the words or letters they are seeing.

Other methods have also been used to identify the size of the perceptual span. Some have simply divided the number of letters on a line by the number of fixations the reader made on it to yield a "span of recognition" (Taylor, 1957; Taylor, 1965) of about 1.1 words for skilled readers. However, Hochberg (1970) has argued convincingly that the number of fixations may reflect the subjects' cognitive operations rather than what they can see on a fixation. Recently, attempts have been made to limit the area of text available to a reader during a fixation by placing a mask over the text, allowing only a certain number of letters to be seen at once. Then either the mask is moved over the text or the text is passed under the mask (Poulton, 1962; Newman, 1966; Bouma & deVoogd, 1974). In these studies, smaller masks greatly disrupt reading. However, the task itself is disruptive to normal eye movements, and it is difficult to know how to estimate the perceptual span from such studies.

It is important here to distinguish between the size of the perceptual spans and the size of the eye–voice span (Levin & Kaplan, 1970). The eye–voice span is a measure of how far the eye is ahead of the voice in oral reading and does not identify the region from which visual information is acquired during a single fixation.

From studies of visual acuity, Gough (1972) suggested that the size of the perceptual span of readers as they read might be about 20 letter spaces on the line fixated. However, what seems to be needed is a way of gaining information about the size of the span as the subject is engaged in a more normal reading task, in which he is attempting to gain information from a passage, and in which his eye-movement behavior is not constrained too severely. That was the goal of the research to be described here.

2.2 Computer Technology in the Study of Reading

The type of equipment used in our research is not generally familiar to people in the reading profession. For this reason, and because we believe it has great potential for research and for diagnosis in reading, we shall describe it here to some degree. Further information can be obtained by consulting Reder (1973) or McConkie and Rayner (1974).

In order to follow the movements of the eye during reading, we used a Biometrics Model-SG Eye Movement Monitor. This equipment detects eye position by illuminating the eye with invisible infrared light and measuring the amount of light reflected from certain portions of the eye's surface. This equipment was attached to a computer which was programmed to check the eye position frequently, in our case 60 times per second. Actually, it is quite possible for the computer to check the position 1,000 times per second or more. The computer was programmed to analyze the eye-position information and decide whether the eye was moving or still, to keep a record of each fixation (where the person was looking and how long it lasted), and to record the duration of each saccade. Thus, the computer kept a complete record of eye-movement behavior, in a form which could be analyzed by other computer programs. With this system, the computer identified where the eye was directed many times a second.

The text for the subjects to read was displayed by the computer on a cathode-ray tube (CRT) much like a television tube. Like a television, the image on the CRT would disappear within a few thousandths of a second if it were not being continually redrawn, usually about 60 times per second. This characteristic makes it possible to rapidly change the image on the CRT within 1/60 sec or less.

Since the computer calculated where the person was looking and also controlled the image on the CRT for the person to see, it was possible to program it to make specific types of changes in the image as the person was engaged in reading. For instance, it was possible for the computer to detect that the eye had completed a saccade, compute where the eye was fixating, and then create a list of instructions for the CRT to place a particular image on the screen at some point in the person's foveal or parafoveal visual area for that particular fixation. The image would appear very shortly after the fixation occurred. The computer can carry out this calculation within a few thousandths of a second or less. This is possible because of the rapid calculation of modern computers; the computer we presently use can carry out at least 250 operations in 1/1000 sec. This technology makes it possible for the researcher to make changes in the display during the period of an eye movement (between 1/50 and 1/10 sec), and to create the exact pattern that he would like the person to see on a particular fixation. It gives us a type of control over the stimulus pattern available to the reader in a manner never before possible. At the same time, we have a complete record of eye behavior and can also use more traditional methods of finding out what effects our manipulations have, such as testing the subject for retention following reading.

The exact manner in which these capabilities were used to investigate the size of the perceptual spans during reading will be described in the next sections. We will present only the major results in summary form here. For added detail see McConkie and Rayner (1975a, b) and Rayner (1975a, b).

2.3   Three Experiments

2.3.1   Window Study: Size of the Perceptual Spans

The first study we shall describe was designed to investigate how far from the point of central vision the reader acquires visual information about individual letters, word shapes, and word lengths during a fixation. Our strategy was to compare the reading pattern of skilled readers when these aspects of the visual pattern were and were not present at different distances into their parafoveal and peripheral visual areas.

In order to do this, a number of passages were selected from a high school psychology text, and then different "mutilated" versions of these passages were produced. Each form of mutilation was designed to produce a text pattern which retained certain visual characteristics of the original passage and changed others. For instance, one mutilated version was produced by replacing every letter with an x. In this version, all visual information about specific letters or word shapes was lost, but word-length patterns were still present. This visual pattern was then displayed on the CRT and the computer began monitoring the subject's eye position. When he oriented his eyes to look at the first line of text, the computer immediately replaced the x's within a certain region around the point of central vision with the corresponding letters from the original passage. Thus, a "window" of normal text was created in the subject's foveal and parafoveal visual region for that fixation. When the subject made a saccadic eye movement and fixated a new location, the old window was returned to its x pattern and a new window of normal text was created at the new eye location. Thus, wherever the reader looked, there was normal text for him to see and he could read quite normally. However, the experimenter could manipulate the size

TABLE 1
An Example of a Line of Text on Four Successive Fixations[a]

Fixation number	Example[b]
1	Xxxxhology means perxxxxxxxx xxxxxxxxx xxxx xxxx xxxxxxx. Xxxx xx x
2	Xxxxxxxxxx xxxxs personality diaxxxxxx xxxx xxxx xxxxxxx. Xxxx xx x
3	Xxxxxxxxxx xxxxx xxxxxxxxxxx xiagnosis from hanx xxxxxxx. Xxxx xx x
4	Xxxxxxxxxx xxxxx xxxxxxxxxxx xxxxxxxxx xxxm hand writing. Xxxx xx x

[a]Each window area is 17 characters wide, with 8 character positions to the left of fixation and 8 character positions to the right of fixation.

[b]Note: The dot represents the location of fixation on four successive fixations.

of the window and, by originally displaying different text mutilations, could determine what visual characteristics of the original passage were present in the reader's parafoveal and peripheral vision.

An example of what a line of text might look like during successive fixations in reading is shown in Table 1. The actual display for the subjects included about 7–9 lines of double-spaced text.

Subjects reported having no difficulty reading under these circumstances unless the window became too small, at which point they reported that reading became difficult, as if some kind of force were holding them back. They did not report seeing the display changes take place (which occurred within 3/ or 4/100 sec after the eye stopped), but did say they sometimes felt like "something funny" was happening in their peripheral vision.

In setting up the study, six types of text mutilation were used. Three involved replacing each letter by some other letter. Already mentioned is the X version, replacing each letter by an x. This maintained word length but destroyed word shape. A "compatible" (C) version was produced by replacing each letter by another letter visually similar to it, replacing ascending letters with other ascending letters, descenders with descenders, etc. Thus, although this version had different letters, the overall shape of the words was the same as in the original passage. Finally, a "noncompatible" (NC) version was produced by replacing each letter by another letter visually very different from it, replacing ascending letters by letters that were not ascending, etc. This produced a version having incorrect word-shape information. All three of these versions maintained the word length and punctuation pattern of the original passage. They were designated "spaces" (S) versions. The final three versions were produced by simply replacing spaces and punctuation marks in these three mutilated versions by the letter a. This eliminated all word-length and punctuation patterns. These were called "filled" (F) versions. An example of each of these six versions is shown in Table 2.

TABLE 2
Window Study 1: An Example of a Line of Text and the Various Text Patterns Derived from It[a]

Text	Graphology means personality diagnosis from hand writing. This is a
XS	Xxxxxxxxxx xxxxx xxxxxonality diagnosis xxxx xxxx xxxxxxxx. Xxxx xx x
XF	xxxxxxxxxxxxxxxxxxxxxxxxXxonality diagnosisxXXXXXXXXXXXXXXXXXXXXXXXXXXXXX
CS	Cnojkaiazp wsorc jsnconality diagnosis tnaw kori mnlflra. Ykle le o
CF	Cnojkaiaqpawsorcajsnconality diagnosisatnawakoriamnlflrqaaaYklealeao
NCS	Hbfxwysyvo tifdl xiblonality diagnosis abyt wfdn hbemedv. Awel el f
NCF	Hbfxwysyvoatifdlaxiblonality diagnosisaabytawfdnahbemedvaaaAwelaelaf

[a]Note: On each line a window of size 17 is shown, assuming the reader is fixating the letter d in "diagnosis."

Subjects read with eight different window sizes. The window was 13, 17, 21, 25, 31, 37, 45, or 100 letter positions in width.[1] A window size of 17 meant that the subject had normal text for the letter directly in central vision and for the eight letters to either side, on the line fixated. Since the lines of text were about 70 letter positions in length, a window size of 100 meant that usually the entire line fixated contained normal text.

In order to understand the strategy used in this research, assume for example that readers of the type we were studying acquire and use letter and word-shape information from a 25-character region, up to 12 letter positions to left and right of the center of vision. Assume further that word-length information is acquired further into the peripheral region, say from a 37-character region or up to 18 letter positions to left and right of the center of vision. How could we discover this from our research? First, if we had subjects read with a window 37 character positions wide or wider, and compared their reading performance under conditions in which word-length patterns were present in the mutilated text outside the window with performance under conditions in which they were not, we would find no difference in their performance. Having or eliminating word-length patterns more than 18 character positions from the center of vision would not affect reading, since (it is assumed) these readers do not pick up this visual information so far into the periphery. However, if we had the subjects read with windows of size 25 or 31, it would make a difference which type of pattern was outside the window. Deleting word-length patterns by using filled text mutilations outside the window would then be deleting visual information from a region from which the readers normally acquired that information. Thus, reading performance would be poorer for subjects having filled text-mutilation patterns outside the window for these size windows. For those subjects having space text mutilations, which preserve word-length patterns, with windows these sizes, it would make no difference whether the mutilations were of the compatible or noncompatible types (whether they preserved or destroyed word-shape patterns), since (it is assumed) the readers do not acquire word-shape information as far as 12 letter positions from the center of vision. However, with smaller windows, we would expect to find subjects reading more easily with the

---

[1] In describing the size of the perceptual span, it is not clear what the units of measurement should be. In this paper, we will report distances in terms of the number of character positions rather than in terms of absolute visual distances measured by visual angle. The experimental conditions were such that 1° of visual angle corresponded to about four letter positions. If the text were made larger, or if the subject were closer to the display, the same number of letter positions would subtend a greater visual angle. Since we did not study subjects reading under such conditions, we cannot say definitely to what degree such changes would have modified our results. We suspect that the results would not have been modified greatly, since enlarging the print, in addition to causing the letters to occupy a greater visual angle, also makes it possible for the reader to identify the letters further into his periphery. This characteristic of vision led us to adopt as our unit of measurement the number of character positions, rather than visual angle.

compatible text pattern outside the window, since it provides accurate word-shape information, than with the noncompatible text pattern.

Thus, by having subjects read the passages with windows of different sizes and with different types of text patterns outside the window, and then by comparing their reading performance for each window size for conditions in which certain aspects of the visual pattern are maintained versus destroyed in the region outside the window, it is possible to specify how far into the periphery particular types of visual information are acquired and used from the text while reading.

Six high school seniors participated in this study, all identified as being among the best readers in their school (Cambridge High and Latin, Cambridge, Mass.). Each read sixteen 500-word passages from a psychology text, each divided into six pages for a total of 96 pages of text. None of the subjects had taken a psychology class. They were asked to read the passages as they would normally do to understand the meaning. After reading each passage, they received multiple-choice questions and they were paid partly on the basis of their performance on these questions. Overall performance was around 80% correct on these tests. All the subjects had participated in an earlier pilot study using the apparatus. Each subject read two pages under each of the 48 conditions involved in the experiment (six types of mutilation and eight window sizes).

A large number of aspects of the subjects' eye-movement behavior were analyzed, as well as their comprehension-test performance. For a detailed examination of these analyses, see McConkie and Rayner (1975a). We will simply summarize the findings here.

Reducing the size of the window had a substantial effect on the subjects' reading speeds and various measures of their eye-movement behavior, increasing their reading time by as much as 60% (from 4.25 sec to 7 sec per 100 characters), but had no effect on their ability to answer the questions about the text. Even reducing the window size to 9 letter positions, which we did in a pilot study, did not significantly affect the subjects' test performance. With a window this small, the reader can hardly see more than a word at a time, which suggests that reducing the size of the perceptual span of a good reader does not destroy his ability to comprehend the passage, it just slows the rate at which he can do it. By implication, this suggests that it is not correct to say that poor readers fail to comprehend because they have a small perceptual span, as has often been suggested (Smith, 1971). The explanation of poor reading must be much more complex.

The evidence indicated that these subjects were acquiring and using specific letter and word-shape information no further than 10 or 11 letter positions from the center of vision; that is, the presence or absence of these types of information in the visual display within this region affected reading performance, but its presence or absence beyond this region did not. On the other hand, word-length information was acquired and used further into the periphery, at least 12 to 15 letter positions from the center of vision and possibly even farther. Word-length patterns in the parafoveal region seemed to be related to the guiding of the eye; eliminating such patterns in this region reduced the median saccade length (from a median of 8 to 6) and particularly reduced the number of long saccades.

Thus, it appears that the subjects were obtaining visual information about letters and word shape from a fairly narrow region during a fixation. However, another question immediately arose. Were the subjects obtaining these sorts of visual information equally far to the left and right of the center of vision? That is, is the perceptual span symmetrical or asymmetrical around the center of vision? This question led to the next study.

2.3.2 Window Study: Asymmetry of the Perceptual Spans

Studies investigating the size of the perceptual span with tachistoscopic methods have typically reported a slight asymmetry to the perceptual span (Mishkin & Forgays, 1952; Heron, 1957; Bryden, 1960). Typically, English-speaking subjects can identify words and letter strings further to the right than to the left. [There has been some controversy over the interpretation of these findings (Neisser, 1967; White, 1969).] Again, however, to understand what is taking place in the act of reading, we felt it necessary to try to use our research techniques to study people who are actually engaged in the act of reading.

In this study we used three window conditions and two types of text mutilation; letters were always replaced by similar letters, but word-length patterns were either present or absent (CS and CF conditions).

The first window condition, called "centered window," used a window size of 41. That is, normal text occurred in the letter position in the center of vision, and for the 20 letter positions to the left and right. The second condition, called "right-shifted window," used a window size of 25 that was offset to the right. It included the position in the center of vision, plus 20 letter positions to the right but only 4 to the left. The other condition, called "left-shifted window," used a window size of 25 offset to the left, which included the position at the center of vision, plus 20 letter positions to the left and 4 to the right. Examples of these different window conditions are shown in Table 3. By comparing reading

TABLE 3

Window Study 2: An Example of the Three Window Conditions Used

Window type	Example[a]
Centered	Cnojkaiazy means personality diagnosis from hand wnlflrz. Ykle le o
Right-shifted	Cnojkaiazp wsorc Jsncaroiity diagnosis from hand wnlflrz. Ykle le o
Left-shifted	Cnojkaiazy means personality diagnaele tnaw dori mnlflrz. Ykle le o

[a]All windows are as they would be if the subject fixated the letter d in the word "diagnosis."

behavior between the shifted conditions and the centered condition, it was possible to determine whether subjects obtained useful visual information more than 4 letter positions to the left and right of the center of vision independently.

Three subjects who had been in previous studies participated in this study as well. They each read six 500-word passages taken from the same source as the earlier passages, and were again tested for retention after each. The results of this experiment are reported by McConkie and Rayner (1975b). For each of the subjects, there was no difference in reading between the centered and right-shifted window conditions. Thus, the subjects did not seem to use visual information more than four letter positions to the left of the center of vision. However, when the window was shifted to the left, great disruption occurred, increasing reading time by at least 24% for all subjects.

Two of the window conditions, the centered window and the right-shifted window, used window sizes extending beyond the area where the presence or absence of spaces between words had an effect in the prior study. Thus, we would not expect any differences between the CS and CF conditions with these windows. However, with the left-shifted window, text patterns outside of the window area were displayed within the region where spaces between words had affected saccade length in the prior study. The saccade-length pattern for this left-shifted window was very similar to the pattern we had observed with small windows in the prior study. In particular, the number of long saccades was consistently reduced for all subjects in the CF condition.

It appears, then, that the region from which visual information was being acquired and used during a fixation by these subjects was highly asymmetrical, extending no more than four letter positions to the left of the center of vision, and possibly even less. This extreme asymmetry is particularly interesting in comparison to results of word-recognition studies. Bouma (1973), using visual displays about the same size as ours, reported that words ending 1½° to the left of the fixation point and words beginning 2½° to the right were identified with 60% accuracy. This region is larger than the region in which we found our subjects to be making semantic identifications (as will be discussed below), gaining visual information no more than 1° to the left and identifying words only if they began no more than 1½° to the right. Bouma's results also showed less asymmetry than ours. These discrepancies may result partially from differences in subjects or characteristics of the display. However, the extent of the discrepancies leads us to conclude that there are substantial differences between the region from which subjects can obtain visual information for word-recognition tasks and the region from which they actually acquire and use visual information during a fixation in reading. This difference indicates that we must be careful about generalizing results from other tasks to the task of normal reading.

There was one additional concern we had about the studies just described that led us to a third experiment in this series. In reading under the window conditions, a reader might be able to narrow his perceptual span in an attempt to keep from using information presented outside the window. If this were so, the size of the perceptual spans obtained from these studies could cause us to greatly underestimate the span size for these same subjects under more-normal reading conditions. This consideration pointed out the necessity of replicating these results by using another method which would not encourage subjects to narrow their effective field of view. The next study was an attempt to meet this problem.

2.3.3 Boundary Study

The technique used in this study was to identify a particular word location in a paragraph, called the "critical word location" or CWL, and then to try to determine if visual information was acquired from that region when subjects fixated at different distances from it. With our apparatus it was quite possible to change the contents of a particular word position in the paragraph from one word to another during a saccade. Thus, if a reader acquired some visual information from the word in the CWL on one fixation, and then found on the next fixation that the word had been changed, we might expect to observe some disruption of the normal reading pattern; particularly we might anticipate a longer-than-normal fixation after the change had been made, since the reader would have to resolve the conflict in his visual information from the two fixations.

In order to explore just what aspects of the visual information were being acquired from various retinal areas, six different stimulus alternatives were prepared for each CWL. One of these six alternatives was initially displayed in the CWL when the subject begin reading, but during some particular eye movement that alternative was replaced by a word, called the base word. Thus, although one of six alternatives could initially be displayed in the CWL when the subject began reading, by the time the display change occurred only the base word could be in the CWL. Each of the initially displayed alternatives had certain similarities and certain differences when compared to the base word itself. The first alternative was to display the base word itself in the CWL, thus leading to no change in the stimulus. This alternative was called W-Ident, W indicating that it was a word, and Ident signifying that the pattern was identical to the base word. The other alternatives were either words (W) or nonword letter strings (N) which had either the same word shape (S) or the same initial and final letters (L) or both (SL). The W-SL alternatives were words which fit both syntactically and semantically into the sentence. Table 4 provides examples of the base word and the other CWL alternatives. The CWL was equally often five, six, or seven letters in length and subject, verb, or object in syntactic function.

An example of the display change is shown in Table 5. Line I shows the sentence as it originally appeared when first displayed. The B marks the location of a boundary set in the computer. The display change occurred on the saccade

TABLE 4

Boundary Experiment: Examples of Base Words and Initially Displayed Alternatives

Grammatical category	Number of letters	Base word	Initially displayed alternatives				
			W–Ident	W–SL	N–SL	N–L	N–S
Subject	5	girls	girls	grads	gvobs	gbfns	pvobr
Subject	6	tailor	tailor	trader	tvobcr	tbfnir	fvobcv
Subject	7	planter	planter	plumber	plmnder	plktrer	qtmndcv
Verb	5	bowed	bowed	bound	bomud	bokdd	damub
Verb	6	tested	tested	tasted	tosted	tflmed	fostab
Verb	7	cracked	cracked	crushed	crmrbed	crklwed	evmrbcb
Object	5	ruler	ruler	rotor	ratar	rymyr	vatan
Object	6	palace	palace	police	pcluce	pyctce	qcluec
Object	7	protest	protest	product	probmet	prynkjt	qvobmel

which crossed this location. The last fixation the reader made prior to crossing the boundary is marked with a 1. Line II shows the same line as it appeared on the next fixation. Here the fixation point is marked with a 2, which is the first fixation after crossing the boundary. Note that the stimulus in the CWL has now been replaced by the base word, palace.

By setting boundaries in the computer which caused the stimulus change to occur when the eye was moving past certain locations on the page at different distances from the CWL, we were able to observe a large number of instances where the reader's eyes fixated different distances left of the CWL on the fixation prior to the stimulus change, and then directly fixated the CWL after the change. It was assumed that if the reader's prior fixation were sufficiently far to the left of the CWL, he would acquire no visual information from that region. If this were the case he would then fail to notice any of the different types of

TABLE 5

Boundary Study: An Example of the Type of Display Change that Occurred in the Boundary Experiment

I. The robbers guarded the pcluce with their guns.
            1   B
II. The robbers guarded the palace with their guns.
                       B 2

Key: B—Location of the boundary which triggers a change in the display.
    1—Location of the last fixation prior to crossing the boundary.
    2—Location of the first fixation after crossing the boundary.

display changes. However, if the prior fixation were closer to the CWL, he might obtain some type of visual information, perhaps word-shape or letter information, and if the stimulus change caused a change in that type of information, a longer fixation would result. However, if the stimulus change were of a type which did not cause a change in the type of visual information he had acquired, he would not detect the change, and no disruption of his reading would occur. This technique allowed us to explore how far to the right of the center of vision visual information was acquired, but not how far to the left.

Ten students at the Massachusetts Institute of Technology participated as subjects in this research and were paid for their participation. They each read 15 blocks of 15 paragraphs each, and were tested for retention of the information after each block. Complete eye-movement data were collected. From these data, we extracted information concerning the duration and location of the fixation just prior to the eye's crossing the boundary, and the duration and location of the fixation just after the crossing of the boundary. Thus, the stimulus change, if one occurred, took place between these two fixations. A full analysis of these data is reported by Rayner (1975a).

Since some of the initially displayed stimuli in the CWLs were nonwords, this raised an interesting question: How near to the CWL did the reader's eye have to be before he noticed that the letter string in the CWL was not a word? We assumed that if the subject encountered a nonword, it would disrupt his reading in some way which would affect the duration of the fixation. Therefore, fixations just prior to the display change were grouped according to how far they were from the CWL, and the average fixation duration at each distance was calculated. The existence of a nonword in the CWL did not affect the fixation duration unless the CWL was no more than three letter positions to the right of the center of vision. It appeared that if the CWL began four or more letter positions to the right of the center of vision, the reader was not discerning whether it contained a word or a nonword.

We then examined the data on the duration of fixations immediately after the display change, classified according to the type of display change that had occurred and to the location of the previous fixation. We considered only fixations in which the CWL lay in the foveal region, so we could be sure that the reader could clearly see the word there following the stimulus change.

First, we found that the readers did not seem to notice the stimulus change if the fixation prior to the change was more than 12 letter positions to the left of the CWL. If the previous fixation was 7 to 12 letters to the left of the CWL, the subjects did seem to pick up information about the word shape and extreme letters of the stimulus in the CWL; if either of these were changed for the next fixation, that fixation was much longer (over 25% longer). At the same time, if the initially displayed stimulus was the N–SL or W–SL, so that the word shape and extreme letters were the same after the stimulus change occurred, very little disruption was noted. Finally, it appeared that the subjects were only identifying the meaning of the word in the CWL if they fixated within four to six letter positions to the left of it. Only if their prior fixation was this close to the CWL did it make any difference whether a W–SL or N–SL alternative occupied the CWL.

Thus, this study indicated that the subjects picked up word-shape and extreme-letter information from words beginning no further than 12 letter positions to the right of their center of vision. Since the average length of the CWL was six character spaces, the results suggest that the subjects may have been picking up these types of cues as much as 14 to 18 character positions from their fixation point. Thus, the results of the boundary study suggest that the region from which information about letters and word shapes are obtained is somewhat larger than that suggested by the window study. This may be due to the differences in subjects and/or techniques used. In the boundary study, the subjects did not seem to identify meanings of words, or distinguish between words and nonwords, for stimuli beginning more than four to six letters to the right of the fixation point. It seems that semantic interpretations are made only for words lying within about 12 character positions to the right of the center of vision. The design of both the window study and the boundary study would have made it possible to obtain evidence that information about the external shapes of the words was obtained further into the periphery than was information about specific letters. For instance, in the window study we might have found that the C condition, providing word-shape information, disrupted reading less than did the other conditions. In the boundary study, we might have found that changes involving the N–L pattern, which changed the word shape in the CWL, were detected when the prior fixation had been further from the CWL than changes involving the N–S pattern, which maintained word shape and changed only specific letters. However, since neither of these data patterns was actually found, we must conclude that we have no evidence that word-shape information is obtained further into the retina by the reader than is specific-letter information. Several other aspects of the data from the boundary study will be mentioned later.

2.4 Size of the Perceptual Spans

These studies begin to provide an answer to the perceptual-span question for reasonably skilled readers who are carefully reading a passage to understand and retain its content. They tend to be able to identify the meaning of words no more than four letter positions to the left of the center of vision and no more than about 10 or 12 letter positions to the right. Thus, semantic interpretation is limited to a rather narrow region. It appears also that the reader is able to obtain some gross visual characteristics of words (word shape and initial and final letters) slightly further into parafoveal vision. Word-length patterns are also identified somewhat further to the right of fixation. Thus, it appears that the readers acquired different aspects of the visual text pattern from different regions: (1) sufficient visual detail to make lexical identifications from a rather limited area; (2) word shape and initial and final letters from an area slightly further into the parafoveal region; and (3) word-length information also slightly further into the parafoveal region and possibly extending to the peripheral region. It will require further research to find out if the sizes of these regions vary or broaden when readers are more or less careful in their reading, or for people who read extremely rapidly.

If an area of no more than 15 to 17 letter positions can be taken as the normal area from which a reader identifies words, it seems evident that the reader seldom identifies more than two or three words on a fixation, and that it is seldom that a text unit as large as a phrase will lie completely within this region. Thus, the reading must be taking place in a rather linear fashion, making contact with perhaps two new words on each fixation. Admonitions to the reader to try to see a phrase or entire sentence at a time seem misdirected. If good readers identify words within a region this small, it does not seem that attempts to use specific exercises to broaden the perceptual span of poorer readers are likely to achieve their goal. It seems unlikely that the size of the perceptual span is a major distinguisher between successful and unsuccessful readers, although further research is needed to establish this point.

These results also indicate that acceptable theories of fluent reading should treat reading as a somewhat linear process, obtaining information about individual words during fixations rather than about whole phrases or larger units. Identifying these larger units must take place at higher, more integrative levels of the processing system.

2.5 Guidance of the Eye

What a person sees in reading is not only determined by the size of his perceptual span, but also by where the eye is sent for its fixations. There has been much speculation about whether the eye is actually carefully guided as one reads, or whether it is simply moved regularly along, just keeping the right distance ahead of the mental processes so that visual information is available when needed. Hochberg (1970), for instance, has argued for guidance based both on certain aspects of the visual information in the peripheral region (peripheral search guidance) and on the reader's knowledge of the structure of language and of what is likely to occur next in the text (cognitive search guidance). Kolers (1976) and Bouma and deVoogd (1974), on the other hand, have argued for a rather random eye-guidance control, simply moving the eye regularly across the line as needed. Certain data from the studies we have described above are pertinent to this question (Rayner & McConkie, 1976).

In the first study, it was found that deleting peripheral and parafoveal information about the word-length pattern tended to shorten saccades. This suggests some use of word-length patterns for guiding the eye. In the last study described, additional analysis of the eye-movement data was carried out to determine where the subjects tended to fixate in the passages. It was found that the frequency of fixating the region between sentences (the last letter or two of the last word in one sentence, the punctuation mark and spaces between sentences, and the first few letters in the next sentence) was much lower than for other areas (Rayner, 1975b). Thus, the readers seemed to avoid fixating this region. Fixations falling in this region also tended to be shorter than those in other regions, and there was some evidence that during fixations in this region the subjects failed to obtain much visual information, even within the usual region for semantic identification. That is, if their fixation prior to the display change occurred in this region, they were less likely to detect the change. Finally, it was found that the likelihood of a letter position's being directly fixated is related to the length of the word in which it lies. Letters in two-letter words were fixated 10% of the time by the subjects. This percentage rose steadily to 13% for six-letter words, a 30% increase, then fell steadily to 11% for words nine letters or more in length. Thus, the eye is not traveling randomly, but is more likely to fixate certain areas of text than others, and the likelihood of being fixated is related to the word-length patterns. These facts provide evidence that the skilled reader's eye is being guided in reading, but they do not answer the further question about the nature of that guidance. Further research is needed on this question.

It is commonly observed that the duration of fixations is related in some degree to aspects of the text being read. The example just cited of particularly short fixations between sentences bears this out. Many researchers have noted that fixations on numbers, new words, and specific names often tend to be quite long (for instance, Woodworth, 1938; Huey, 1908). Also, in the last study described above, the occurrence of stimulus pattern changes from one fixation to the next produced lengthened fixation durations, indicating longer fixations when difficulties in cognitive processing occur. Actually, there is a great deal of variability in the durations of fixations, ranging from 1/10 to 1 sec for a single person reading a single passage. These differences may be reflecting the types of cognitive processes occurring at these specific points in the text. If so, theories of the cognitive processes in reading may be tested by identifying where in the text they indicate that particularly heavy mental activities take place, and then by examining eye-movement data to see if fixations tend to be particularly long in those regions. Incidentally, it appears that decisions concerning where to direct the eye and how long to keep it there for a fixation are independent. There is essentially no correlation between the durations of fixations and the lengths of the saccades either preceding or following them (Rayner & McConkie, 1976).

It appears that an adequate cognitive processing theory of reading must provide a set of rules that determine where the eye is to be directed, and how long it should remain in that position for a fixation. It is not yet clear how these should be linked to the cognitive processes involved in identifying the meaning of the text, but there is the strong possibility of a very close relationship.

2.6 When Is a Word Identified?

Another question about the nature of silent reading has sometimes been asked: How long is it after the visual information is obtained from a word that the word itself is identified? It may be that word identification in reading occurs almost immediately upon encountering the stimulus, or it may be that the visual information is taken in and processing is initiated, but actual identification of the word does not occur for some time, perhaps not until the next fixation or two. The boundary experiment seems to provide some evidence on that question. It appears that the decision of whether the reader is viewing a word or nonword is made early enough during a fixation to cause that fixation to be lengthened if a nonword is encountered. Also, when a subject has seen one word on one fixation, and he encounters another word in the same location on the next, during that second fixation the discrepancy is noted, resulting in a lengthened fixation duration. Thus, it appears that at least to some degree, the meaning of the words encountered on a fixation are identified during the period of that fixation.

3 CONCERNING THEORIES OF READING

The data from the studies described above begin to answer some important questions about the nature of skilled reading. Assuming that future research upholds these "facts," they can assist us in selecting among possible theories of the cognitive processes in reading, as indicated earlier. Thus, theories postulating a large perceptual span, essentially random eye movements, or delayed identification of words do not seem to be supported by the present data.

One type of theory that has been particularly popular recently (Levin & Kaplan, 1970; Hochberg, 1970) is based on the notion that subjects form a guess or hypothesis about what is likely to appear next in the text, and then they fixate the next region, obtain just enough visual information to confirm their hypothesis, and then form their next hypothesis. Occasionally the reader's hypothesis will be wrong, and this may require a regressive movement of the eye to investigate the reason for the error and generate a correct hypothesis. Thus, the reader is believed to spend his time during a fixation in testing his previous hypothesis and generating a new one. This approach to reading is epitomized in the title of a popular article by Goodman (1970), "Reading: A Psycholinguistic Guessing Game." This type of theory views the fluent reader as primarily a good guesser.

There are several facts about reading which have been used to argue for the validity of this type of theory. First, it explains how a person can read so quickly. Assuming that input of visual information is the bottleneck in reading, this type of theory allows the person to read with a minimum of visual input, taking in only that amount needed to test hypotheses. The model also accounts for reading-speed changes with more or less difficult text. Presumably difficult text is text which is less predictable, thus causing the reader's hypotheses to fail more often, requiring more regressions and a general slowing of the reading process. Finally, it is consistent with the observation that when people misread a word, the substituted word tends to be syntactically and semantically appropriate for that word position. This is presumably because the erroneous word was generated as a hypothesis as to what would occur, and the visual information obtained by the reader failed to reject it as an incorrect word.

We would like to point out, however, that the facts presently available about reading, including those just cited, do not necessarily require the adoption of a hypothesis-testing view of reading. For example, one alternative position, which we will call the "direct-perception" view of reading, seems consistent with the same set of facts as the "hypothesis-testing" view. We know that it is possible for a person to find words in his memory strictly on the basis of prior information and his knowledge of the language: people are able to read a sentence up to some point and then to supply a string of words which would complete it in a reasonable way. We also know that people can find words in memory strictly on the basis of visual patterns: they can read a word presented in isolation. It is therefore reasonable to believe that people can also identify words on the basis of some combination of these two types of information. Thus, as a person makes a fixation, he has some contextual information from the text up to that point. However, that information is not sufficient to specify what the next word is going to be. In fact, if a person is allowed to read a passage up to some point, and then is asked to guess what the next word will be, he tends to be wrong far more often than he is right, for most texts. During the fixation, however, the reader begins to take in certain visual information about the word in some order (Brown, 1970). At some point, enough visual information is acquired so that this, in conjunction with the contextual information, identifies a particular word as being the word on the page. At that point, input of visual information can cease for that word. The identification may be wrong, of course, but the person is committed to it. When the words within the region of the perceptual span have been identified so far as possible, and other meaning integration tasks carried out as needed, the eye can be sent to the next location.

This view of processing during the fixation is consistent with the same facts and assumptions which have given credence to the hypothesis-testing position. Rapid reading is possible without complete visual analysis of the text. If the text is more difficult or less predictable, contextual information will be less useful in identifying the words and the reader will have to depend more upon visual information, thus slowing the reading process. If the reader makes an error in identification, since the word was identified partially on the basis of the contextual information, it will tend to be semantically and syntactically appropriate. Finally, if a misreading occurs, this may set up an inappropriate context for identifying words later on. Thus, the combination of contextual and visual information will not specify a word in memory and the reader will finally have to identify the word on the basis of its visual features alone. Since the word identified does not fit in with the context, he will return his eye to an earlier-encountered region of the text in an attempt to find the point where he was led astray in his interpretation.

Thus, the direct-perception position view of reading accounts for the same phenomena as the hypothesis-testing view, without requiring guessing or hypothesis testing. In addition, several features of the hypothesis-testing view of reading which we find quite objectionable are described in an earlier report (McConkie & Rayner, 1976). Finally, if readers use visual information only to test hypotheses, it is difficult to see why they were able to detect changes in the stimulus displays from one fixation to the next as they did in the boundary experiment.

Clearly, additional research is needed to determine whether the reader is spending the time during his fixation primarily in testing and generating hypotheses or is using visual information, together with contextual information, to identify the words within his field of view and to integrate their meaning into memory structures. If further work casts doubt on theories of the hypothesis-testing type, this would question the validity of teaching children to guess as a means of increasing their reading ability (Smith, 1973).

4 SUMMARY

We have attempted to accomplish several purposes in this chapter. We have argued the importance of coming to understand the nature of fluent reading, and have suggested that such understanding take the form of the development of a cognitive processing theory of reading. We have indicated the general way in which such a theory can develop. We have described a new technology for the study of some aspects of reading which has great promise for identifying a number of important facts about the reading process and which may also become useful in diagnosis as we come to understand reading better. Finally, we have described three studies, using this technology, which provide specific information about the sizes of the perceptual spans and some other questions about reading, and we have attempted to point out the implications of the results from these studies for an understanding of the nature of fluent reading.

ACKNOWLEDGMENTS

Preparation of this chapter was supported in part by Public Health Research Grant MH25868 from the National Institute of Mental Health to K. Rayner and by Office of Education Grant OEG 2-71-0531 to G. W. McConkie. The research described in this paper was conducted at the Artificial Intelligence Laboratory of the Massachusetts Institute of Technology. We gratefully acknowledge the assistance of Dr. Marvin Minsky, Russell Noftsker, and David Silver during our stay at that facility.

REFERENCES

Bouma, H. Visual interference in the parafoveal recognition of initial and final letters of words. *Vision Research*, 1973, *13*, 767–782.

Bouma, H., & deVoogd, A. H. On the control of eye saccades in reading. *Vision Research*, 1974, *14*, 272–284.

Brown, R. Psychology and reading. In H. Levin & J. P. Williams (Eds.), *Basic studies on reading*. New York: Basic Books, 1970.

Bryden, M. P. Tachistoscopic recognition of non-alphabetic material. *Canadian Journal of Psychology*, 1960, *14*, 78–86.

Ditchburn, R. W. *Eye-movements and visual perception*. London, England: Oxford University Press, 1973.

Goodman, K. S. Reading: a psycholinguistic guessing game. In H. Singer & R. B. Ruddell (Eds.), *Theoretical models and processes of reading*. Newark, Del.: International Reading Association, 1970.

Gough, P. B. One second of reading. In J. F. Kavanagh & I. G. Mattingly (Eds.), *Language by ear and by eye*. Cambridge, Mass.: MIT Press, 1972.

Heron, W. Perception as a function of retinal locus and attention. *American Journal of Psychology*, 1957, *70*, 38–48.

Hochberg, J. Components of literacy: speculations and exploratory research. In H. Levin & J. P. Williams (Eds.), *Basic studies on reading*. New York: Basic Books, 1970.

Huey, E. B. *The psychology and pedagogy of reading*. New York: Macmillan, 1908. Republished: Cambridge, Mass.: MIT Press, 1968.

Kolers, P. A. Buswell's discoveries. In R. A. Monty & J. W. Senders (Eds.), *Eye movements and psychological processes*. Hillsdale, N.J.: Lawrence Erlbaum Assoc., 1976.

Levin, H., & Kaplan, E. L. Grammatical structure and reading. In H. Levin & J. P. Williams (Eds.), *Basic studies on reading*. New York: Basic Books, 1970.

McConkie, G. W., & Rayner, K. Identifying the span of the effective stimulus in reading. Final report, Office of Education, Grant No. OEG-2-71-0531, July, 1974.

McConkie, G. W., & Rayner, K. The span of the effective stimulus during a fixation in reading. *Perception and Psychophysics*, 1975, 17, 578–586. (a)

McConkie, G. W., & Rayner, K. Asymmetry in the perceptual span. Paper presented at the meetings of the American Educational Research Association, Washington, D.C., 1975. (b)

McConkie, G. W., & Rayner, K. Identifying the span of the effective stimulus in reading: literature review and theories of reading. In H. Singer & R. B. Ruddell (Eds.), *Theoretical models and processes of reading* (2nd ed.). Newark, Del.: International Reading Association, 1976.

Mackworth, N. H. Visual noise causes tunnel vision. *Psychonomic Science*, 1965, *3*, 67–68.

Marcel, T. The effective visual field and the use of context in fast and slow readers of two ages. *British Journal of Psychology,* 1974, *65,* 479–492.

Mishkin, M., & Forgays, D. G. Word recognition as a function of retinal locus. *Journal of Experimental Psychology,* 1952, *43,* 43–48.

Morton, J. The effect of context upon the visual duration threshold for words. *British Journal of Psychology,* 1964, *55,* 165–180.

Neisser, U. *Cognitive psychology.* New York: Appleton-Century-Crofts, 1967.

Newman, E. B. Speed of reading when the span of letters is restricted. *American Journal of Psychology,* 1966, *79,* 272–278.

Poulton, E. C. Peripheral vision, refractoriness and eye movements in fast oral reading. *British Journal of Psychology,* 1962, *53,* 409–419.

Rayner, K. The perceptual span and peripheral cues in reading. *Cognitive Psychology,* 1975, *7,* 65–81. (a)

Rayner, K. Parafoveal identification during a fixation in reading. *Acta Psychologica,* 1975, *39,* 271–282. (b)

Rayner, K., & McConkie, G. W. What guides a reader's eye movements? *Vision Research,* 1976, in press.

Reder, S. M. On-line monitoring of eye-position signals in contingent and noncontingent paradigms. *Behavior Research Methods and Instrumentation,* 1973, *5,* 218–228.

Smith, F. *Understanding reading.* New York: Holt, Rinehart & Winston, 1971.

Smith, F. *Psycholinguistics and reading.* New York: Holt, Rinehart & Winston, 1973.

Taylor, E. A. The spans: perception, apprehension, and recognition. *American Journal of Ophthalmology,* 1957, *44,* 501–507.

Taylor, S. E. Eye movements in reading: facts and fallacies. *American Educational Research Journal,* 1965, *2,* 187–202.

Tulving, E., & Gold, C. Stimulus information and contextual information as determinants of tachistoscopic recognition of words. *Journal of Experimental Psychology,* 1963, *66,* 319–327.

White, M. J. Laterality differences in perception: a review. *Psychological Bulletin,* 1969, *66,* 387–405.

Woodworth, R. S. *Experimental psychology.* New York: Henry Holt, 1938.

5

Phonetic Segmentation and Recoding in the Beginning Reader

Isabelle Y. Liberman[1]
Donald Shankweiler[1]
Alvin M. Liberman[2]
Carol Fowler
F. William Fischer

University of Connecticut

1 INTRODUCTION

The beginning reader—the child of six or thereabout—is an accomplished speaker–hearer of his language and has been for a year or more. Why, then, should he find it hard to read, as so many children do? Why does he not learn to read as naturally and inevitably as he learned to speak and listen? What other abilities, not required for mastery of speech, must he have if he is to cope with language in its written form?

If the beginning reader is to take greatest advantage of an alphabet and of the language processes he already has, he must convert print to speech or, more covertly, to the phonetic structure that in some neurological form must be presumed to underlie and control overt speech articulation. In the first part of the chapter we will say why it might be hard to make the conversion properly— that is, so as to gain all the advantages that an alphabetic system offers. But the conversion from print to speech, whether properly made or not, may be important to the child also in reducing that which is read to a meaningful message. That is so because of a basic characteristic of language: the meaning of

[1] Isabelle Y. Liberman and Donald Shankweiler are also associated with Haskins Laboratories, New Haven, Connecticut.
[2] Alvin M. Liberman is also associated with Haskins Laboratories and Yale University.

the longer segments (for example, sentences) transcends the meaning of the shorter segments (for example, words) out of which they are formed. From that it follows that the shorter segments must be held in some short-term store until the meaning of the longer segments has been computed. In the second part of the chapter we will consider the possibility that a phonetic representation may be particularly suited to that requirement.

In referring to the conversion of print to speech, which is what much of this presentation is about, we will not be especially concerned to make a distinction between overt speech and the covert neurological processes (isomorphic, presumably, with the phonetic representation) that govern its production and perception. We should only note that the beginning reader often converts to overt speech and the skilled reader to some more covert form; conversion to the covert form does not, of course, limit the reader to the relatively slow rates at which he can overtly articulate. Nor will we be concerned with the distinction between the phonetic and the more abstract phonological representations. Like many alphabetically written languages, English makes contact, not at the phonetic level, but at some more abstract remove, closer surely to the level of systematic phonologic structure (Chomsky, 1970; Klima, 1972; see also Gleitman & Rozin, this volume) or, in the older terminology, to the phonemic and morphophonemic levels. That is an important consideration for students of the reading process, but it happens not to be especially relevant to our purposes here. For convenience, then, we will speak of phonemes, phonetic segments, and phonetic structure without meaning to imply any differences in the abstractness of the units being referred to.

2   USING THE ALPHABET TO FULL ADVANTAGE

2.1   The Need to Segment Phonetically

For the moment we will concern ourselves only with the first problem: what a child needs in order to read an alphabetic language properly. In that connection, let us look at the strategies the beginning reader might use to recover a phonetic representation of the written word. In the early stages of learning to read, there are at least two possibilities: the child might work analytically, by first relating the orthographic components of the written word to the segmental structure of the spoken word, or he might do it holistically, as in the whole-word method, by simply associating the overall shape of the written word with the appropriate spoken word.[3] In the whole-word strategy, the child not only does not analyze

---

[3] We do not contend that the use of either strategy is necessarily tied to a particular method of instruction. For example, a child may have arrived by induction at the mapping principles required to use the analytic strategy without having been taught the rules as such. Moreover, in later stages of reading, these strategies are not mutually exclusive. There are undoubtedly many words, and even whole phrases, that are recognized as gestalts by the expert, mature reader, who is able to switch to a more analytic strategy as the circumstances require.

words into their phonetic components, but need not necessarily even be aware that such an analysis can be made. There are, however, several problems with this strategy. An obvious one, of course, is that it is self-limiting; it does not permit the child to read words not previously encountered in print. In the whole-word strategy, each new word must be learned as a unit, as if it were an ideographic character, before it can be read. Only if the child is able to use the more analytic strategy can he realize the important advantages of an alphabetically written language. Given a word that is already in his lexicon, the child can read it without specific instruction although he has never before seen it in print; or given a new word which he has never before heard or seen, the child can closely approximate its spoken form and hold that until its meaning can be inferred from the context or discovered later by his asking someone about it. In connection with the latter advantage, one might ask why the child cannot similarly hold the word in visual form. Perhaps he can. We know, however, that the spoken form can be retained quite easily and, indeed, that it can be readily called up. As to what can be done with a purely visual representation, we are not so sure. At all events, and as we will say at greater length later, spoken language, or its underlying and covert phonetic representation, seems particularly suited for storage of the short-term variety.

What special ability does the child need, then, if he is to employ the analytic strategy and thus take full advantage of the alphabetic way our language is written? In our view, it is the ability to become more explicitly aware of the fact that speech consists of phonetic segments. Consider, for example, what is involved in reading a simple word like *bag*. Let us assume that the child can (visually) identify the three letters of the word. Let us assume further that he knows the individual letter-to-sound correspondences—that the sound of *b* is /bʌ/, that *a* is /æ/, and that *g* is /gʌ/. But if that is all he knows, he will sound out the word as *buhaguh,* a nonsense trisyllable containing five phonetic segments, and not as *bag,* a meaningful monosyllable which has only three phonetic segments. It is patent that if he is to map the printed three-letter word *bag* onto the spoken word *bag* which is already in his lexicon, he must know that the spoken syllable also has three segments.

2.2   The Difficulties of Making Phonetic Segmentation Explicit

Given that the child must be able to make explicit the phonetic segmentation of the word, is there any reason to believe that he might encounter difficulties? There is, indeed, and it comes directly from research on acoustic cues for speech perception. The relevant finding is that there is most commonly no acoustic criterion by which the phonetic segmentation of a given word is dependably marked (Liberman, Cooper, Shankweiler, & Studdert-Kennedy, 1967). Phoneme boundaries are not marked acoustically because the segments of the phonetic message are often coarticulated with the result, for example, that a consonant segment will, at the acoustic level, be encoded into—that is, merged with—the vowel. The word *bag*, for example, has three phonetic segments but only one acoustic segment. Thus, there is no acoustic criterion by which one can segment the word into its three constituent phonemes. Analyzing an utterance into syllables, on the other hand, may present a different and easier problem. We should expect that to be so because every syllable contains a vocalic nucleus and thus will have, in most cases, a distinctive peak of acoustic energy. These energy peaks provide audible cues that correspond approximately to the syllable centers (Fletcher, 1929). Although such auditory cues could not in themselves help a listener to define exact syllable boundaries, they ought to make it relatively easy for him to discover how many syllables there are and, in that sense, to do explicit syllable segmentation.

We should remark here that the encoding or merging of phones at the level of sound not only complicates the task of explicit segmentation but also makes it impossible to read by sounding out the letters one by one. In the example of *bag* offered earlier, sounding out produces *buhaguh.* Hence, the analytic strategy we have been talking about does not—indeed, cannot—mean reading letter by letter. To recover the spoken form the reader must, before making the conversion to speech, take into account all the letters that represent the several phonetic segments that are to be encoded. In the example of *bag,* the coding unit is obviously the syllable. But coding influences sometimes extend across syllables, and in the case of prosody such influences may cover quite long stretches. We should think, therefore, that the number of letters that must be apprehended before an attempt can be made to recover the spoken form may sometimes be quite large. In fact, we do not now know exactly how large these coding units are, only that they almost always exceed one letter in length. To identify such units is, in our view, a research undertaking of great importance and correspondingly great difficulty.

We should also remark here that the child who finds it difficult to make explicit the phonetic segmentation of his speech need not have any problems at all in the regular course of speaking and listening. Children generally distinguish (or identify) words like *bad* or *bag* which differ in only one phonetic segment. Indeed, there is evidence now that infants at one month of age discriminate *ba* from *pa* (and *da* from *ta*) and, moreover, that they make this discrimination categorically, just as adults do (Eimas, Siqueland, Jusczyk, & Vigorito, 1971). The child has no difficulty in speaking and listening to speech because there the segmentation of the largely continuous acoustic signal is done for him automatically by operations of which he is not conscious. In order to speak and listen, therefore, he need have no more conscious awareness of phonetic structure than he has of syntactic structure. In that connection, we all know that the child can speak grammatical sentences without being able to verbalize their structure. Similarly, he can readily distinguish *bad* from *bag* without being able to analyze the underlying phonetic structure—that is, without an explicit understanding of the fact that each of these utterances consists of three segments and that the difference lies wholly in the third. But reading, unlike speech, does require a more explicit analysis if the advantages of an alphabet are to be realized.

That explicit phonetic analysis might be difficult is suggested also by the history of writing (Gelb, 1963).[4] In the very earliest systems, the segment that the orthography represented was the word. Present-day approximations to that kind of writing are to be found in Chinese characters and in the very similar kanji that the Japanese use. Writing with meaningless units is a more recent development, the segment size represented in all the earliest forms being the syllable. An alphabet, representing the shortest meaningless segments (phones or phonemes), developed still later and apparently out of a syllabary. Moreover, all the other systems, whether comprising meaningful or meaningless segments of whatever size, seem to have appeared independently in various places and at various times, but all the alphabets were derived from a single source. It seems reasonable to suppose that the historical development of writing systems—from word, to syllable, to phoneme—might reflect the ease or difficulty of explicitly carrying out the particular type of segmentation that each of these orthographies requires. More to the point of our present concerns, one would suppose that for the child there might be the same order of difficulty and, correspondingly, the same order of appearance in development.

2.3 Development of the Ability to Analyze Speech into Phonemes and Syllables

There is thus reason to suppose that phonetic segmentation might be a difficult task, more difficult than syllabic segmentation, and that the ability to do it might, therefore, develop later. To test that supposition directly, we have recently resorted to an experiment. The point was to determine how well children in nursery school, kindergarten, and first grade (4-, 5-, and 6-year-olds) can identify the number of phonetic segments in spoken utterances and how this compares with their ability to deal similarly with syllables (Liberman, Shankweiler, Fischer, & Carter, 1974). The procedure was in the form of a game which required of the child that he indicate, by tapping a wooden dowel on the table, the number (from one to three) of segments (phonemes in the case of one group, syllables in the other) in a list of test words. In order to teach the child what was expected of him, the test list was preceded by a series of training trials in which the experimenter demonstrated how the child was to respond. The test proper consisted of 42 randomly assorted individual items of one, two, or three segments, presented without prior demonstration and corrected, as needed, immediately after the child's response. Each of the 42 items occurred once in

---

[4] This point is discussed at greater length in Liberman, Shankweiler, Fischer, and Carter (1974), and in Gleitman and Rozin, this volume.

the test list. Testing was continued through all 42 items or until the child reached a criterion of tapping six consecutive trials correctly without demonstration. The children of each grade level were divided into two experimental groups, the one performing phoneme segmentation and the other, syllable segmentation. Instructions given the two groups were identical, except that the training and test items required phoneme segmentation in one group and syllable segmentation in the other.

The results showed in more than one way that the test words were more readily segmented into syllables than into phonemes. At all grade levels, the number of children who were able to reach criterion was markedly greater in the group required to segment by syllable than in the group required to segment by phoneme. At age four, none of the children could segment by phoneme, whereas nearly half (46%) could segment by syllable. Ability to carry out phoneme segmentation successfully did not appear until age five, and then it was demonstrated by only 17% of the children. In contrast, almost half (48%) of the children at that age again could segment syllabically. Even at age six, only 70% succeeded in phoneme segmentation, while 90% were successful in the syllable task.

The proportions of children at each age who reached criterion level in the minimum number of trials is another measure of the contrast in difficulty of the two tasks. For the children who worked at the syllable task, the percentage reaching criterion in the minimum time increased steadily over the three age levels. It was 7% at age four, 16% at age five, and 50% at age six. By contrast, we find in the phoneme group that no child at any grade level attained the criterion in the minimum time.

The data were also analyzed in terms of mean errors. In Fig. 1, mean errors to passing or failing the criterion of six consecutive correct trials without demonstration are plotted by task and grade. Errors on both the syllable and phoneme tasks decreased monotonically at successive grade levels, but the greater difficulty of phoneme segmentation at every level was again clearly demonstrated.

2.4   Segmentation and Reading

The difficulty of phonetic segmentation has been remarked by a number of investigators besides ourselves (Calfee, Chapman, & Venezky, 1972; Elkonin, 1973; Gibson & Levin, 1975; Gleitman & Rozin, 1973; Rosner & Simon, 1970; Savin, 1972). Their observations, together with ours described in the experiment above, also imply a connection between phonetic segmentation ability and early reading acquisition. This relationship is suggested in our experiment by the increase in the number of children passing the phoneme-counting task, from only 17% at age five to 70% at age six. Unfortunately, the nature of the connection is in doubt. On the one hand, the increase in ability to segment phonetically might result from the reading instruction that begins between five

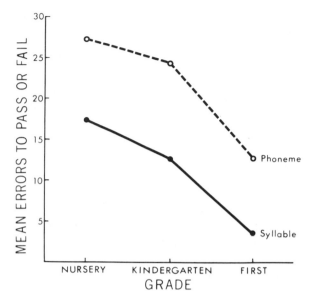

FIG. 1.   Mean number of errors to passing or failing a criterion of six consecutive trials without demonstration in phoneme and syllable segmentation.

and six. Or, alternatively, it might be a manifestation of some kind of intellectual maturation. The latter possibility might be tested by a developmental study of segmentation skills in a language community such as the Chinese, where the orthographic unit is the word and where reading instruction therefore does not demand the kind of phonetic analysis needed in an alphabetic system.[5]

In any event, since explicit phoneme segmentation is harder for the young child and develops later than syllable segmentation, one would expect that syllable-based writing systems would be easier to learn to read than those based on an alphabet. We may thus have an explanation for the assertion (Makita, 1968) that the Japanese kana, roughly a syllabary, is readily mastered by first-grade children. One might expect, furthermore, that an orthography which represents each word with a different character (as is the case in Chinese logographs and in the closely related Japanese kanji) would obviate the difficulties in initial learning that arise in mastering an alphabetic system. The relative ease with which reading-disabled children learn kanjilike representations of language, while being unable to break the alphabetic code (Rozin, Poritsky, & Sotsky, 1971), may be cited here as evidence of the special burden imposed by an alphabetic script.

[5] Unfortunately, a pure test will be hard to make. Children in the People's Republic of China are now being taught to read alphabetically before beginning their study of logographic characters.

However, we need not go so far afield to collect indirect evidence that the difficulties of phoneme segmentation may be related to early reading acquisition. Such a relation can be inferred from the observation that children who are resistant to early reading instruction have problems even with spoken language when they are required to perform tasks demanding some rather explicit understanding of phonetic structure. Such children are reported (Monroe, 1932; Savin, 1972) to be deficient in rhyming, in recognizing that two different monosyllables may share the same first (or last) phoneme segment, and also in speaking Pig Latin, which demands a deliberate shift of the initial consonant segment of the word to initial position in a nonsense syllable added to the end of the word.

We, too, have explored directly, if in a preliminary way, the relation between an ability to segment phonemes and reading. For that purpose we measured the reading achievement of the children who had taken part in our experiment on phonetic segmentation, described above. Testing at the beginning of the second school year, we found that half of the children in the lowest third of the class in reading achievement (as measured by the word-recognition task of the Wide Range Achievement Test; Jastak, Bijou, & Jaskak, 1965) had failed the phoneme segmentation task the previous June; on the other hand, there were no failures in phoneme segmentation among the children who scored in the top third in reading ability (Liberman, 1973).

Data from the analysis of children's reading errors also may be cited as additional evidence for the view that failure to perform explicit phoneme segmentation may be a serious roadblock to reading acquisition. If a chief source of reading difficulty is that the child cannot make explicit the phonetic structure of the language, he might be expected to show success with the initial letter—which requires no further analysis of the syllable—and relatively poor performance beyond that point. If he knows some letter-to-sound correspondences, and that he must scan in a left-to-right direction, he might simply search his lexicon for a word, any word, beginning with a phoneme that matches the initial letter. Thus, presented with the word *bag,* he might give the response *butterfly.* Such a response could not occur if the child were searching his lexicon for a word that has three sound segments corresponding to the letter segments in the printed word. If, however, the child is unaware that words in his lexicon have a phonetic structure, or if he has difficulty in determining what that structure is, then he will not be able to map the letters to the segments in these words. On these grounds, we would expect that in reading words such a child would make more errors on final consonants than on initial consonants. We have observed just this error pattern in a number of beginning and disabled readers, ages 7 to 11 (Shankweiler & Liberman, 1972; Liberman, 1973; Fowler, Liberman, & Shankweiler, in press). Similar findings have been reported by other investigators (Daniels & Diack, 1956; Weber, 1970) who examined error patterns in reading connected text. It is worth noting that the initial—final error pattern in reading is contrary to what would be expected in terms of left-to-right sequential probabilities (Miller, Bruner, & Postman, 1954). If the child at the early stages of beginning to read were using the constraints built into the language, he would make fewer errors at the end than at the beginning of words, not more.

2.5 The Contribution of Orthographic Complexity

In stressing the difficulty of phonemic segmentation, we do not intend to imply that no other problems are involved in reading an alphabetic language. For example, we realize that the mapping in English between spelling and language is sometimes complex and irregular.[6] Although that undoubtedly contributes to the difficulties of reading acquisition, we do not believe that the complexity of the orthography is the principal cause. Indeed, we know that it cannot be the only cause since many children continue to have problems even when the words are carefully chosen to include only those which map the sound in a consistent way and are part of the child's active vocabulary (Savin, 1972). Moreover, reading problems are known to occur in countries in which the writing system maps the language more directly than in English (Downing, 1973).

In any event, the major irregularities of English spelling which confront the young child in the simple words he must read have to do mainly with the vowels (Dewey, 1970; Heilman, 1964; Monroe, 1932). Although we believe it to be of interest to examine the relation of orthographic complexity of the vowels to the problems of reading acquisition, and we are doing so (Fowler et al., in press), we suspect that getting the vowel exactly right may not be of critical importance in reading (though, of course, it is in spelling). If in the conversion to sound the child gets the phonetic structure correct except for errors in vowel color, he would not be too wide of the mark, and many such errors would be rather easily corrected by context or by information obtained at a later time.

3 THE PHONETIC REPRESENTATION, SHORT-TERM MEMORY, AND READING

3.1 Phonetic Recoding in Reading as a Way to Tap Primary Language Processes

Although beginning readers must surely recode phonetically if they are to cope with new words, we should wonder what they do with words (and phrases) they have read many times. Do they, in those cases, construct a phonetic representa-

---

[6] It is recognized that the "irregularities" of English spelling are more lawful than might appear, as in the spellings of "sign" and "signal" for example, which reflect morphological structure quite accurately (Chomsky, 1970). However, it must be said that this lawfulness can be appreciated only by the skilled reader and probably does not aid the beginner.

tion using either of the two strategies we described earlier, or do they, as some believe (Bever & Bower, 1966), go directly from print to meaning?

One can think of at least two reasons why phonetic recoding might occur even with frequently read materials. A not very interesting reason is that, having adopted the phonetic strategy to gain advantages in the early stages of learning, the reader continues with the habit although it may have ceased to be functional or even have become, as some might think, a liability. There is a more interesting reason, however, and one we are inclined to take more seriously. It derives from the possibility that working from a phonetic base is natural and necessary if the reader (including even one who is highly practiced) is to take advantage of the primary language processes that are so deep in his experience and, indeed, in his biology. Consider, for example, that the normal processes for storing, indexing, and retrieving lexical entries may be carried out on a phonetic base. If so, it is hard to see why the reader should develop completely new processes suited for the visual system and less natural, presumably, for the linguistic purposes than the old ones. Or consider what we normally do in coping with syntax, an essential step in arriving at the meaning of a sentence. Although we do not know much about how we decode syntax, it is virtually certain that we are aided significantly by the prosody, which marks the syntactic boundaries. What, then, is the cost to our understanding of what we read if we do not recover the prosody, using for that purpose the marks of punctuation and such subtle cues as skillful writers may know how to provide (Bolinger, 1957)? We find it hard to imagine how the reader could construct the prosody except upon a phonetic base.

There are, of course, other natural language processes that the reader can best exploit by constructing a phonetic representation. Among them is short-term storage, and it is that process that we will be concerned with in the remainder of this chapter. As we had occasion to point out earlier, it is characteristic of language that the meaning of longer segments (e.g., sentences) transcends the meaning of the shorter segments (words) out of which they are formed. It follows, then, that the listener and reader must hold the shorter segments in some short-term store if the meaning of the longer segments is to be extracted from them. Given what we know about the characteristics of the phonetic representation, we might suppose that, as Liberman, Mattingly, and Turvey (1972) have suggested, it is uniquely suited to the short-term storage requirements of language. But apart from what we or they might suppose, there is relevant experimental evidence.

3.2 Phonetic Representation of Visually Presented Material in Short-Term Memory

Some of the evidence comes from a class of experiments in which it has been found that when lists of letters or alphabetically written words are presented to be read and remembered, the confusions in short-term memory are phonetic rather than optical (Baddeley, 1966, 1968, 1970; Conrad, 1963, 1964, 1972; Conrad, Freeman, & Hull, 1965; Conrad & Hull, 1964; Dornič, 1967; Hintzman, 1967; Kintsch & Buschke, 1969; Sperling, 1963; Thomasson, 1970 reported in Conrad, 1972). From that finding it has been inferred that the stimulus items had been stored in phonetic rather than visual form. Indeed, the tendency to recode visually presented items into phonetic form is so strong that, as Conrad (1972) has emphasized, adult subjects consistently do so recode even in experimental situations in which it is clearly disadvantageous to do so.

A similar kind of experiment (Erickson, Mattingly, & Turvey, 1973) suggests that exactly the same kind of phonetic recoding occurs even when the linguistic stimuli are not presented in a form (alphabetic) that represents the phonetic structure. For the purposes of that experiment the investigators used lists of kanji characters, which are essentially logographic, and Japanese subjects who were readers of kanji. As in the experiments with alphabetically spelled words, there was evidence that the stimulus items had been stored in short-term memory in phonetic rather than visual (or semantic) form.

There is also evidence that even nonlinguistic stimuli may, under some circumstances, be recoded into phonetic form and so stored in short-term memory. That evidence comes from work by Conrad (1972) who found that in short-term recall of pictures of common objects, confusions by older children and adults were clearly based on the phonetic forms of the names of the objects, rather than on their visual or semantic characteristics.

Although none of the experiments cited here dealt with natural reading situations, they are nevertheless relevant to the assumption that even skilled readers might recode phonetically, and that in so doing they might gain an advantage in short-term memory. It remains to be determined whether and to what extent readers rely on phonetic recoding for the short-term memory requirements of normal reading. Less generally, it remains to be determined also whether good and poor readers are distinguished by greater or lesser tendencies toward phonetic recoding. In the next section we will describe our first attempt to gain evidence bearing on this question.

3.3 Phonetic Recoding in Good and Poor Beginning Readers: An Experiment

Given the short-term memory requirements of the reading task and evidence for the involvement of phonetic coding in short-term storage, we might expect to find that those beginning readers who are progressing well and those who are doing poorly will be further distinguished by the degree to which they rely on phonetic recoding. To our knowledge no one has investigated this possibility; consequently, we set out to do so. The experiments we have done are outlined in detail elsewhere (Shankweiler & Liberman, in press). For our purposes, we will report briefly on only one experiment.

We used a procedure similar to one devised by Conrad (1972) for adult subjects in which the subject's performance is compared on recall of phonetically confusable (rhyming) and nonconfusable (nonrhyming) letters. Our expectation was that phonetically similar items would maximize phonetic confusability and thus penalize recall in subjects who use the phonetic code in short-term memory. Sixteen strings of five upper-case letters were presented to the subjects by projector tachistoscope. Eight of the five-letter strings were composed of rhyming consonants (drawn from the set B C D G P T V Z) and eight were composed of nonrhyming consonants (drawn from the set H K L Q R S W Y). The two series of five-letter strings (confusable and nonconfusable) were randomly interleaved. An exposure time of 3 sec was adopted after preliminary studies had shown that even adult subjects require exposures in excess of 2 sec in order to report all five letters reliably. The test was given twice: first with immediate recall, then with delayed recall. In the first condition, recall was tested immediately after presentation by having subjects print as many letters as could be recalled in each letter string, in the order given. In order to make the task maximally sensitive to the recall strategy, we then imposed a 15-sec delay between tachistoscopic presentation and the response of writing down the string of letters. The children were requested to sit quietly during the delay interval; no intervening task was imposed. We have reason to believe that subjects used this period for rehearsal. Many children were observed mouthing the syllables silently; other tapped their feet rhythmically; some could hardly be restrained from repeating the letters aloud.

As can be seen in Table 1, the subjects included three groups of school children who differed in level of attainment in reading as estimated by the word-recognition subtest of the Wide Range Achievement Test (WRAT) (Jastak et al., 1965). All were nearing completion of the second grade at the time the tests were conducted. There was no overlap in WRAT scores among the three groups. The first group, designated as the superior readers, comprised 17 children who were reading well ahead of their grade placement, having scored a mean grade equivalent of 4.9 on the WRAT. The second group, whom we call

TABLE 1
Estimated Mean Reading Grade,[a] Mean Age, and IQ[b] for
Second-Grade School Children Grouped According to
Reading Attainment

Group	n	Age	IQ	Reading grade
Superior	17	8.0	113.9	4.9
Marginal	16	8.1	101.7	2.5
Poor	13	8.2	111.6	2.0

[a]Reading-grade equivalent score on reading subtest of Wide Range Achievement Test.
[b]Peabody Picture Vocabulary Test.

marginal readers, included 16 children who averaged slightly less than one-half year of lag in reading achievement (grade 2.5). The third group, 13 children in number, whom we call poor readers, obtained a mean WRAT equivalent of 2.0, indicating nearly a full year of retardation in reading. The three groups did not differ significantly in mean age. Their intelligence level, as measured by the Peabody Picture Vocabulary Test (Dunn, 1965), was closely matched in the two extreme groups, the superior and poor readers. The difference in IQ level in the marginal group is apparently of no serious consequence since, as will be seen below, the performances of the marginal and poor groups on the experimental tasks were not appreciably different from each other.

The responses were scored in two ways, with and without regard for serial position. In the first procedure, only those items listed in the correct serial position were counted correct. Thus, credit was given for incomplete strings only if the positions of the omitted items were indicated by blank spaces. The second procedure credited any items which occurred in the stimulus set regardless of the order in which they were written down. An analysis of variance was performed on each set of scores. The pattern of results was remarkably similar for data derived from each method of scoring. We display here the results of only the scoring procedure that takes account of serial position.

In Fig. 2, which displays the data in terms of mean errors summed over all serial positions in the letter strings, the upper plot gives the results for superior readers, while the middle and lower plots show the results for the marginal and poor readers, respectively. We see at once that the main differences are between the superior readers and the other two groups. It was found, in fact, that the marginal and poor readers did not differ significantly in their overall performance. For this reason, we need not consider them separately here and will therefore refer to them collectively instead, as the "inferior" readers.

It is immediately apparent that the superior group tends, overall, to make fewer errors in recall than the inferior readers. More notable, however, are the differences in the effects of phonetic similarity on the recall performance of the two reading groups. First, it is seen that, although phonetic similarity caused some deterioration in immediate recall for all the children, the effect was much greater for the superior group than for the inferior readers. Second, the differential effect of phonetic similarity is even more marked in the delay condition. For the superior group, the interposition of a delay interval steeply increased errors of recall of the phonetically confusable strings but produced no effect on the recall of nonconfusable strings. We may suppose that in both groups the phonetic similarity of the confusable strings caused interference with rehearsal during the delay interval. For the superior readers the interference effect is large, for the inferior readers it is small. In the latter group, there was no interaction of the effects of confusability with delay. Recall of both confusable and nonconfusable strings deteriorated with delay by nearly equal amounts. This tells us that, for whatever reason, the inferior readers have a less efficient recall strategy

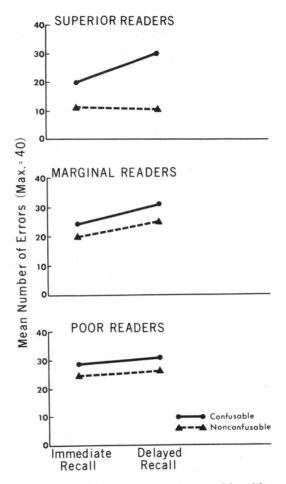

FIG. 2.   Mean recall errors summed over serial position.

than the superior readers. We would suggest that the better recall of the superior readers is due to their more efficient use of phonetic recoding, a strategy that ordinarily works to their advantage, but not in the special case of rhyming strings.

The differential effect of phonetic similarity on the superior readers is again apparent in Fig. 3, where the data are replotted as a function of serial position. An examination of the two graphs in the lower half of the figure shows that, after delay, the superior readers are sharply distinguished from the inferior groups in their better recall of nonconfusable strings but are nearly indistinguishable from the others in their recall of confusable strings. Taken together, the two lower graphs make manifest the much greater penal effect of phonetic confusability on the superior readers. The same differentially penal effect on this

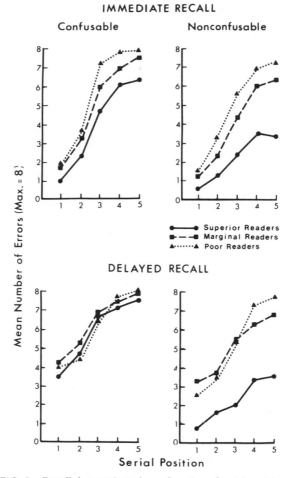

IMMEDIATE RECALL

Confusable   Nonconfusable

●——● Superior Readers
■– –■ Marginal Readers
▲┈┈┈▲ Poor Readers

DELAYED RECALL

Mean Number of Errors (Max. = 8)

Serial Position

FIG. 3.   Recall data replotted as a function of serial position.

group is found also in the case of immediate recall, as seen in the upper graphs of Fig. 3, but there the difference is less striking.[7]

In summary, then, the superior readers are strongly penalized by the phonetic

[7] An analysis of variance performed on the data showed all main effects to be significant at $p < .001$ (reading group: $F(2, 43) = 22.67$; delay: $F(1, 43) = 29.77$; confusability: $F(1, 43) = 73.00$). (The significance of the reading group factor is accounted for by the differences between the superior readers and the other two groups; the marginal and poor readers do not differ significantly from each other in recall.) The three-way interaction, reading group × delay × confusability, is statistically significant at $p < .001$ (where $F(2, 43) = 8.24$). Newman–Kuels post-hoc means tests reveal that for the superior readers, delay has a significantly greater effect on recall of confusable sequences than on recall of nonconfusable sequences. Among the marginal and poor readers, on the other hand, delay did not differentially affect performance on the two types of sequences.

similarity of the confusable strings of letters. The penalty is apparent in immediate recall and more marked in the delay condition. We should conclude from these findings that the superior group is using a phonetic code in short-term memory. This is not to say, however, that the inferior readers are not recoding phonetically at all. Phonetic similarity does impair their performance somewhat, although the effect is clearly less than for the superior group.

There may be several interpretations of this difference between the two reading groups in our study. One possibility is that the inferior readers rely less on phonetic recoding than does the superior group and use other codes concurrently (visual codes, for example), which are unaffected by phonetic confusability. Another possibility, suggested by R. G. Crowder (personal communication), is that they may simply rehearse at a slower rate than the superior readers, thereby giving the confusable items less opportunity to interfere. Whatever interpretation is accepted (and the answers must await further investigation), we would emphasize that the failure of the superior readers to maintain their advantage over the inferior group in short-term memory when the items are phonetically confusable cannot be accounted for by assuming that the groups differ only with respect to a general memory capacity.

An auditory analog of our experiment would be one way to clarify the nature of the difference in short-term memory between the two groups of readers.[8] Since phonetic coding, as we said earlier, presumably cannot be avoided when the linguistic material arrives auditorily, auditory presentation might force the inferior reader into a phonetic mode. If an important component of his difficulty is that he is deficient in recoding visual symbolic material into phonetic form, then the phonetic similarity of auditorily presented stimuli should affect him as much (or as little) as it does the superior readers. While quantitative differences in memory capacity between the two groups may still show up in the general level of recall on the auditory presentation, the interaction of reading group and phonetic confusability should be diminished. If, on the other hand, the poor reader tends generally in memory to rely, where possible, on nonphonetic codes or to rehearse phonetically but at a slower rate, the interaction should remain.

Obviously, many other refinements of the experimental task remain to be made. In particular, we should hope in the future to use tasks which resemble more closely what happens in actual reading. At the very least, we should like to

[8] Since the auditory experiment would, of course necessitate serial presentation, an additional visual condition employing serial presentation would be required to achieve comparability. In a pilot experiment, we have found virtually identical patterns of performance for the two types of presentation, the auditory and the visual. In both cases, phonetic similarity again hurts both groups of readers, especially in delayed recall, but the effect is again greater, although perhaps not clearly so, for the good readers than for the poor. It would seem from these results that the difference between the good and poor readers might be more general than we had assumed. That is, the difference might be related not so much to the visual or auditory source of the linguistic material but rather more generally to the way the two groups process linguistic information in short-term memory.

repeat the kind of experiment reported here using words instead of letters. Only after that, could we have a very high degree of confidence in the conclusion that seems to be suggested by the results of the present experiment—namely, that phonetic recoding is characteristic of skilled reading.

4 SUMMARY

By converting print to speech the beginning reader gains two advantages: he can read words he has never seen before, and he can, as he reads, fully exploit the primary language processes of which he is already master. If he is to realize the first advantage, he must make the conversion analytically, not by whole words. That analytic conversion requires, in particular, an explicit awareness that speech is segmentable into units of phonemic size. Given what we know about the relation of speech sounds to phonetic structure, we can see why explicit segmentation might be hard to achieve. Recent research by us has shown that for young children such explicit segmentation is, in fact, difficult, more difficult in any case than segmentation into syllables, and that such difficulty may be related to success, or the lack of it, in the early stages of reading.

Among the primary language processes that the child can exploit by conversion to speech (either analytically or holistically) is the use of a phonetic representation to store smaller segments (words, for example) until the meaning of larger segments (phrases or sentences) can be extracted. Research on speech perception suggests that the phonetic representation may be uniquely suited to such storage. That the phonetic representation is, in fact, so suited is suggested by the outcome of many experiments on short-term memory. Now we have evidence from a similar experiment that, among second graders, good readers rely more on a phonetic representation than poor readers do.

ACKNOWLEDGMENTS

We should like to express our thanks to the University of Connecticut Computer Center for their assistance in processing our data and to the school authorities in Andover, East Hartford, Mansfield, and Tolland, Connecticut without whose generous cooperation the research reported here could not have been done.

REFERENCES

Baddeley, A. D. Short-term memory for word sequences as a function of acoustic, semantic and formal similarity. *Quarterly Journal of Experimental Psychology,* 1966, *18,* 362–365.
Baddeley, A. D. How does acoustic similarity influence short-term memory? *Quarterly Journal of Experimental Psychology,* 1968, *20,* 249–264.

Baddeley, A. D. Effects of acoustic and semantic similarity on short-term paired associate learning. *British Journal of Psychology,* 1970, *61,* 335–343.

Bever, T. G., & Bower, T. G. How to read without listening. *Project Literacy Reports,* 1966, *No. 6,* 13–25.

Bolinger, D. L. Maneuvering for accent and position. *College Composition and Communication,* 1957, *8,* 234–238.

Calfee, R., Chapman, R., & Venezky, R. How a child needs to think to learn to read. In L. W. Gregg (Ed.), *Cognition in learning and memory.* New York: Wiley, 1972.

Chomsky, C. Reading, writing and phonology. *Harvard Educational Review,* 1970, *40*(2), 287–309.

Conrad, R. Acoustic confusions and memory span for words. *Nature,* 1963, *197,* 1029–1030.

Conrad, R. Acoustic confusions in immediate memory. *British Journal of Psychology,* 1964, *55,* 75–84.

Conrad, R. Speech and reading. In J. F. Kavanagh & I. G. Mattingly (Eds.), *Language by ear and by eye: The relationships between speech and reading.* Cambridge, Massachusetts: MIT Press, 1972.

Conrad, R., Freeman, P. R., & Hull, A. J. Acoustic factors versus language factors in short-term memory. *Psychonomic Science,* 1965, *3,* 57–58.

Conrad, R., & Hull, A. J. Input modality, acoustic confusion and memory span. *British Journal of Psychology,* 1964, *55,* 429–432.

Daniels, J. C., & Diack, H. *Progress in reading.* Nottingham: University of Nottingham Institute of Education, 1956.

Dewey, G. *Relative frequency of English spellings.* New York: Teachers College Press, 1970.

Dornič, S. Effect of a specific noise on visual and auditory memory span. *Scandinavian Journal of Psychology,* 1967, *8,* 155–160.

Downing, J. *Comparative reading.* New York: Macmillan, 1973.

Dunn, L. M. *Peabody Picture Vocabulary Test.* Circle Pines, Minnesota: American Guidance Service, 1965.

Eimas, P. D., Siqueland, E. R., Jusczyk, P., & Vigorito, J. Speech perception in infants. *Science,* 1971, *171,* 303–306.

Elkonin, D. B. U.S.S.R. In J. Downing (Ed.), *Comparative reading.* New York: Macmillan, 1973.

Erickson, D., Mattingly, I. G., & Turvey, M. T. Phonetic activity in reading: An experiment with kanji. *Haskins Laboratories Status Report on Speech Research,* 1973, *33,* 137–156.

Fletcher, H. *Speech and hearing.* New York: Van Nostrand Co., 1929.

Fowler, C. A., Liberman, I. Y., & Shankweiler, D. On interpreting the error pattern in beginning reading. *Language and Speech,* in press.

Gelb, I. J. *A study of writing.* Chicago: University of Chicago Press, 1963.

Gibson, E. J., & Levin, H. *The psychology of reading.* Cambridge: MIT Press, 1975.

Gleitman, L. R., & Rozin, P. Teaching reading by use of a syllabary. *Reading Research Quarterly,* 1973, *8,* 447–483.

Heilman, A. W. *Phonics in proper perspective.* Columbus, Ohio: Charles E. Merrill, Inc., 1964.

Hintzman, D. L. Articulatory coding in short-term memory. *Journal of Verbal Learning and Verbal Behavior,* 1967, *6,* 312–316.

Jastak, J., Bijou, S. W., & Jastak, S. R. *Wide Range Achievement Test.* Wilmington, Delaware: Guidance Assoc., 1965.

Kintsch, W., & Buschke, H. Homophones and synonyms in short-term memory. *Journal of Experimental Psychology,* 1969, *80,* 403–407.

Klima, E. How alphabets might reflect language. In J. F. Kavanagh & I. G. Mattingly (Eds.),

Language by ear and by eye: The relationships between speech and reading. Cambridge, Massachusetts: MIT Press, 1972.

Liberman, A. M., Cooper, F. S., Shankweiler, D., & Studdert-Kennedy, M. Perception of the speech code. *Psychological Review,* 1967, *74,* 431–461.

Liberman, A. M., Mattingly, I. G., & Turvey, M. T. Language codes and memory codes. In A. W. Melton & E. Martin (Eds.), *Coding processes in human memory.* Washington, D.C.: Winston, 1972.

Liberman, I. Y. Segmentation of the spoken word and reading acquisition. *Bulletin of the Orton Society,* 1973, *23,* 65–77.

Liberman, I. Y., Shankweiler, D., Fischer, F. W., & Carter, B. Reading and the awareness of linguistic segments. *Journal of Experimental Child Psychology,* 1974, *18,* 201–212.

Makita, K. Rarity of reading disability in Japanese children. *American Journal of Orthopsychiatry,* 1968, *38*(4), 599–614.

Miller, G. A., Bruner, J. S., & Postman, L. Familiarity of letter sequences and tachistoscopic identification. *Journal of General Psychology,* 1954, *50,* 129–139.

Monroe, M. *Children who cannot read.* Chicago: University of Chicago Press, 1932.

Rosner, J., & Simon, D. P. *The auditory analysis test: An initial report.* Pittsburgh: University of Pittsburgh Learning Research and Development Center, 1970.

Rozin, P., Poritsky, S., & Sotsky, R. American children with reading problems can easily learn to read English represented by Chinese characters. *Science,* 1971, *171,* 1264–1267.

Savin, H. B. What the child knows about speech when he starts to learn to read. In J. F. Kavanagh & I. G. Mattingly (Eds.), *Language by ear and by eye: The relationships between speech and reading.* Cambridge, Massachusetts: MIT Press, 1972.

Shankweiler, D., & Liberman, I. Y. Misreading: A search for causes. In J. F. Kavanagh & I. G. Mattingly (Eds.), *Language by ear and by eye: The relationships between speech and reading.* Cambridge, Massachusetts: MIT Press, 1972.

Shankweiler, D., & Liberman, I. Y. Exploring the relations between reading and speech. In R. Knights & D. J. Bakker (Eds.), *Neuropsychology of learning disorders: theoretical approaches.* Baltimore: University Park Press, in press.

Sperling, G. A model for visual memory tasks. *Human Factors,* 1963, *5,* 19–31.

Thomasson, A. J. W. M. *On the representation of verbal items in short-term memory.* Nijmegen: Drukkerij, Schippers, 1970. Cited by R. Conrad (1972).

Weber, R. A linguistic analysis of first-grade errors: A survey of the literature. *Reading Research Quarterly,* 1970, *4,* 96–119.

6
Reading Comprehension as a Function of Text Structure

Walter Kintsch

University of Colorado

> POLONIUS: What do you read, my lord?
> HAMLET: Words, words, words.

INTRODUCTION

There appears to be a general trend among students of memory to be concerned more and more with texts rather than with the traditional nonsense syllables or word lists. Since it is very convenient in an experiment to present a text visually to a subject, we suddenly find ourselves doing research on "reading." Thus, we enter the area of reading research by the back door, and more by coincidence than by design. I am quite aware that this does not make me an expert on reading; but I believe that the traditional academic research on learning, memory, and psycholinguistics, now that it is finally beginning seriously to study textual materials, has something to offer to specialists in reading. Exactly how much, or even precisely what, it is too early to tell, but I am sure it is worthwhile for students of memory and students of reading alike to familiarize themselves with each other's research methods, results, and special problems.

Ultimately, the final skill of the fluent reader is the highly developed process of acquiring information from a richly structured visual display. But that most essential aspect of the reading process seems to be the one least accessible to our research techniques. The reason for this failing is that psychologists have found it very difficult to give a precise meaning to the phrase "acquiring information." Everyone knows that it is insufficient simply to consider the actual words that a person reads, but various attempts to score "idea units" or the like have not been very satisfactory. I believe that the only solution lies in adopting a

227

theoretical approach in order first to work out a general theory for the representation of meaning in memory and knowledge, and then to use that theory as a tool for empirical investigation. The trouble with this proposal is, of course, that it is easier said than done; indeed, it may be foolhardy to attempt such goals. In any case, suppose one tries approaching the problem that way, looking for ways to reduce it somehow to manageable proportions. There is, after all, a great deal of nonpsychological knowledge that can be used for that purpose. Philosophers, logicians, and linguists have long been concerned with the representation of meaning, and although we do not want to solve their problems for them, we can use some of their results for our purposes. There have been several efforts in that direction in recent years, some within the field of artificial intelligence (Winograd, 1972), others from within psychology, such as Rumelhart, Lindsay, and Norman (1972) and Anderson and Bower (1973). I have been working along these lines for several years, and a fairly comprehensive presentation of the results of that work is now available (Kintsch, 1974). This is not the place to summarize that work. Instead, what I want to do in this chapter is to outline briefly some aspects of my theory for the representation of the meaning of texts, and to discuss in some detail experiments on reading comprehension and recall which depend upon that theory, in that the theory provides the independent variables to be investigated in the experiments.

1 PROPOSITIONAL TEXT BASES

The theory assumes that a text is derived from a text base which is a representation of the meaning of the text. Text bases are ordered lists of propositions. A proposition, in turn, consists of an n-tuple of word concepts. Text, text base, proposition, and word concept are, therefore, the central terms of the theory, and the specification of the relationships among these terms is the main objective of the theory.

1.1 The Lexicon

Semantic memory contains as one of its principal components a listing of all word concepts that a speaker knows, together with information about their meaning and use. This is the subjective lexicon. The meaning of a word concept is not strictly defined in the subjective lexicon, but its relationships with other concepts in the lexicon are indicated, the presuppositions and implications of its use are noted, and various possible uses of the word concept are listed in the lexicon. A propositional frame, or frames, specifies for each word concept the ways in which it may be used, together with the necessary conditions for each use, its implications, and consequences. In addition to such propositional information, a lexical entry also contains sensory (smell of the rose) and motor information (how to pick the rose) that is associated with a word concept and, of course, the linguistic information about how this word concept is expressed in the language. Usually a word concept is expressed by a word but if no single word is available a phrase can be used. Because of the existence of synonyms, homophones, and homographs in the language, the relationship between words and word concepts is, in general, many to many.

Propositions are n-tuples of word concepts, one of which serves as a predicator and the other as arguments. The predicator specifies a relationship that holds among the arguments of the proposition. Syntactically, the predicator is usually a verb, adjective, or sentence conjunction, while the arguments are nouns. Also, propositions may serve as arguments of other propositions. It is the task of the lexicon to specify which combinations of word concepts constitute semantically acceptable propositions and which do not. An explicit listing of lexical constraints is, of course, not available, and will not be for a long time. However, for present purposes one may very well rely upon linguistic intuition for the specification of acceptable propositional frames: for the most part, people's intuitions in this respect are not controversial, and we shall simply disregard the relatively few controversial cases. Two examples will illustrate the notion of lexical constraints.

Consider the word concept FEEL, which is discussed more fully in Kintsch (1974). FEEL may be used as a predicate in two separate ways, first in the sense of "to touch," second in the sense of "to perceive, be aware of." In the first sense, it may combine in propositions of the form (FEEL, AGENT, OBJECT), where AGENT is a class of word concepts, designated as such in the lexicon, which may be used in the role of agent, and OBJECT is similarly defined in the lexicon as word concepts which may be used in an object role. The agent class includes, for instance, all word concepts that belong to the classes of human beings, while the object class includes physical objects, among others. Thus, an acceptable proposition would be (FEEL, JOHN, CLOTH), *John feels the cloth.* The second way in which FEEL may be used is in the frame (FEEL, EXPERIENCER, INSTRUMENT). The classes EXPERIENCER and INSTRUMENT are also lexically defined, with EXPERIENCER again including human beings, among others, and INSTRUMENT being restricted to three disjoint sets of word concepts in this case, one including certain physical objects which may serve as an instrument, one including emotional objects, and one including intellectual objects, as for instance in *John felt a warm body, John felt a vague desire,* and *John felt he was right.* Note that all these uses of FEEL have somewhat different implications, which must be stated explicitly in the lexicon to assure that the meaning of FEEL is completely represented. Furthermore, there are uses of FEEL as an argument rather than as a predicator; these however, may be transformationally derived from the expressions already listed ("X feels" → "X's feel").

As a second example, take another predicator, the word concept CONTRAST, which may be expressed in English as an intransitive verb, a transitive verb, a noun, or a sentence connective. A few examples will illustrate these possibilities. The general propositional frame for CONTRAST contains an optional AGENT and two obligatory OBJECTS: (CONTRAST, AGENT, OBJECT$_1$, OBJECT$_2$). Consider, for instance, the proposition (CONTRAST, REPORTER, COWARD-ICE, BRAVERY). Deleting the optional AGENT we might obtain the sentence (1a), or the noun phrase (1b):

(1)　(a)　*Cowardice contrasted with bravery.*
　　　(b)　*The contrast between cowardice and bravery . . .*

With the AGENT slot filled, the (slightly awkward) sentence (2a) might be generated, or the corresponding phrase (2b):

(2)　(a)　*The reporter contrasted cowardice with bravery.*
　　　(b)　*The contrast made by the reporter between cowardice*
　　　　　 and bravery . . .

With propositions instead of single word concepts in the OBJECT slot, we obtain some further possibilities, as for instance with (CONTRAST, REPORTER, (COWARDLY, POLICE), (BRAVE, SOLDIER)). Several paraphrases of this proposition are presented with the AGENT deleted in (3), and without this deletion in (4):

(3)　(a)　*The cowardice of the police contrasted with the bravery*
　　　　　 of the soldiers.
　　　(b)　*The police were cowardly, but (whereas) the soldiers*
　　　　　 were brave.
　　　(c)　*The police were cowardly. In contrast (however), the*
　　　　　 soldiers were brave.

(4)　(a)　*The reporter contrasted the cowardice of the police with*
　　　　　 the bravery of the soldiers.
　　　(b)　*The reporter wrote that the police were cowardly, but the*
　　　　　 soldiers were brave.

In the last example the predicator CONTRAST is expressed by the English phrase *"wrote that . . . but . . ."* Clearly, this expression is highly context dependent. The verb *"wrote"* can be used only because we know that the AGENT in this case was a REPORTER. The point that I am trying to make is that any sentence constitutes an acceptable expression of the underlying proposition, as long as it communicates the concept that some REPORTER in the role of AGENT produced a certain CONTRAST. Which of the many possibilities an actual speaker would use depends upon the context of the whole communication act, the speaker's intentions, his assumptions about what the addressee already knows, etc. In this presentation we shall not investigate the factors which determine how a particular expression is selected for a given proposition.

Obviously, the lexicon must contain fairly complicated linguistic rules to permit the correct derivation of all these expressions. Furthermore, it must also contain rules specifying the proper implications of CONTRAST, as well as the proper conditions for its use, which are met, for instance, by (4) but not by (5):

(5)   *The police were cowardly, but Carol ate melons.

Specifying precisely what these requirements are is by no means a trivial problem, but it is more properly linguistic rather than psychological. For present purposes it is enough to study the form which such lexical descriptions take, and to make sure that at least in principle it is possible to state lexical descriptions in detail. With this in mind, we can go on to study interesting psychological problems without having to wait for the completion of the lexicon.

1.2 Types of Propositions

The examples discussed so far already indicate that the lexicon, as envisaged here, permits several different types of propositions. Without aspiring to completeness, I shall list just a few examples here to prepare the reader for the propositional text bases used in the experiments below.

(6)   (EAT, ANN, STRAWBERRY)
         Ann eats a strawberry.

(7)   (FRESH, STRAWBERRY)
         The strawberry is fresh, or *fresh strawberry.*

(8)   (MANY, STRAWBERRY)
         Many strawberries.

(9)   (CONTRAST, (EAT, ANN, (MANY, STRAWBERRY)),
         (EAT, CAROL, MELON))
         Ann eats many strawberries but Carol eats a melon.

(10)   (TIME: YESTERDAY, (BLOW, WIND))
         The wind blew yesterday.

(11)   (LOCATION: IN, (BLOW, WIND), BOULDER)
         The wind blew in Boulder.

In all examples the predicator is written first in a proposition, and arguments are separated by commas. In (6) and (7) a verb and an adjective serve as predicator, respectively. In (8) a quantifier is used as predicator; (9) uses a sentence connective; (10) and (11) contain a special type of TIME and LOCATION predicators. The rationale for using connectives, quantifiers, time, and location as predicators, as well as the assignments of tenses in the sentences used above, are discussed in detail in Kintsch (1974); here I shall simply employ the theory as developed there, without further justification.

1.3   Acceptability and Metaphor

The notion of a semantically acceptable proposition is central to the present theory. The lexicon states the semantically acceptable propositions for each predicator by listing the class of possible arguments as well as the conditions for their use. A proposition such as (CONTRAST, COWARDICE, BRAVERY) is understood by noting that COWARDICE plays the role of $OBJECT_1$ and BRAVERY that of $OBJECT_2$ in the lexical expression, and that the necessary relationship between $OBJECT_1$ and $OBJECT_2$ (which I have not tried to specify here) is fulfilled. But what about a sentence like (5), where the latter condition is not fulfilled, and which is, therefore, semantically unacceptable? Such propositions cannot always be treated as nonsense. Instead, a metaphorical interpretation will be attempted for unacceptable propositions on the supposition that people do not ordinarily communicate nonsense, and that if they say something that is unacceptable semantically, the very violation of semantic constraints has a communicative function. How this may be done cannot be discussed here. I have suggested earlier (Kintsch 1972, 1974) how at least some types of metaphor can be interpreted within the present theory. In the texts used for our studies we have avoided metaphors, and I am only bringing up this topic here in order to point out that the reliance upon semantically acceptable propositions is not a fatal limitation of the present theory, but that propositions violating semantic constraints can still be understood, although such understanding requires different ways of processing than the understanding of semantically acceptable propositions.

1.4   Lexical Decomposition

A feature which distinguishes the present theory from several other approaches, particularly in artificial intelligence (e.g., Schank, 1972), is that word concepts are not decomposed into their lexical constituents when used as the arguments of a proposition; lexically complex constituents are used as arguments of propositions in precisely the same way as simple elements. Thus, we admit *builder* instead of *someone-who-builds, the soldier's bravery* instead of *the-soldier-is-brave, kill* instead of *cause-to-die.* Naturally, the lexicon must contain in some form the information about the relationship between a decomposable word and its decomposition; but in principle this information is no different than other types of lexical information, such as implications, presuppositions, or consequences; a decomposition is not automatically substituted for a complex word concept in a text. Therefore, what a reader deals with in comprehending a text are propositions constructed from word concepts, regardless of whether they are lexically simple or complex.

For a detailed discussion and rationale for this practice the reader must be referred to Kintsch (1974, Chapter 11) once again, but it is nevertheless important here to mention this point. In the experiments to be reported we shall be concerned, for instance, with the number of propositions in a text as an experimental variable, and obviously, whether or not all lexically complex concepts are automatically decomposed into their semantic elements makes a rather substantial difference in how many propositions one counts in a text.

1.5   Texts and Text Bases

A text base is an ordered list of propositions. The salient properties of text bases are best explained by an example. Suppose we have the following five-proposition text base, which may be thought of as the beginning of a longer paragraph about the Greeks' love of art:

(12)   #(LOVE, GREEK, ART) & (BEAUTIFUL, ART) &
        (WHEN, (CONQUER, ROMAN, GREEK),
        (COPY, ROMAN, GREEK)) . . .

First a comment on notation: propositions in a text base are connected by the symbol &. A # is used to indicate the beginning of the text. Usually, it is more convenient not to write out propositions with their embeddings in a continuous line, but to write each proposition on a separate line, and using the line number to refer to it when it is used as an argument in some other proposition [as is done in (14)].

A possible English version of (12) might be

(13)   *The Greeks loved beautiful art. When the Romans*
        conquered the Greeks, they copied them.

Text bases are structured hierarchically by the repetition rule. Given a set of propositions and the designation of one (or more) of them as the topical or thematic elements, this rule specifies which propositions are connected to which other propositions: all propositions that share a common argument are connected. Thereby, a levels hierarchy of propositions is implied. At the top of the hierarchy are the specified thematic propositions; subordinated to this level are all propositions that share an argument with a level 1 proposition; a third level of propositions is obtained by taking all propositions that share an argument with any of the second-level propositions (but not with a first-level proposition). In this way levels of subordination can be determined objectively by noting the argument overlap that exists in a set of propositions. As yet, the theory has no way to account for the choice of the most superordinate proposition in a paragraph, and this is done intuitively. Note that whenever we speak of subordination in the present paper, we mean subordination as defined above, by means of the repetition rule, not, for instance, syntactic subordination.

If one draws lines between connected propositions, the graph structure of (12) can be made explicit:

(14)   1   (LOVE, GREEK, ART)
        2   (BEAUTIFUL, ART)
        3   (CONQUER, ROMAN, GREEK)
        4   (COPY, ROMAN, GREEK)
        5   (WHEN, 3, 4)

What is the relationship between a text base and the corresponding text, say, between (12) and (13)? There are two aspects to this question which must be strictly separated. First of all, one would like to have formal procedures which allow one both to derive texts from text bases and to construct a text base from a given text While a complete set of such rules is not yet available, this presents no insurmountable problem for the psychologist: in those cases where formal derivation rules are lacking, texts which adequately represent a given text base can be generated on the basis of agreement among speakers of a language in this respect. In fact, this is the procedure which we use in all of our experiments: we start out with a given text base, and then make the text fit that base. Given the meaning, it is relatively easy to find *a* way to express it in English. The converse, however, is much more difficult; given an arbitrary text, it is often very difficult (in the sense that people will disagree about it) to construct the corresponding text base. The development of formal rules for this purpose is, of course, one of the important goals of linguistics, artificial intelligence, and theoretical psychology, but we are still far from a general solution to this problem. I myself have neglected this question, and have chosen to work around it by always starting with a given text base.

The second question, much more interesting to the psychologist, is how people generate texts from meaning and infer meaning from texts. The ways in which people perform these tasks may be quite different from the formal procedures referred to above. Indeed, it may be that people do not employ algorithmic procedures at all in interpreting a text or sentences, but use various heuristic methods, as argued, for instance, by Bever (1970). Little is as yet known about this question. The experiments reported in this chapter are addressed to some aspects of this problem.

What the present theory, as outlined here, aspires to, is to provide the psychologist with a way to represent meaning so that the meaning of texts can become the subject of experimental investigation. In the remainder of this chapter, a few examples of such investigations will be discussed.

2 READING RATE AND RECALL AS A FUNCTION
OF THE NUMBER OF PROPOSITIONS
IN A TEXT BASE

Theories like the one outlined in the previous section cannot be tested in a strict way; they are too general for that, and too incomplete. In fact, the theory merely concerns the representation of meaning—it does not contain specific processing models. However, with the theory as a background, it is possible to design experiments that can provide some of the information necessary for the eventual formulation of processing models in the area of text comprehension and memory. At this point, our ignorance concerning these questions is so great that processing models either are restricted to very specific tasks or, if they are general, are more inspired guesses than well founded models. I propose to defer the development of processing models until more extensive experimental results about the processing of meaningful materials become available, and to concentrate first upon the establishment of an experimental data base.

The first study that was directly inspired by the propositional theory for the representation of meaning was done in collaboration with Jan Keenan (Kintsch & Keenan; 1973, also reprinted in Kintsch, 1974). The goals of this study were straightforward: we wanted to test some obvious implications of the propositional theory, and in the process find out as much as we could about memory and comprehension of text. The obvious implication that we chose for the initial test of the theory was that the mere number of propositions in a text base should have predictable psychological effects. If reading consists in reconstructing a text base from a given text, then reading time should increase as the number of propositions to be processed increases. Of course, the number of propositions in a text base is normally correlated with the number of words in a text, and so our first task was to construct texts that were all of the same length, that is, they contained the same number of words, but that derived from text bases of different lengths, that is, different numbers of propositions. Table 1 shows two sample sentences from a ten-sentence set in which all sentences had the same number of words (16 or 17), but in which the number of propositions in the underlying text bases varied from 4 to 9. The *Romulus* sentence has four rather simple propositions, while the sentence on *Cleopatra* is derived from eight propositions. The experimental task was an easy one for our subjects: they had to read each sentence as it was projected on a screen and press a button when they were finished. That made the sentence disappear from the screen and they attempted to recall it in writing. They were instructed that recall need not be verbatim. There were other sentences and paragraphs differing in length which were also used in this experiment; these will be discussed later. The first analysis simply plotted the average reading time for each of the ten sentences against the number of propositions in its base structure. In spite of the fact that the number of words was constant in all cases, reading time quite clearly depended upon the

TABLE 1
Two Sample Sentences and Their Base

I. Romulus, the legendary founder of Rome, took the women of the
Sabine by force.
1   (TAKE, ROMULUS, WOMEN, BY FORCE)
2   (FOUND, ROMULUS, ROME)
3   (LEGENDARY, ROMULUS)
4   (SABINE, WOMEN)

II. Cleopatra's downfall lay in her foolish trust in the fickle
political figures of the Roman world.
1   (FELL DOWN, CLEOPATRA)
2   (CONSEQUENCE, 1, 3,)
3   (TRUST, CLEOPATRA, FIGURE)
4   (FOOLISH, TRUST)
5   (FICKLE, FIGURE)
6   (POLITICAL, FIGURE)
7   (PART OF, FIGURE, WORLD)
8   (ROMAN, WORLD)

number of propositions in the base structure: each proposition added about 1
sec to the total reading time.

Actually this analysis is a little misleading since we have no guarantee that a
reader processes all the propositions in a given text. A better estimate of his
processing rate can be obtained by plotting reading rate not against the number
of presented propositions but against the number of propositions recalled. Since
the sentences used here are short and since the recall test is immediate, there is
probably very little forgetting; thus, recall can be assumed to mirror quite
accurately what the reader actually got out of the sentence. These data are
shown in Fig. 1. A least-squares line indicates that readers needed about 1.5 sec
of additional processing time for each proposition recalled. In this graph complete recall of all the propositions in a sentence has been combined with partial
recall from sentences with a greater number of propositions. Figure 2 shows that
this procedure introduced no artifacts: the data are plotted separately here for
partial recall and complete sentence recall, and the two curves overlap very
nicely. Recall was scored here by comparing each subject's recall protocol with
the proposition list for that sentence and deciding for each proposition whether
or not it was fully expressed in the protocol regardless of whether it was
expressed in the same form as in the original text or it was paraphrased. The
only problem arose with embedded propositions. For instance, how should one
score the second proposition in the *Cleopatra* sentence of Table 1 given the
following recall protocol: *Cleopatra's downfall lay in her foolish trust of the
Romans.* Clearly, (FELL DOWN, CLEOPATRA) can be scored as correct and
(TRUST, CLEOPATRA, FIGURE) as incorrect. The consequence proposition
was also scored as correct, even though one of the embedded propositions was

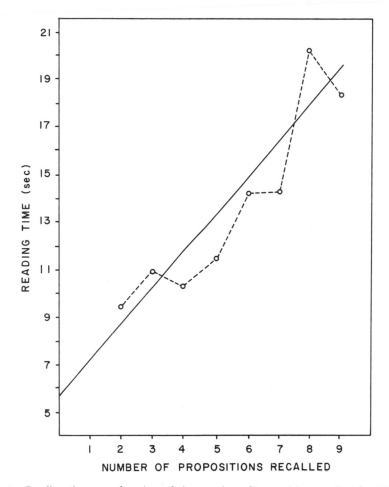

FIG. 1.   Reading time as a function of the number of propositions recalled for 16-word sentences.

incorrect. The rationale for this scoring procedure is that although the subject did not know precisely what was related, he knew that the FALL DOWN proposition and the TRUST proposition were related by CONSEQUENCE, hence he should be given credit for the latter even though an error was made in an embedded proposition. On the other hand, we would not score the CON-SEQUENCE proposition as correct if one or both embedded propositions were absent (e.g., the protocol consists only of *Because*), or if the wrong proposition had been used (a sample protocol might be *Cleopatra fell down because of the political figures,* where the second proposition related by CONSEQUENCE does not contain the correct predicator TRUST). This scoring procedure could be executed with very high reliability (the two experimenters agreed on 95% of all

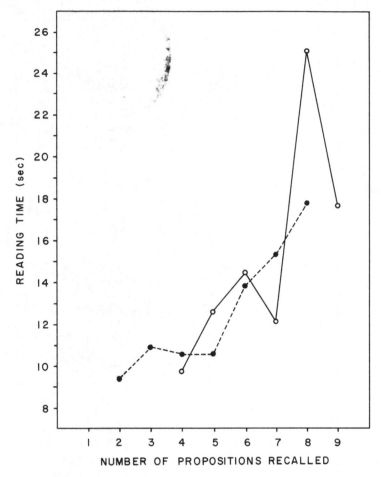

FIG. 2. Reading time as a function of the number of propositions recalled when the whole sentence was recalled (———) and when only a part of the sentence was recalled (– – –).

cases). Of course, it throws away data about the nature of errors, inferences, elaborations, etc., but it is a good way to start our investigation.

There are some subsidiary results in this experiment which should be mentioned. First, the function relating reading time to the number of propositions in the base is not due to syntactic confounding. The nine-proposition sentence in Table 1 is more complex syntactically than the four-proposition sentence. However, the results do not change if one plots reading time against number of propositions recalled separately for each sentence (except of course, that the variability is even higher). Second, the 1.5-sec reading time per additional proposition is not a constant. Other sentences and paragraphs, in addition to the ten already discussed, were also used in the same experiment. These texts ranged in length from

7 to 58 words. Separate plots for each text of reading time against number of propositions recalled revealed a tendency for both the intercepts and slopes of the functions to increase with length. For the short test sentences, only about 1 sec additional reading time was required for each proposition recalled, while for 50-word paragraphs as much as 4.3 sec were required for each proposition.

There is another incidental result from this study that is interesting. If one looks at the proportion of times that each proposition was recalled, a very wide variation is found between propositions that were recalled by almost everyone and others that were very rarely recalled. Is there anything in the theory that might be correlated with recall likelihood? First, propositional structure (Section 1.2) may influence recall likelihood, such as the number of arguments which a proposition contains, the types of argument, and the type of predicator. Since this factor varied unsystematically in the material used here, it could not be considered (but see Kintsch, 1974, Chapter 7, for some experiments designed to investigate such questions). A second factor which may influence recall likelihood is the position of a proposition in the text hierarchy. We shall consider the data with respect to this factor.

One way of measuring the position of a proposition in a text hierarchy has already been indicated in Example (14): propositions can be classified according to their level in the hierarchy, as shown in (14). When we computed the probability of recall for propositions at various levels, we found a pronounced dependence upon level: superordinate propositions were recalled better than subordinate ones. The effect was quite strong, with recall being over 90% for the most superordinate propositions and decreasing regularly to about 70% for the most subordinate ones. An ad hoc result like this, naturally, must be treated with great caution, but I shall show later that the levels effect holds up very well in other experiments.

Before concluding this section I should state why I find a demonstration that study time is related to amount recalled so important: it is because this is the first piece of experimental datum to indicate that the theoretical notions derived from the present theory have, in fact, something to do with experimental facts. Perhaps looking at reading comprehension in terms of propositional units really is a fruitful way of proceeding. In any case, it looked promising enough to go on.

3   READING RATE AND THE REPETITION OF ARGUMENTS

A study like the one just reported needs, above all, replication. At the same time, it is obvious that the mere number of propositions in a text base is only one of many factors that determine comprehension difficulty; it accounted for only about 25% of the variance in reading times. It seemed worthwhile to make a dent in the remaining 75%.

Together with G. McKoon and E. Kozminsky, we recently performed a new experiment which is still unpublished. Thus, I would like to report it in some detail. The experimental procedure was exactly as in the first study: the subject read a paragraph projected on a screen, pressed an advance button when he was through, and then recalled in writing as much of the material which he had just read as he could, although not necessarily verbatim. Thus, reading time and number of propositions recalled were, again, the dependent variables in this experiment. Two aspects of the text bases upon which the reading material was based provided the independent variables for the experiment: the number of propositions was again varied, as well as the number of arguments used. There were six short paragraphs based upon either 8 or 9 propositions and ranging from 21 to 23 words in the surface structure, and six long paragraphs based upon text bases containing between 23 and 26 propositions and ranging from 64 to 67 words. The reason this slight variation in words and propositions was permitted in our paragraphs is that it is very hard to construct natural-sounding texts which fulfill all of the necessary constraints, and we judged slight variations in these measures to be a lesser evil than stilted passages. All texts were about classical history and were adapted from paragraphs taken from "A Child's History of the World." In other words, they were rather simple texts for our college student subjects, which turned out to be an important factor. The second variable in the study was actually the main variable of interest: it concerned the nature of the propositions from which the texts were constructed rather than

TABLE 2

The *Greek Art* Paragraph

The Greeks loved beautiful art. When the Romans conquered the Greeks, they copied them, and, thus, learned to create beautiful art. (21 words)

1 (LOVE, GREEKS, ART)
2 (BEAUTIFUL, ART)
3 (CONQUER, ROMANS, GREEKS)
4 (COPY, ROMANS, GREEKS)
5 (WHEN, 3, 4)
6 (LEARN, ROMANS, 8)
7 (CONSEQUENCE, 3, 6)
8 (CREATE, ROMANS, 2)

Arguments	Argument count:	
	Repetitions	Totals
GREEKS	2	3
ART	1	2
ROMANS	3	4
Propositions appearing as arguments		6
		15

their number. Half of the paragraphs, both long and short, were constructed from propositions containing only a few different arguments, while the other paragraphs were based upon propositions containing many different arguments.

I can illustrate the distinction best by means of examples. Table 2 shows one of the short paragraphs, together with the 8 propositions from which it was derived. The argument count is also included in the table. The eight propositions which make up this text base contain only three different arguments: GREEKS, ART, and ROMANS. These arguments are all repeated and propositions containing these arguments are embedded as arguments in other propositions. Now contrast this with the text base in Table 3: again there are eight propositions containing a total of 15 arguments, just as before, but now there are eight different arguments, many of which are not repeated at all, and only one proposition is used as an argument. Half of our texts were like the *Greek art* paragraph, and I shall call these texts few-different-arguments texts; half were like the *Babylonian garden* paragraph, and I shall call those the many-different-arguments texts.

TABLE 3

The *Babylonian* Paragraph

The Babylonians built a beautiful garden on a hill. They planted lovely flowers, constructed fountains and designed a pavillion for the queen's pleasure. (23 words)

1 (BUILD, BABYLONIANS, GARDEN)
2 (BEAUTIFUL, GARDEN)
3 (LOCATION: ON, GARDEN, HILL)
4 (PLANT, BABYLONIANS, FLOWERS)
5   (LOVELY, FLOWERS)
6 (CONSTRUCT, BABYLONIANS, FOUNTAINS)
7 (DESIGN, BABYLONIANS, PAVILLION, 8)
8   (HAS, QUEEN, PLEASURE)

	Argument count:	
Arguments	Repetitions	Totals
BABYLONIANS	3	4
GARDEN	2	3
FLOWERS	1	2
HILL		1
FOUNTAINS		1
PAVILLION		1
QUEEN		1
PLEASURE		1
Propositions appearing as arguments		1
		15

Examples of long paragraphs with few and many different arguments are shown in Tables 4 and 5. The differences between the two types of paragraphs become much more apparent with the longer texts. For long paragraphs, "few different arguments" means either 7 or 8, while "many different arguments" means either 16 or 17. Repetitions of arguments have been indicated in Tables 4 and 5 by only the first letters. If one contrasts Tables 4 and 5, a striking difference is the much higher incidence of reference numbers incidating repetitions of whole propositions: on 15 occasions, propositions are embedded as arguments of other propositions in the *Joseph* paragraph, versus only 3 such embeddings in the *Assyria* paragraph.

Another way of describing the difference between the two types of paragraphs is in terms of their graph structures instead of the number of different arguments, or the number of propositional embeddings. Tables 6 and 7 show the

TABLE 4
The *Joseph* Paragraph (Repeated Arguments Are Indicated Only by the First Letter)

Although Joseph was a slave in Egypt and it was difficult to rise from the class of slaves to a higher one, Joseph was so bright that he became a ruler in Egypt. Joseph's wicked brothers, who had once planned to kill him, came to Egypt in order to beg for bread. There they found that Joseph had become a great rules. (66 words)

```
 1 (BECOME, JOSEPH, RULER)
 2   (IS A, J, SLAVE)
 3     (LOC: IN, 2, EGYPT)
 4     (RISE, S, CLASS)
 5       (HIGHER, C)
 6       (DIFFICULT, 4)
 7     (CONJUNCTION, 2, 6)
 8     (CONCESSION, 7, 10)
 9   (BRIGHT, J)
10   (CAUSALITY, 9, 1)
11   (LOC: IN, 1, E)
12   (GREAT, R)
13   (HAVE, J, BROTHER)
14     (SEVERAL, B)
15     (WICKED, B)
16     (PLAN, B, 17)
17   (KILL, B, J)
18     (TIME: PAST, 17)
19     (COME, B, E)
20     (BEG, B, BREAD)
21       (FINALITY, 19, 20)
22   (FIND, B, 1)
23     (LOC: IN, 22, E)
```

Different arguments: JOSEPH, RULER, SLAVE, EGYPT, CLASS, BROTHER, BREAD (7)

Total number of arguments: 39

graph structures of both paragraphs in matrix form: whenever there is a connection between two propositions (that is, a shared argument) a "1" has been entered in the corresponding cell of the matrix. Propositions are numbered in the same way as in Tables 4 and 5, and next to each number the first letters of the arguments of each proposition are shown. The difference between the two paragraphs is quite striking. Not only does the *Joseph* paragraph have somewhat more connections, but these connections are distributed all over the text. In the *Assyria* paragraph, on the other hand, most of the connections are to adjacent propositions in the list. In fact, if one draws a band of 12 propositions (about

TABLE 5

The *Assyria* Paragraph[a]

The rich country of Assyria was ruled by a king who lived at Nineveh. This king loved luxury and he built a wonderful palace. On the roadway that led to the palace he placed many huge and fantastic statues, depicting bulls with wings and lions with the heads of men, just as a rich man nowadays might plant trees along the driveway that leads to his home. (67 words)

```
 1 (RULE, KING, ASSYRIA)
 2   (IS A, A, COUNTRY)
 3     (RICH, C)
 4   (LOC: AT, K, NINEVEH)
 5   (LOVE, K, LUXURY)
 6   (BUILD, K, PALACE)
 7     (WONDERFUL, P)
 8   (PLACE, K, STATUE, ROAD)
 9     (LEAD, R, P)
10   (MANY, S)
11   (HUGE, S)
12   (FANTASTIC, S)
13   (DEPICT, S, BULL)
14     (HAVE, B, WING)
15   (DEPICT, S, LION)
16     (HAVE, L, HEAD)
17       (PART OF, H, MAN)
18 (PLANT, MAN', TREE)
19   (MANNER: AS, 8, 18)
20   (RICH, M)
21   (TIME: NOW, 18)
22   (LOC: ALONG, 18, DRIVEWAY)
23   (HAVE, M, HOME)
24     (LEAD, D, H)
```

Different arguments: KIND, COUNTRY, ASSYRIA, NINEVEH, LUXURY, PALACE, STATUE, ROAD, BULL, WING, LION, HEAD, MAN, MAN', TREE, DRIVEWAY, HOME(17)

Total number of arguments: 42

[a]Repeated arguments are indicated only by their first letter.

TABLE 6
Connections among Propositions in the Joseph Paragraph

	1 J, R	2 J, S	3 2, E	4 S, C	5 C	6 4	7 2, 6	8 7, 10	9 J	10 9, 1	11 1, E	12 R	13 J, B	14 B	15 B	16 B, 17	17 B, J	18 17	19 B, E	20 B, Br	21 19, 20	22 B, 1	23 22, E	C[a]	D[b]
1 JOSEPH, RULER		1							1	1	1	1	1				1					1		8	8
2 JOSEPH, SLAVE			1	1			1		1				1											6	5
3 2,EGYPT											1								1				1	4	3
4 SLAVE, CLASS					1	1																		3	2
5 CLASS																								1	0
6 4																								1	0
7 2, 6								1																3	1
8 7, 10										1														2	1
9 JOSEPH										1			1				1							5	3
10 9, 1																								3	0
11 1, EGYPT																			1			1	1	6	3
12 RULER																								1	0
13 JOSEPH, BROTHER														1	1	1	1		1	1		1		10	7
14 BROTHER															1	1	1		1	1		1		7	6
15 BROTHER																1	1		1	1		1		7	5
16 BROTHER, 17																	1		1	1		1		7	4
17 BROTHER, JOSEPH																			1	1		1		10	3
18 17																								1	0
19 BROTHER, EGYPT																				1	1		1	10	3
20 BROTHER, BREAD																					1	1		8	2
21 19, 20																								2	0
22 BROTHER, 1																								10	0
23 22, EGYPT																								4	0

[a] C = row sum.

TABLE 7

Connections among Propositions in the *Assyria* Paragraph

	1 K, A	2 A, C	3 C	4 K, N	5 K, L	6 K, P	7 P	8 K, S, R	9 R, P	10 S	11 S	12 S	13 S, B	14 B, W	15 S, L	16 L, H	17 H, M	18 8, 19	19 M', T	20 M'	21 18	22 18, D	23 D, H	24 M', H	C	D
1 KING, ASSYRIA																									5	5
2 ASSYRIA, COUNTRY	1																								2	1
3 COUNTRY		1																							1	0
4 KING, NINEVEH	1																								4	3
5 KING, LUXURY	1			1																					4	2
6 KING, PALACE	1			1	1																				6	3
7 PALACE						1																			2	1
8 KING, STATUE, PALACE	1			1	1	1	1																		10	6
9 ROAD, PALACE						1	1	1																	3	0
10 STATUE								1																	5	4
11 STATUE								1		1															5	3
12 STATUE								1		1	1														5	2
13 STATUE, BULL								1		1	1	1													6	2
14 BULL, WING													1												1	0
15 STATUE, LION								1		1	1	1	1												6	1
16 LION, HEAD															1										2	1
17 HEAD, MAN																1									1	0
18 8, 19								1																	4	3
19 MAN', TREE																		1							2	2
20 MAN'																			1						2	1
21 18																		1							1	0
22 18, DRIVEWAY																		1							2	1
23 DRIVEWAY, HOME																						1			2	1
24 MAN', HOME																			1	1			1		3	0

half of the total number in each text), 6 on either side of the diagonal, it includes 95% of all connections in the *Assyria* paragraph but only 61% in the *Joseph* paragraph. With few different arguments, connections among propositions occur throughout the list, while with many different arguments the text moves along in such a way that most connections are restricted to neighboring propositions.

Why did we choose to look at many versus few different arguments as a variable? Simply because, of the many things that might make a difference, that one was an obvious candidate. Given the very important role which the repetition of arguments plays in the theory [not only paragraph structure depends upon it, but the continuity of a text as well, and the whole account of definite and indefinite description and particularization (see Kintsch, 1974, Chapter 2)], we expected *some* psychological effect of this variable. We had no precise prediction as to the outcome; at this stage we are merely concerned with getting together some facts about reading comprehension as a basis for future attempts to formulate explicit processing models.

At an intuitive level, one can come up with plausible reasons for predicting both that few-different arguments should be harder than many-different arguments, as well as that they should be easier. The first prediction derives from a more or less well formulated parallel with double-function paired-associate lists. According to this idea, the few-different-arguments texts should be harder to learn because of greater intratask interference (many different things are predicated about the same few arguments), but long-term retention should be good. Alternatively, one might think that the frequent use of propositional arguments might be a source of difficulty. Syntactic embeddings are notoriously difficult, perhaps propositional embeddings are difficult, too.

The opposite view is that a repetition of an argument is easier to deal with in the comprehension process than an entirely new argument, and hence the few-different paragraphs should be easier to comprehend and recall. This prediction would appear to be a reasonable extension of the HAM (Human Associative Memory) model of Anderson and Bower (1973). The HAM model is too different from the present approach to make unambiguous predictions about these texts, but one may note, nevertheless, that the main difficulty which HAM

TABLE 8
Average Reading Times

Paragraphs	Average reading time (sec) for:	
	Few different arguments	Many different arguments
Short paragraphs	9.41	10.22
Long paragraphs	18.54	23.09

TABLE 9
Average Number of Propositions Recalled

| Paragraphs | Average number of propositions recalled for: | |
	Few different arguments	Many different arguments
Short paragraphs	5.44 (65%)	4.79 (59%)
Long paragraphs	11.47 (49%)	11.39 (47%)

experiences in encoding a sentence into memory is in establishing new nodes. Since more than twice as many nodes are necessary to represent the many-different-arguments sentences in HAM's format than the few-different-arguments sentences, the many-different paragraphs might be harder for HAM to encode.

As it turns out (see also Kintsch, Kozminsky, Streby, McKoon, & Keenan, 1975), the many-different paragraphs were the harder ones, indeed, as shown by the average reading times of 35 subjects for the four different paragraphs in Table 8. There is, of course, a trivial length effect and not much difference for the short paragraphs. For the long paragraphs, however, the many-different-arguments texts require significantly more reading time than the few-different-arguments texts, $F(1,327) = 33.18$, $p < .001$. When we look at recall (Table 9), the differences between the two types of texts disappear. Especially in the case of the long paragraphs, many- and few-different-arguments paragraphs are recalled equally well. In fact, the variation in amount recalled ranged only between 10.6 and 11.8 propositions for the six long paragraphs—which shows that our efforts to construct texts of equal difficulty were successful beyond expectations.

Table 10 shows the main results of this experiment in an especially clear way: for both short and long texts, the mean number of seconds of reading time per proposition recalled was considerably higher when the propositions contained many different arguments than when they contained only few different arguments. It appears that our subjects decided to study each paragraph until they

TABLE 10
Average Reading Time per Proposition Recalled

| Paragraphs | Average reading time (sec) per proposition recalled for: | |
	Few different arguments	Many different arguments
Short paragraphs	1.73	2.13
Long paragraphs	1.62	2.03

reached a certain level of comprehension (about 60% for the short ones, almost 50% for the long ones); then they quit and recalled what they could—but to do so required more time for the many-different texts than for the few-different texts.

What this experiment demonstrates is that a second aspect of the proposed representation of meaning is psychologically relevant. Another few percentage points of the unexplained variance of reading times has been accounted for: the confidence in our theoretical speculations has been strengthened a little. But the experiment has done more than that: there are some fairly rich ancillary results which are just as important as the main results discussed so far, in that they replicate and extend various earlier findings. These results will be presented in the next section.

4   FURTHER ANALYSES

4.1   Reading Rate

The main result of the Kintsch and Keenan (1973) study described in Section 2 is that the number of propositions recalled is more or less linearly related to reading time. Figure 3 shows the corresponding result from the new experiment. The data from the few- and many-different-argument paragraphs had to be combined in order to obtain sufficiently reliable estimates of the slopes and intercepts of the functions. For short paragraphs the regression line shown in Fig. 3 is

$$(15) \quad Rt_s = 7.09 + .51P,$$

where Rt is the mean reading time in sec and P is the number of propositions recalled. The corresponding equation for the long paragraph is

$$(16) \quad Rt_l = 10.90 + .98P.$$

Qualitatively, these results replicate our earlier ones in every respect. The linear correlation between study time and recall is highly significant statistically for both short and long paragraphs ($r_{short} = .82$ and $r_{long} = .79$, respectively). Previously we had reported that subjects needed about 1.5 sec per proposition for 16-word sentences and considerably more time for longer texts. The fact that the slopes obtained in the present experiment are all considerably lower is understandable: texts from a children's history book ought to be easier to read than the adult reading material used before. On the other hand, that the slope for the long paragraphs is almost double the slope for the short paragraphs agrees well with earlier findings that the amount of processing time per proposition correlates positively with the length of the text involved.

It was necessary in Fig. 3 to combine the data from the two paragraph types used in the experiment. Separate plots for many- and few-different-arguments

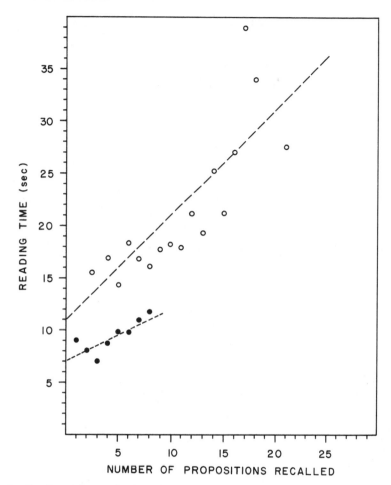

FIG. 3. Reading time as a function of the number of propositions recalled for long (open circles) and short (filled circles) paragraphs.

paragraphs show that, for both short and long paragraphs, the former generally require longer reading times for each number of propositions recalled, in agreement with the means presented in Table 8. However, deviations from linearity occur, presumably because the data points are based upon too few observations, so that no meaningful estimates of the processing times per proposition can be obtained.

4.2 Levels Effects

Another result from our first study was that superordinate propositions were recalled better than subordinate ones, what I have called the "levels effect." In the sample texts (Tables 2 to 5), the level of each proposition in the text

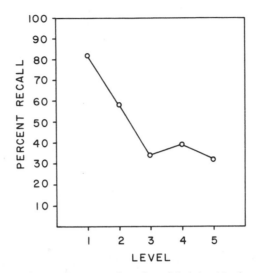

FIG. 4.   Recall of propositions as a function of their level in the text hierarchy.

hierarchy has been indicated by indentation, and the manner in which level is determined has been described in detail in Section 1. A plot of the probability of recall as a function of level is shown for the long paragraphs in Fig. 4. Recall likelihood depends quite strongly upon the level in the hierarchy of a proposition, decreasing from .82 for the most superordinate propositions to an asymptote slightly above .30 for the three most subordinated levels. This decrease is statistically significant, $F(4,138) = 22.92$, $p < .001$, according to an analysis in which the recall probability of propositions is treated as a random variable. Comparable results are obtained for short paragraphs, although there are fewer levels in that case.

In the paragraphs used here, the level of a proposition in the text hierarchy tends to be correlated with serial position in the actual text: superordinate propositions tend to come early in the paragraph. It is, therefore, possible that the levels effect reported here is due in part to serial position effects. To determine whether this was indeed the case all propositions were rank ordered according to their serial position in the surface structure (more precisely, the words corresponding to the predicators were ranked). Levels were reduced to superordinate propositions (levels 1 and 2) and subordinate propositions (levels 3, 4, and higher); serial positions were lumped into five groups. For each of the resulting 10 cells, the number of propositions in each cell and the likelihood that these propositions would be recalled are shown in Fig. 5. There are two notable aspects of this figure. First, it is indeed true that level in the text base and serial position in the surface structure are correlated. A chi-square test yielded a value of $\chi^2 = 12.48$, $p = .014$, which is sufficient to reject the hypothesis of independence. Second, it is obvious from Fig. 4 that the superior recall of

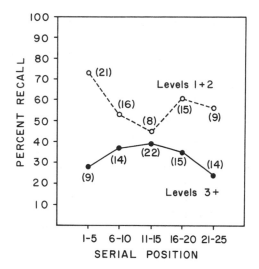

FIG. 5. Recall of propositions as a function of their level in the text hierarchy and their serial position in the surface structure.

superordinate propositions is not an artifact of serial position: for all serial positions, superordinate propositions were recalled better than subordinate ones. An analysis of variance of the data shown in Fig. 5 yielded a significant main effect for the levels variable, $F(1,333) = 48.76$, $p < .001$, a nonsignificant main effect for serial position, $F(4,113) = 1.16$, and a significant serial position by levels interaction, $F(4,133) = 2.81$, $p = .028$. The curves in Fig. 5 are quite noisy because some points are based upon very few observations, but it appears that the main reason for the significant interaction is that, for superordinate propositions, there was a decided primacy effect, but no such effect was obtained for the subordinate propositions. The recall of a proposition was facilitated when it appeared early in the text if it was an important one, that is, a superordinate proposition, but primacy in the surface structure was of no help in these data for propositions from lower levels of the text hierarchy. One should also note that there is no indication whatsoever for any kind of a recency effect in Fig. 5.

Figures 4 and 5, together with our earlier results, indicate that the level of a proposition in a text hierarchy is an important variable in determining immediate recall and thus, presumably, comprehension. This variable, however, may not be the only important structural variable. We have investigated two other possible structural variables. Their nature is best illustrated with reference to Tables 6 and 7. The matrix form used to list all interconnections among propositions, as defined by the repetition rule, suggests that the total number of connections C might be a significant variable. This number is shown as the row sum for each proposition in Tables 6 and 7. The second variable of possible significance is the number of descending connections of each proposition D that is the sum of the above-diagonal entries for each row in the tables. If the recall probability R of each proposition is correlated with these two indices, then correlations of $r_{RC} = .276$ and $r_{RD} = .253$ are obtained. These values are not very large but for 141 df they are highly significant statistically. (For comparison, the recall-and-levels correlate $r_{RL} = -.469$.) However, both of these indices correlate significantly with levels, and if one removes the levels effect from these correlations by calculating partial correlation coefficients between recall and connections and descending connections, respectively, they are effectively reduced to zero: $r_{RC/L} = .092$, $p = .28$, and $r_{RD/L} = .100$, $p = .24$. This result agrees entirely with an earlier analysis of the Kintsch and Keenan data (1973), where we have shown that the number of "descendants" of a proposition in a text hierarchy (a variable related to, but not identical with, D as defined here) does not affect recall likelihood except insofar as it is correlated with levels.

4.3 Argument Recall

There are some interesting analyses possible with respect to the recall of arguments as opposed to propositional recall. It certainly should be the case that the more often an argument is repeated in a paragraph, the greater should be the likelihood of its recall. But repeated *where*—in the text base or as an actual word in the surface structure? Figure 6 shows the answers to both questions. Clearly, there is a strong effect of base-structure repetitions in the expected direction, and again we can use this piece of information as an indication that the kind of theoretical analysis which we have made does, indeed, have something to do with the real world. There is also a very strong surface-structure effect, in that repeated words were recalled much better than words which appeared only once

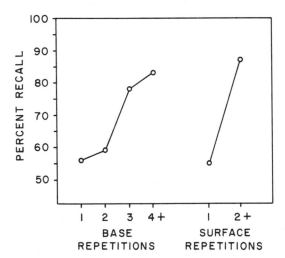

FIG. 6. Recall of arguments as a function of the number of repetitions in the text base and in the surface structure.

in a text. Needless to say, the two effects are not independent. The correlation of the number of surface-structure repetitions and base-structure repetitions for the arguments in the long paragraphs is $r = .53$. Because of the restricted range of the variables involved, and because of the strong ceiling effects in the recall of arguments noticeable in Fig. 6, there is no statistically satisfactory way of separating the contributions of base repetitions and surface repetitions, and the present results must, therefore, be regarded as tentative. An analysis of variance of recall scores as a function of number of base-structure repetitions, including only arguments represented in the surface structure exactly once, yielded a marginally significant F value, $F(2,46) = 3.09$, $p = .055$. Further research using longer texts containing more base and surface repetitions and having lower argument recall is needed to settle this question.

Why should the number of surface repetitions matter in addition to base-structure repetitions? It must be remembered that this was an immediate-recall task; even if memory for text includes a propositional level, as argued here, it certainly also includes additional levels, such as memory for the actual words used when testing is immediate. It is impossible to understand the results of experiments on memory for text unless one recognizes the multilevel character of the processing during text comprehension and the resulting multilevel memory traces. The effects of base repetitions as well as surface repetitions in Fig. 6 are a further demonstration of the importance of multilevel memory traces. It should also be noted here that, according to the theory outlined in Kintsch (1974), nonpropositional memory traces are less stable when the recall task is incidental, and hence one might expect surface effects to disappear in a delayed test while the effects of base-structure repetitions should still be observable.

5 TEXT BASES AND READING

The theory I have outlined appears to provide an adequate way of representing what a text means. While it is an incomplete theory, and certainly many of its features will need to be changed as our understanding of the problems involved improves, I think it has already proven its usefulness as a framework for generating experiments. The experiments reported here (plus some others described in Kintsch, 1974) are only a beginning; yet we have already learned some things, and even replicated a few findings, and there are enough interesting open problems around. In conclusion I would like to review what these studies mean with respect to the general question of the relationship between the meaning of a text and reading difficulty, and then comment upon some methodological problems.

The first fairly solid result that we have is that reading time can be expressed as a linear function of the number of propositions processed during reading. The processing time per proposition varies with the text in ways not yet systematically explored, from about .5 sec in short simple historical narratives to over 4 sec for the longest psychological definitions used in the Kintsch and Keenan study (1973). One source of variability appears to be the length of the text: if other characteristics remain unchanged, longer paragraphs require more processing time per proposition than shorter ones. It must be noted, however, that as yet the longest paragraphs used in these studies were merely 60 words long.

It has also been shown that the manner in which subjects process a text is related to the structural relationships among the propositions in the text base: superordinate propositions, as defined here, are recalled best, and as the level of a proposition in the text hierarchy decreases, the likelihood of recall also decreases. Again, because we have studied only relatively short texts, the limits of this phenomenon remain unspecified. Furthermore, we have demonstrated that this levels effect is not a surface-structure serial-position effect. Superordinate-level propositions were recalled better regardless of serial position. In fact, the only surface-structure serial-position effect obtained was a primacy effect for superordinate propositions. No primacy effect was observed for subordinate propositions, and no recency effects were observed at all.

Other plausible indices of structural complexity, such as the total connectivity with other propositions in the text or the connections with later propositions in the text base, did not affect recall except insofar as they were correlated with the level of a proposition in the text base. Clearly, such findings are the kind of data needed for the eventual construction of a model of the reading process.

The final result to be discussed concerns the differences in reading time for paragraphs based upon propositions containing many different arguments and those with few different arguments. This result, too, is of considerable importance for our understanding of how the reader processes the meaning of a text. Apparently, introducing new word concepts into a text added to reading time, while some other manipulations which occurred in these texts did not. For instance, the embedding of propositions as arguments of other propositions did not prove to be a source of difficulty and, somewhat surprisingly, texts in which interconnections among propositions occurred throughout the text base were in fact easier to read that texts in which there was a more definite progression of topics, with interconnections largely restricted to neighboring propositions in the text base.

Note that it would be inaccurate to say that the few-different-arguments paragraphs were more redundant than the paragraphs in which many different word concepts appeared as arguments. The same number of propositions were used in both types of paragraphs, that is, the same number of statements occurred in them, except that in one case these statements tended to be all about the same few things, while many different things were talked about in the other. I presume that redundancy, however it is to be measured, makes a text easier to read, but in the texts we used one cannot talk about redundancy at all: each proposition in the text base was expressed exactly once in the text, and each proposition, with a few accidental exceptions, added "information," that is, it said something new. In the few cases where it did not, the effects upon recall were striking. For instance, in the *Babylonians* paragraph (Table 3) there was a proposition (LOVELY, FLOWER). Two subjects out of 35 recalled this proposition, while 22 subjects recalled, on the average, the other propositions of that paragraph. I think this is because subjects just did not bother to write down patently redundant phrases: flowers are supposed to be lovely in our culture, and are probably marked so in the subjective lexicon; there seemed no need for these subjects to write this down on their recall sheets. This interpretation of the data is, of course, merely a speculation, but recently similar effects have been reported in an experiment specifically designed to investigate this phenomenon (Ehri & Muzio, 1974).

None of the information in our paragraphs was strictly new. We intentionally selected texts about widely known topics from classical history, in order to control the familiarity of the material (although I found out that not all college students have heard about Joseph and his brothers). What is new and what is old information, and how the two are related and expressed, probably are very interesting and powerful experimental variables awaiting study.

Another variable that I would like to study is the abstractness of the material. Again, I do not believe that an atheoretical approach (ratings, Flesch's formula, etc.) will get us very far in this respect: before we can study the abstractness of reading material, considerable theoretical work is needed to determine exactly what factors make a text base abstract. This requires a very specific notion of "abstract," which I think should not be conceived of in terms of visual imagery but in terms of specificity of meaning. There are, of course, further variables that are important in determining reading rate which are neglected in our work but which must be controlled. We have done, for instance, some pilot work with materials including both the kind of irrelevant historical stories used above and topics that really interested our student subjects (e.g., sex—treated quite abstractly): we found that the differences in interest value of the material had such powerful effects upon reading rate and recall that all other effects were overshadowed and insignificant in comparison.

A few remarks need to be made concerning methodology, in particular the practice of scoring as correct only recall of complete propositions. Obviously this procedure underestimates actual recall. Subjects often recall statements that are apparently derived or inferred from actual text propositions which themselves are not recalled. There are two ways to go. One could develop some scoring system, based upon intuition, which captures such occurrences. I regard such a course of action as fairly hopeless. What I would like to do is to develop the theory to such a point that it includes inference rules that allow one to decide with some degree of objectivity whether a statement is derived from the text or not, just as we are now able to tell whether a certain proposition is or is not recalled. This is the long and hard way and the theoretical developments required are far from realization, but in the long run it may be the only promising approach.

The claim that I made at the beginning of this paper, that the essence of fluid reading consists in acquiring information from a text, can now be restated with somewhat greater precision as a result of the studies reported here. We are now able to characterize the process of acquiring information during reading as the extraction of propositions from the text and the organization of these propositions into coherent, well-structured text bases. The data reviewed here on the relationship between number of propositions and reading time, or on the likelihood of recalling sub- and superordinated propositions in the text base, certainly suggest that the approach taken may be a feasible one.

ACKNOWLEDGMENTS

This research was supported by Grant MH 15 872 from the National Institute of Mental Health. I thank Jan Keenan and Eileen Kintsch for their help with this chapter.

REFERENCES

Anderson, J. R., & Bower, G. H. *Human associative memory.* Washington, D. C.: Winston, 1973.

Bever, T. G. The cognitive basis for linguistic structures. In J. R. Hayes (Ed.), *Cognition and the development of language.* New York: Wiley, 1970.

Ehri, L. C., & Muzio, I. M. The influence of verb meanings on memory for adjectives. *Journal of Verbal Learning and Verbal Behavior,* 1974, *13,* 265–271.

Kintsch, W. Notes on the structure of semantic memory. In E. Tulving & W. Donaldson (Eds.), *Organization of memory.* New York: Academic Press, 1972.

Kintsch, W. *The representation of meaning in memory.* Hillsdale, N. J.: Lawrence Erlbaum Associates, 1974.

Kintsch, W., & Keenan, J. Reading rate and retention as a function of the number of propositions in the base structure of sentences. *Cognitive Psychology,* 1973, *5,* 257–274.

Kintsch, W., Kozminsky, E., Streby, W. J., McKoon, G., and Keenan, J. M. Comprehension and recall as a function of content variables. *Journal of Verbal Learning and Verbal Behavior,* 1975, *14,* 196–214.

Rumelhart, D. W., Lindsay, P. H., & Norman, D. A. A process model of long-term memory. In E. Tulving & W. Donaldson (Eds.), *Organization of memory.* New York: Academic Press, 1972.

Schank, R. Conceptual dependency: A theory of natural language understanding. *Cognitive Psychology,* 1972, *3,* 552–631.

Winograd, T. Understanding natural language. *Cognitive Psychology,* 1972, *3,* 1–191.

7
Building Perceptual and Cognitive Strategies into a Reading Curriculum

Joanna Williams

Teachers College, Columbia University

1 INTRODUCTION

Reading is an active, constructive process. In order to become a fluent reader, a child must acquire not only what might be called the basic content of reading, such as the correspondences between sound and symbol, but also a set of complex strategies. The skilled reader is commonly described as one who does not read every word on the printed page. Rather, he samples; and the limited amount of information he gets from what is actually in front of him, together with the information that he brings with him to the task of reading, provide sufficient information for him to generate and confirm hypotheses and to comprehend the printed material. Many techniques are acquired as proficiency develops: the reader gradually develops the ability to get maximal information from his sampling; he begins to focus on words that appear just before a mark of punctuation and to focus on words that contain a relatively large amount of information. He learns to recognize phrase boundaries whether or not they are marked in any direct way by the orthography. Much more research is needed before we are able to specify all the diverse strategies that constitute "fluent reading" (Gibson & Levin, 1975).

2 LEARNING STRATEGIES AND INSTRUCTIONAL STRATEGIES

Strategies are involved even in the very beginning stages of reading. The large literature on word recognition—a classic topic over the years—indicates the potential involvement of many strategies. However, we still cannot delineate the ones a reader actually uses when he identifies a word (Levin & Williams, 1970; Venezky, 1974).

It would be an immense task, and quite outside the scope of this paper, to review the findings on this vast topic. I should, however, like to touch on several general points. First, most of this work falls in the category of "laboratory studies" and must be evaluated as such. People have often been too quick to overgeneralize about data collected under carefully specified artificial and arbitrary laboratory conditions. It is important to keep in mind the dangers of doing this, although naturally the temptations are great for the experimenter. One excellent way to develop hypotheses about the nature and sequencing of instructional materials is to make comparisons in the laboratory, where crucial variables can be isolated and manipulated. It is true that a significant difference between experimental treatments may wash out under the actual classroom conditions and also that effects may be statistically significant and yet so small as to be of no practical significance. Nevertheless, the opposite sometimes holds: there can be situations (Marsh & Desberg, 1973) in which a small-scale laboratory study will yield only a very small effect or even no effect at all, and yet, when the study is conducted over an extended time period, the larger amounts of the same experimental treatment will lead to substantial and important effects. This type of work, of course, is only an initial stage in the development of materials and techniques to be used in the classroom.

One of my own experiments can serve as an illustration (Williams, Blumberg, & Williams, 1970). Using a delayed matching-to-sample procedure, subjects chose matches for three-letter and five-letter nonsense words from an array of choices that were structured such that each choice represented one of a systematic series of possible errors. Kindergarten children, who had had no reading instruction, showed no systematic preference for any of the cues. First-grade children, who had begun receiving instruction in reading and who were competent at naming the letters of the alphabet, matched on the basis of first and last letters significantly more often than on the basis of middle letters or the configuration (overall outline) of the word.

Adults, whom we were able to question after the experiment, reported the use of a variety of strategies. Although the task as presented seemed wholly visual, almost half the adult subjects reported some use of an "aural" strategy—rhyme, in most cases. For example, they matched trigrams on the basis of second and third letters. The other subjects reported that they used a purely visual strategy and again, surprisingly, they often described their strategy (and the data confirmed their description) as one in which they tried to match on the basis of overall shape. This had been the least salient cue for the children.

On the basis of these as well as other findings, there seems to be no justification for developing instructional methods or primer materials based on the use of configuration as a cue. Configuration seems a poor choice after reading training is begun, for when children have been taught by word analysis methods, individual letters become quite salient. Moreover, if one's instructional strategy were to attempt to capitalize on tendencies seen before any instruction is given, configuration would still be a poor choice. There was no special tendency to use this (or any other) cue in the kindergarten (nonreading) children. More crucial is that fact that it is unreasonable to rely on configuration as a cue for effective transfer. Even if a child were in fact skilled in this strategy, a simple transfer from lower-case to upper-case letters would remove the possibility of utilizing that strategy.

The results of this experiment remind us that it should not be assumed that adults and children behave in the same manner on simple tasks like this one. Implications for instruction based on data collected on adult readers can be seriously misleading. Indeed, it is interesting to note the fact that while many widely used reading methods over the past 40 years (the "look–say" or "whole-word" method) have stressed identification of words on the basis of overall shape, it is adults and not children who sometimes show this strategy in word recognition. We know that educational methods and materials have been developed too often on the basis of armchair speculation alone, without actual data. Perhaps they have also been based on the results of empirical investigations that cannot yield worthwhile information because the wrong subjects have been studied!

In a second study (Kuenne & Williams, 1973) we used the same experimental technique to explore the question of what cues might be used in identifying a word aurally. This experiment dealt with a different set of cues that are particularly relevant to auditory processing, but essentially it raised the same issues. Kindergartners showed no systematic tendencies, but by the second grade, children demonstrated a rather clear pattern of cue choices. There was significantly more matching on the basis of CV (consonant–vowel) or VC segments than to single consonants. There was also no clear-cut preference for position as a cue; to the extent that position was at all important, it appeared that the final position was more salient, as opposed to the initial position as in visual word recognition. Girls showed clearer patterns than boys did at each grade level, reflecting the typical finding that girls are more advanced in verbal tasks and show more differentiated behaviors at an earlier age.

Thus, what appears to be a highly salient perceptual or cognitive strategy may vary as a function of age, type of instruction, modality, and probably a large number of other factors. One cannot easily generalize across subjects or situations without careful investigation.

The identification of those strategies that are relevant and useful in the acquisition of reading is a crucial first question for curriculum design. After the strategies have been identified, the obvious follow-up question is whether we can provide instruction that will enhance the development of certain of them, so that competence in reading will be more quickly and more effectively achieved (Williams, 1973). Sometimes a strategy can be taught directly. For example, some teachers for years have been suggesting to children that, when faced with an unfamiliar word, they should identify the first letter and then guess. The first letter, plus the context, is indeed often sufficient for word identification. Samuels, Dahl, and Archwamety (1974) have described this strategy explicitly and have had some success in teaching it to retarded children who do not ordinarily utilize such techniques.

Some strategies, however, cannot be taught directly. For example, the perceptual learning underlying the differentiation of alphabet letters involves a search for the distinctive features of the letters. How do we get children to focus on the distinctive features so that they will differentiate them appropriately? To some degree, we can describe and point out the differences between two letters, but we are not really certain that we know what are the actual critical features people use. To a great extent, therefore, we approach the task indirectly. We provide many opportunities in which cognitive strategies may occur and may be practiced. We try to manipulate attention to the task in general, hoping that this will lead to the use of a strategy that we cannot manipulate directly.

Another important distinction must be made: there are strategies of learning that the child develops and, on the other hand, there are strategies of instruction which, it is hoped, will lead to the development of appropriate perceptual and cognitive strategies in the learner. One simple example should make clear what I mean by strategies of instruction. Knowing that the initial letter is a highly salient cue in visual word recognition, one might adopt an instructional strategy that seeks to capitalize on this tendency and design materials and procedures accordingly. On the other hand, one could argue that it would be more effective to focus instruction on aspects of the task that were not particularly salient prior to instruction, that is, to provide materials that make the middle of the word more salient. Such simple distinctions have sometimes proved very important in the development of the programs of instruction and the theories that I shall discuss in this paper.

3 THE LEARNING-DISABLED READER

More often than not, instructional strategies in reading have been developed with specific reference to poor readers. This does not mean, however, that what we learn is unrelated to the nature of the reading task in general and to the typical processes involved in reading acquisition. On the contrary, as Gibson (1971) has pointed out, proficient readers make such economical use of all of their perceptual, cognitive, and linguistic abilities that it is sometimes difficult to tease out the ways in which they utilize their various skills.

How can these poor readers be described? In early work, experimental samples were not very carefully selected or easily described. Recently, investigators have become more interested in adequate definition; they usually report scores on individually administered intelligence tests and standardized reading tests, and they also make sure that comparisons between poor and normal readers are based on groups that are equivalent in terms of such variables as age, sex, and socioeconomic status. Terminology changes regularly. It seems fair to say that the currently popular label for the poor reader is "learning disabled." More and more emphasis lately within the field of special education is focused on those children who appear to have potential for achievement but who nevertheless do not demonstrate adequate achievement.

The term "learning disabled" has been accepted by most specialists as the most descriptive and most palatable of the many labels that have been used to describe this population. During the 1930s and 1940s, when the first spurt of books devoted to the development of remedial educational procedures appeared, the same types of children were typically labeled "brain injured," following a medical model that hypothesized that there had been some damage to the central nervous system (Strauss & Lehtinen, 1947). Very rarely were there actually any "hard" signs of neurological impairment. Rather, inferences were drawn from behavior, for the most part in terms of fairly gross categories. Atypical test performance soon appeared as part of the description. Uneven profiles on the Wechsler Intelligence Scale for Children (WISC) were considered to mirror uneven underlying neurological processing, for example. Other tests, such as the Illinois Test of Psycholinguistic Abilities, were developed more specifically for diagnostic purposes.

Over the years, there has been little increase in our understanding of the learning-disabled child from advances in neurology—although Sperry's recent work in the differentiated functions of the two hemispheres of the brain (Sperry, 1964; Gazzaniga, 1970) might modify this conclusion in the relatively near future. Moreover, this "medical model" has often been seen as a rather pessimistic one from the point of view of remediation. Today the field is characterized by what might be called an "educational model," focusing on the underachievement of the child and on consideration of more direct (educational) remediation possibilities (Bryant, 1972).

The learning-disabled child demonstrates a significant discrepancy between his estimated intellectual ability and his school performance, a discrepancy that is not secondary to mental retardation, educational or cultural deprivation, emotional disturbance, or sensory loss (Myers & Hammill, 1969). Despite average or above-average intelligence, it is difficult or impossible for such a child to learn in a normal classroom situation. Characteristic of this population are "various combinations of impairment in perception, conceptualization, language, memory, and control of attention, impulse, or motor function" (Myers & Hammill, 1969).

The population is indeed a heterogeneous one. Among the specific problems usually mentioned are the following: confusion of time, space, and direction; hyperkinesis; uneven performance of WISC subtests with substantial differences between verbal and performance IQ; awkwardness; poor perceptual—motor skills; inadequate perceptual abilities; poor intersensory integration; late and deficient language development; difficulties in reading, writing, spelling, and arithmetic (Chalfant & Scheffelin, 1972). Difficulties in one or several of these characteristics may be noted in a particular child. These children may sometimes find it impossible to follow a series of directions. They often have poor short-term auditory memory, may not be able to distinguish between left and right, or they may have difficulty maintaining attention for age-appropriate lengths of time. They show highly erratic performance from one day to the next.

Whatever general definition is accepted, however, certain questions remain. How is any particular disorder to be assesed? What reading test, for example, is to be specified as one that acceptably identifies and presents the appropriate content to be tested? And, when we are satisfied with such measures—which we certainly are not, at present, what level of severity of a given disorder must be reached before the child is considered disabled?

Today there are almost as many answers to these questions as there are specialists in the field, and for this reason it is difficult to determine how widespread learning disability may be. Surveys of teachers, principals, and other specialists vary tremendously in their reports of incidence, some identifying 1—3% of the school population as learning disabled, and others reporting 15% or even higher. More than anything else, such figures reflect the basic confusion about the definition (Bryant, 1974).

Not all learning-disabled children have difficulty in learning to read. However, this skill represents the single most important source of failure for elementary-grade children. There are two important reasons for this: reading requires that cognitive and perceptual faculties be intact and integrated; and reading is heavily stressed in the early grades. How the child develops the extensive set of cognitive skills that must combine both hierarchically and sequentially in fluent reading is far from clear. Because of this lack of basic knowledge about the normal reader, we would expect an even greater lack of knowledge when it comes to understanding the problem reader. We *can* say that the disabled reader (sometimes called "dyslexic," although this term is at other times reserved for the most severely disabled) may exhibit disorders in any or all of the basic skills upon which reading depends. There may be difficulties in visual and auditory discrimination, memory, and sequencing, as well as in the integration of auditory and visual perception (Samuels, 1973). In particular, learning-disabled children may have problems in the identification of words as wholes, so that they lack an adequate sight vocabulary; and/or they may be unable to synthesize a word out of its letter units. Typical errors include: reversing and transposing, adding or dropping of phonemes or syllables, substituting one word for another with a similar meaning, confusing similar letter sounds, and being unable to blend and analyze word parts (Vellutino, 1974). Nondisabled children, of course, also make the same errors when they are learning to read, but they make many fewer, and the patterns of error do not persist as long.

4 INSTRUCTIONAL PROGRAMS

One important early type of educational treatment derives from the point of view that inherent dysfunctions must be remediated before any academic training is given; for example, one area of the brain might be lagging behind in development, so that one sensory modality might be operating at an immature level. Although often there was a conceptualization of this sort of developmental lag, others held simply that a particular part of the brain might be damaged and so lead to dysfunction. Treatments within this category attempted to work directly on the neurological deficits and thereby to promote perceptual learning. For example, Orton (1937) was concerned with making sure that hemisphere dominance was established. His educational treatment consisted of very systematic perceptual–motor training, and it was particularly emphasized for children who demonstrated such relevant symptoms as reversing letters, words, and so forth. Strauss (Strauss & Lehtinen, 1947) was particularly interested in the hyperactive child, who presumably suffered from a brain dysfunction which led to distractibility and perceptual and cognitive difficulties. His remediation stressed the necessity of minimizing distracting stimuli, both aural and visual, so that the child's environment was made extremely stable and quiet.

Other types of treatment focused more on the need for providing opportunities to learn certain prerequisite skills that, for some reason, were not present. That is, it was the lack of these skills rather than the lack of neurological functioning per se. These treatments can be considered readiness programs. Kephart (1960) was a major theorist within this tradition: all learning, he said, has a sensory–motor base, and the developmental stages go from there through perceptual–motor learning, intersensory integration, up to pure cognitive learning. To provide for the lags in achieving these developmental skills, a wide variety of tasks, mostly multisensory, must be provided. Before anything related to letters and numbers, or any other symbolic material, is introduced, the child should be given a program that involves balance boards, trampolines, and other gross motor activities, as well as rhythm activities and fine motor training, ocular-control training, and so forth.

Frostig's approach (Frostig & Horne, 1964) is not too different. Her program provides remedial perceptual training in various visual functions: eye–motor coordination, figure–ground perception, perception of constancy of shape, perception of position in space, and perception of spatial relationships. Frostig's work is a model for this kind of approach. She emphasizes the importance of individualized instruction and of continuous monitoring of the child's progress. She insists on explicitness in diagnostic procedures and in the evaluation of remediation so that, as the child's achievement pattern is modified, the teacher can be responsive with new decisions about instruction. While some of the early training activities involve motor tasks and body-concept development, her training program is for the most part a paper-and-pencil program that focuses on the visual–perceptual skills outlined above.

There are many other educational programs of this variety; in general, both in theoretical rationale and in instructional treatment, they are rather similar to the ones I have mentioned. That is, the basic assumption was usually made that there was some inherent psychological dysfunction that must be remedied *before* regular academic training should be started. Presumably, transfer to the acquisition of cognitive skills such as reading would occur as a consequence of this type of training.

Empirical Evidence

What kind of empirical evidence was used to justify these instructional programs? There was some, although it should be made clear that it was not so much any hard data that convinced people of the worth of these approaches. It was, rather, the eminently reasonable, though untested, assumption that neurological deficits existed and that they could be corrected or at least alleviated by such procedures. And even more important than the rationale was the incontrovertible fact that the proponents of these approaches were indeed helping disabled children. Frostig (Frostig & Horne, 1964) again provides a model. A skilled teacher, she founded a most successful school. Was her success with children really due to her treatment as I have described it? The claim was indeed that the training program itself led to improvement. It is perhaps significant that case studies have been offered where such training, presented in the absence of other treatment, did lead to improvement; but it was improvement on the Frostig test, which included the same type of tasks as did the training. It was not improvement in reading—it was not necessary to test that; it was assumed. And yet a child in Frostig's school received, along with the specified visual–perceptual training, real reading instruction, language and mathematics, motor training and psychotherapy. No use taking any chances!

Let us turn to more straightforward empirical data. Much of the justification for these approaches rests, rather uneasily, on correlations found between performance on perceptual tests and reading achievement, usually assessed at the end of first grade. Goins (1958), for example, correlated scores on fourteen visual–perceptual tests given to beginning first graders and reading achievement assessed several months later. There were indeed some correlations between most of the tests and reading. None, however, was higher than .50. Tasks other than what can perhaps best be described as visual discrimination tasks have also been used, including visual memory (Lyle & Goyen, 1968) and visual sequencing (Kass, 1966). While a large number of the many studies that report correlations between visual–perceptual abilities and reading involve visual–motor tasks, which complicates the conclusions that can be drawn, some studies have been reported that investigate visual tasks that are free of motor-skill requirements (e.g., tests of figure–ground relationships and of visual closure), and these, too, are correlated with early reading achievement (Bell & Aftanas, 1972; Goins,

1958). However, it is rare that any of these correlations exceed .60 (Bryant, 1972).

Of course, perceptual tests based on other types of tasks, especially auditory tasks (Samuels, 1973), also correlate to some extent with early reading achievement, but the traditional instructional programs focused almost totally on visual perception. In any event, it is obviously not appropriate to use this sort of correlational evidence as a basis for the point of view that reading failure can be corrected or prevented if visual–perceptual training is given first.

There has been relatively little substantive research in the area, and the evaluations of these compensatory programs have often been based more on faith than on solid evidence. The developers of these well-elaborated remediation systems have not often shown interest in objective evaluation; after all, they are already convinced. And a look at the general literature on remediation is not more convincing. Few of the studies describe the remediation techniques used with any degree of specificity; and few are exemplary with respect to other basic research considerations, such as experimental design, the selection of criteria for the tests utilized, and so forth. In general, one can say that giving special instructional help in reading itself does seem to lead to improvement, and that such improvement seems to be more likely if children are fairly young—possibly because the lessons focus on decoding skills rather than comprehension. But there is no evidence that any one technique is better than any other. With respect to the specific evaluation of visual–perceptual–motor curricula, there does not seem to be any evidence that these lead to improved reading performance. In a recent review of 12 studies assessing the Frostig materials (Hammill & Wiederholt, 1973), 11 found no difference in reading achievement as a function of training—although most did show improvement on the Frostig items themselves. The twelfth study rather unaccountably did show reading gains—but no improvement on the Frostig test! In the last couple of years, faced with the inescapable fact that children given these types of programs have *not* responded as had been hoped—that is, the expected transfer to reading did not occur—the tremendous popularity of the perceptual–motor-skills curriculum has started to wane.

Unfortunately, there is nothing to put in its place. Classrooms are still using this type of approach, although, in the more sophisticated classrooms, the rationale has changed. Perceptual–motor activities are now recommended as a help in the development of motor functions for their own sake, as opportunities to provide important socialization experiences, to enhance body image, and to help with classroom management. For these reasons, they are presented as legitimate components of instruction.

All of this has left behind those of us who are concerned with cognitive deficits and poor reading ability. What type of instruction would be most effective? Most recently, there has been a shift toward the point of view that academic training, that is, instruction in reading, should be attempted directly, without waiting for, and without trying to develop, neurological patterns or readiness skills. It is felt that both the essential skills and the relevant perceptual and cognitive strategies will be better learned within the context of reading itself.

5 MATCHING INSTRUCTIONAL TREATMENT
TO DIAGNOSTIC CATEGORY

The notion that education ought to be individualized is, today, a real ideal. Individualization seems even more important when we think of learning-disabled children or any other group with distinctive yet heterogeneous difficulties. The very term "special education" suggests that there is a relationship between certain specified characteristics of the child on the one hand and instructional techniques on the other. This surely means that optimizing learning for the slow learner will involve the use of carefully worked-out procedures. But there is another common, though not necessary, implication: that we should look for the right "match" between pupil type and instruction type. Indeed, if highly recommended, fervently believed-in remedial techniques cannot be demonstrated to be effective, perhaps the reason is *not* that they are not effective, but rather that they are differentially effective. That is, they do work, but only for certain limited categories of children, so that in overall comparisons the positive results wash out.

Is this a reasonable point of view? If so, we would expect that there would be an interaction between pupil category and instruction type, that is, that the effectiveness of instruction would depend on the type of pupil. For this to make sense, of course, we must observe a particular kind of interaction. Only if it can be shown that one method of treatment is superior to another for one group of children, and that a second method is superior to the first for a different group of children, would it make sense to talk about prescribing different educational treatments for different children. Cronbach and Snow (1969) have alerted us to the difficulties of actually finding such disordinal interactions within the general field of educational research. Heedless of the difficulties, many educators hold, at least in theory, to an instructional strategy that first requires the identification of a particular child's cognitive style and then seeks to identify or develop appropriate instruction based on that style.

Within the specific field of reading, a most provocative—and, indeed, intuitively a very reasonable—notion is that it is useful to characterize a child with reading disability in terms of the discrepancy between his visual and his auditory modalities. Some children appear to be "eye oriented" and have difficulty with tasks involving auditory analysis. Others seem to be "ear oriented"—they have no trouble with auditory tasks, but their visual perceptual abilities are wanting. One approach that has come to be called in the literature "modality matching" suggests that instruction might be more effective for these children if it is geared to their dominant modality. Wepman (1968), a leading proponent of this point of view, feels that all early learning (i.e., in the preschool and elementary school year) is modality bound, and that some children suffer from lags in the development of the neurological pathways of one or another modality, leading to discrepancies not in auditory or visual acuity but rather in the ease of processing and storing information received through the various modalities.

It would seem plausible, on the basis of this theorizing, that perhaps the visiles (the eye-oriented children) would respond favorably to reading instruction stressing an essentially whole-word approach and requiring little analysis of sounds. Audiles, on the other hand, might do well with an approach that is heavily oriented toward phonics. Here we have a hypothesis that is straightforward and, in fact, unusual in that the distinctions between the two groups of subjects and between the two instructional methods are, conceptually at least, fairly clear-cut.

Empirical Evidence

There is very little empirical evidence for the notion. DeHirsch, Jansky, and Langford's (1966) longitudinal study attempted to predict reading failure at grade 2 from tests administered in kindergarten. It was noted that of the ten children (19% of the sample) who showed discrepant modality scores at the kindergarten level, seven indicated a dominance in the auditory modality. All five of these children who could be later categorized as good readers had received phonics instruction, and the other two, who turned out to be poor readers, had not. On the basis of this rather casual observation, the authors recommended that "modality strength and weakness" should be considered seriously in the selection of instructional methods. On the basis of correlations between auditory perceptual tests and visual perceptual tests in a sample of children followed from the first to the third grade, Morency (1968) argued that the improvement of one modality over the course of development is usually, but not necessarily, related to improvement in the other modality; he, too, emphasized the importance for instruction of information about modality dominance or preference.

However, most attempts to test the hypothesis have failed. It should first be noted that there is no generally accepted way of assessing audiles and visiles. Rather, children with discrepant scores, for example, relatively high on visual tests and relatively low on auditory tests, are identified. Since there is no consensus about what tests are appropriate or how large the discrepancies between scores must be and, for the most part, no attention to such matters as reliability and validity, it is difficult to generalize about the work that has been done.

There are two types of study. One is a large-scale long-term study that examines the hypothesis directly in an instructional setting. The other is a short-term laboratory analog, usually further from the real question of interest but more rigorously controlled. Let us look at a few of the laboratory studies first. Bruinicks (1970) studied audiles and visiles in a sample of eight-year-old black males whose mean IQ was 90 and mean reading (grade equivalent) score was 2.74. Subjects were trained to recognize 15 unknown words by a sight–word procedure and another 15 by a phonics procedure. No interaction between method and modality group was found on either immediate or delayed recall. There was an overall difference in favor of the visual presentation, however, which approached significance. Waugh (1973), working with second graders, found that the audiles' performance was superior over all the different instructional groups on a word-recall task; audiles and visiles performed equally well, however, on word recognition. Ringler and Smith (1973) used the New York Modality Test to identify auditory and visual as well as tactile learners. Within each modality group, subjects were assigned to one of four treatment groups— auditory, visual, tactile, and combination—or to a control group. Fifty familiar words were taught over the course of 7½ months in the following ways: the auditory group listened to the sound of the whole word both in isolation and in context and listened to segments of the word; the visual group focused on word configuration; and the tactile group traced words outlined with pipe cleaners. No differences on a test of word recognition were found, except that all treatment groups were significantly better than the control group. No modality-group differences or interactions were found.

Of the studies conducted in an instructional setting (e.g., Bateman, 1968; Harris, 1965), I shall discuss just one by Robinson (1972), which is one of the most thorough studies of this type. At the beginning of first grade, children in four Chicago school systems were given an extensive battery of visual perceptual tests, including a portion of the Goins Battery, the Wepman Auditory Discrimination Test, and the SRA Primary Mental Abilities Test, as well as several reading measures, including the Metropolitan Test and the Gray Oral Test.[1] Of the 448 children tested, Robinson could classify only 11% as having discrepant modality patterns. That is, there were only 26 children who scored high on visual and low on auditory ability and 24 who scored high on auditory and low on visual ability. In two of the four school systems, a sight–word approach (Ginn and Scott-Foresman) was taken; in the other two, a phonics approach (Lippincott and Hay-Wingo) was used. A rather unusual aspect to this study was the fact that Robinson monitored the classrooms regularly in order to ensure that teachers were indeed holding to their particular instructional method.

The children's progress in reading was evaluated at the end of the first grade and again at the end of the third grade. The first-grade analysis indicated that the audile children tended to score higher on the Metropolitan Achievement Test when taught by the phonics method; this finding came close to statistical

---

[1] Readers who would be interested in a complete description of the specific tests mentioned are referred to Buros (1968).

significance ($p < .06$). However, there was no suggestion at all of an interaction in the third grade. (It could be argued, of course, that tests at the third-grade level measure comprehension and intelligence rather than the decoding skills that presumably are sensitive to modality differences.) There were some overall differences between methods. In the first grade the children who had been taught by a sight–word method scored significantly higher than the phonics-taught children on the Gray Oral Reading Test, whereas the phonics-taught children showed a tendency toward superiority on the Metropolitan. In the third grade, the phonics-taught group tended to surpass the sight–word group over all the criteria measures. Although Bateman (1968) had previously found phonics-taught children superior to sight–word-trained children (but no interaction between instructional method and modality group), Robinson was cautious in her conclusions as to the superiority of a phonics approach. In sum, it must be concluded that there is no firm empirical support for the "modality-matching" hypothesis.

Perhaps in concentrating on modality strengths and weaknesses, we have been looking at the wrong variables. Stallings (1970), for example, found a significant interaction between performance on the sequencing subtests of the Illinois Test of Psycholinguistic Abilities and type of initial reading instruction, such that low scorers were better with a whole-word method while high scorers were better with a linguistic (i.e., structured phonics) method. This finding does not solidly establish a relationship between the two variables, but it is intriguing and it certainly deserves to be followed up. While it is premature to draw any final conclusions, we must admit that so far there is no convincing evidence that matching instructional treatment to diagnostic category will enhance learning. To focus the development of curriculum methods and materials on such interactions seems unproductive right now.

6 THE TACTILE-KINESTHETIC MODALITY

After reviewing the literature, one aspect of the modality question, however, seemed rather interesting. It has often been claimed that beginning reading instruction that stresses the tactile-kinesthetic modality is highly effective. Fernald (1943), Spalding and Spalding (1957), and others recommend one or another variation of such training, emphasizing its usefulness in the early steps of reading acquisition and also for slow learners. In the Fernald method, for example, a great deal of instructional time is spent in having the child trace over the letters of a word at the same time that he is saying the word aloud.

Research evidence of the value of these approaches is equivocal and inconclusive. Many of the studies that have investigated the effectiveness of tactile-kinesthetic training have done so in the context of rather complex situations, using a measure such as word recognition or word retention and involving one or another variation of a paired-associates paradigm (Jensen & King, 1970; Ofman & Shaevitz, 1963; Williams, 1974). Even if such studies indicated a strong superiority for tactile-kinesthetic training, it would be difficult to identify the specific mechanisms by which the effect occurred.

We have done some work on this topic that focuses on a relatively more straightforward (although still quite complicated) question: how effective is such training for improving simple visual discrimination? Our plan was to develop a laboratory analog of the educational procedures in which the effectiveness of such training could be demonstrated. Then, using that experimental situation, we would try to determine the reasons underlying its effectiveness.

We reasoned that possibly the technique is effective because it provides a means of ensuring that the children will focus on their task. What, actually, must the child learn in order to differentiate those letters and words on the printed page? Presumably, he must notice and retain the information inherent in those marks, which can be described in terms of distinctive features—whether a letter is curved or has only straight lines, whether it is symmetrical, etc. No one has come up with a satisfactory list of such critical features yet, although Gibson's (1970) analysis makes a substantial contribution to the question. The features will turn out to be considerably more complicated than the examples I have given, to be sure. But we can ask the question of what training methods would be most effective in ensuring that the child's attention is focused on the distinctive features, whatever they may be. It is quite likely that tracing or copying—some form of reproduction training—would force a child to look more closely at what he was doing and to attend to more criterial attributes. Then he would have available more of these features to aid him in word recognition.

Furthermore, it seemed reasonable to expect that whether or not reproduction training would force closer attention to the form would depend on the similarity of the standard form and other stimuli from which it must be distinguished. For example, if the child must discriminate a circle from a triangle, he needs only to notice that one of the forms has an angle. If, however, his task is to distinguish an upright triangle from an inverted one, he is required to notice more. Hence, the use of training items involving stimuli that are only minimally different will force the child to attend closely and thereby focus on many attributes of the stimulus. In the process he will be likely to abstract features which are critical for its differentiation.

6.1   Effects on Recognition

In our first experiment (Williams, 1969), the training task consisted of a delayed matching-to-sample task in which urban kindergarten children were asked to identify the standard after it was removed from view. This visual memory task was used because it approximates the perceptual learning tasks involved in actual reading more closely than does simple discrimination training (Wohlwill &

Wiener, 1964). Three of the standards (chosen randomly from the six) were placed in an array in front of the child. Twelve cards, on each of which were two forms (one of the standards and another form), were presented in sequence, and the child was asked to choose the form on each card that was exactly the same as one of the three standards. The correction method was used. There were five such presentations, with the twelve cards presented in a different random order on each trial.

There were three discrimination-training groups (n = 8 in each group), which varied with respect to the comparison stimuli used (see Fig. 1). In group D-1 (difficult), the comparison stimuli were right–left reversal (R–L) and 180°-rotation transformations. In group D-2 (difficult), they were up–down reversal (U–D) and 90°-rotation transformations. In group S (simple), they were four forms completely different from the standards. The fourth condition (group R), also containing eight subjects, consisted of reproduction training. The three standards were placed in an array as in the other conditions, but no other forms were presented. Each child traced and copied each standard for a period of time matched with the time taken by a child in one of the discrimination-training groups.

A series of three tests, graded in difficulty, was administered immediately upon the completion of training and was repeated 24 hr later. Test 1 (and Retest 1) consisted of 24 cards on each of which were drawn two forms, one standard and one other, either a dissimilar form or a transformation of one of the

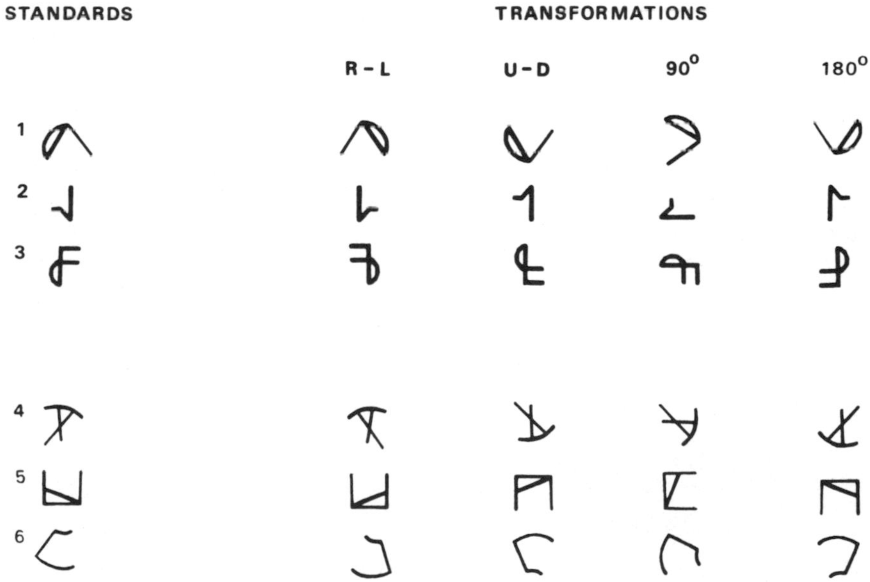

FIG. 1. The standards and their transformations.

standards. Test 2 (and Retest 2) consisted of 15 cards, on each of which were printed two sets of three forms each: one set contained one of the three standards and the other set, a transformation of that standard. Test 3 (and Retest 3) consisted of 12 cards, each of which contained two pairs of forms. One pair was composed of standard only, and the other pair was composed of one standard and one transformation. On each of these tests the child was required to point to the card that contained the standard(s).

The results are presented in Table 1. Analysis of variance indicated that on all three tests, differences among training methods were significant:

Test 1: $F = 4.27$, $p < .05$;
Test 2: $F = 9.57$, $p < .01$;
Test 3: $F = 3.27$, $p < .05$;

all $df = 3, 24$. The two sets of standards did not differ: the respective $F(1,24)$ were 2.88, 2.11, and 1.00. On Test 1, there were fewer errors on the retest than on the original test, $F(1,24) = 5.17$, $p < .05$, and there was a tendency for the retest to show fewer errors on the other two tests, although those differences did not reach significance. None of the interactions reached significance. Specific comparisons on Test 1 indicated that the two difficult training procedures were not different, $F(1,28) < 1$, but were significantly superior to the simple-discrimination and the reproduction training, $F(1,28) = 12.90$, $p < .01$, which did not differ from each other, $F(1,28) = 1.23$. Exactly the same pattern was seen on the other tests. We concluded that discrimination training methods, if they provided an opportunity to make certain types of discriminations, were more effective than training involving a tactile-kinesthetic component.

It is important to note that the criterion test in this experiment was a recognition, not a reproduction, test. The effectiveness of the educational methods endorsed by Fernald and others might well be demonstrated on reproduction tasks, that is, on writing. Therefore, in our next experiment we compared the two types of training on both discrimination and reproduction tests.

TABLE 1
Number of Errors as a Function of Type of Training

	Discrimination			Reproduction
	(D-1)	(D-2)	(S)	(R)
Test and Retest 1	45[a]	35	79	65
Test and Retest 2	53	41	85	70
Test and Retest 3	52	56	86	76
Total errors	150	132	250	211

[a]Each entry represents the total number of errors for eight subjects.

6.2 Effects on Reproduction

In order to evaluate how well children were able to reproduce letterlike forms, a scoring system was needed. We had previously developed a technique for scoring both upper-case and lower-case alphabet letters (Williams, 1974) which proved adaptable to the letterlike forms we used in these experiments. First, the method of reproduction was evaluated on the basis of deviations from

1. the optimal number of lines used in reproducing a form,
2. the order in which the lines were drawn, and
3. the direction in which they were drawn.

Second, the overall appearance of the form was rated on a series of criteria relevant to that particular form (placement of intersections, degree of angularity, etc.). The total score for each form was composed of the two subscores for method and appearance, equally weighted.

In addition to comparing visual discrimination training with tactile-kinesthetic training on the ability both to discriminate letterlike forms and to reproduce them, the experiment (Williams, 1974) had another purpose. Would the effectiveness of the training generalize to novel forms of the same type as used in training?

Forty children, four and five years old and enrolled in Philadelphia day-care centers, served as subjects. A two-part pretest was administered which featured one of the sets of three letterlike forms used in our previous study. (These three forms were used also in the training.) In the first part of the pretest, the child was asked to draw two copies of each of the three forms on unlined paper. In the second part, there were 18 simultaneous matching-to-sample items. Six of these involved choosing a match to a standard consisting of a single form, where the four alternatives consisted of transformations (rotations and reversals) of that standard. Another six items consisted of a pair of letterlike forms as the standard; the four alternatives consisted of pairs of correct forms and their transformations. The last six items presented all three forms as the standard with a similar set of alternatives, that is, the forms and transformations of them presented in triples. The posttest was exactly the same as the pretest. In addition, a second posttest was administered consisting of the same format (six reproduction items and 18 matching-to-sample items) but utilizing three equally difficult letterlike forms that had not been used in training.

Each subject was seen five times; for the pretest, for three 15-min training sessions (one per day), and for the posttest. The children were randomly assigned to one of four training conditions: (1) reproduction training; (2) discrimination training; (3) a combination of reproduction and discrimination training; and (4) a no-training control. Reproduction training consisted of copying the three letterlike forms that had served as the pretest standards. When errors were made, feedback was given by the experimenter as to the correct method of drawing the letters, using the same criteria as were built into the scoring system. Discrimination training consisted of simultaneous matching-to-sample practice on the items that had appeared on the discrimination pretest. Combination training consisted of both discrimination and reproduction training; this experimental condition was identical in format and content to the other two groups except that half as much time for each type of training was given.

Analysis of covariance, using the pretest score as the covariate, indicated that there was a significant difference among training groups on the discrimination posttest, $F(3,31) = 3.10$, $p < .05$, and specific comparisons indicated that discrimination training was superior to the other three training conditions, $F(1,31) = 8.10$, $p < .01$, which did not differ among themselves. There were no differences between trained and nontrained forms, and there were no interactions. Similar analyses were performed on the reproduction data. Again, the main effect of training method was significant, $F(3,31) = 7.11$, $p < .05$. Performance on trained forms was superior to that on untrained forms, $F(3,31) = 8.905$, $p < .01$, which, when further evaluated, revealed that on the trained forms only, reproduction and combination training did not differ from each

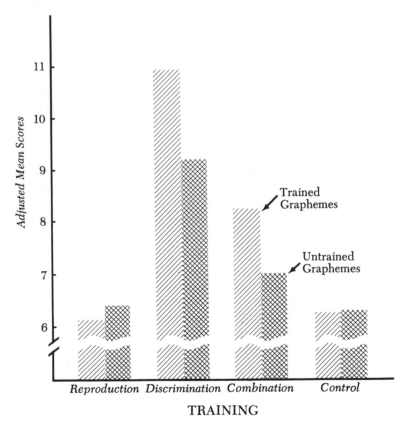

FIG. 2. Effects of training condition on discrimination posttest (adjusted means).

other but were significantly superior to the other two training groups, which did not differ from each other, $F(1,31) = 26.38$, $p < .001$. Figures 2 and 3 present the adjusted means.

The results of this experiment indicated that effects of training were quite specific: that is, discrimination training improved performance on the discrimination test but not on the reproduction test, and reproduction training led to superior performance on the reproduction test and not on the discrimination test. The combination training was as effective as the reproduction training on the reproduction test, however, which suggests that half as much reproduction training was as effective as the total amount that was given to the reproduction groups. It might be, of course, that the addition of some discrimination training enhances the effectiveness of reproduction training on a reproduction criterion; further study is needed to validate completely the specificity hypothesis.

The implications for instruction in reading and writing seem clear. One cannot rely on the transfer of training on one task to that on another, even though both deal with the same content. Rather, the perceptual learning involved in the

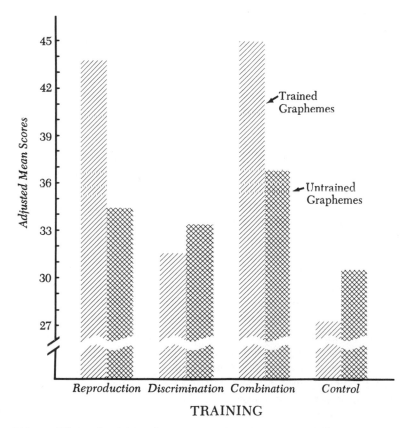

FIG. 3. Effects of training condition on reproduction posttest (adjusted means).

development of the ability to differentiate between letters and the acquisition of the ability to copy letters must be considered, in terms of optimal curriculum development, as separate tasks. Presumably, whatever is learned in the training of letter discrimination—the ability to identify and contrast the distinctive features—will transfer to novel letters. But the letter-formation training to be pursued in the development of good handwriting must focus specifically on each of the letters; improvement on novel forms cannot be expected.

I believe that this specificity of training effects is important to keep in mind. The dismaying lack of success of the perceptual—motor curricula, I think, can be explained in terms of their failure to consider that simple fact. It would appear to be considerably more fruitful to study carefully the task that is to be taught, do a careful analysis of the components of the task, and design instruction that attacks each of these components directly.

7 PSYCHOLINGUISTIC FACTORS

The recent disillusionment with perceptual theories, perceptual—motor programs, and modality-specific instruction has indeed left a gap, for we are without answers to some important questions. However, it is fairly easy to predict how that gap will be filled over the next few years. More and more investigators have been concerned with the language skills of reading-disabled children, and a rather substantial amount of evidence has been collected that indicates that these children are poorer in many aspects of language than are normal readers. This is hardly surprising since, as Miller (1972) has observed, reading skills must ultimately derive from linguistic skills. In both receptive and expressive speech, children with reading problems are less fluent, know fewer words, and give less-mature definitions; that is, poor readers give more descriptive definitions, such as that a bicycle has wheels, and fewer categorical definitions, such as that a bicycle is a vehicle (DeHirsch et al., 1966; Fry, Johnson, & Muehl, 1970).

Problem readers also do not perform as well in processing grammatical structure. Steiner, Weiner, and Cromer (1971), for example, found that, given prior information about material they were to read, good readers could be led into making more anticipation errors than poor readers made. The poor readers appeared to respond word by word, ignoring prior context and therefore making fewer anticipation errors. Other studies demonstrate also the greater influence of linguistic organization on good readers. For example, Weinstein and Rabinovitch (1971) asked children to learn sentences composed of English function words, English bound morphemes, and nonsense-syllable items, either organized into English sentence frames or not so organized. While both good and poor readers learned the unstructured list in about the same number of trials, good readers needed significantly fewer trials to learn the structured lists.

Of course, we must not assume that reading problems invariably have direct correlates in oral speech production and reception. For example, Shankweiler and Liberman (1972) found that errors in the oral repetition of monosyllables were quite different from errors in reading those monosyllables. It also should be noted that evidence for specific linguistic problems in reading disability does not necessarily rule out a contribution to reading problems from perceptual dysfunction. Often, however, apparent perceptual errors (for example, *b/d* reversals, or sequencing errors such as *from/form* and *was/saw*) are specifically linguistic (Vellutino, Steger, Moyer, Harding, & Niles, 1974).

These and other similar data suggest that it might be of some value to design remedial curricular materials focused on improving the language skills of poor readers. However, it is too early to predict exactly what types of remediation might be useful. Given our experience over the years with the perceptual–motor curricula, we must be very careful. It would be wasteful and indeed unfortunate if people jumped on a bandwagon, declaring that training on linguistic skills was the answer, without taking the time to evaluate the notion—*or* to examine the relationship of whatever language abilities were to be trained to actual reading performance. We would probably be in for a repeat of 25 years of, first, excitement, followed by disillusion, and finally, an admission of "no progress."

8   CURRICULUM DESIGN

Unfortunately, sometimes a curriculum developer may take a promising new idea that is as yet untested, and in his enthusiasm to implement the idea, he may forget the old tried-and-true principles of instruction. They are not "interesting," and admittedly, it often takes considerable time and effort to implement them effectively. Yet we do know a substantial amount about what a good program of instruction looks like: it is structured and organized; it minimizes possibilities of failure; it starts out with simple, high-contrast, highly cued items and progresses toward complex items that have stringent response requirements. We have knowledge about learning strategies that can be built into instruction: for rehearsal, for organization, for rule learning. We know something about engineering attention in the classroom. We are pretty sure that we should concentrate our efforts for the most part on direct instruction, and that we should not rely on what will be achieved through transfer. And we can provide for individual differences in rate of learning and, to some extent, preference. Practical curriculum development *must* utilize what is known, as a priority.

We are attempting to follow these ideas in our work at the Research and Development Center for the Handicapped at Teachers College, Columbia University, where we are developing materials and procedures for teaching decoding skills to learning-disabled children. For many such children, the initial encounter with reading may have ended in failure simply because they could not contend with the complexity of the task (that is, they suffer from "sensory overload"). Other children, perhaps, are highly distractible and so they, too, cannot perform well unless the task is considerably simplified. For such reasons we feel that a systematic and highly structured approach to instruction, based on sound principles of learning, is essential.

Our program is designed to teach the fundamental skills of decoding, that is, analysis and synthesis (blending). It is not intended as a complete reading program. Rather, it is to be used as a supplement to whatever reading program is utilized in the classroom, and it probably will be used most often as remedial instruction.

In the beginning stages of instruction, we take a completely auditory approach. All instruction, practice, and games involve sounds and their relationships. Symbols (letters) are not introduced until proficiency is reached on the auditory tasks. This approach should be useful not only for learning-disabled children who have not had extensive training in reading, but also for those children who have had substantial exposure to reading (prior to being diagnosed as learning disabled, for example) and who have failed to achieve certain skills, either those requiring auditory processing or those requiring visual processing. Their earlier difficulties may have been due to overloading or to the lack of explicit emphasis on the auditory components of reading, which are slighted in most programs.

I shall present a brief outline of the program, and then I shall explain why we have chosen to develop our program in this way. First, in a short introductory section of the program, the child learns the very elementary concept that words have parts. The child learns the concepts of analysis (breaking words apart) and synthesis (putting them together); and at the end of this sequence, he can analyze and synthesize at the syllable level. He learns to attend to syllables and can tell what syllable occupies the initial, medial, and final positions in a whole word. Analysis and synthesis of syllables is an easier task than is that of segmenting and blending phonemes (Hardy, Stennett, & Smythe, 1973; Liberman, Shankweiler, Fischer, & Carter, 1974). Indeed, it is an extremely simple task, and this introductory section moves very quickly. It is included not because we suppose that this skill will greatly decrease the amount of instruction necessary for phoneme blending; on the contrary, there is some evidence that success with syllable synthesizing does not transfer directly to phoneme synthesis (Desberg, Marsh, & Givendo, 1973). It is included primarily as an introduction to the general concepts of analysis and synthesis, that is, to demonstrate that words can be broken apart and put together (Holden & MacGinitie, 1972). Our instructional program includes a variety of interim tasks, with extensive practice on each of them, between blending syllables and blending phonemes.

There is a second reason for beginning with compound words and syllables. Because the sequencing of sounds is a temporal phenomenon, it is wise (Elkonin, 1963; Kuenne & Williams, 1973) to provide some sort of visual "marker." Movable wooden squares which provide tactile and visual representation of sounds are used to facilitate auditory analysis and synthesis. The child learns to identify auditorally first, middle, and last syllables (or word parts) and to associate them visually with left, middle, and right markers, respectively. This visual representation is introduced on a task that represents very little challenge to the child and is therefore accomplished easily. (If a child's previous instruction has included some work on individual phonemes, introducing our program in terms of syllables may well prove unnecessary. If so, this part of the program can be omitted.)

8.1 Aspects of the Program

8.1.1 Phoneme Analysis

In this section of the curriculum, phoneme analysis is taught, again, as a strictly auditory task. The wooden squares are now utilized as visual representations of phonemes, as an aid in focusing on the number and the order of sounds, which has been found to be a difficult task for children (Calfee, Lindamood, & Lindamood, 1973).

All of the auditory analysis and sequencing practice in this section of the program is done with a limited number of phonemic units so that the child can concentrate on process. It may be instructive to describe the way in which we selected the first set of nine phonemes (and therefore, later in the program, letters), as an illustration of how very simple decisions can get quite complicated. We considered the following factors:

1. avoidance of auditory confusability,
2. avoidance of visual confusability,
3. ease of blendability of the phonemes in combination,
4. productivity of phonemes in creating real-word trigrams,
5. ability of children to produce sounds,
6. ease of learning grapheme—phoneme associations, and
7. regularity of phonemes in spelling patterns.

Each of the seven considerations suggested a different set of "most appropriate" letters, so compromises had to be made on some points. Because of our emphasis on auditory skills, we decided that the visual considerations would be of relatively low priority and that avoiding auditory confusability would be our highest priority.

The short vowels (o and a) were selected primarily because of their adherence to regular spelling rules in consonant—vowel—consonant (CVC) trigrams and secondarily because of their productivity. Long vowels, while more easily discriminable and blendable (Coleman, 1970), were ruled out because of the irregularity of long-vowel spelling patterns in English. The selection of consonants proved to be at least as difficult as that of vowels. Miller and Nicely (1955) divided consonant phonemes into four basic groups; within each one there is considerable potential for confusion in discrimination, whereas between groups there is little. Thus, for ease of discrimination, we chose one consonant from within each group, the one which best satisfied the requirements of

1. production of many real word trigrams, and
2. children's ability to produce the sound without error (Marsh & Sherman, 1971).

The ease of sound–symbol association learning (Coleman, 1970) was also considered, and the letters chosen were acceptable in this respect. On this basis the initial set consisted of *m, b, s,* and *p.* Then in violation of several considerations but in order to provide enough real-word trigrams for meaningful instruction, the letters *c, g,* and *t* were added. Thus the nine letters are *a, o, m, b, s, p, c, g,* and *t.*

Another advantage of using only a small number of phonemes that are chosen for maximum discriminability is that if a child moves ahead rapidly in analysis and synthesis and yet finds auditory discrimination difficult, he can still proceed in the program. Furthermore, the program may well improve his discrimination abilities as a side effect because it works to increase attention to detail.

8.1.2 Phoneme Blending

The next section of the program presents phoneme blending of the same CVC units. The CVCs are broken at different points. Initially, only the last phoneme is separated from the rest of the word, then only the first phoneme is separated from the rest of the word, and later all three phonemes are presented separately. This sequence is based on research by Coleman (1970). To facilitate learning to blend, broken words are first presented in a sentence context. Semantic constraints limit the range of appropriate responses. Later, the semantic context is dropped and instruction proceeds to the point where individual phonemes in isolation are the units to be blended.

8.1.3 Letter–Sound Correspondences

Moving along concurrently with the basic instructional sequence on auditory analysis and synthesis described above is another instructional sequence which teaches grapheme–phoneme correspondences for the nine phonemes used in the auditory section. Thus, the child will be thoroughly familiar with the nine letters he will need for the initial decoding section before he gets to that point in the program.

8.1.4 Sight Words

Twelve short words are then introduced. The introduction of this type of content is not a necessary element in a program with the purpose that has been described. However, to avoid the possibility that the decoding skills taught here will be isolated and therefore not able to be applied in an actual reading context, words that have been decoded are immediately used in sentences and short paragraphs which incorporate simple comprehension activities. Obviously, some simple words that are not easily decodable—words like *is, the,* and *of*—are necessary for this purpose.

8.1.5 Decoding

The next section of the program pulls together the auditory skills and the grapheme–phoneme correspondences that the child has been practicing. Thus, he must integrate the skills that he has learned in isolation. Again using the wooden squares, which now have letters on them, the child learns to decode bigrams and trigrams (both meaningful words and nonsense syllables). They are made up of the same nine letters with which he has already become familiar in two ways: (a) in purely auditory analysis and synthesis, and (b) in isolated sound–symbol correspondences. He receives extensive practice in the manipulation of these letters so that he can decode (read) and construct from squares (spell) all possible CVC combinations of these letters. Through this extensive practice with limited content, the child will have learned to attend to the details required for accurate decoding and he will have learned the fundamental processes and strategies that will enable him to apply decoding skills to other content.

Subsequent sections of the program will repeat the same sequence of decoding tasks and very slowly introduce more complex units for decoding as additional letter–sound correspondences are introduced. After six additional sound–symbol correspondences are introduced (*f, l, r, n, h,* and *i*), they are used in additional trigram decoding. In this way the child gets further practice in the basic processes and strategies as well as carefully guided application of these processes to additional content.

Following this section of the program, longer words (first CCVC patterns and then CVCC and CCVCC patterns) are introduced, and then two-syllable words made up of the same basic patterns are included. The final unit of instruction, as the program is now outlined, introduces a second phoneme for each of the three vowels already presented. Practice in decoding words and nonsense combinations in two patterns (CVCC and CVCe) proceeds concurrently (Williams, 1968).[2]

8.1.6 Organization

The instruction outlined above is organized into 12 units. Each unit begins with a story read to the children by the teacher. This story is designed to capture the

---

[2] We hope also to incorporate instruction in copying and writing letters into our program. The design of this instructional component, which really could be regarded as a separate program, is in its initial stages. Just as we developed the decoding lessons in view of (1) the needs of the field, that is, the lack of availability of certain types of teaching material, (2) a general well-established theory of instruction, and (3) implications drawn from specific relevant research, so we are going about the development of instructional techniques for handwriting. However, we are going to have to base this instruction more centrally on our own research (some of which was presented earlier in the chapter), since there has been so little work in the area. This forces us to proceed more slowly, but we hope to be able to have the program developed next year.

child's interest and it incorporates a demonstration of the skills to be mastered in the unit. For example, a child must guess the "magic" word which unlocks a secret door when the magician can only say a word broken into syllables. The same cast of characters—Isabel, whose nickname is Wisebell because she is a little know-it-all, along with her friends Tom and Mac, and Sam the janitor—appear throughout the program in stories and games and provide a continuing theme and focus of interest, which increases the appeal of the program.

Following the story, a teaching procedure is presented for each objective. This is a complete and very explicit script for the teacher along with appropriate examples. Each unit also contains a variety of materials for practice. There are worksheets, some of which are designed to be completed under the supervision of the teacher and others of which can be done independently. There are also various activities that can be pursued independently. And there are competitive games designed to provide small groups of children with the opportunity for extensive practice of skills in a variety of contexts. Since they are based on the theme of the story presented at the beginning of the unit, they also provide for continuity and a high level of pupil interest.

8.1.7 Maintenance

Our program is process oriented, and our basic concern is that children acquire the essential blending skills with limited content and that they be able to apply the skills to new content, that is, additional sound–symbol correspondences. After this goal is achieved, we introduce "maintenance" activities. Since we expect that most children will be exposed to some sort of decoding instruction as part of their regular classroom routine (although we also expect that many of them may not be gaining greatly from it), it is reasonable to expect that teachers will be using reading materials in which the content is introduced and sequenced in a particular way. Thus, for those classrooms the best procedure consists of their putting their own classroom content (letter–sound correspondences) in the framework of our process program. Therefore, our practice materials are designed to be adaptable to any sequence of decoding of phonics instruction. (On the other hand, because some regular classrooms may not be teaching decoding at all, we do provide a suggested sequence for introducing new content.)

8.1.8 Individual Differences

It is obvious that individual and group differences exist in the degree to which some of these abilities are deficient and in the amount of training that will be required. The program is designed to be maximally flexible in dealing with these differences. For example, the sound–symbol and sight–word sequence may be begun early or late; and it, or any of the units, may be extended for whatever length of time is required to attain competence. Some children may prefer competitive games and others may achieve more readily with individual activities.

In summary, our program simplifies presentation in the beginning stages by taking a completely auditory approach. In addition, we introduce concepts and skills using only a carefully limited amount of material, stressing skill development that can be generalized to larger word patterns that are introduced later. Recognizing that instruction must be tailored to individual requirements, we include a set of practice options, that is, a variety of alternative strategies from which (when feasible) both teacher and child can choose an optimal program. And we are careful not to violate traditional principles, such as the importance of repetitive practice within a variety of contexts.

8.2 The Program Rationale

Our decision to introduce decoding through auditory skills and concepts was made for several reasons. First of all, it does simplify the child's task. In addition, auditory deficits seem to be more characteristic of learning-disabled children than are visual or intersensory problems (Zigmond, 1969). Among those reported are defects of auditory discrimination, memory, sequencing ability, analysis, and synthesis. It is generally recognized that each of these problems may lead to difficulty in learning to read.

Even though methodological problems, conflicting results in different studies, and the difficulties inherent in interpreting correlational data lessen the weight the research would otherwise be given (Samuels, 1973), we believe that the importance of auditory abilities for learning to read has been amply demonstrated. Over the years, correlational studies have proliferated. An early study by Monroe (1932) found significant differences between children with reading disabilities and younger controls in both auditory discrimination and the acquisition of auditory–visual associations. Later work revealed relationships between a variety of auditory tasks and reading readiness or first- and second-grade reading achievement (e. g., Dykstra, 1966; Flynn & Byrne, 1970; Harrington & Durrell, 1955).

Recently, there has been considerable emphasis on the importance of the abilities of blending and segmentation in the initial reading task. Elkonin (1963) has suggested, "To learn to read, the child must be able to hear and distinguish the separate sounds in words." MacGinitie (1967) added that the child must "discriminate and manipulate sequences of sounds." According to Vernon (1957), "The commonest feature of reading disability is the incapacity to perform the cognitive processes of analyzing accurately the visual and auditory structures of words . . . the severe cases of disability seem to have a deeply rooted incapacity to perform the process of analysis with facility, and to synthesize or blend phonetic units to form complete words." Several studies have shown the importance of these skills. Chall, Roswell, and Blumenthal (1963) found substantial correlations between blending ability in grade 1 and later reading achievement. Balmuth (1972) found significant correlations between blending phonemes into nonsense syllables and silent reading achievement; Calfee, Lindamood, and Lindamood (1973) found considerable predictive ability of reading achievement through grade 10 in a test that required students to manipulate phonemes; and Liberman et al. (this volume) suggests that the ability to segment into phonemes is predictive of beginning reading achievement.

Given that there is a relationship between auditory skills and reading, we may ask certain other questions:

1. To what extent can the auditory skills which are faulty be improved through training?

2. Will the results of this training transfer to beginning reading? The evidence is inconclusive but promising.

Several studies have been reported which show that training in auditory skills may have positive effects on reading. For example, in an early study, Durrell and Murphy (1953) reported that training children to notice sounds in words improved their reading scores and that greatest gains were found for children with lowest initial scores. More recently, Elkonin (1963) taught kindergarten children to identify the sounds in words by using counters to represent each phoneme. After practice with the counters the children could progress to word analysis without aid. Rosner (1973, 1974) has reported an instructional program which develops word analysis skills to a high level in young children. Preliminary results are encouraging, showing transfer of these skills to the reading task. Thus there seems to be adequate evidence for the potential of a highly structured reading-related auditory-skills program for children who are deficient in these skills.

However, we are *not* proposing that training in auditory perceptual skills, generally speaking, will lead to better achievement in reading. The lessons from the past two or three decades on the relationship of visual–perceptual skills and reading have convinced us otherwise. When we reviewed several recently developed and popular auditory programs (many of which are listed by Kass, 1972), we were dismayed to find content coverage or methodology which, on the basis of current knowledge about perceptual skills and instructional methodology, was surprisingly poor. For example, there is often excessive emphasis on material unrelated to that of early reading skills (e. g., children are asked to identify the animals who make different barnyard sounds). Sometimes language tasks are presented in a context quite different from that of initial decoding. For example, two voices present two separate messages concurrently and the child must focus his attention on only one of the conflicting messages. Sometimes relevant tasks are presented, but in a way which would tax the child's memory or confuse him. In addition, one program, dealing with the important skill of auditory analysis, develops tasks to a level of difficulty far beyond that required for initial decoding; some programs present what could be classified as practice material but no instruction; and blending as a process is not taught in any of the programs.

We are attempting to avoid such pitfalls. We are limiting our instruction to skills and content that are themselves believed to be important components of the reading task and which are currently not often covered in depth elsewhere. As far as possible, we are teaching those skills directly and explicitly. Moreover, we are not attempting to prescribe the materials for any particular type of learner. We expect that, like with most instructional programs, some pupils will respond more appropriately and more enthusiastically to the program than will others. But we are realistic: the program is offered as an instructional option. It is not offered as a panacea either for all or for any particular subset of learning-disabled children.

Researchers are just beginning to develop genuine understandings of the complexities of the reading process and the way in which skills and strategies are acquired. We should look forward to going much further. In large measure, the extent to which we make further progress will depend on future developments in the broad area of perceptual and cognitive development. In equally large measure, further progress will depend on advances in the area of instruction, so that as new knowledge about perception and cognition is attained, we shall be able to utilize it effectively in the development of curriculum and teaching strategies.

ACKNOWLEDGMENTS

This work was supported in part by a grant to Teachers College, Columbia University (U. S. Office of Education, OEG-O-72-5458) and in part by a grant to the University of Pennsylvania (U. S. Office of Education, OEG-3-71-0124).

REFERENCES

Balmuth, M. Phoneme blending and silent reading achievement. In R. C. Aukerman (Ed.), *Some persistent questions on beginning reading.* Newark, Delaware: International Reading Association, 1972.

Bateman, B. The efficacy of an auditory and a visual method of first-grade reading instruction with auditory and visual learners. In H. K. Smith (Ed.), *Perception and reading.* Newark, Delaware: International Reading Association, 1968.

Bell, A. E., & Aftanas, M. S. Some correlates of reading retardation. *Perceptual and Motor Skills,* 1972, *35,* 659–667.

Bruinicks, R. H. Teaching word recognition to disadvantaged boys. *Journal of Learning Disabilities,* 1970, *3,* 28–37.

Bryant, N. D. Subject variables: definition, incidence, characteristics, and correlates. In *Leadership training institute in learning disabilities* (Vol. 1). Final Report, USOE Grant No. OEG-0-71-4425 604, 1972.

Bryant, N. D. Learning disabilities: a report on the state of the art. *Teachers College Record,* 1974, *75,* 395–404.

Buros, O. K. *Reading tests and reviews*. Highland Park, New Jersey: Gryphon Press, 1968.

Calfee, R. C., Lindamood, P., & Lindamood, C. Acoustic–phonetic skills and reading: Kindergarten through twelfth grade. *Journal of Educational Psychology,* 1973, *64,* 293–298.

Chalfant, J. D., & Scheffelin, M. Central processing dysfunction syndromes in children through profile analysis. *Journal of Consulting and Clinical Psychology,* 1972, *2,* 251–260.

Chall, J., Roswell, F. G., & Blumenthal, S. H. Auditory blending ability: A factor in success in beginning reading. *Reading Teacher,* 1963, *17,* 113–118.

Coleman, E. B. Collecting a data base for a reading technology. *Journal of Educational Psychology,* 1970, *61,* 1–23.

Cronbach, L. J., & Snow, R. E. *Individual differences in learning ability as a function of instructional variables.* Final report, USOE Contract No. OEG-4-6-061269-1217. Stanford, California: Stanford University, 1969.

Desberg, P., Marsh, G., & Givendo, D. Transfer between compound words, syllables and phonemes in blending. Unpublished manuscript, 1973.

DeHirsch, K., Jansky, J., & Langford, W. *Predicting reading failure.* New York: Harper & Row, 1966.

Durrell, D., & Murphy, H. The auditory discrimination factor in reading readiness and reading disability. *Education,* 1953, *73,* 556–560.

Dykstra, R. Auditory discrimination abilities and beginning reading achievement. *Reading Research Quarterly,* 1966, *1,* 5–34.

Elkonin, D. B. The psychology of mastering the elements of reading. In B. & J. Simon (Eds.), *Educational Psychology in the U.S.S.R.* London: Routledge and Kegan Paul, 1963.

Fernald, G. M. *Remedial techniques in basic school subjects.* New York: McGraw-Hill, 1943.

Flynn, P. T., & Byrne, M. C. Relationship between reading and selected auditory abilities of third-grade children. *Journal of Speech and Hearing Research,* 1970, *13,* 731–740.

Frostig, M., & Horne, D. *The Frostig program for the development of visual perception.* Chicago: Follett Publishing Co., 1964.

Fry, M. A., Johnson, C. S., & Muehl, S. Oral language production in relation to reading achievement among select second graders. In D. Bakker & P. Satz (Eds.), *Specific Reading Disability.* Rotterdam: Rotterdam University Press, 1970.

Gazzaniga, M. S. The bisected brain. *Neuroscience series #2.* New York: Appleton-Century-Crofts, Meredith Corporation, 1970.

Gibson, E. J. The ontogeny of reading. *American Psychologist,* 1970, *25,* 136–143.

Gibson, E. J. Perceptual learning and the theory of word perception. *Cognitive Psychology,* 1971, *2,* 351–368.

Gibson, E. J. & Levin, H. *Psychology of Reading.* Cambridge, Mass: MIT Press, 1975.

Goins, J. T. Visual perceptual abilities and early reading progress. *University of Chicago Supplemental Educational Monographs,* 1958, No. 87.

Hammill, D. D., & Wiederholt, J. L. Review of the Frostig visual-perception test and the related training program. In L. Mann & D. A. Sabatino (Eds.), *The first review of special education* (Vol. 1). Philadelphia: J. S. E. Press, 1973.

Hardy, M., Stennett, R. G., & Smythe, P. C. Auditory segmentation and auditory blending in relation to beginning reading. *Alberta Journal of Educational Research,* 1973, *19,* 144–158.

Harrington, S. M. J., & Durrell, D. Mental maturity vs. perceptual abilities in primary reading. *Journal of Educational Psychology,* 1955, *46,* 375–380.

Harris, A. J. Individualizing first grade reading according to specific learning aptitudes. Research report, Office of Research Evaluation, Division of Teaching, City University of New York, 1965.

Holden, M., & MacGinitie, W. Children's conceptions of word boundaries in speech and print. *Journal of Educational Psychology,* 1972, *63,* 551–557.

Jensen, N., & King, E. Effects of different kinds of visual-motor discrimination training on learning to read words. *Journal of Educational Psychology,* 1970, *61,* 90–96.

Kass, C. Psycholinguistic disabilities of children with reading problems. *Exceptional Children,* 1966, *2,* 533–539.

Kass, C. E. Methods and materials in learning disabilities. In *Leadership Training Institute in Learning Disabilities* (Vol. 1). Final report, USOE Grant No. OEG-0-71-4425 604, 1972 (N. D. Bryant, Director).

Kephart, N. *The slow learner in the classroom.* Columbus, Ohio: Charles E. Merrill, 1960.

Kuenne, J. B., & Williams, J. P. Auditory recognition cues in the primary grades. *Journal of Educational Psychology,* 1973, *64,* 241–246.

Levin, H., & Williams, J. P. (Eds.). *Basic studies on reading.* New York: Basic Books, 1970.

Liberman, I. Y., Shankweiler, D., Fischer, F. W., & Carter, B. Explicit syllable and phoneme segmentation in the young child. *Journal of Experimental Child Psychology,* 1974, *18,* 201–212.

Lyle, J. G., & Goyen, J. Visual recognition, developmental lag and strephosymbolia in reading retardation. *Journal of Abnormal Psychology,* 1968, *73,* 25–29.

MacGinitie, W. Auditory perception in reading. *Education,* 1967, *87,* 532–538.

Marsh, G., & Desberg, P. Current basic research in beginning reading. Paper presented at the meetings of the American Educational Research Association, New Orleans, 1973.

Marsh, G., & Sherman, M. Kindergarten children's discrimination and production of phonemes in isolation and in words. *Southwest Regional Laboratory Technical Memorandum* No. TM-2-71-07, 1971.

Miller, G. A. Reflections on the conference. In J. F. Kavanaugh & I. G. Mattingly, (Eds.), *Language by ear and by eye.* Cambridge, Massachusetts: MIT Press, 1972.

Miller, G. A., & Nicely, P. E. An analysis of perceptual confusions among some English consonants. *Journal of the Acoustical Society of America,* 1955, *27,* 338–352.

Monroe, M. *Children who cannot read.* Chicago: University of Chicago Press, 1932.

Morency, A. Auditory modality–research and practice. In H. K. Smith (Ed.), *Perception and reading.* Newark, Delaware: International Reading Association, 1968.

Myers, P., & Hammill, D. *Methods for learning disorders.* New York: John Wiley and Sons, 1969.

Ofman, W., & Shaevitz, M. The kinesthetic method in remedial reading. *Journal of Experimental Education,* 1963, *31,* 317–320.

Orton, S. T. *Reading, writing, and speech problems in children.* London: Chapman and Hall, 1937.

Ringler, L., & Smith, I. Learning modality and word recognition of first grade children. *Journal of Learning Disabilities,* 1973, *6,* 307–312.

Robinson, H. M. Visual and auditory modalities related to methods for beginning reading. *Reading Research Quarterly,* 1972, *8,* 7–39.

Rosner, J. Language arts and arithmetic achievement, and specifically related perceptual skills. *American Educational Research Journal,* 1973, *10,* 59–68.

Rosner, J. Auditory analysis training with prereaders. *Reading Teacher,* 1974, *27,* 379–384.

Samuels, S. J. Success and failure in learning to read: a critique of the research. *Reading Research Quarterly,* 1973, *8,* 200–239.

Samuels, S. J., Dahl, P., & Archwamety, T. Effect of hypothesis test training on reading skill. *Journal of Educational Psychology,* 1974, *66,* 835–844.

Shankweiler, D., & Liberman, I. Misreading: a search for causes. In J. F. Kavanaugh & I. G.

Mattingly (Eds.), *Language by ear and by eye*. Cambridge, Massachusetts: MIT Press, 1972.

Spalding, R. B., & Spalding, W. T. *The writing road to reading*. New York: Whiteside, 1957.

Sperry, R. W. The great cerebral commissure. *Scientific American*, 1964, *210*, 42–52.

Stallings, J. A. *Reading methods and sequencing abilities: an interaction study in beginning reading*. Unpublished doctoral dissertation, Stanford University, 1970.

Steiner, R., Weiner, M., & Cromer, W. Comprehension training and identification for good and poor readers. *Journal of Educational Psychology*, 1971, *62*, 506–513.

Strauss, A., & Lehtinen, L. *Psychopathology and education of the brain-injured child* (Vol. 1). New York: Grune and Stratton, 1947.

Vellutino, F. R. Psychological factors in reading disability. Paper presented at American Educational Research Association, Chicago, 1974.

Vellutino, F. R., Steger, B. M., Moyer, S. C., Harding, C. J., & Niles, J. A. Has the perceptual deficit hypothesis led us astray? Paper presented at the Council for Exceptional Children, New York, 1974.

Venezky, R. L. Theoretical and experimental bases for teaching reading. In T. A. Sebeok (Ed.), *Current trends in linguistics,* Vol. 12. The Hague: Mouton, 1974.

Vernon, M. D. *Backwardness in reading*. Cambridge, England: Cambridge University Press, 1957.

Waugh, R. P. Relationship between modality preference and performance. *Exceptional Children*, 1973, *39*, 465–469.

Weinstein, R., & Rabinovitch, M. Sentence structure and retention in good and poor readers. *Journal of Educational Psychology*, 1971, *62*, 25–30.

Wepman, J. M. The modality concept—including a statement of the perceptual and conceptual levels of learning. In H. K. Smith (Ed.), *Perception and reading*. Newark, Delaware: International Reading Association, 1968.

Williams, J. P. Successive vs. concurrent presentation of multiple grapheme–phoneme correspondences. *Journal of Educational Psychology*, 1968, *59*, 309–314.

Williams, J. P. Training kindergarten children to discriminate letter-like forms. *American Educational Research Journal*, 1969, *6*, 501–514.

Williams, J. P. Learning to read: a review of theories and models. *Reading Research Quarterly*, 1973, *8*, 121–146.

Williams, J. P. *Training kindergarten children in tactile-kinesthetic skills assumed to be related to reading*. Final report, USOE Grant No. OEG-3-71-0124. Philadelphia: University of Pennsylvania, 1974.

Williams, J. P., Blumberg, E. L., & Williams, D. V. Cues used in visual word recognition, *Journal of Educational Psychology*, 1970, *61*, 310–315.

Wohlwill, J. F., & Wiener, M. Discrimination of form orientation in young children. *Child Development*, 1964, *35*, 1113–1125.

Zigmond, N. Auditory processes in children with learning disabilities. In L. Tarnopol (Ed.), *Learning disabilities: Introduction to educational and medical management*. Springfield, Illinois: Charles C Thomas, 1969.

8
Assessment of Independent Reading Skills: Basic Research and Practical Applications

Robert C. Calfee

Stanford University

1 INTRODUCTION

The ability to read with fluency is a fundamental skill for citizens in our society. Although hundreds of thousands of children learn to read in our schools every year, there is great concern in many quarters about the number of children who fail to acquire this skill, and about the low level of skill achieved by many of those who do learn to read.

Just how serious are these problems? How can we judge the merits of the dozens of innovative ideas proposed every year for improving reading instruction? How can the classroom teacher monitor what an individual student has learned about reading? How can he decide what else the student needs to learn and to practice? Answers to these questions all hinge on the adequacy of instruments for precise assessment of students' knowledge and skills in reading. Existing instruments are woefully inadequate for this purpose. To be sure, the readiness tests, achievement tests, diagnostic tests, and criterion-referenced tests now available to researchers and program evaluators possess great predictive validity and stability. Success in school (and success in taking other such tests) can be reliably predicted from a student's performance on almost any given instrument in the reading-test armamentarium. But we need to do more than predict success or failure.

In the summer of 1973, the Study Group on Linguistic Communication, a group of distinguished scholars under the direction of George Miller, reviewed our knowledge of reading and reading instruction, and reported to the National Institute of Education (NIE) their recommendations for future research and evaluation projects. The first of several recommendations was this:

That NIE should establish criteria by which to measure functional literacy, and develop special competence in the assessment of functional literacy and its underlying skills. In particular, the NIE should develop alternatives to the present widely used grade-level criteria [Miller, 1974, p. 5].

In a recently published volume on assessment of reading competence, MacGinitie (1973) emphasizes a critical property of any assessment system—the reliable generation of selective information about different skills. He points to the practical difficulty of gaining such information using current tests.

One of the most persistent of the many issues raised by the papers in this volume involves the reliability of difference scores. Several of the papers stress the importance of diagnostic testing or diagnostic judgments. It is important to good teaching to realize how fallible such differential test results or judgments ordinarily are, so that instructional decisions can be kept appropriately tentative. Most reading skills—especially the more advanced comprehension skills—are highly correlated with one another, and only when the subskill scores are quite different from each other can diagnostic judgments of practical usefulness be made.

Since a teacher's judgments are likely to be at least as unreliable and as highly intercorrelated as test subscores are, the sobering message of Thorndike's tables (Thorndike, 1973) applies in full measure to teachers' judgments as well. The teacher should be at least as tentative about diagnostic judgments formed from his own observations as those formed from test scores and be ready to change both appraisal and treatment as new evidence warrants. The references in several articles to the value of systematic observation, anecdotal records, and teacher-made diagnostic instruments suggest the need for more training in these skills in teacher education [MacGinitie, 1973, pp. 2–3. Reprinted with permission of W. H. MacGinitie and the International Reading Association].

It should be noted that these remarks apply to the evaluation of teachers, schools and programs, as well as individual students. If a principal, superintendent, or program director is to make informed, rational decisions about the strengths and weaknesses of the teaching and learning that take place under his supervision, information about specific strengths and weaknesses—something more than a gross characterization of success or failure—is necessary.

Differential assessment of specific skills may be an impossible goal. Reading is a language-related skill, and thought and language are closely linked. We may be dealing with a "black box," a complex network of interactive systems not capable of analysis into simple components. The high correlations between reading subtests with different labels ("vocabulary," "comprehension"), high correlations of reading achievement with intelligence and aptitude measures, and high correlations between achievement tests in such diverse areas as reading and mathematics all may mean that reading, language, and problem solving depend on a single complex cognitive system (Calfee & Venezky, 1968).

Assessment typically falls within the province of educational psychologists, test-construction experts, and reading specialists. I want to propose that these questions can also interest experimental and cognitive psychologists and linguists. Moreover, the expertise that these scholars bring to bear on these areas may affect much-needed innovations in the theory and practice of reading assessment.

2   AN EXAMPLE OF A READING TEST

Let us examine a reading-assessment instrument. I have chosen the California First-Grade Entry-Level Test, which is currently administered to all California students at the beginning of first grade. This test is part of a system to "provide the public, the legislature, and school districts with information for evaluating the strengths and weaknesses of educational programs" (California State Department of Education, 1973). It consists of five subtests "selected to represent a range of skills." It is designed to provide information about groups of students (schools or districts) rather than individuals. The results have been used for differential assessment of skills at the school level. For instance, if a principal learns that the school is below average on the Auditory Discrimination test, then he might presumably seek to strengthen kindergarten and first-grade instruction in that area.

Although innovative in concept and purpose, this test has much in common with other reading-readiness instruments now on the market; whether these are labeled norm-referenced, criterion-referenced, or diagnostic is not a significant distinction.

One laudable innovation is the provision of a practice test, which can be given prior to the actual test as many times as necessary to assure that each student understands how to take the test. To be sure, the effectiveness of this innovation depends on the sensitivity and industriousness of the classroom teacher, and the time and resources at his or her disposal.

In Fig. 1 is a page from the practice version of this test. The group-administered, multiple-choice format is typical. The task seems straightforward:

On this page are some pictures and letters. Put your marker under the first row of letters, the row that begins with the picture of the sun. I am going to say the name of a

LETTER RECOGNITION

FIG. 1. Sample items from practice test, letter recognition, California First-Grade Entry-Level Test. (Reproduced with permission of the California State Department of Education.)

letter; find the letter that I say and make an "X" on it. Make an "X" on the letter C (Pause.) Find the letter C; make an "X" on C [California State Department of Education, 1973, p. 26].

Performance on this test is a remarkably accurate predictor of later reading ability. Children who do poorly on it will very likely be less successful readers at the end of the first grade. And there is an obvious instructional response to this test—if a student (or group of students) does poorly, then he needs an opportunity to learn the letter names. But teaching to the test will not help. Lack of knowledge of letter names at entrance to kindergarten or first grade is not the cause of reading failure, but an index that reflects a variety of other causal factors—children from low-income homes, low-academic homes, children who have not watched *Sesame Street,* all tend to do poorly on this test. Simply teaching letter names to children with this history will not make much difference (e.g., Silberberg, Silberberg, & Iverson, 1972).

In the Visual Discrimination test in Fig. 2, the child is asked to "look at the letter in the first box. Find another letter in the row that is like the one in the first box."

To understand performance on this task we need to consider the instructions ("first box," "like"), visual short-term memory (Sperling, 1960), and familiarity with the letter symbols. Suppose the student proceeds as follows: he first looks at the target letter on the left, then moves his eye to the first test item on the right, and compares his image of the target with the test item. This takes about one-quarter to one-half a second. Then the eye is moved to the second test item to the right. By now, about 1 sec has passed, and the visual image of the target has decayed to a tattered, ragged vestige. By the time the third test item is examined, the student has only the faintest cues as to what he is looking for.

VISUAL DISCRIMINATION

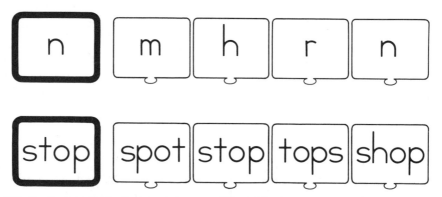

FIG. 2. Sample items from practice test, Visual Discrimination, California First-Grade Entry Level Test. (Reproduced with permission of the California State Department of Education.)

This model predicts that the further to the right the test item is located, the higher should be the probability of an error. Preliminary data from the California test confirm this prediction, although the test is not designed to permit a rigorous examination of the point.[1]

There is more to the story. Some first graders can read when they enter school, or at least they know the names of the letters. This gives them a distinct advantage—they can recode the target into an auditory form, which can be rehearsed in verbal short-term memory (Atkinson & Shiffrin, 1968). In this form, the target can be retained for 30 sec or so, more than enough time for the eye to move from the leftmost test item to the rightmost item. In other words, a *reader* is at a distinct advantage in performing this task, and hence the correlation between this test and later reading achievement. But the causal chain is awry. The Visual Discrimination subtest is simply an inefficient way to find out how much a child already knows about reading.

In Fig. 3 are sample items from the other subtests. They all have different labels. If you ignore these, you will notice that every one of them makes substantial demands on vocabulary-conceptual knowledge—they are all, to some extent, "picture vocabulary" tests. Verbal fluency in young children measured in this fashion is known to be a potent predictor of verbal intelligence and of school achievement.

Undoubtedly this test will predict school success for districts, for schools, for classes, and even for individual students. And I must applaud several features of the instrument—the availability of a practice form, a length appropriate to the information needed (it is a very short test), above-average attention to clarity of the format and instructions, and a concerted effort at comprehensiveness in the selection of materials.

My quarrel with the test is twofold. First, I suspect that the subtest scores will be highly intercorrelated (preliminary data have confirmed this) and hence it is misleading to report results broken down by "skill" areas. The only informative result is the total test score. Second, I believe that a test could be created that would provide differential information of a practically useful and theoretically interesting sort, without any increase in testing time or complexity.

3 INDEPENDENT SKILLS IN READING

What does a child have to know in order to perform well on a test? This question is at the core of research that our group has conducted for the past several years. We have assumed that during the acquisition of reading a student makes use of a

---

[1] The serial-position effect may reflect also a shift in criterion from left to right. As the student begins to run out of choices, he may become more willing to accept a "close" match.

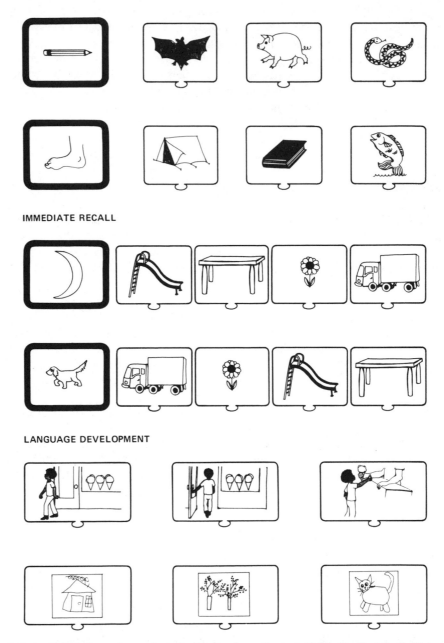

FIG. 3. Sample items from selected subtests of practice test, California First-Grade Entry Level Test. (Reproduced with permission of California State Department of Education.)

set of independent cognitive and language skills. The mind of the reader is better described by a digital computer analogy than a black box or a bowl of "gestalt jello" (Fig. 4). The "jello" model is consistent with the all-too-frequent characterization of an individual student by general descriptors. These latter, whether commonplace ("dumb" or "smart") or technical ("learning disabled," "minimal brain damage," or "mentally gifted minor") have the same implication—any description of the child's specific strengths and weaknesses is forestalled.

In this presentation, I will spell out what is meant by an *independent process,* will point to research in cognitive psychology that support an independent-process theory, and will examine the implications for educational research and practice. I will introduce the notion of a "clean" test—one constructed to measure a selected skill as precisely as possible, and will discuss how such tests might be used for differential diagnosis. Finally, I will present distributional data that are all-or-none in character; under certain conditions a test may show that the skill is either present or absent, a result which greatly simplifies diagnostic decision making.

Most existing tests demand a complex variety of skills and knowledge. This is illustrated by task analysis of reading readiness tests (Calfee & Venezky, 1968). Carver (1973) analyzed what a student must do when confronted with a typical comprehension test. What does a test measure? In both these instances, the answer is that many skills must be brought to play.

In our research we have sought to identify a range of skills directly related to early reading acquisition—visual perception of letter strings, auditory–phonetic analysis of spoken words, learning of letter–sound correspondences, associating a

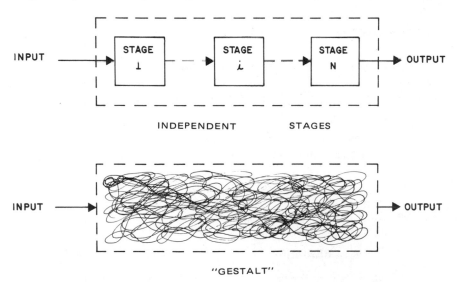

FIG. 4.   Independent-stage and Gestalt "models" of cognitive processes.

letter string with a lexical node in memory (understanding the meaning of a written word), and a variety of comprehension skills. In addition, we have identified subsidiary skills of a general character which may influence a student's performance on virtually any assessment task. These general skills include knowledge of how to take a test, a set toward speed versus accuracy, and availability of coding systems for processing incoming information and reducing short-term memory load.

The subsidiary factors play an important role in most existing tests, which is one reason for high intertest correlations. The child who has difficulty in understanding instructions will do poorly no matter what "skill" a test is designed to measure. A similar problem exists for the child who comes to every task with a set for speed rather than accuracy [i.e., is impulsive rather than reflective, to use Kagan's labels (Kagan, Rosman, Day, Albert, & Phillips, 1964)].

The situation is similar to the one faced by cognitive psychologists and psycholinguists when they seek to isolate and measure independent cognitive and linguistic processes. Sternberg (1969) suggested a methodology to deal with the problem. The basic idea in Sternberg's independent-stage analysis of reaction time is simple: the time required to perform a cognitive task is the sum of the times taken by each of several underlying stages. Factorial experiments provide a ready means for testing the independence of the proposed stages under these conditions (Calfee & Floyd, 1973).

For instance, consider a situation in which the subject's task is to read a list of words and memorize them for later recall. In Fig. 5 is an independent-stage model for this task. There are two stages:

1. *Reading* is assumed to be affected by factors such as word familiarity ("euchre" is less familiar than "house," and should take longer to read),

2. *Organizing* is assumed to be affected by factors such as the categorizability of a list of words (the list "pea, cow, radish, red, goat, yellow" is quickly organized, while "glass, nail, paper, tea, bulb, switch," is not).

For an additive measure such as reaction time, independence implies no interaction between factors affecting different stages. The time parameters associated with each factor should show up only as main effects, as illustrated in

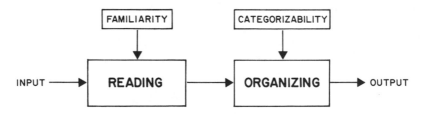

FIG. 5.   Relation of factors to processes in "study" model.

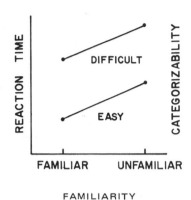

FAMILIARITY

	FAMILIAR	UNFAMILIAR
EASY	f + e	u + e
DIFFICULT	f + d	u + d

CATEGORIZABILITY

PREDICTED
REACTION TIMES

FAMILIARITY

FIG. 6. Algebraic and graphical predictions based on "study" model with two independent processes.

Fig. 6. Any substantial interaction means that the analysis is faulty somewhere: the stages are not independent and have to be treated as a single complex process; the factors as represented in the design are confounded in some way; the stages do not operate in a strict serial order. A substantial number of studies has supported the independent-stage hypothesis; many tasks are performed as if the information passes through a series of independent stages, each stage affected by a unique set of factors.

This approach has considerable promise. The empirical support for a parsimonious theoretical system, the existence of a well developed methodology in the analysis of variance, and the value of the concept for directing research on complex cognitive processes all add to the attractiveness of the idea. The basic concepts can be extended to other measurement systems than reaction time (Calfee, 1974), and would seem to have practical value in the development of assessment systems for educational research and evaluation. To my knowledge this approach has seen little application in reading research (however, compare Lucas, 1974), but I foresee considerable development of this paradigm in the future.

4 "CLEAN" TESTS

Another approach, first described in Calfee, Chapman, and Venezky (1972), focuses on the construction of "clean" tests. The task demands are minimal, and the context and materials are chosen so that the student makes very few errors. If the error rate is too high, this means that the testing conditions are not suitably "clean," and further task analysis is required. If the error rate is

BASIC

LETTER SET

UNMARKED
REVERSALS

MARKED
REVERSALS

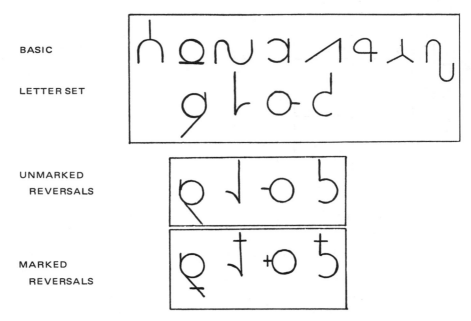

FIG. 7. Synthetic orthography used in tests of letter-matching skills (Calfee et al., 1971).

satisfactorily low, then one can investigate the effect of systematically introducing sources of difficulty that are related either to task factors or to skill factors.

For example, to investigate "visual perceptual" tests like those used in reading-readiness instruments, we first established conditions under which young children make virtually no errors in selecting a letter string to match a target string. And we then learned why this task is difficult to perform under other conditions.

The studies used the synthetic alphabet in Fig. 7, which incorporates distinctive features and rules of combination typical of lower-case English orthography. The 12 basic characters are relatively distinct. Mirror-image reversals for four of the letters are either unmarked or marked with a cross-hatch.

4.1 Letter Matching

One study of visual matching tested perception of single synthetic letters from this set (Calfee, Cullenbine, dePorcel, & Royston, 1971). The subjects were kindergartners and first graders from schools in the San Jose Unified School District. Schools were classified as middle or low income from demographic analysis of the neighborhood; students were classified as Spanish surname or "other." Students from different grades and schools were tested at different times of the year, so there is a partial confounding of background variables with time of testing. Details of the design of the study and characteristics of the students can be found in the original report.

The student was seated beside the tester, who showed him a target letter and five other test letters; the student's task was to select any test letters that looked like the target. Testing began with a sample item using a simple geometric form. The child was instructed to "mark any that are exactly the same as this one" (pointing to the target). Two test forms matched the target in the example. If the child marked only one of these, he was prompted with "look carefully, sometimes more than one is exactly the same." This procedure minimizes the influence of decision processses—if two alternatives look correct to you, and only one can be selected, then you have to decide which one to pick.

After successfully completing the sample items, the student proceeded through the rest of the items. Four of the 12 items are of interest here. Each contained two correct matches, an unmarked or a marked reversal, and two mismatches. One of the three formats in Fig. 8 was used. The target letter was circled as shown. A left-to-right (e.g., Fig. 2) arrangement was not used because of the

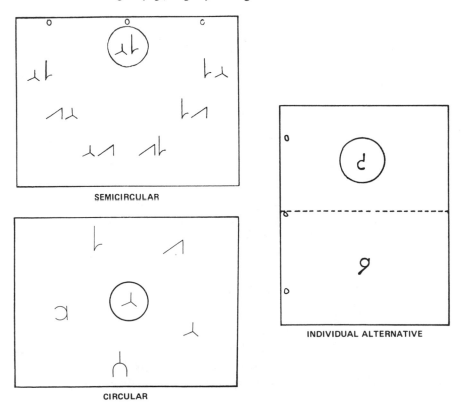

FIG. 8. Examples of items and formats used in single- and double-letter matching tests (Calfee et al., 1971).

TABLE 1
Choice of Marked and Unmarked Reversals[a,b]

Group	N^c	Unmarked reversal (%)					Marked reversal (%)				
		Correct[d]			Mismatch[d]		Correct[d]			Mismatch[d]	
		1	2	Rev.	1	2	1	2	Rev.	1	2
Middle income[e]											
First grade	138	98	97	48	0	1	98	99	4	1	1
Kindergarten	132	97	96	78	4	2	98	98	14	2	1
Lower income, kindergarten											
Spanish surname	72	97	92	70	3	1	94	96	8	0	2
Other white	72	97	94	67	2	0	97	98	7	2	2

[a]On single-letter matching test for designated school groups.
[b]Data from Calfee et al. (1971).
[c]Number of children.
[d]Column headings 1 and 2 are the first and second test letters respectively, in these categories.
[e]The number of Spanish-surname children in the middle-income group was negligible.

possible involvement of visual short-term memory described earlier. The individual-alternative format was considered optimal. The target remained in view at all times, while the five alternatives were flipped into view, one at a time. The student had a minimal amount of information to process in what was effectively a same–different task. The two other procedures were chosen from pilot work as likely to produce successive scanning between target and each alternative. The individual-alternative format provides a baseline for measuring the efficiency of the other formats.

Feedback was given only on the practice item. If a child changed his mind about a response, he was allowed to erase it. There was no time pressure, but most children spent no more than 4 or 5 sec per page after they got started.

The results are shown in Table 1 for several groups of students. The data are averaged over format, which had no differential effect on task performance. The correct alternatives were chosen with a very high probability (better than 96% of the time in all groups), and the incorrect (nonreversal) alternatives were seldom selected. These results hold for all groups of students. Unmarked reversals were selected with a relatively high probability, which ranged from about 50% for entering first-graders to about 75% for entering kindergartners. Marked reversals were much less likely to be selected—marking a small crossbar on a reversed synthetic letter form reduced by almost an order of magnitude the probability that a young child falsely chose a mirror-image reversal of the target.[2]

[2] Error patterns of subjects who chose both the correct figure and a mismatch were not examined. The proportion of errors other than reversals was so small that detailed analysis seemed pointless.

A great deal of research has aimed at understanding of letter-reversal problems in nonreaders (for a recent report see Sidman & Kirk, 1974). The child who has not learned to read is more likely to confuse *b* and *d* than one who can read. Many reading specialists and other practitioners, as well as researchers, attach significance to this finding. Training a child to notice and remember abstract mirror-image reversals is quite difficult—an adult has similar problems under certain conditions (Huttenlocher, 1967; Sekuler & Houlihan, 1968). We find this whole problem rather uninteresting. There is no correlation between rate of mirror-image reversals and later reading achievement in our study.[3] Minor modifications of the orthography seems the easiest way to solve this problem— minor variations between *b* and *d* in the DISTAR reading program (Engelmann & Bruner, 1968) exemplifies this technique. The modification can be eliminated after four to six months of reading instruction, by which time context cues resolve any remaining confusions.

Here, then, is an illustration of a "clean" test in which extraneous sources of difficulty have been minimized and selected sources of errors introduced in a systematic fashion. The result in this instance is that a long-standing "problem" in reading readiness appears to be spurious. Children who have learned to read or who know the letter names can distinguish *b* from *d*; children without this learning will confuse what are for them abstract characters. Thus, the *b–d* "visual perceptual confusion" is an indirect, inefficient, and misleading method of finding out whether a child knows his ABCs.

4.2 "Word" Matching

A *double-letter* test was also part of the assessment battery administered to the groups of students who took the single-letter test. The synthetic orthography was used to construct a set of 12 items, each with a two-letter target and six alternatives in a 3 × 2 factorial arrangement. Where *AB* is the target, the alternatives comprised all combinations of *AB, A* only, or *B* only present, and synthetic letters in original placement (*AB*) or in reversed placement (*BA*). This design generates as alternatives to an *AB* target the following: *AB, AX, YB, BA, XA, BY*. An example of an item in the synthetic orthography is shown in the upper left panel of Fig. 8. It looks forbidding to many adults who imagine it through a child's eyes. However, previous work had suggested that simpler arrangements were easily handled by kindergartners without errors. Variation in format was also included in the experimental design. The procedure was similar to that used in the single-letter test; for instance, the child could select as many

---

[3] Auditory–phonetic skills are stronger predictors of success in learning to read than visual perceptual skills when both are measured. For instance, Robinson found that "auditory discrimination had a strongly significant effect on reading scores regardless of the method used for teaching . . . Visual perception made no significant contribution to reading with *CA* [chronological age] and *MA* [mental age] controlled" (Robinson, 1972, p. 33).

TABLE 2

Choice of Each Alternative in Word-Matching Test for Designated School Groups and Presentation Format[a]

Group	Number per cell	Presentation format[b]	Alternatives (%)						Average error per alternative (%)
			AB	BA	AX	YB	XA	BY	
Middle income									
First grade	46	S	90	61	10	15	14	16	21
		C	93	63	21	22	21	21	26
		I	96	33	14	18	7	4	13
Kindergarten	44	S	83	31	14	14	10	10	16
		C	79	28	14	14	8	9	16
		I	88	25	15	17	8	9	14
Lower income, kindergarten									
Spanish surname	24	S	78	28	13	10	7	8	15
		C	82	37	16	16	13	14	19
		I	91	15	10	9	3	3	8
Other white	24	S	91	16	9	6	1	2	7
		C	81	18	9	6	4	3	10
		I	98	16	8	10	3	4	7

[a]Data from Calfee et al. (1971).
[b]Code: S is semicircular rowwise presentation format; C is circular format; and I is individual or single-alternative-at-a-time format.

of the six alternatives as he wanted. As in the earlier study, feedback was given for the practice item only.

The results are shown in Table 2. These data are from a subsample of students drawn randomly from the groups described earlier; the subsample provided equal-cell sizes in the presentation-format factor for convenience in computing the analysis of variance.

Discrimination accuracy was high. The correct alternative (AB) was marked with a high percentage (generally 85% or better, M [mean] = 88%) under all conditions. Alternatives with an inappropriate letter (AX, YB, XA, and BY) were marked infrequently (generally 20% or less, M = 12%). The error rate was lowest when one letter was changed and the position of the other letter was moved (XA and BY, M = 9%). There was some effect of format. Performance was poorest with the circular format (19% errors), the semicircular format was next (16% errors), and the "optimal" individual-alternative format was best (12% errors).

In order to determine the locus of individual differences, orthogonal contrasts in the analysis of variance were employed. The results of this procedure are shown in Table 3 for each school and grade in the study. Two contrasts account for all but a negligible amount of systematic variance—the difference between the number correct and all errors combined (AB versus BA + AX + YB + XA + BY), and the difference between BA order-reversal errors and all other error types (BA versus AX + YB + XA + BY). These are contrasts C1 and C2, respectively; the remaining variability between alternatives within each student's record is C3.

The other entries in the table are measures of individual differences. The mean square for the $N(\cdot)$ source is an estimate of between-subjects variability in the total scores. In the last column to the right is the mean square for $I \times N(\cdot)$, which is a minimum estimate of the variance of each test item. Differences between students contribute negligibly to this variance estimate. Three other variance estimates, $C1 \times N(\cdot)$, $C2 \times N(\cdot)$, and $C3 \times N(\cdot)$, are based on individual differences in the three contrasts described above. To the extent that each of these estimates approaches $I \times N(\cdot)$, the source contains no significant individual differences. To the extent that the estimate approaches $N(\cdot)$, students differ greatly on the contrast. The estimates for C1, C2, and C3 are based on the average effects of these contrasts over subjects, and can be used to evaluate the statistical significance of differences between average percentages in Table 2.

All main effects in the table, when tested against the corresponding subject-treatment error term to the right, are statistically significant at better than the .001 level. However, it is clear that C1 and C2 account for the bulk of the systematic variability. Of more interest for our purposes are the ratios of the C1 $\times N(\cdot)$ and C2 $\times N(\cdot)$ estimates to the $I \times N(\cdot)$ estimate. These reveal that the interindividual variance for the first two contrasts is from 5 to 15 times as large as the minimum variance. The $C3 \times N(\cdot)$ estimate is approximately equal to

TABLE 3

Analysis of Variance of Word-Matching Test[a,b]

Group	df for N(·)	N(·)	C1	C1 × N(·)	C2	C2 × N(·)	C3	C3 × N(·)	I × N(·)
					Variance estimates (mean square from analysis of variance)				
Middle income									
First grade									
School C	60	2.31	312.0	.56	87.8	.70	1.2	.05	.09
School T	66	2.08	350.3	.59	94.5	1.38	.4	.14	.08
Kindergarten									
School C	66	1.62	276.0	.64	27.4	.53	.8	.11	.11
School T	54	.48	335.7	.88	9.7	.33	.5	.09	.06
Lower income, kindergarten									
School L	66	1.11	384.0	.70	14.6	.31	1.0	.05	.06
School M	66	.57	448.0	.48	12.9	.41	.1	.05	.07

[a]Entries are mean squares for orthogonal contrasts and student-by-contrast interactions for six school groups. Contrast C1 compared AB alternative with all others; C2 compared BA with all other incorrect; C3 is the residual term for AX, YB, XA, and BY alternatives. $I \times N(\cdot)$ is the student-by-item variance source, which is a close estimate of the standard variance of each item. C1 and C2 have 1 df (degree of freedom) each, C3 has 3 df and I has 11 df.

[b]Note: Sex and format were also in the design for each school, so the number of subjects in each school is 6 more than the indicated df. Neither of these sources nor their interactions was consistently large.

the $I \times N(\cdot)$ estimate; once interindividual differences in performance measured by $C1$ and $C2$ are extracted, no substantial variation remains.

Interpretation of these results is straightforward. There are large interindividual differences in the overall error rate—this is, in essence, what is measured by comparison $C1$. When the errors are further divided into BA errors versus all others—this is comparison $C2$—large interindividual differences are also found in all groups. These two measures account for all significant variations between students.

The largest source of errors comes from order-reversal (BA) alternatives. These are noticeably higher in the first-grade than in the kindergarten sample, most likely because of the following difference in testing procedure. The first graders, who were tested first, were given no clear instructions on what constituted a match. They were told, "Mark it [an alternative] if it looks exactly the same as that one [the target]." If a child asked for clarification, as happened frequently, these instructions were repeated. The testers became increasingly dissatisfied at the inadequacy of the instructions. Subsequently, when testing of kindergartners began, revised instructions and an example made it explicit that order reversals were *not* a correct match in this task. The order-reversal error rate in the kindergarten sample was about half that in the first-grade sample, which speaks to the effectiveness of the instructional variable. Clear instructions were especially important when the format was less than optimal (compare error rates for first graders in the S and C formats compared with the I format).

The most striking effect of the change in instructions is not the average reduction in the order-reversal error rate, however, but in the changed character of the errors. This can be seen in Fig. 9, which shows the frequency distribution for order-reversal errors. The first-grade distribution is strikingly bimodal; about half the students marked the BA alternative on the 10 or more of the 12 test items, while the other half chose this alternative on two or less of the 12 items. In the kindergarten sample, which received explicit instructions, order-reversal errors were less frequent overall, and the distribution was unimodal. A reasonable interpretation of this finding is that under vague instructions, about half the children assumed that "same" meant both letters present in any order and marked their tests accordingly; the remaining children assumed that order was a relevant feature. What is impressive about this shift in performance is the relatively small amount of training required to produce a substantial change in performance—two to five minutes of pretraining stressing the importance of order with examples and feedback.

Incidentally, these word-matching errors do not contribute substantially to the prediction of reading performance. The order-reversal errors are not at all correlated with later reading achievement for the students described above, and overall error rate (correct versus others) was not a substantial component of the multiple regression equation relating various readiness tests to reading achievement at the end of first grade (Calfee et al., 1971; Calfee, 1972).

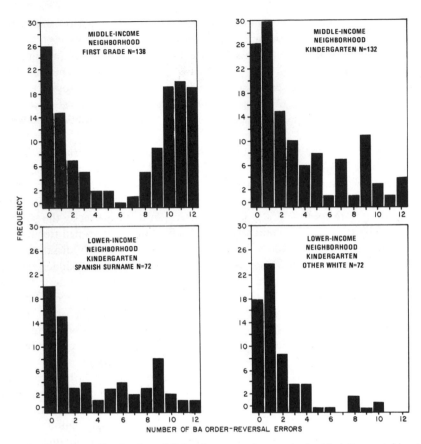

FIG. 9. Frequency distribution of *BA* order-reversed errors in double letter matching test (Calfee et al., 1971).

4.3 Situational Factors in Letter Matching

The role of task and contextual variables was further examined in a later study (Curry, Ross, & Calfee, 1973). Students performed a word-matching task with the synthetic alphabet, following the same general procedures described above. The design provided control over a number of *materials, task,* and *student* factors.

The materials variables were *number of letters, type of distractor,* and *spacing.* A word had two, three, or four letters. The six or seven alternatives for each target word always included one correct choice (an exact match), and one or more alternatives with either an order change (two letters interchanged), a replacement (one letter replaced with a different one), or an order-and-replacement change (two letters interchanged and one letter replaced with a different one). For a three-letter target, *ABC,* these variations can be represented as *ACB* (order). *ABX* (replacement), and *AXB* (order and replacement). This variation was balanced over subjects and testing conditions.

The letters were separated by a quarter or full letter space. The spacing variable was designed to examine the effects of variation in number of letters under conditions that promoted perception of a word as an integrated "whole" (close spacing) or a string of letters (wide spacing). This factor had no effect at all and will be disregarded.

The task factors included: *memory* (the target either remained in view while the child marked the alternatives, or was displayed for a few seconds and then covered during the marking of alternatives); *instructions* (the student was given explicit instructions about the criteria for a correct match, including order, followed by examples and a tryout with examples, or was told to mark only those alternatives that were "exactly the same"); and *format* (a single alternative was presented at a time, or six alternatives in a semicircular array).

The student factors included *age, ability,* and *sex.* The 64 subjects were four and five years old, judged to be above or below average ability by the teacher, separately for boys and girls. Age and grade were confounded: the four-year-olds were preschoolers and the five-year-olds were kindergartners. The sex variable did not affect performance and will not be discussed further.

The children were tested on two separate occasions with a week intervening. Format and spacing were between-subject factors, as were age and ability. Memory and instructions were between-session factors, balanced by a con-founded-blocks design for the effects of order. In each session, subjects were tested on 24 items consisting of a target word plus six or seven alternatives. Eight items were two-letter words, eight items were three-letter words, and eight were four-letter words.

The general instructions were to select the alternatives that were "the same" as the target. For each item only one of the alternatives was an exact match. Thus a subject could make four types of errors: He could fail to choose the correct match, or he could choose a misordered alternative, an alternative with a replacement, or a misordered alternative with a replaced letter. For all conditions, testing was subject-paced. Multiple responses were allowed, but not especially encouraged.

The major results of the study are in Fig. 10, and the analysis of variance is in Table 4. The finding of most relevance here is the error rate under optimal presentation conditions. These are conditions in which the instructions are clear, there is no memory requirement, and a single alternative is compared with the target. Five-year-olds seldom made errors, even with four-letter words. Four-year-olds had more trouble, especially those rated low in ability. Several of these latter children seemed to persevere in marking every alternative, or the right- or leftmost alternative; they all happened to be in the single-alternative condition,

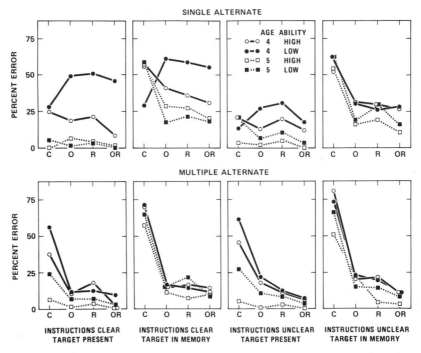

FIG. 10. Average error rate on word-matching task as a function of grade, ability, memory, instructions, and format (Curry, Ross, & Calfee, 1973). Error codes: C = failure to mark correct alternative, O = order change marked, R = replacement change marked, OR = order and replacement change marked.

which accounts for the rather unusual pattern of results in the top panel of the figure. Incidentally, the notion of a "chance" level of performance is poorly defined in this task, because the student could mark as many alternatives as he wished.

When the task demanded memory, the error rate increased substantially, slightly more so for low-ability than for high-ability students, and to the same extent whether the instructions were clear or not. All kinds of errors became more likely, but the greatest increase was in failure to mark the correct alternative; it appears that the children simply forgot what they were looking for.

The design does not allow statistical tests of the memory-by-instruction interaction; the main effect of instruction was not significant. However, certain patterns in the data warrant comment. When the instructions were unclear and there were no memory requirements, high-ability children did about as well as under optimal conditions, whereas low-ability children made more errors. The latter were more likely to miss the correct alternative and to mark an incorrect

TABLE 4
F Ratios and Error Mean Squares[a]

		Within contrasts[b]					
				Error type			
				E_1	E_2		
Between contrasts	Total score	Memory (*M*)	Instruction (*I*)	Correct vs. others	O, R vs. OR	List length linear (*L*)	$M \times E_1$
Main effects		212.2	ns	134.4	74.7	52.2	29.
Grade/age (G)	31.1	15.1	ns	ns	ns	ns	ns
Ability (A)	7.5	5.8	ns	ns	ns	ns	ns
Format (F)	5.7	10.3	ns	ns	ns	ns	ns
Error mean square	1616.9	512.4		1442.2	113.3	139.1	1719.4

[a]From analysis of variance of word-matching study (Curry et al., 1973).
[b]Note: Interactions of memory, instructions and session are block confounded. Two-way interactions of between-subject factors were extracted but were negligible. Error is pooled residual. Nonsignificant abbreviated as ns in table.

alternative, especially one that differed from the target only in the order of the letters. Children rated high in general ability understood that, by convention, order is a relevant feature of sameness, whereas many low-ability children did not seem to have this understanding.

These same patterns are observed whether there is one alternative or several present at the same time. When several alternatives are available simultaneously students tend to mark only one of them; if an incorrect one is marked then the correct one is not marked, especially in the memory conditions. When the alternatives are presented one at a time, the tendency is to mark more than one alternative as the series is presented. This reduces the likelihood that the correct alternative is missed, but increases the probability of marking an incorrect alternative.

The results of this study are comparable to earlier findings for similar instructions, memory, and age. Students do better in single-alternative conditions than in multiple-alternative conditions. This difference is reflected both in the number of failures to mark the correct alternative and in the number of mismarkings of incorrect alternatives. The major sources of individual differences are in the overall handling of correct and incorrect alternatives, in the effects of the memory variable on performance, and in the contrast between order and replacement errors (not shown in the table, but the error mean square for this source, 265.4, is about twice as large as the other error terms). These conclusions are based on comparison of the error mean squares in Table 4.

The effects of list length are substantial and consistent over subjects: there is a linear increase in errors as the number of letters goes from two to four.

The data from this experiment illustrate several points. First, it was possible to find optimal conditions under which most children satisfactorily performed the task involving particular kinds of materials, and then to degrade the testing environment to the point where performance was quite poor. Second, children of varying levels of general ability are differentially sensitive to such task variations. Complicating a test causes relatively more difficulty for the low-ability than the high-ability child. If a test constructor's purpose is to measure general ability, then he should create a task environment in which conditions are less than optimal. If general ability is to be minimized in a test of a specific skill, it is important to arrange conditions so that all children are on an equal footing.[4]

5   MODIFIABILITY OF TEST PERFORMANCE

Suppose that, under what seem reasonable circumstances, most children cannot perform a given task with any degree of accuracy. An underlying competency may appear if the child receives a little training. Posttraining performance may yield a better assessment than the student's initial performance under these circumstances.

For example, Kamil and Rudegeair (1972; Rudegeair & Kamil, 1970) looked at the effects of repeated test sessions on the auditory–phonetic discrimination ability of young children (kindergartners and first-graders). The purpose of the testing was to measure students' ability to perceive similarities and differences in minimal phonetic contrasts, as in "pat" versus "bat." A variety of task formats was used, including the popular Wepman Auditory Discrimination Test (Wepman, 1958). Children were tested for six days in succession on different lists of materials. There was never any feedback. Nonetheless, the error rate on day 2 was about half that on day 1. Errors continued to fall over the next four days until they reached a negligible level.

As no training occurred during the test–retest interval, it seems unlikely that the children were undergoing rapid and spontaneous change in their acoustic–phonetic discrimination abilities during this period. A more reasonable suggestion is that some children needed time to understand the task. Day 1 performance is undoubtedly a good measure of how quickly the child can figure out what the situation is all about; it is a poor measure of underlying acoustic–phonetic discrimination skills.

[4] For further thoughts along this line see Goodnow (1972). The term "general ability" here refers to the teacher ratings. Its meaning here is vague but probably includes verbal fluency, ability to concentrate, and preparation for the routine of school.

5.1 Miniature Training on Acoustic—Phonetic Skills

A second example comes from research on acoustic—phonetic segmentation skills conducted originally in collaboration with Venezky and Chapman at Wisconsin (Calfee et al., 1972) and followed up later with others at Stanford (Calfee et al., 1971). This test was designed to measure a student's ability to strip off the initial consonant portion of a monosyllable and pronounce the vowel—consonant remainder. Thus if I say "greet," you should say "eat," if I say "ties" you should say "eyes," and so on. This task resembles Pig Latin (Savin, 1972).

Our earliest efforts to elicit kindergartners' segmentation skills proved altogether fruitless. We then devised a five-trial rote-teaching sequence. The child was told the correct response to each word in the training list. Then followed a transfer test on a new set of words. The results (Calfee et al., 1972) were disappointing. We found, as have others (Rozin & Gleitman and Liberman et al., this volume), that young children experience great difficulty handling phonological relations. Performance changed only slightly over trials, and there was virtually no transfer.

Our initial reaction was similar to that expressed by other researchers. We thought that the measurement and development of auditory—phonetic skills was a significant matter in beginning reading, but could find no effective means of communicating with children about this task—of course, once a child acquired rudimentary decoding skills, the task was duck soup.

5.2 Training Based on Task Analysis

We launched another attack on the problem, combining task analysis à la Gagné (Gagné & Briggs, 1974) with the miniature training paradigm. The results were considerably more promising (Calfee et al., 1971). We asked ourselves: What does a child have to be able to do to achieve success in this task, and where might difficulties arise? For one thing, the target stimulus (*greet, ties,* etc.) has to be remembered during the comparison process: "If I say *'greet'* . . . you say 'eat.'" To eliminate this potential source of difficulty, we backed up each target word with a supporting picture which remained in view until the end of a trial. (Our subsequent experience suggests this support is unimportant.)

The second task requirement was response availability. Until he has formed the segmentation concept, the child has to remember which responses are appropriate, and must produce the one that seems best for a target stimulus. To reduce this source of difficulty, the child was provided with a response card with pictures for the response words "eat" (a person eating), "ache" (a person in obvious discomfort), and "eyes" (a pair of eyes). The child was taught to point and name each picture until the response was given quickly and easily. During subsequent training and testing he had only to point to the answer that he thought was correct.

TABLE 5

Percentage of Correct Responses on Phonetic-Segmentation Work for Selected Groups of Students[a]

Group	Training	Transfer			
		I–Old stimuli	I–New stimuli	II–New response	III–No response cards
Middle income					
First grade, $N = 138$	94	95	85	88	71
Kindergarten, $N = 132$	93	94	84	84	66
Lower income, kindergarten					
Spanish surname, $N = 72$	90	88	72	72	52
		$(t = 1.9)$	$(t = 3.0*)$	$(t = 3.1*)$	$(t = 3.6**)$
Other white, $N = 72$	92	95	85	86	69

[a]Transfer test I used the same responses as training, test II used a new response set, and in test III the child had to generate the response on his own. Data from Calfee et al. (1971). (Significance of Spanish-surname vs. other-white differences is shown by t tests. This is one of the few sources of significant differences between groups in this testing program.)

*$p < .05$.
**$p < .01$.

Paired-associate training was then carried out as the next step in the sequence of tasks. The list consisted of nine stimuli, three assigned to each response (e.g., *cake, rake,* and *lake* were each assigned *ache* as a response). Some variations in training procedure were incorporated in the design, but they all followed a common format: "If I say 'pies,' you point and say 'eyes.' " Training consisted of an initial study-only trial followed by three test-study trials.[5]

Several transfer tests were then administered. Transfer test I consisted of the old stimulus words, together with a new set of stimulus words which went with the old (i.e., original) response set (e.g., *break* and *cake*). In transfer test II a new response card was shown to the child, who was told the name of each of the three pictured response segments (e.g., *ice, itch, old*); a new set of stimulus pictures was presented without any additional paired-associate training, and the child was asked to point to the proper response picture for each and pronounce the segment (e.g., "If I say 'mice,' you point and say?" The correct answer would be "ice"). On transfer test III the response card was completely eliminated. The tester pronounced six words (*spies, make, heat, dice, fold,* and *stitch*), each accompanied by a picture, following the format "If I say 'spies,' you say?" The vowel–consonant segment for each of these words had been used earlier, so the child was familiar with them.

The subjects were the kindergartners and first-graders from Calfee et al. (1971) described earlier (compare Fig. 9 for other data on these students).

After the considerable difficulty we had experienced in trying to teach young prereaders to produce segmental responses to monosyllables, the success of the new procedures was rewarding (Table 5). Training performance was almost perfect in all groups. Learning was, to all intents and purposes, instantaneous. The success rate was 90% or better on the first anticipation trial, and increased only slightly over the next two trials.

The interesting questions concern transfer performance, also shown on Table 5. Generalization of the segmentation training was very substantial, except for transfer III, a totally oral test. Even there, students were correct 70% of the time on the average.[6]

[5] Children sometimes seemed to interpret the task as rhyming. Thus the word *fold* might be answered with *told* on transfer test III. This suggests that performance reflected phonological awareness. This understanding rather than precise segmentation seems the important indicator.

[6] More than half of the training errors were on *ache,* which all groups found difficult. There were no consistent differences as a function of sex, surname, or variations in training procedures which were part of the design. The one exception to this generalization is seen in the Spanish-surname kindergartners. Their training performance was not significantly different from the other groups. But as the transfer task became increasingly demanding and dissimilar from the training conditions, their performance became relatively poorer than that of the other groups. The reason for this finding are not clear. All of the children spoke fluent English with little apparent dialect; the Spanish-surname children in this area of San Jose were probably from a somewhat lower socioeconomic level than the other children, but we were unable to obtain any reliable evidence on this variable.

The point of this study and the work of Kamil and Rudegeair (1972) is *not* to suggest that children can acquire new skills. That would be worth little note. Rather, it is that under suitable training conditions, performance may change quickly and abruptly, as if the training provided an extended set of instructions. The child demonstrates substantial competence in what earlier appeared to be a nonexistent skill. Responsiveness to such training might well be a more interesting measure than the initial performance level in many areas of cognition.

It should also be noted that phonetic segmentation skills, when measured in kindergarten, do predict later reading achievement reasonably well. The kindergarten students were tested on the Cooperative Primary Test at the end of first grade, and it was found that phonetic segmentation transfer scores in kindergarten contributed substantially to the multiple regression equation predicting reading achievement; this contribution was over and above the total test score for all skills combined (Calfee, 1972).

6 ALL-OR-NONE DISTRIBUTIONS OF TEST SCORES

We examine frequency distributions for scores on the various component tests in our battery as a matter of course. The findings have proved most interesting. One such distribution has already been presented in Fig. 9; others are shown in Fig. 11.

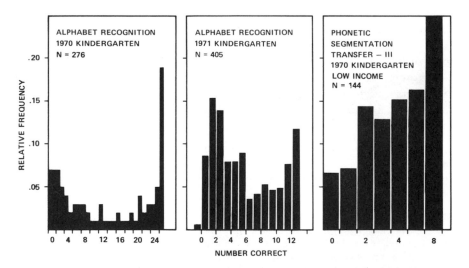

FIG. 11. Frequency distribution of alphabet-recognition and phonetic-segmentation scores, showing nonnormality and bimodality (Calfee et al., 1971; Calfee, 1972). The 1970 sample was individually tested on all letters of the alphabet; the 1971 sample was tested in small groups on 12 letters spanning a range of difficulty. The phonetic segmentation data are from lower-income schools, a subset of those represented in the panel on the left.

These distributions are not normal bell-shaped functions, nor can they be fitted by a single-parameter binomial function. Rather the BA-reversal errors in Fig. 9 and the alphabet-knowledge scores in Fig. 11 are noticeably bimodal. The phonetic-segmentation scores from transfer III also differ significantly from a single-parameter binomial distribution, largely because there are far too many extreme scores—too many children who are mostly right or mostly wrong.

Let us reflect for a moment on some possible consequences of non-normality. For one thing, it suggests more frequent investigation of distributional data might prove informative. Second, it may be a mistake to examine only omnibus scores, in which a number of subtests are combined into a single measure. It is well known that the sum of a number of (more or less) independent random variables is normally distributed, no matter what the distribution of the individual variables. The total-test score may be normal even though none of the subtests are. Third, a large body of work on test theory rests fairly heavily on an assumption of normally distributed measures; the results are not applicable to non-normal data.

It is beyond the scope of this presentation to consider this last point in any detail, but let us look at one instance—Thorndike's (1973) recent treatment of the problem of reliable diagnosis of specific skill deficits. Suppose we have two tests which we think measure different underlying competencies, A and B. Ideally we would like to answer such questions as: Does an individual need help with A or B, or both? How should we divide available instructional time between improving A and improving B? Thorndike focuses on the reliability of differential judgments, given that A and B might be partly correlated (perhaps due to general factors affecting performance in both tests), and given that the tests for both A and B are likely to be unreliable (both are "subtests" and hence relatively short).

Suppose that, in the case of a particular student, the difference between performance on A and B equals X standard-score units. The likelihood that X is a "real" difference rather than an error of measurement depends, among other things, on the reliability of A and B and the correlation between the two. Thorndike summarizes his findings:

> The tables and illustrations that we have examined illustrate the impact of reliability, intercorrelation, and score difference upon the confidence that one can logically place in an observed difference between two scores. They illustrate that over the realistic range of test reliabilities, and using the kinds of pairs of measures that we are likely to want to use in diagnostic studies, the confidence [we can place in such decisions] is distressingly low [Thorndike, 1973, p. 66].

I have no quarrel with the argument—it is proper and directly applicable to most "diagnostic" tests. But the analysis hinges strongly on the assumption of normality of the test scores, and the conclusions do not necessarily hold for other cases.

In fact, Thorndike's analysis is a strong argument for developing alternative approaches to diagnostic testing. The construction of instruments that tap relatively independent component skills in an all-or-none fashion is one such alternative. This effort will work only if (1) the component skills actually exist, and (2) the instrument is designed to measure the skills in a precise, uncontaminated fashion. The first presumption may not be true, and the task may be practically impossible, but the effort seems worthwhile.[7]

6.1   The Practical Use of All-or-None Tests

For the classroom teacher, a test may serve several purposes. Most often it is used for evaluation. The teacher needs to assign a grade, and the test score is convenient for this purpose. Standardized tests are often administered because of a mandate from the school district, principal, or some other authority.

Teachers occasionally test a student because they need to find out something about him. The teacher may suspect that the student is in trouble, and seeks evidence to substantiate the prediction. The teacher wants to "diagnose" a problem; he seeks evidence about specific deficiencies so that instructional efforts can be precisely focused on areas of greatest need.

Both evaluation and diagnosis are legitimate aims, and teachers are poorly served by the instruments presently available. I will concentrate here on the first question—how can we help a teacher obtain practically useful information of a general, predictive nature about individual students? The latter problem—specific diagnostic information—is a significant problem and one that we are working on, but detailed discussion is beyond the scope of this chapter.

The usual approach to prediction in educational settings is by the venerable Pearson correlation coefficient. It assumes that two normally distributed covariates share some common variance in the form of a linear relation. This solution is elegant, and most teachers learn something about correlation during their preservice training.

The technology is straightforward. If we know (1) a student's score on the predictor test A, (2) the mean and variance of A, (3) the correlation between A and the criterion or to-be-predicted test B, and (4) the mean and variance of B, then we can readily compute an estimate of the student's probable performance on B, along with confidence bounds on the estimate. Standard procedures include the assumption of normality.

Teachers do not do this sort of thing very often, to be sure. They are not comfortable with statistics, they do not have the time, the requisite information, nor the formula for computation. Thus, knowing that the correlation between a child's score on a readiness test at the beginning of kindergarten and his reading achievement at the end of first grade is .7 is likely to be of little help to the typical classroom teacher, no matter how dedicated he or she might be. The situation is even more difficult if the predictive relation has been established by

[7] Carver's (1974) distinction between psychometric and edumetric tests speaks to these same issues.

more sophisticated techniques such as stepwise multiple regression, discriminant analysis, factor analysis, or the like.

Our research group has been exploring alternative approaches to prediction based on all-or-none tests, with interesting consequences. The general technique is most conveniently presented by a concrete example. A kindergartner's knowledge of the names of the letters of the alphabet is known to be predictive of subsequent performance on reading achievement tests. (See, for example, Gibson & Levin, 1975, p. 250.) The reasons for this relation are complex and undoubtedly have more to do with home environment, general ability, amount of time spent watching *Sesame Street,* and so on, than with specific training on letter names. Alphabet knowledge is an indicator, not a cause, of reading success or failure.

Here is a technique for applying all-or-none test scores in prediction. Early in the school year, ask a group of kindergartners to name each letter of the alphabet; the result will be a prediction score. Then measure reading achievement of these children two years later when they leave the first grade. Divide the students into two groups: those who read at or above grade level and those who are below grade level. The former group has succeeded by current standards. The children in the latter group are below acceptable level of performance and might have profited from additional instruction during kindergarten and first grade. This then is the problem: the kindergarten teacher wants to sort children into those who will probably succeed and those who probably need additional help. Using the child's knowledge of letter names, what decision rule should be used for sorting, how complicated does it have to be, and how accurate will it be?

We have some data on this question. The kindergarten children who were tested in 1970 were also asked to name each of the 26 upper case English letters.[8] Two years later when they left first grade, they took the Cooperative Primary Reading Test (Educational Testing Service, 1970) as part of the California Testing Program. We obtained complete records for 144 children from the original sample of 276. There is a strong relation between alphabet knowledge and reading achievement in this group of students; the correlation is .50.

But a more interesting pattern appears if we examine the frequency distribution of alphabet scores for the children above and below grade level (Fig. 12). Children who are below grade level at the end of the first grade are disproportionately represented at the low end of the bimodal distribution of the alphabet-knowledge test (they do not know their ABCs at the beginning of kindergarten),

---

[8] Earlier in the chapter it was argued that a test that combined several independent components would be normally distributed. Knowledge of the alphabet, it is also argued, is sensitive to a number of background variables; why is it not normally distributed? The first-mentioned argument presumes that the items on the test tap a number of components in a random, haphazard fashion. Knowledge of the letter names is homogeneous in the sense that they tend to be learned as a batch together. The probability that the letters will be learned depends on a number of background variables. But as is obvious from the data, once more than a few of the letters are learned, all of the others tend to be acquired.

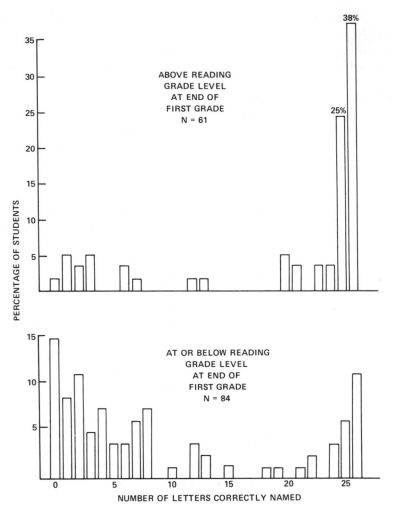

FIG. 12. Frequency distribution of kindergarten alphabet scores for students above and below grade level in reading achievement at end of first grade (Calfee, 1972).

whereas the children who were above grade level are disproportionately represented at the upper end of the alphabet knowledge test. Let us see what we can do with this information.

6.2   A "Cut-Point" Approach to Assessment

Suppose we sort children into two groups by a "cut point" on the alphabet-knowledge distribution. For instance, we classify as "in need of additional instruction" all children who identified 10 or fewer letters. Then 12 of the 61 children who are at or above grade level would be misclassified as needing additional instruction (they knew 10 or fewer letters when they entered kindergarten, but met the grade level criterion at the end of the first grade); 28 of the 84 children who were below grade level would be misclassified as *not* needing additional instruction (they knew more than 10 letters on entry to kindergarten, but failed to meet the grade-level criterion). This means that a cut point at 10 or fewer letters correctly identified misclassifies 12 out of the total 144 students, or 8%, as needing instruction when they would end up doing all right; 28 out of 144, or 19%, are misclassified as not needing instruction, but end up below criterion. The total misclassification rate is thus 27% at this cut point.

Figure 13 shows what happens as the cut point is moved from one extreme to another for this set of data. If the cut point is at the extreme left of the abscissa, then even if a child cannot identify a single letter, he is given no supplementary instruction. All of the children who fail to reach criterion are misclassified under this condition; none of the children who met criterion are misclassified, of course, since by definition they need no additional help. As the cut point is moved to the right, more and more students are assigned to supplementary instruction. At first, most are from the below-criterion subgroup. There is then a wide flat spot in the misclassification function, reflecting the small number of students in the middle portion of the bimodal distribution of alphabet-knowledge scores. At a cut point of 10 in the figure, the percentages mentioned above can be seen; 8% of the students are falsely classified as needing more help and

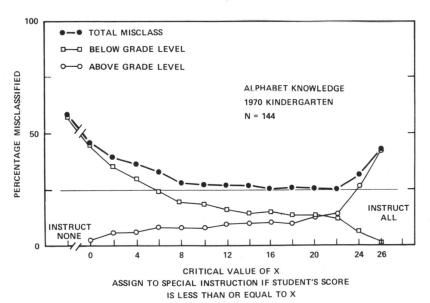

FIG. 13. Cut-point results based on kindergarten alphabet scores and first-grade reading achievement (Calfee, 1972).

19% of those that need help are not so classified, for a cumulative misclassification rate of 27% (the sum of the previous two percentages). Eventually, at the rightmost side of the abscissa, all students receive supplementary instruction, even those who know all the letter names. This means that all of the above-criterion students are, by definition, misclassified.

Two features of this procedure warrant emphasis. First, it is simple. We can say to the teacher: "Give the child a test. If he makes more than X successes, he's probably going to do all right (this can be made more precise). If he makes X successes or less, then he's probably going to be in trouble and you had better plan action to prevent failure." There are no complicated statistics.

Second, it is robustly accurate. The total misclassification rate in Fig. 13 drops to a low of 25%, and stays at that level over a broad range of cut points. [Incidentally, Feshbach, Adelman, and Fuller (1973), using a predictive test battery or teacher judgment or both, found that the misclassification rate from their measures and procedures ranged around 25% for a sample of almost 600 students.] These data and a number of other data sets we have examined suggest that for middle- and lower-class kindergartners, a good rule of thumb is this: if a child misses more than five or six letter names when he enters school, chances are that he (or she) will be below grade level at the end of first grade. And Bloom's (1964) analysis of academic stability suggests that the child is likely to stay behind unless some special effort is made.

It should be stressed that nothing in the present analysis of alphabet-knowledge scores and reading achievement implies the most appropriate action of a child in need. This is clearly not a diagnostic test that calls for a specific treatment. It is probably acting as a general indicator of a variety of abilities and skills; the instructional response can be only a general one. The development of more specific independent component tests is one aim of our current work, along with extension of the cut-point procedure to multidimensional test scores.

7   SUMMARY

What, then, is the current status of research findings on independent cognitive skills in beginning reading? The emphasis in this chapter has been more on methodology than on substance. Adequate methodology is required to establish the existence and operation of cognitive skills; we think the ideas discussed above are a step forward (compare Calfee, 1974, and Sternberg, 1969, for related developments).

Some substantive results do come from the research discussed here. The situation in beginning reading, as we see it (Calfee et al., 1971; Calfee 1972), is this. Visual matching skills when clearly measured are largely independent of other cognitive skills such as phonological awareness and verbal fluency. Visual matching is well developed in young children, and such individual differences as exist are not consistently predictive of later reading ability. Phonological awareness is moderately correlated with verbal fluency; these two skills are strongly related to later reading achievement. General skills such as atttentional concentration, an active set to remember what someone says to you, and the tendency to respond reflectively rather than impulsively (Kagan, 1965) are also important components in the prediction of reading performance. These general skills need to be tested in a variety of contexts to be measured validly; much work remains to be done. Whether they would then prove to be independent of other skills is not known at present.

The development of more adequate testing methodology seems to us of signal importance. We think it is possible to construct tests that are sufficiently selective so that performance is virtually the all-or-none type. This means that if a student has mastered the skills being tested, then he makes no mistakes; if he has not mastered the skills then he performs at a chance level. We have reason to believe that if a skill is precisely defined and general factors are minimized, numerous skills related to acquisition of reading will prove to be of all-or-none type.

The finding has interesting implications for test theory and important implications for classroom practice. Normal distribution theory is inappropriate when test scores are bimodally distributed. Test length becomes a less-critical determinant of test reliability. Fairly short tests may serve to identify a student's competence in a given skill area. Using a cut-point method, classroom teachers can use tests to make decisions about individual students. To the extent that these research efforts prove successful, continuous classroom assessment may become a realizable goal in the near future.

I hope to have given you some feel for the interplay in our research of practical and theoretical elements, of cognitive psychology and classroom teaching, and of educational and experimental psychology. Cognitive psychologists have learned much in the past decade about how to probe the mind. The analytic rigor and experimental tools developed by this discipline need to be put to work in support of the efforts of classroom teachers, who every day are charged with a great ongoing social experiment.

ACKNOWLEDGMENTS

Preparation of this paper was supported by a grant from the Carnegie Foundation. I am grateful to Annalee Elman and Leonard Fisk, Jr., for their assistance in the preparation of this paper.

REFERENCES

Atkinson, R. C., & Shiffrin, R. M. Human memory: A proposed system and its control processes. In K. W. Spence & J. T. Spence (Eds.), *The psychology of learning and motivation*, Vol. 2. New York: Academic Press, 1968.

Bloom, B. S. *Stability and change in human characteristics.* New York: Wiley, 1964.

Calfee, R. C. Diagnostic evaluation of visual, auditory and general language factors in prereaders. Paper presented at the American Psychological Association Convention, Honolulu, Hawaii, September 1972.

Calfee, R. C. The application of mathematical learning theories in educational settings: Possibilities and limitations. Paper presented at the Seventh IPN Symposium, Kiel, West Germany, 1975.

Calfee, R. C. Sources of dependency in cognitive processes. In D. Klahr (Ed.): *Cognition and instruction.* Hillsdale, New Jersey: Lawrence Erlbaum Assoc., 1976.

Calfee, R. C., Cullenbine, R. S., dePorcel, A., & Royston, A. Further exploration of tests of basic prereading skills. Paper presented at American Psychological Association Convention, Washington, D.C., 1971.

Calfee, R. C., & Floyd, J. Independence of cognitive processes: Implications for curriculum research. In *Cognitive Processes and Science Instruction.* Berne, Switzerland: Verlag Hans Huber, 1973.

Calfee, R. C., & Venezky, R. L. Component skills in beginning reading. In K. S. Goodman & J. T. Fleming (Eds.), *Psycholinguistics and the teaching of reading.* Newark, Delaware: International Reading Association, 1968.

Calfee, R. C., Chapman, R., & Venezky, R. L. How a child needs to think to learn to read. In L. W. Gregg (Ed.), *Cognition and learning in memory.* New York: Wiley, 1972.

California State Department of Education. *First grade entry level test California assessment program: Teacher's manual.* Sacramento, California: State Department of Education, 1973.

Carver, R. P. Reading as reasoning: Implications for measurement. In W. H. MacGinitie (Ed.), *Assessment problems in reading.* Newark, Delaware: International Reading Association, 1973.

Carver, R. P. Two dimensions of tests: Psychometric and edumetric. *American Psychologist,* 1974, *29,* 512–518.

Curry, L., Ross, R., & Calfee, R. C. Components of visual matching skills in prereaders. Paper presented to American Psychological Association, Montreal, 1973.

Educational Testing Service. *Cooperative primary reading test.* Princeton, New Jersey: Educational Testing Service, 1970.

Engelmann, S., & Bruner, E. *DISTAR: Direct instruction system for teaching arithmetic and reading.* Chicago: Science Research Associates, 1968.

Feshbach, S., Adelman, H., & Fuller, W. W. Early identification of children with high risk of reading failure. Paper presented to American Educational Research Association, New Orleans, 1973.

Gagné, R. M., & Briggs, L. J. *Principles of instructional design.* New York: Holt, Rinehart and Winston, 1974.

Gibson, E. J., & Levin, H. *The psychology of reading.* Cambridge, Massachusetts: MIT Press, 1975.

Goodnow, J. J. Rules and repertoires, rituals and tricks of the trade: Social and informational aspects of cognitive and representational development. In S. Farnham-Diggory (Ed.), *Information processing in children.* Pittsburgh: Carnegie-Mellon University Press, 1972.

Huttenlocher, J. Children's ability to order and orient objects. *Child Development,* 1967, *38,* 1169–1176.

Kagan, J. Reflection–impulsivity and reading ability in primary grade children. *Child Development,* 1965, *36,* 609–628.

Kagan, J., Rosman, L., Day, D., Albert, J., & Phillips, W. Information processing in the child: Significance of analytic and reflective attitudes. *Psychological Monographs,* 1964, *78,* (1, whole No. 578).

Kamil, M. L., & Rudegeair, R. E. Methodological improvements in the assessment of phonological discrimination in children. *Child Development,* 1972, *43,* 1087–1089.

Lucas, J. F. A stage processing model of reading for elementary school pupils. Technical Report, Children's Research Center, University of Illinois, Urbana, Illinois, 1974.

MacGinitie, W. H. An introduction to some measurement problems in reading. In W. H. MacGinitie (Ed.), *Assessment problems in reading.* Newark, Delaware: International Reading Association, 1973.

Miller, G. A. (Ed.). *Linguistic communication: Perspectives for research.* Newark, Delaware: International Reading Association, 1974.

Robinson, H. M. Visual and auditory modalities related to methods for beginning reading. *Reading Research Quarterly,* 1972, *8,* 7–39.

Rudegeair, R. E., & Kamil, M. L. Assessment of phonological skills in children. Technical Report 118, Research and Development Center for Cognitive Learning, University of Wisconsin, 1970.

Savin, H. B. What the child knows about speech when he starts to learn to read. In J. F. Kavanaugh & I. G. Mattingly (Eds.), *Language by eye and ear.* Cambridge, Massachusetts: MIT Press, 1972.

Sekuler, R. W., & Houlihan, K. Discrimination of mirror-images: Choice time analysis of human adult performance. *The Quarterly Journal of Experimental Psychology,* 1968, *20,* 204–207.

Sidman, M., & Kirk, B. Letter reversals in naming, writing, and matching to sample. *Child Development,* 1974, *45,* 616–625.

Silberberg, N. E., Silberberg, M. D., & Iverson, I. A. The effects of kindergarten instruction in alphabet and numbers on first-grade reading. *Journal of Learning Disabilities,* 1972, *5,* 7–12.

Sperling, G. The information available in brief visual presentations. *Psychological Monographs,* 1960, *74* (11, whole No. 498).

Sternberg, S. The discovery of processing stages: Extension of Donders' method. In W. G. Koster (Ed.), *Attention and performance II.* Amsterdam: North-Holland Publ., 1969.

Thorndike, R. L. Dilemmas in diagnosis. In W. H. MacGinitie (Ed.), *Assessment problems in reading.* Newark, Delaware: International Reading Association, 1973.

Wepman, J. M. *Auditory discrimination test: Manual of directions.* Chicago: Language Research Associates, 1958.

Author Index

The numbers in *italics* refer to pages on which the complete references are listed.

A

Adelman, H., 320, *322*
Aftanas, M. S., 264, *285*
Albert, J., 296, *323*
Allen, M. W., 99, *136*
Anderson, J. R., 228, 246, *256*
Archwamety, T., 260, *287*
Atkinson, R. C., 293, *321*

B

Baddeley, A. D., 217, *223, 224*
Balmuth, M., 284, *285*
Baron, J., 70, 78, 79, 82, *136,* 149, *180*
Bateman, B., 268, 269, *285*
Bell, A. E., 264, *285*
Beller, H. K., 155, *180*
Bellugi, U., 64, *136*
Benson, F., 75, *136*
Bever, T. G., 48, *52,* 72, 84, 99, *136, 140,* 216, *224,* 234, *256*
Bijou, S. W., 214, 218, *224*
Blank, M., 88, *136*
Bloch, B., 23, 28, 32, *51*
Bloom B. S., 320, *322*
Bloomfield, L., 21, 23, 26, *51*
Blumberg, E. L., 258, *288*
Blumenthal, S. H., 283, *286*

Bolinger, D. L., 216, *224*
Bond, G. L., 102, *136*
Bouma, H., 186, 194, 199, *204*
Bower, G. H., 228, 246, *256*
Bower, T. G., 70, *136, 180,* 216, *224*
Bransford, J. D., 81, *136*
Bressman, B., 93, *140*
Briggs, L. J., 311, *322*
Brill, L., 92, *136*
Brown, D. L., 99, *136*
Brown, R., 202, *204*
Bruce, D. J., 96, *136*
Bruinicks, R. H., 268, *285*
Bruner, E., 301, *322*
Bruner, J. S., 78, *139,* 215, *225*
Bryan, W. L., 61, *136*
Bryant, N. D., 261, 262, 265, *285*
Bryden, M. P., 193, *204*
Budiansky, J., 74, *140*
Buros, O. K., 268, *286*
Buschke, H., 217, *224*
Byrne, M. C., 283, *286*

C

Calfee, R. C., 87, 94, 97, 105, 107, *136,* 212, *224,* 279, 284, *286,* 290, 295, 296, 297, 298, 299, 300, 302, 305, 306, 308, 309, 311, 312, 313, 314, 318, 319, 320, *322*
Carter, B., 93, *138,* 211, *225,* 278, *287*

Carver, R. P., 295, 316, *322*
Cattell, J. Mck., 77, *136*
Cazden, C., 3, *51*
Chalfant, J. D., 262, *286*
Chall, J., 102, 105, 135, *136,* 283, *286*
Chao, Y-R., 15, 16, 17, 18, 23, 30, 33, *51,* 65, *136*
Chapman, R., 87, 94, *136,* 212, *224,* 297, 311, *322*
Chomsky, C., 21, 22, 38, *51,* 89, *136, 137,* 208, 215, *224*
Chomsky, N., 22, 23, 28, 30, 31, 33, 34, *51*
Clark, C. R., 116, *141*
Cole, R. A., 41, 42, 48, *51*
Coleman, E. B., 279, 280, *286*
Coleman, J. S., 101, *137*
Coltheart, M., 173, *181*
Conrad, C., 155, *181*
Conrad, R., 66, 69, 95, *137,* 217, 218, *224*
Cooper, F. S., 41, 42, 43, 44, 45, 47, 48, 49, *51, 52,* 209, *225*
Cromer, W., 276, *288*
Cronbach, L. J., 266, *286*
Cronnell, B., 75, *140,* 172, *181*
Cullenbine, R. S., 298, 299, 300, 302, 305, 306, 311, 312, 313, 314, 320, *322*
Curry, L., 306, 308, 309, *322*

D

Dahl, P., 260, *287*
Dale, P. S., 89, *137*
Daniels, J. C., 214, *224*
Davies, C. O., 116, *141*
Day, D., 296, *323*
DeHirsch, K., 95, *137,* 267, 276, *286*
Delattre, P. C., 41, 42, 43, *51, 52*
dePorcel, A., 298, 299, 300, 302, 305, 306, 311, 312, 313, 314, 320, *322*
Desberg, P., 258, 278, *286, 287*
deVoogd, A. H., 186, 199, *204*
Dewey, G., 215, *224*
Diack, H., 214, *224*
Diringer, D., 9, *51*
Ditchburn, R. W., 185, *204*
Dorničˇ, S., 217, *224*
Downing, J., 2, 3, *51,* 86, 89, 93, *137,* 215, *224*
Dunn, L. M., 219, *224*
Durrell, D., 283, 284, *286*
Dykstra, R., 95, 102, *136, 137,* 283, *286*

E

Ehri, L. C., 255, *256*
Eichelman, W. H., 155, *181*
Eimas, P. D., 88, *137,* 210, *224*
Elkonin, D. B., 93, 98, *137,* 212, *224,* 278, 283, 284, *286*
Engelmann, S., 301, *322*
Erickson, D., 217, *224*

F

Fant, C. G. M., 30, *52*
Feigenbaum, E. A., 76, *137*
Ferguson, C. A., 67, 99, *137*
Fernald, G. M., 269, *286*
Feshbach, S., 320, *322*
Fillenbaum, S., 81, *137*
Firth, I., 67, 96, 97, 104, 105, 106, *137*
Fischer, F. W., 93, *138,* 211, *225,* 278, *287*
Fischer, S., 64, *136*
Fletcher, H., 210, *224*
Floyd, J., 296, *322*
Flynn, P. T., 283, *286*
Forgays, D. G., 193, *205*
Foulke, E., 64, *137*
Fowler, C. A., 214, 215, *224,* 278, *287*
Francis, W. N., 22, 34, *51*
Franks, J. J., 81, *136*
Freeman, P. R., 217, *224*
Freeman, R., 173, *181*
Friedman, E. A., 69, *139*
Frostig, M., 263, 264, *286*
Fry, E., 147, *181*
Fry, M. A., 276, *286*
Fujimura, O., 69, *140*
Fuller, W. W., 320, *322*
Furth, H. G., 66, *137*

G

Gagné, R. M., 311, *322*
Gazzaniga, M. S., 261, *286*
Gelb, I. J., 8, 9, 10, 11, 13, 14, 16, *51,* 211, *224*
Geschwind, N., 75, 94, *136, 137*
Gibson, E. J., 66, 78, 79, 87, 101, *137,* 212, *224,* 257, 260, 270, *286*
Givendo, D., 278, *286*
Gleitman, H., 3, *51,* 89, 90, 92, *137, 138*

Gleitman, L. R., 3, 8, 21, 36, *51,* 57, 89, 90, 92, 93, 99, 106, 114, 116, 117, 118, 120, 121, 122, 124, 128, *136, 137, 138, 140,* 212, *224*
Goins, J. T., 264, *286*
Gold, C., 186, *205*
Gollmer, C. A., 9, *51*
Goodman, K. S., 3, 21, 36, 38, *51,* 61, 65, 72, 73, 80, *138,* 201, *204*
Goodnow, J. J., 310, *322*
Gough, P. B., 64, 74, *138,* 187, *204*
Goyen, J., 264, *287*

H

Halle, M., 23, 28, 30, 31, *51, 52*
Hammill, D. D., 261, 265, *286, 287*
Hammond, M., 78, *137*
Harding, C. J., 277, *288*
Hardy, M., 278, *286*
Hardyck, C. D., 65, *138*
Harrington, S. M. J., 283, *286*
Harris, A. J., 59, 87, 107, *138,* 268, *286*
Harris, Z. S., 23, 24, *52*
Harter, N., 61, *136*
Heilman, A. W., 215, *224*
Heron, W., 193, *204*
Hintzman, D. L., 217, *224*
Hochberg, J., 72, 73, *138,* 186, 199, 201, *204*
Hoenigswald, H. M., 26, *52*
Holden, M. H., 93, 98, *138,* 278, *287*
Horne, D., 263, 264, *286*
Houlihan, K., 301, *323*
House, A. S., 41, 44, 47, *53*
Huey, E. B., 21, 38, *52,* 61, 64, *138,* 186, 200, *204*
Hull, A. J., 217, *224*
Huttenlocher, J., 301, *322*

I

Iverson, I. A., 292, *323*

J

Jakobson, R., 30, *52*
Jansky, J. J., 95, *137,* 267, 276, *286*
Jastak, J., 214, 218, *224*

Jastak, S. R., 214, 218, *224*
Jeffery, L. H., 20, *52*
Jensen, H., 9, 10, *52*
Jensen, N., 270, *287*
Johnson, C. S., 276, *286*
Johnson, M. C., 74, *140*
Johnson, N. F., 73, *138*
Johnston, J. C., 77, 82, *138, 139*
Jusczyk, P., 88, *137,* 210, *224*

K

Kagan, J., 296, 321, *322, 323*
Kamil, M. L., 310, 314, *323*
Kaplan, E. L., 73, *138,* 186, 201, *204*
Kass, C. E., 264, 284, *287*
Keen, R. H., 107, *138*
Keenan, J. M., 235, 247, 248, 252, 254, *256*
Kephart, N., 263, *287*
King, E., 270, *287*
Kintsch, W., 217, *224,* 228, 229, 231, 232, 234, 235, 239, 246, 247, 248, 252, 253, 254, *256*
Kirk, B., 301, *323*
Klima, E. S., 2, 22, *52,* 208, *224*
Kolers, P. A., 73, *138,* 149, *181,* 199, *204*
Kozminsky, E., 247, *256*
Kroeber, A. L., 20, *52*
Krueger, L. E., 107, *138,* 155, 163, *181*
Kuenne, J. B., 259, 278, *287*

L

LaBerge, D., 61, *138*
Labov, W., 89, *138*
Langford, W. S., 95, *137,* 267, 276, *286*
Lashley, K. S., 106, *138*
Lehtinen, L., 261, 263, *288*
Lenneberg, E. H., 2, *52,* 66, 89, *138*
Leong, C. K., 2, 15, *52,* 65, *138*
Levin, H., 73, *138,* 186, 201, *204,* 212, *224,* 257, 258, *286, 287,* 317, *322*
Lewis, J. Z., 155, *181*
Liberman, A. M., 3, 41, 42, 43, 44, 45, 46, 47, 48, *51, 52,* 209, 216, *225*
Liberman, I. Y., 3, *52,* 93, 97, 98, 105, *138, 140,* 211, 214, 215, 217, *224, 225,* 276, 278, *287, 288*
Lieberman, P., 3, *52, 138*

Lindamood, C., 97, 105, 107, *136,* 279, 284, *286*
Lindamood, P., 97, 105, 107, *136,* 279, 284, *286*
Lindsay, P. H., 228, *256*
Lorge, I., 68, *140*
Lott, D., 75, *140,* 172, *181*
Lucas, J. F., 297, *323*
Lyle, J. G., 264, *287*

M

MacGinitie, W. H., 93, 98, *138,* 278, 283, *287,* 290, *323*
Mackworth, N. H., 186, *204*
Makita, K., 99, 100, *139, 140,* 213, *225*
Marcel, T., 186, *205*
Markman, E., 89, *139*
Marsh, G., 258, 278, 280, *286, 287*
Marshall, J. C., 75, *139*
Martin, S. E., 15, *52,* 65, *139*
Mattingly, I. G., 3, *52,* 93, *139,* 216, 217, *224, 225*
McClelland, J. L., 77, 78, 79, 82, *138, 139*
McConkie, G. W., 187, 188, 192, 194, 199, 200, 203, *204, 205*
McKoon, G., 247, *256*
Meyer, D. E., 158, *181*
Miller, G. A., 69, 78, *139,* 215, *225,* 279, 279, *287,* 290, *323*
Mishkin, M., 193, *205*
Monroe, M., 214, 215, *225,* 283, *287*
Morency, A., 267, *287*
Morton, J., 186, *205*
Moskowitz, A. I., 89, *139*
Moskowitz, B. A., 35, *52,* 88, *139*
Moyer, S. C., 277, *288*
Muehl, S., 276, *286*
Murphy, H., 284, *286*
Muzio, I. M., 255, *256*
Myers, P., 261, *287*

N

Neisser, U., 69, 72, *139,* 149, *181,* 193, *205*
Newcombe, F., 75, *139*
Newman, E. B., 186, *205*
Nicely, P. E., 279, *287*
Niles, J. A., 277, *288*
Norman, D. A., 228, *256*

O

Ofman, W., 270, *287*
Oliver, P., 93, *137*
Orton, S. T., 263, *287*
Osherson, D., 89, *139*
Osser, H., 78, *137*

P

Petrinovich, L. F., 65, *138*
Phillips, W., 296, *323*
Pick, A., 78, *137*
Poritsky, S., 2, 8, 12, *52,* 66, 87, 98, 117, 126, *140,* 213, *225*
Posner, M. I., 77, *139,* 155, *181*
Postman, L., 78, *139,* 215, *225*
Poulton, E. C., 186, *205*

Q

Quadfasel, F. A., 94, *137*

R

Rabbitt, P. M., 168, *181*
Rabinovitch, M., 276, *288*
Rayner, K., 187, 188, 192, 194, 197, 199, 200, 203, *204, 205*
Read, C., 2, 35, *52,* 88, *139*
Reber, A. S., 83, *139,* 166, *181*
Reder, S. M., 187, *205*
Reed, S. K., 158, *181*
Reicher, G. M., 77, *139*
Ringler, L., 268, *287*
Robinson, H. M., 268, *287,* 301, *323*
Rosman, L., 296, *323*
Rosner, J., 57, 93, 96, 97, 99, 129, *139,* 212, *225,* 284, *287*
Ross, R., 306, 308, 309, *322*
Roswell, F. G., 283, *286*
Royston, A., 298, 299, 300, 302, 305, 306, 311, 312, 313, 314, 320, *322*
Rozin, P., 2, 3, 8, 12, 21, 36, *51, 52,* 57, 66, 87, 93, 94, 98, 99, 106, 114, 116, 117, 118, 120, 121, 122, 124, 126, 128, *136, 138, 139, 140,* 212, 213, *224, 225*
Rublevich, B., 107, *138*
Ruddy, M. G., 158, *181*
Rudegeair, R. E., 310, 314, *323*
Rumelhart, D. W., 228, *256*

S

Sachs, J. S., 81, *140*
Sainte-Beuve, 57, *140*
Sakamoto, T., 99, 100, *140*
Samuels, S. J., 61, *138,* 260, 262, 265, 283, 287
Sasanuma, S., 69, *140*
Savin, H. B., 40, 48, *52,* 57, 84, 93, 99, *140,* 212, 214, 215, *225,* 311, *323*
Schank, R., 232, *256*
Scheffelin, M., 262, *286*
Schvaneveldt, R. W., 158, *181*
Scott, B., 41, 42, 48, *51*
Segarra, J. M., 94, *137*
Sekuler, R. W., 301, *323*
Selfridge, O. G., 76, *140*
Shaevitz, M., 270, *287*
Shankweiler, D. P., 41, 42, 43, 44, 47, *52,* 93, 97, 105, *138, 140,* 209, 211, 214, 215, 217, *224, 225,* 276, 278, *287, 288*
Shatz, M., 92, *140*
Shaw, G. B., 21, *52*
Shen, E., 64, *140*
Shepard, R. N., 158, *181*
Sherman, M., 280, *287*
Shiffrin, R. M., 293, *321*
Shipley, E., 3, *51,* 92, *138*
Shurcliff, A., 66, 79, *137*
Sidman, M., 301, *323*
Silberberg, M. D., 292, *323*
Silberberg, N. E., 292, *323*
Simon, D. P., 93, 96, 99, *139,* 212, *225*
Singer, H., 6, *53,* 58, 107, *140*
Siqueland, E. R., 88, *137,* 210, *224*
Smith, F., 3, 21, 22, *53,* 61, 63, 66, 68, 75, 80, *140,* 148, 172, *181,* 192, 203, *205*
Smith, I., 268, *287*
Smith, J. A., 94, 98, *140*
Smythe, P. C., 278, *286*
Snow, R. E., 266, *286*
Sotsky, R., 2, 8, 12, *52,* 66, 87, 98, 117, 126, *140,* 213, *225*
Southgate, V., 146, *181*
Spalding, R. B., 269, *288*
Spalding, W. T., 269, *288*
Sperling, G., 74, *140,* 217, *225,* 292, *323*
Sperry, R. W., 261, *288*
Spivak, J. G., 74, *140*
Stallings, J. A., 269, *288*
Steger, B. M., 277, *288*

Steiner, R., 276, *288*
Stennett, R. G., 278, *286*
Sternberg, S., 296, 320, *323*
Stevens, K. N., 41, 44, 47, *53*
Sticht, T. G., 64, *137*
Strauss, A., 261, 263, *288*
Strawson, C., 82, *136*
Streby, W. J., 247, *256*
Studdert-Kennedy, M., 41, 42, 43, 44, 47, *52,* 209, *225*
Szumski, J. M., 175, *181*

T

Taft, M., 93, *140*
Taylor, E. A., 186, *205*
Taylor, S. E., 186, *205*
Thomasson, A. J. W. M., 217, *225*
Thompson, D. M., 168, *181*
Thorndike, E. L., 68, *140*
Thorndike, R. L., 107, *141,* 290, 315, *323*
Thorndike, W. E., 2, *53,* 58, *141*
Thurston, I. M., 78, *136,* 149, 168, *180, 181*
Tinker, M. A., 143, 147, 155, *181*
Tulving, E., 168, *181,* 186, *205*
Turvey, M. T., 216, 217, *224, 225*

V

Vellutino, F. R., 262, 277, *288*
Venezky, R. L., 22, *53,* 87, 94, *136,* 146, *181,* 212, *224,* 258, *288,* 290, 295, 297, 311, *322*
Vernon, M. D., 283, *288*
Vigorito, J., 88, *137,* 210, *224*

W

Walker, W., 15, *53,* 99, *141*
Warburton, F. W., 146, *181*
Warren, R. M., 48, *53*
Waugh, R. P., 268, *288*
Weber, R., 73, 107, *141,* 214, *225*
Weiner, M., 276, *288*
Weinstein, R., 276, *288*
Wepman, J. M., 88, *141,* 267, *288,* 310, *323*
Wheeler, D. D., 77, 78, *141*
White, M. J., 193, *205*
Wiederholt, J. L., 265, *286*
Wiener, M., 270, *288*

Wijk, A., 146, *181*
Williams, D. V., 258, *288*
Williams, J. P., 258, 259, 270, 273, 278,
  281, *287, 288*
Winograd, T., 228, *256*
Wohlwill, J. F., 270, *288*
Woodcock, R. W., 116, *141*
Woodworth, R. S., 200, *205*

Y

Yonas, A., 66, 79, *137*

Z

Zigmond, N., 283, *288*

Subject Index

A

Acronymic principle, 18, 20
Acuity, *see* Span, perceptual
Alphabets, 2–3, 19–21, 44–48, 111, 123,
    131, 143–181, 208–215, 270–276,
    297–310, 314–321, *see also* English
    orthography
  appearance of, 20–21, 49, 55
  artificial, 143–181, 270–276, 297–310
  as ciphers, 2
  compared with syllabaries, 19–20
  difficulty in learning, 50, 56–58, 134,
    270–276, 301
  and phonetic recoding, *see* Phonetic
    recoding; Phonetic segmentation
  as phonological mnemonics, 35
  and phonological principles, 38, 131–135,
    215
  and speech production, 44–48
Anagrams, 91
Analysis by synthesis, 44
Anomalous sentences, detection of by
    children, 92
Aphasia in Japanese, 69–71
Articulation, *see* Speech production
Assessment of reading skills, 5–7, 58,
    183–205, 227–256, 289–323
  additive factors analysis, 296–297
  adequacy of testing, 289–293, 314–316,
    320–321
  "all-or-none" tests, 314–320
    applications, 316

Assessment of reading skills, *(contd.)*
  alphabet knowledge, 314–320
  auditory abilities, 211–212, 215–223,
    266–269, 301, 310–314
  California First-Grade Entry-Level Test,
    291–293
  "Clean" tests, 295, 297–310
  component abilities, 289–297, 310–314
  Cooperative Primary Reading Test, 317
  diagnosis, 217–223, 260–262, 289–321
  and distribution of test scores, 314–321
  individual differences, 217–223, 257–269,
    303–310
  instructional variables, 291–293, 301–314
  letter identification, 269–276, 291–293,
    297–301, 314–320
  matching tasks, 269–272, 291–293,
    298–310
  modifiability of performance, 310–314
  reliability, 315–320
  task analysis, 311–314
  tests, 289–293, 297–298, 314–321
  visual discrimination, 269–276, 291–293,
    298–310
Audiles, *see* Modality matching
Auditory Analysis Test, 96
Auditory discrimination in infants, 88, 210
Auditory recoding, *see* Phonetic recoding;
    Phonetic segmentation
Aural coding, *see* Phonetic recoding;
    Phonetic segmentation
Automatization of reading skill, *see* Fluent
    reading

B

Beginning reader, *see* Preliterate child
Blending, 43, 62, 108, 113, 128–129,
    209–210, 280, 283–285, *see also*
    Phonetic segmentation; Syllables,
    segmentation
"Buh-ah-guh" problem, 208–210

C

California Reading Achievement Tests, 125,
    291–293
Cherokee, 15, 99
Chinese, 11, 12, 16, 213
    classical, 16, 17
    phonetic compounds in, 13–15
    reading of, 64–67, 131
    reading rate, 65
Chunking, 74, 80, *see also* Span, perceptual
    and levels of organization, 60–61
Cognitive strategies, *see* Learning strategies
Comprehension, *see* Propositions, theory of
    meaning
Complementary distribution, 25
Consonants, 20, 25
Cooperative Primary Reading Test, 317
Cryptograms, 91
Cuneiform, 11–14, 55
Curriculum design, *see* Reading curricula

D

Deaf, *see* Reader, deaf
Decoding
    auditory, 3
    in Chinese, 15
    manipulative, 107
    phonological, 102–105, 107, 108, *see also*
        Phonological recoding
    visual, 3
Diacritical Marking System, 146
Diagrams, 10, 11
Digraphs, 17
DISTAR program, 301
Dyslexia, *see* Learning disabilities

E

Egyptian, 11, 13, 16, 21
English orthography, 22–39, 143–181, 215
    levels of, 33–38, 133–134
    logographic aspects, 35–36

English orthography, *(contd.)*
    phonemic aspects, 38–39
    phonographic aspects, 35–37
    and systematic phonemics, 31–33
EPAM, 76
Ewe, 8, 10
Eye fixations, *see* Span, perceptual
Eye movements, 106, 186, 193, *see also*
    Span, perceptual
    control of, 199–201
    measurement of, 187–188
Eye–voice span, *see* Span, perceptual

F

Features, phonological, 30, 44–45, 48
Fernald method, 269
Fluent reading, 6, 63–71, 148–150,
    178–180, 183–187, 198–203, 253–256,
    see also Span, perceptual; Reader,
    average adult
    automatization, 61, 74, 78–81, 85,
        106–107
    and contextual information, 59–60, 202,
        260
    definition of, 6
    and perceptual span, 185–186, 188–201
    theories of, 58–86, 148–150, 201–203
    and visual pattern, 143–180, 195–199
Formants, 40–41
Foveal fixation, 60, 72, 185, *see also* Span,
    perceptual
Frostig method, 263–264

G

Glyphs, 154–167, *see also* Logograms;
    Logographies; Word recognition, visual
    pattern
Gray Oral Reading Test, 268–269
Greek, 8, 20

H

Haskins Laboratory, 41, 44, 46–48
Hebrew, 18
Hiragana, 18, 36–37, 69
Hittite, 16
Homographs, 70, 116
Homonyms, 70, 116
    nonhomographic, 81

I

Ideograms, 11, 13
Illinois Test of Psycholinguistic Abilities, 261, 269
Illiteracy, 58, 111, 113, *see also* Literacy
  functional definition, 58
  in United States, 58
Implicit learning, 83–84, 166
  of orthographic rules, 83
Independent stage analysis, *see* Assessment
  of reading skills, component abilities
Initial Teaching Alphabet, 146
Instructional programs, *see* Reading
  curricula

J

Japanese
  logographic orthography, 16–17, 36–37,
    99–100
  syllabary orthography, 16–19, 36–37,
    99–100
Jello model of the mind, 295
Jotto, 91

K

Kana, *see* Katakana
Kanji, 36–37, 69, 213
Katakana, 17, 36–37, 69, 213
  compared with Kanji, 99–100
Korean, 30

L

Lateralization, 94, 261–264
Learning disabilities, 260–262, *see also*
  Reading disabled child
  auditory and visual skills, 266–269
  correlates of, 260–262
  diagnosis, 217–223, 260–262, 316–321
  and neurology, 261–262
  psycholinguistic factors, 276–277
Learning strategies, 257–260
  and auditory coding, 215–223, 257–260
  and curriculum design, 257–260
  in matching tasks, 257–260, 301–310
  relation to instruction, 257–260, 297–314
  variables influencing, 257–260, 297–314
Letter blindness, 75
Letter case alternation, reading of, 75–77

Letters

Letters
  identification, 74, 76–79, 87–88, 291,
    314–321
  scanning, 74
  as units in reading, 74
Lexical representation, 28–29, 228–231
  decomposition of, 232–233
Linguistic method, *see* Reading curricula
Literacy, 5–7, 101–130, *see also* Illiteracy
  and intelligence, 58
  in Japan, 100
  problems in achieving, 101–130
  problems in defining, 110
  tests of, 5–7
Logograms, 10, 13–14, 113, *see also* Glyphs
  in English, 35
  in syllabary curriculum, 112–113
  visual distinctiveness, 66
Logographies, 11–13, 36, 99–100, 111
  compared with alphabets, 65, 131, 134
  learnability, 100, 134
  in reading curriculum, 115–116, 126, 131

M

Mayan, 11
Meaning, *see* Propositions, theory of
  meaning
Metropolitan Achievement Test, 268–269
Memory
  propositional, *see* Propositions
  semantic, *see* Propositions
  short-term, 215–223
    auditory coding, 293
    beginning reader, 95, 217
    fluent reader, 216
    and phonetic recoding, 216
    visual coding, 292
Metalinguistics, 3, 38, 91
Metaorthographic joke, 83
Minimal pair, 24–25
Modality matching, 266–269
Morpheme, 4, 11, 16, 34, 111
  phonological representation of, 28–29
Morphology, 32
Morphophonemic(s), 32–35, 82, 111
  deep representations of, 34–35
  writing, 32–33
Motor–speech acts, 44

N

Nonstandard English, 89

O

Orthography, 7–21, 143–180, *see also,*
    Alphabets; Diagrams; English
    orthography; Logographies; Pictogra-
    phies, Rebus; Semasiographies;
    Syllabaries
  arbitrary components, 83
  history of, 4–5, 7–21, 49–50
  and phonological relevance, 82–83
  representations, 81–84, 126, 143–180,
    215

P

Pandemonium, 76
Parallel processing, 61–63, 85
Peabody Picture Vocabulary Test, 219
Peabody Rebus Reading Program, 116
Perceptual Skills Curriculum, 129
Perceptual strategies, *see* Learning strategies
Phone, 4, 22–49, 82
  as feature bundle, 44–45
  invariant acoustic cues, 41–42
  relation to acoustic stimulus, 22–23,
    39–49
  relation to alphabet, 114
  segmentation problem, 39–49
  shingling in speech, 45–48
  surface, 28–29, 34
  transitions between, 47
Phonecian, 20, 26
Phoneme, 4, 18, 22–39, 49, 56, 82,
    131–132, 208, 279–281
  as abstract representation, 28–29, 56
  as cognitive-perceptual category, 22–23,
    28–31
  descriptive linguistic formulation, 23
  and dialects, 24–25
  generative transformational formulation,
    23, 28–29
  as independent of meaning, 23–24
  as perceived sound, 24–25
  and phonological processes, 28
  relation to phone, 22–23
  shingling in speech, 132
  as simple perceptual category, 23–28
  systematic, 28–29
Phoneme deletion task, 96, 311–314
Phoneme segmentation, 57, *see also*
    Phonetic segmentation
Phonetic complement, 12, 13–15, 19, 20

Phonetic compounds, 13, 15
Phonetic recoding, *see* Phonetic segmenta-
    tion; Phonological recoding
Phonetic segmentation, 39–49, 207–223
  and awareness, 210–211
  in beginning reader, 208–209
  developmental ability, 211–212
  orthographic complexity, 215
  and phonemes, 212
  and reading, 207–223
  and reading errors, 214
  relation to acoustic cues, 209
Phonetization, 112–113, *see also* Blending;
    Phonetic segmentation
  in reading curriculum, 116–117
Phonographies, 13–22, 36
  as derived from logographies, 35
Phonological awareness, 4, 45, 57, 97–98,
    101, 133, *see also* Phonetic segmenta-
    tion
Phonological recoding
  bypassing of, 105–107
  Kant versus Spillane, 107
  in teaching reading, 102–105
Phonology, 32, 34–35
  context effects, 46–47
  deep, 38
  generative, 22
  organization
    in adults, 34
    in children, 35
  role in reading, *see* Reader, average adult,
      phonological issues
  and spelling, 27–29
Phrases as reading units, 79–81
Pictograms, 11
Pictographies, 7–8, 111
Pictorial representations and reading
    curricula, 112–130
Pig Latin, 214, 311
Preliterate child, 86–101, 211–215,
    257–260, 269–276, 291–293
  accessing meaning, 90–93
  access to linguistic knowledge, 89–98,
    210–211
  auditory–perceptual skills, 88–89, 310
  letter naming skills, 87–88, 314–320
  phonological awareness, 93–98, 209–212,
    310–314
  predicting reading success, 96, 314–320
  previous knowledge, 86–89
  semantic skills, 89

Preliterate child, *(contd.)*
and short-term memory, 95
syllabic knowledge, 98–99
syntactic skills, 89
visual perceptual skills, 87–88, 301
Proofreader's effect, 68–69
Propositions, 227–256
acceptability and metaphor, 232
definition, 229
propositional frames, 228
and reading speed
effect of argument repetition, 239–248
effect of number of propositions, 235–239, 248–249
recall
effect of argument repetition, 239–248, 252–253
effect of number of propositions, 235–239, 248–249
and reading rate, 248–249
effect of subordination, 249–253
serial position effects, 250–252
theory of meaning, 227–234
relation to text, 234
text base, 233–234, 253–256
types of, 231–233
Protowriting, 55
Psycholinguistic factors, *see* Learning disability
"Puh-ah-tuh" problem, 43
Puns, 91
Pygmalion, 26

R

Radical, *see* Ideogram
Readability, 253–256
Reader, average adult, 36, 58–86, 90–92, 105–107, 183–205, 227–256
compared with beginning readers, 105–107, 179–180
definition of, 58–59
as "explorer," 59–63, 85, 97, 132, 201–203, 257
and eye movements, 183–205
individual differences, 90–91, 96–97, 111, 303, 307–310
and IQ, 97
phonological awareness, 97–98
as "plodder," 59–63, 85, 132, 201–203, 257
semantic tasks, 96
word segmentation tasks, 97

Reader average adult, *(contd.)*
phonological issues, 62, 63–71, 97, 150–167
bypassing phonology, 70–71, 148–167
neurological factors, 69–70
problem of novelty, 67–68
reading errors, 68–69
print-to-meaning hypothesis, 21, 63–67, 79–81, 148–149, 201–203, 215–217
scanning strategies, 62–63, 189–203
text comprehension, 227–256
Reader, deaf, 64–67
fluency level, 66
phonological bypass, 66
Reader, fluent, *see* Reader, average adult
Reading
compared with speaking, 1–5, 89
in preliterate child, 89
definition of, 6–7
as hierarchical process, 4, 73–85, 111
as psycholinguistic guessing game, 72, 201–203
of meanings, *see* Reader, average adult, print-to-meaning hypothesis
text sampling, 72–73, 80, 199–203
cognitive search guidance, 72–73, 199–201
peripheral search guidance, 72–73, 199–201
Reading acquisition, 2–5, 39–40, 101–135, 179–180, 207–215, 277–279, *see also* Preliterate child; Reading curricula
compared with language acquisition, 1–5
learning to "explore," 105–107
learning to "plod," 102–105
motivational factors, 129–130, 281–283
Reading comprehension, 5–6, 227–256
correlation with IQ, 6
Reading curricula, 50–58, 101–135, 179–180, 263–285
alphabets via syllabaries, 57–58
design of, 111–114, 277–285
auditory training, 116–117, 279–281, 283–284
decoding issues, 111–124, 280–281
and individual differences, 282–283
and organization, 114–123, 281–283
evaluation of, 108–111, 124–130, 264–277
Hawthorne, 109
extracurricular factors, 101–102

Reading curricula, (contd.)
  Frostig method, 263–264
  historically oriented, 50, 57–135
  individualized instruction, 277, 282–283
  readiness programs, 263–266
  role of teacher, 108–110, 125, 264–266
  tactile–kinesthetic training, 269–276
  transfer of training, 270–276
Reading deficiency, see Learning disability
Reading disabled child, 87–89, see also
    Learning disabilities
  and dialects, 89
  and logographic reading, 87
Reading errors, 73, 202–203, 300, 305
Reading rate
  average adult, 5, 58–60, 64–65, 235–256
  in Chinese, 64–67
  compared with compressed speech, 64–65
  in deaf, 64–67
  difficulty of material, 64, 235–256
Reading readiness, 125, 263–266
Rebus, 15, 116
Remedial techniques, see Learning
    disabilities; Reading curricula

S

Saccades, see Eye movements
Scrabble, 91
Semantic memory, see Propositions, theory
    of meaning
Semantic complements, 11–12, 13–15
Semasiogram, 10
Semasiographic devices, 113
Semasiographies, 9–11, 21, 111
  in reading curriculum, 115
Sememe, 9
Semitic language, 18–19
Sentence perception
  and automatization, 81
  role of phrases, 73
Sequoyah, 99
Sight-word method, 148–149, 268–269,
    280–281, see also Reading curricula
Span of apprehension, see Span, perceptual
Span of recognition, see Span, perceptual
Span, perceptual, 183–203
  and acuity, 185
  asymmetry of, 193–194
  and comprehension, 192–193
  eye–voice, 73, 186
  and fluent reading, 188–192, 199–203

Span, perceptual, (contd.)
  and word identification, 195–198, 201
  word shape, 185, 195–201
Speaking compared with reading, 1–5
Spectrogram, sound, 39–42
Speech perception, 44, 209–212
  relation to speech production, 44
Speech production, 44–49
  articulation, 44–45
  Haskins' model of, 46
  higher levels of organization, 48
  parallel transmission in, 46–48
  relation to the alphabet, 44–48
Speed reading, 63, 65, 71, 201–203
Spelling
  Chomsky's claims, 33
  irregularities in, 19, 22, 145–148,
    159–172, 215
  in reading curriculum, 121–122, 279–281
  reforms, 21
  systematic phonemic, 28–29, 31
SRA Primary Mental Abilities Test, 268
Stanford Language Arts Test, 96
Subjective lexicon, see Lexical representation
Sumerian, 16
Syllabaries, 15–19, 36, 98–100, 111–130
  compared with alphabets, 99
  compared with logographies, 16
  invention of, 99, 111
  learnability of, 98–100, 134
  and morphology, 16
  and phonology, 16
  in reading curriculum, 111–130
Syllabary curriculum, see Reading curricula,
    historically oriented
Syllable, 4, 45–48, 98–100, 117–130, see
    also Phonetic segmentation; Syllabaries;
    Blending
  number in English, 84
  segmentation, 85, 108, 118–122,
    126–128, 210–212
  as sequence of phones, 45–48
  in speech perception, 41, 48–49
  in speech production, 48–49
  as unit in reading, 84–85
Syllable deletion task, 96
Syntax, 4, 68–69, 111, 238–248

T

Tactile-kinesthetic modality, see Reading
    curricula

Task analysis, *see* Assessment of reading
  skills
Text complexity, 238–256
Tongue twisters, 40
Transfer of training, *see* Reading curricula
Typography, *see* Word recognition, visual
  pattern

V

Visiles, *see* Modality matching
Visual search, *see* Word recognition
Vowels, 32, 45–46

W

Wampum, 8
Wechsler Intelligence Scale for Children,
  261
Wepman Auditory Discrimination Test, 88,
  94–95, 268, 310
Whole word technique, 38, 103–104,
  148–149, 209, 258, *see also* Word
  recognition
Wide Range Achievement Test, 95, 214,
  218–219
Woods, Evelyn, *see* Speed reading
Word concepts, 228–233
Word recognition
  lexical access, *see* Fluent reading, theories
    of
  phonics, 149, *see also* Word recognition,
    visual pattern
  visual pattern, 143–181
    artificial alphabets, 151–181
    case of letters, 165–167, 172–178

Word recognition, (*contd.*)
  glyphs, 151–167
  letters, distinctiveness of, 143, 181
  linguistic translation, 149–150
  and pronunciation, 145–148, 150–153,
    159–167
  and reading instruction, 179–180, 260
  specific stimulus learning, 148–149,
    172–178
  speed of recognition, 153–159,
    167–178
  and visual search, 154, 172–178
  words, distinctiveness of, 144–145,
    153–159
Word shape, 144–145, 148–149, 153–159,
  195–203
Word superiority effect, 77–79, 82–84
  and automatization, 107
  and bigram frequencies, 82
  in deaf readers, 79, 83–84
  and phonological irregularities, 83
  and pseudowords, 78–79, 81, 84
  theories of, 78
Words as units in reading, 75, 77–79
Writing
  of meanings, *see* Semasiographies
  of morphemes, *see* Logographies
  of sounds, *see* Phonographies
  of syllables, *see* Syllabaries
  systems, *see* Orthographies
  of words, *see* Logographies

Y

Yoruba, 9